Odyssey

Travels On A Bucket List

Ron Culley

Edited by John McManus

Scottish chapters edited by George Cuthbert

Book cover by Alexander Tarbet

**Grosvenor House
Publishing Limited**

This book is published by
Grosvenor House Publishing Ltd
Link House
140 The Broadway, Tolworth, Surrey, KT6 7HT.
www.grosvenorhousepublishing.co.uk

A CIP record for this book
is available from the British Library

ISBN 978-1-78623-194-9

Previous books by Ron Culley

The Kaibab Resolution. Kennedy & Boyd 2010.
I Belong To Glasgow (foreword by Sir Alex Ferguson)
The Grimsay Press, 2011
A Confusion of Mandarins. Grosvenor House. 2011.
Glasgow Belongs To Me. Grosvenor House
(electronic media only) 2012
The Patriot Game. Grosvenor House 2013
Shoeshine Man. A one-act play. SCDA. 2014.
One Year. Grosvenor House 2015
Alba: Who Shot Willie McRae? Grosvenor House 2016
The Never Ending Story (Editor) Downie Allison Downie 2018

Web address
www.ronculley.com

Celebrity Reviews

"I laughed until I wet myself. But then I am a very old man."
The Dalai Lama.

"Just the funniest and most informative book I've ever read."
Stevie Wonder.

"These travel writings are right up there with Michael Palin, Stephen Fry and Bill Bryson. Very funny and interesting."
Mrs. Culley

Culley's down-home reviews of Nashville's Country and Western tradition are somewhat at odds with my own experience last time I had a few beers at Moe's Bar!
Luciano Pavarotti

"I prefer the Kindle edition."
Abraham Lincoln.

Contents

Your intrepid author. Inside the Arctic Circle in Tromsø.

Odyssey

Travels On A Bucket List

Odyssey. (noun) /ˌödd.is.ē/

1. A Greek hexameter epic poem traditionally ascribed to Homer, describing the travels of Odysseus.

2. *(Colloquial).* Long journeys, especially when filled with adventure and fuelled by Guinness and whisky.

Acknowledgements

I suspect that every author with a few books under their belt is sustained by positive feedback received from readers of earlier works and given that I have now had seven books and a play sent out to the world to be enjoyed and commented upon, my first expression of gratitude is to those who not only have read my work but who have taken the time and trouble to comment upon it. Affirmation is important to every sentient being but as a consequence of writing being such an isolated task, endorsement of the effort put in to creating a literary work is of particular significance. It's been much appreciated, highly sustaining and very warming.

Friends and family have also been helpful in ways that may not immediately be apparent to them but they have provided the nourishment that encouraged me to continue to put pen to paper or, perhaps more accurately these days, to press finger to keyboard. I love them all and hope that in my writing they catch a glimpse of aspects of my character that is new to them. Thank you also to my wonderful editor John McManus, the exceptionally talented Alexander Tarbet who designed the book's cover and to the supremely knowledgeable George Cuthbert who commented helpfully on those visits I made to Scottish destinations. They have been great friends to me and have been hugely supportive. My gratitude is boundless.

This book, being comprised of travel writings, could not have been written with any flavour had it not been for the many wonderfully serendipitous dealings I had with people on my journeys. Almost everyone was kind and helpful. But even when I was presented with circumstances of a less savoury, indeed positively unpleasant nature - yes, Mr. Yorkshire in Berwick-upon-Tweed, I'm thinking of you - it's been exhilarating, fascinating and hugely enjoyable.

I also hope I've also managed to convey something of the humour I found in these exchanges.

Introduction

Odysseus travelled for ten years before being able to lend his name to the notion of an *'odyssey'*. Well, mine took fewer years and was much less random but, like Odysseus, it brought me back home, for a while anyway.

They say that travel broadens the mind. Well, so goes the old adage. Mark Twain also reckoned that 'travel is fatal to prejudice, bigotry, and narrow-mindedness'; and as an unprejudiced, liberal, Glasgow-born man, those sentiments don't apply to me in the slightest - except when I visit Edinburgh.

Travel for most of my adult life has been of immeasurable pleasure and has sated my need to attend my curiosity about cultures other than my own. I love travel. Like Henry David Thoreau once remarked, 'I do not seek merely safely to reach death only to discover that I had not lived'.

You need only open a newspaper or watch the evening news to be fully aware of the horrors and depredations of modern society, but we also live in a wonderful world that is full of beauty, charm and adventure and it has never been enough for me merely to set foot on the turf of another country. I've always been keen to enjoy the food, understand the customs, religion and the people of anywhere I've visited - whether the far-flung jungles of Vietnam or the closer villages of Scotland. Finding myself with the time and resources to visit places I'd always wanted to see, I took the opportunity and set about devising a bucket list of countries and cities I intended visiting. Occasionally in company but more often on my own, I set off and made good on the promise to myself that I'd visit every last destination on my list.

Rudyard Kipling said that the first condition of understanding a foreign country was to *smell* it and I think I know what he was getting at. It's not uncommon to visit a country for the first time but to so ensconce oneself in the trappings of home that the experience becomes neutered, dulled and familiar. Travelling, in my view, forces us to trust strangers, leave behind the familiar comforts of home and to place ourselves slightly off-kilter. Not that I eschew comfort when travelling. I don't feel the need to sleep overnight in a bus station when there's an alternative but also when travelling I don't feel the need to sip cocktails in sumptuous surroundings - except in Ho Chi Minh City where, as I recount later, I let myself down badly.

In this book, I've only included visits to places where I wrote contemporaneously. That is to say, my writings reflected the happenings of the day recorded shortly upon their having taken place. This provides a diaried flavour and content that would be denied the reader if I captured events some time afterwards. Consequently, I've not mentioned my argument with armed security guards in Moscow's Kremlin, being stood up by Vice-President Dan Quayle in Washington D.C. the day I was scheduled to meet him for a one-on-one chat about local economic development in the Eisenhower Executive Office Building located next to the West Wing on the White House premises, standing on the Great Wall of China, meeting Fidel Castro in Havana, being shown round the safe house used by Stalin and Lenin in St Petersburg before the Russian Revolution (something to this day denied the Russian people), being flown over the rooftops of Paris in a Police helicopter because the pilot liked the Scots, having my ear set on fire by a barber in Istanbul, being held at gunpoint in Palestine by three Israeli soldiers when I crossed the border illegally and sitting in the Flight Director's chair in Johnson Space Centre during a joint American/Russian space mission and saying in my best cod-American accent the words, "Houston, we hevv a praablem," only to be told by a stern-faced older man standing nearby, "Son, I heard those words for real!".

These stories and more can only be prised from my lips if over a beer in a decent bar somewhere. And where I *have* reminisced, my words are based upon notes or writings I made at the time.

My own travel-writing inspirations, Bill Bryson, Stephen Fry and Michael Palin, have tended to write about journeys which have a beginning, middle and an end. There's cohesion to their perambulations. Not me. Not here. I tend to take an interest in a place on the bucket list, consult my diary and take off. It has allowed me to find reason to journey to Tromsø in the Arctic Circle and then swan off to New Delhi and Kathmandu, visit Jerusalem then take an interest in Country and Western music in Nashville; the only cohesive feature being my interest in somewhere. I've found it fascinating, met lots of lovely people and had great fun. I hope I've communicated as much in these pages

Having commenced this introduction with an old adage, it seems appropriate to end with one; a Scottish one. *'We're a' Jock Thomson's bairns'*...which attempts to suggest that we're all the same under the sun and that Abraham Maslow had a point when he suggested that wherever we hail from, all humankind seeks clean air, healthy food, unpolluted water, shelter, warmth, sex, sleep, protection from the elements, security, order, stability, freedom from fear, friendship, intimacy, trust, acceptance, love, independence, self-respect and personal growth. Certainly when on my travels whether in the Arctic Circle or in a desert, I've found humanity to be humanity and that Maslow's hierarchy of needs are well-founded if slightly deficient in ignoring the need of a decent glass of whisky now and again.

*Some of the words that follow have appeared in the columns of the Big Issue magazine.

Odyssey

Travels On A Bucket List

An Atheist Goes To Lourdes

Bordeaux, Lourdes

Most husbands have a wife who would be somewhat irked at the prospect of their other half regularly heading off for a distant shore. Mine helped me pack and drove me at speed to the airport! I'm personally convinced that these generous acts were to do with her empathic understanding of my innate wanderlust although I did often notice collections of new handbags and high-heeled shoes upon my return.

Anyway, finding myself with the time and resources to travel to places on the globe I'd always sought to visit, I made a list; north beyond Iceland deep into the Arctic Circle, west to the Pacific Ocean, east to the South China Sea and south to Africa at the Indian Ocean below the equator. I'd made a list of places all over the world that I'd love to visit along with a second list of small locations mostly in Scotland that I wanted better to understand… and I wanted to write about my experiences. I love my nation of Scotland, but first, I decided to pay a visit to the other member of 'the Auld Alliance', France.

I rose early to catch the 6.30am train to Euston and thence to Bordeaux which I'll use as a base for my visit to Lourdes on which town I'm writing an article for *The Big Issue*. Upon arrival in London, I was delighted to see an earlier *Big Issue* article I'd written on Sir Alex Ferguson which featured on the front cover being waved about by vendors on street corners in London. Nice to think my efforts will be read by a goodly number of readers across the UK and generate sales to address the issue of homelessness – although the *Big Issue* seller whose neck was warmed by an Arsenal scarf may have been waving the magazine less enthusiastically than others.

An uneventful journey south, although Eurostar, the hi-speed channel train disappointed in comparison to the earlier Virgin Pendolino from Glasgow. Practical and bland, it just made 'serviceable' standard. Once underway, I found myself irritated in the on-train cafe when buying a coffee. The coach had been commandeered by around a dozen 'Hooray Henrys' all drinking Champagne at a pace that suggested that they'd just been informed that an asteroid was speeding towards earth. One of them behaved as if a Keith Moon impersonator out on a bender and being pretty raucous and silly. Nothing outrageous but small children in Glasgow are taught whilst still in the cradle to narrow their eyes, manufacture a level stare and in an enhanced Glasgow accent, make their requirements known. I began formulating some words something along the lines of, "Make way, you bunch of raggabrash scobberlotchers or somesuch taunt understandable only by Old Etonians before returning to my seat. However, I worried there'd be a future Chancellor among them who'd have been scarred by the confrontation and who might have messed about with the Barnet Formula so I desisted.

The cross-Paris Metro trip from *Gare du Nord* to *Montparnasse* railway stations was undertaken with ease despite earlier dire on-line warnings about its complexity and physical test. I'd been so looking forward to my Bordeaux wine–tasting but while awaiting the train, a visit to the station café bar saw me reduced to a spluttering hapless as I was served up what can only be described as a glass of sweetish, warmish vinegar. As I looked around to confer with anyone who might catch my eye, I noticed that all the regulars were each sipping at a small glass of local beer. It's easy to be wise after the event.

As it powered muscularly through the night at colossal speed, the TGV served up a wonderfully elegant, chilled *Viognier* which I drained rather too quickly to persuade fellow travellers that I was a *connoisseur*. You can take the man out of Glasgow...

It did rather occur to me as a consequence of an article I was reading on the train about the *travails,* the illnesses, the weather and the threat of robbery experienced by travellers who made their way slowly south from Paris in days of yore that *my* sole discomfort was trying to secure a second glass of *Viognier* as I sped towards Bordeaux in cushioned comfort!

One surprise was that the much vaunted French TGV - and it deserves its status as a first class rail experience - didn't have ticket barriers at Montparnasse. Nor were there station guards in evidence on the open platform. I'd read that all tickets had to be authenticated through having them verified by scanning them in a yellow machine before boarding the train or a fine would be levied. I'd sweated buckets over making sure I'd remember to do this and did so...but if there was a ticket collector on board, he didn't trouble me. I could have made the entire journey through France free! But I got pretty edgy when everyone - and I do mean *everyone* - got up and prepared to detrain leaving me the only person on the coach. Could this be Bordeaux half an hour early? It turned out to be a place called Libourne...a *popular* place called Libourne in northern Aquitaine, given that most people on the train had travelled the length of France to get there! I could determine no reason why this should be so.

I arrived at Bordeaux bang on time and in no little comfort. That changed immediately when my overconfidence saw me walk in circles for an hour and in darkness to find my accommodation which was actually only yards from the station. Eegit!

I slept very poorly as a consequence I guess, of the interminable cups of strong coffee consumed on the day's fleet of trains. Invariably I take decaffeinated everything but having accepted on the trains what had been on offer, I lay awake staring wide-eyed at the ceiling most of the night. As might then have been predicted, I fell asleep approaching 6.00am and was half an hour late for my 8.00am breakfast.

Out at 9.00am to take the measure of Bordeaux in weak spring sunshine; a handsome city, obviously wealthy although populated by a higher number of Eastern European-looking beggars than I'd have anticipated. I walked towards the old city. The French have an old saying, *'If you step in dog shit with your left foot, it's lucky. If you step in dog shit with your right foot, it's unlucky.'*...Now *there's* an old French saying that merits review! Cursing and wrinkling my nose, I prodded and scooped at my left shoe with a stick as best I could and soldiered on.

Their transport system is simply marvellous. A combination of a first class integrated metro system; trams, buses, river-taxis, bicycles (as a consequence of being as flat as Amsterdam) acres of underground parking and lots of pedestrianisation results in a city centre largely free from traffic jams and pollution. I enjoyed a brief trip to the small *Stade Chaban Delmas*, home of Bordeaux FC and emailed a photograph to my youngest sons who have an abiding interest in all things football.

I'd a bit of trouble working out how to catch *Le Bateaux de Cub* - the Bordeaux river-taxi - but the Tourist Office sorted me out and most impressive it was. Despite this being intended as a trip to some cold and windswept destination I ventured that my wife would abhor, Bordeaux was bathed in warm sunshine all afternoon. As I sat sunning myself at the rear of the good ship *l'Hirondelle*, it occurred to me that I'd better not return with a tan or my wife would never again believe my protestations of great hardships on my adventures.

Sur le bateaux, a man in his late sixties with a beer gut that threatened to knock over unwary passengers as he turned, was photographing a tall, leather-clad, red-headed young lady whom I'd initially imagined must be his niece. Not classically pretty enough to be a model, she was nevertheless dressed alluringly. His prowess behind the camera was either questionable or excellent as he continually shot her with the sun directly behind her. Perhaps he thought her too ugly to view properly. Whatever their relationship, she was obviously a very *affectionate* niece!

The boat made easy work of the chocolate coloured, swift-flowing River Garonne that lies at the heart of Bordeaux's success as a city, permitting as it has done for centuries, the export of the now world famous Bordeaux wine. I read that per annum, average vintages produce over 700 million bottles of Bordeaux wine, made by more than 8,500 *châteaux* ranging from large quantities of everyday table wine, to some of the most expensive and prestigious wines in the world. However, the wine industry in Bordeaux has been experiencing economic problems in the face of strong international competition from New World wines and a reduction in French consumption. Over-production now threatens the industry and there are plans to uproot 17,000 hectares of the 124,000 hectares of vineyards in Bordeaux. Bugger! I was beginning to imagine good Claret at thirty bob a pop!

I headed off to Lourdes this morning in my rented car but turned on to the wrong motorway and ended up in Biarritz - only some one hundred and five miles in the wrong direction. My intended article: '*An Atheist Goes To Lourdes*' was under threat. An article entitled '*An Atheist Goes To Biarritz And Has A Chilled Glass Of Wine On The Beach,*' doesn't have quite the same ring to it!

I wandered the streets of the very pretty, up-market town of Biarritz before returning to my hired car. I headed along a road that ran in the shadow of the mountains for most of the journey and eventually, in mid-afternoon, drove into the town at which I'd meant to arrive some five hours earlier.

Hugging tight to the tree-lined foothills of the Pyrenees, there is at first nothing remarkable about the small commune of Lourdes in the Hautes-Pyrénées Département of South-west France. Despite a couple of forgotten Christmas lights hanging from lampposts and snow-capped mountains looming over the village, it was quite warm despite winter beginning to acknowledge the arrival of spring and with it, Easter...and with Easter, pilgrims.

On entering Lourdes, I was guided helpfully by a large McDonalds' sign which directed the hungry to their fast-foods and the pious to the Grotto at Massabielle; an area of the township that was more commercialised than I'd imagined. Stalls selling all manner of religious bric-a-brac crowded the sidewalk.

Not unprepossessing, Lourdes might otherwise be indistinguishable from any other French *ville* were it not for the majestic castle that dominates its skyline - and an international reputation claimed back in 1858 when over a period of twelve weeks, a fourteen year old local girl, Bernadette Soubirous claimed to have seen some eighteen separate apparitions of a woman in a white dress. Although the spectre was invisible to older persons who were standing nearby, Bernadette told how it wore a blue waistband and had a yellow rose on each foot. On the sixteenth visit of the apparition, in front of ever-increasing crowds, it allegedly spoke and said in the local *Bigourdan* dialect, *"Que soy era immaculada concepciou."* (I am the Immaculate Conception.) Now at this point, rationalists like me would reach for a book on psychology and turn to the chapter on the neuro-psychological theory of hypnotic suggestion; but I suppose that it should also be born in mind that at that time in 19th Century France, there was a culture of popular piety that was common throughout the Pyrenean region. In the years leading up to 1858, there were reports of several children in small local villages who claimed to see apparitions.

However, to the faithful, the events alleged to have taken place in the grotto were very real and after water began to flow and has purportedly surged from the Grotto ever since Bernadette had dug in the earth, healings began to be claimed and the shrine began to earn a national and international reputation for therapeutic powers.

Over the years, countless miracle cures have been claimed but only a total of sixty-seven miraculous healings have been recognised by the church. However, it would appear that miracles are nowadays less frequent, having become somewhat more difficult to authenticate. Back in 2008, Monsignor Jacques Perrier, the Bishop of Tarbes and Lourdes, announced that there would be a new approach taken that would take account of the advances of modern science. So nowadays, there are some significant hurdles to be overcome as Vatican rules now demand that the illness healed must have been incurable and that the healing must be sudden, instantaneous, complete, without any subsequent relapse and without the benefit of earlier medication.

Lists can be examined that detail the various cures that have occurred which have matched these criteria - but it is populated with examples of people who have been restored having been diagnosed with pulmonary tuberculosis, peritonitis, rheumatic mitral valvular heart disease, abdominal tumour and the like - but with not a re-grown severed limb among the sixty-seven miracles. Perhaps that looks a bit too *unambiguous* a wonder to behold!

Since 1858, some two hundred million people have made the pilgrimage to Lourdes and the church has claimed that sixty-seven have been cured of their ailment; that's a success rate of something like one in three million. I'd wager that at least the same proportion might make a similar claim of Irn Bru or Red Bull (other miracle curative drinks are available). And scientists who have analysed the miracle waters of Lourdes have determined that there can be shown to be no scientific or medicinal properties in its peculiarity although you can purchase an entire litre of the stuff from one of the local vendors for only one hundred Euros....that's *one hundred* Euros!

Nevertheless, the faithful return and return again. In Lourdes there are around fifteen thousand residents but this number is inflated each year as some five million pilgrims and tourists swell its footways. However, with just under three hundred hotels, the commune has the greatest number of hotels, apartments, bed & breakfast establishments and guest houses per square mile in France after its capital city and is well prepared to cope with the numbers that crowd its streets each year.

However, many remain sceptical about Lourdes and its alleged healing power. Some argue that the health improvements claimed by those visiting the Grotto at Massabielle are little other than as a consequence of the placebo effect. Moreover, they dismiss the 'Catholic Disneyland' experience as little more than faith-healing. But in the commune of Lourdes, the faithful; the believers in the story of Bernadette Soubirous and her apparition, would certainly demur - although it has to be said that the phenomenon that is Lourdes brings sufficiently substantial tourist Euros to the town to provide a mild vested interest in them maintaining pilgrim visiting numbers.

So is there any substance to the Lourdes apparition? Well, two hundred million people can't be wrong, can they? But I'll say this about apparitions. They're not daft; they seem to prefer a warm welcome. You don't see many Catholic apparitions appearing in Mecca or Amritsar, just in places where the faithful might doff their cap like Knock in Ireland, Fátima in Portugal, Garabandal in Spain or Guadalupe in Mexico.

There are people who believe that Elvis is still alive and that's fine by me so long as I'm not required to believe similarly. So, if there are those who take comfort from the story told by Bernadette Soubirous, that's equally fine by me. I merely regret the impact that belief in the supernatural has over science and logic. As I left Lourdes in my rental car, I reminded myself of the comment made by Belgian philosopher Etienne Vermeersch who averred that of the numbers who have visited and who have claimed to have been cured, a greater proportion must have been killed or injured on the way to or returning from the township. I decided to use my mirrors, obey speed limits and drive carefully rather than ask St Christopher to bless my journey.

Although I spent more time than I'd anticipated on the French motorway system and although it cost a small fortune at each *péage*, thoughtfully situated at what seemed like one hundred yard intervals, the roads were uncongested and lined by beautifully scented pine trees. The sun was out and behind me, making driving a pleasure - even at the brisk and assertive pace at which I drove.

Returning me home, the TGV, leaving Bordeaux half an hour late, headed north under a greying sky. I subdued my disappointment in the absence of a clear blue heaven due to my Glaswegian roots, as a 'greying sky' is usually a precursor of cries to fire up the barbecue in consequence of such fine weather! The train was very agreeable and commodious, in direct proportion to the subsequent discomfort of boarding the Metro from *Montparnasse* to *Gare du Nord* once I'd arrived in Paris. It was as if passengers had been packed in like sardines - other than the fact that we were upright and not horizontal, not dressed in brine and didn't smell of fish... although the gentleman standing next to me...

The complex convolutions required of travellers between stations caused me to reflect upon my current poor assessment of the ability of my youngest boys, Conor and Ciaran, to plan ahead. There was no way I'd have been able to travel between Bordeaux and my home station of Williamwood without choreographing the journey down to the finest detail. As I shook my head in regret, hoping that maturity and the years would be kind to them in this regard, I noticed that the zip on the compartment in my bag containing all of my tickets and my passport lay wide open to the elements...so make that choreographing the journey down to the finest detail and not being an eegit!

I had an hour and a half to spare at *Gare du Nord* and decided upon a lunch of *Croque Monsieur* and a *quatre carafe de Beaujolais Nouveaux* in a pavement café close by in order to speed me on my way from Paris. I'd my mouth shaped for a cheeky wee glass of chilled white wine when I became the day's entertainment as having been delivered of a glass container of red wine, I protested that I'd ordered white. Who knew *Beaujolais Nouveaux* was red? Much merriment from the waiting staff. Fortunately, I overheard myself described as *l'Anglais*". Much further merriment from *me*, however, when I discovered that as a consequence of my poor schoolboy French, I'd inadvertently ordered and consumed a half-carafe instead of a quarter-carafe. Unsteadily, I made my way to Eurostar across the road.

Upon arrival at Euston Station, my heart sank as I joined a queue to negotiate the fact that I'd appeared to have lost my rail ticket and couldn't produce it in time for the 16.30 train to Glasgow. My thoughts turned to the earlier open pouch in my rucksack containing my tickets. As I neared the front of the queue, my strategy of producing all of the supporting documentation proving I'd bought the ticket ebbed in persuasiveness as I began to appreciate that they'd charge the full fare given that it would have been a simple task for a bad man to give the correct ticket to a pal in order that both might claim boarding rights with the twin documentation. I was correct in my presumption and had to cough up a further £101 to travel home. I resigned myself to my fate and decided to be honest when later recounting the sorry tale to my youngest sons, whom I'd often accuse of carelessness and having no understanding of the value of money! *Mea culpa, mea culpa, mea máxima culpa.*

I sat back in my seat, relaxed and headed northwards contemplating the world as I sipped at a Gin & Tonic that had been poured by a steward as one drink from a can...a *can*! They'll call it progress and I suppose it is but when they start offering me Guinness in tablet form, I'm arming myself. Some welcome rest and recuperation beckoned and I made the most of it as, my appetite whetted, I prepared for my next trip – this time, a longer rail journey through Europe.

A European Rail Trip

Brussels, Cologne, Warsaw, Krakow, Auschwitz,
Vienna, Bratislava, Budapest

How's this for serendipity?

I was invited to take part in an exercise to review a new fleet of sleeping carriages to be brought into use by the Caledonian Rail Sleeper which would travel between Glasgow and London in 2017. For some reason the mock-up carriages were concealed in a disguised warehouse in darkest Broxburn near Livingston in Scotland, protected by armed guards and machine gun turrets at each corner of the compound. (I made that bit up about the armed guards...and the turrets.)

I was of particular interest to my hosts as I had to leave the meeting at 8.00pm sharp because I was bound for the *real* Caledonian Sleeper departing Glasgow at 11.40pm and would be travelling thereafter through seven different countries on mainland Europe where I'd be able to compare train interiors at first hand. 'Could they contact me upon my return?' I was asked.

I found the New Caledonian Sleeper mock-up compartments frustratingly modern, worryingly efficient and deeply unlovely. Space had been tightened; the fabric instead of faded leather seemed to be a type of Harris Tweed whose complex, multi-lined design strobed wildly, threatening an epileptic fit to all who viewed it. It would be like sitting inside a very long, very fast caravan. I offered my opinions over a two hour interrogation and drove home. I showered in anticipation of having to go without one for two days before my wife, Jean drove me to Central Station in Glasgow where I boarded the train early in order to dine prior to taking to my solo cabin and sleep.

The lounge car was comprised of leather sofas and tables and chairs that were not affixed to the floor...the only such arrangement permitted these days by UK rail authorities where Health and Safety regulations otherwise require furnishings nailed to the floor. It reeked of the faded glory of days gone by. I enjoyed a small plate of haggis and a brandy before retiring to my comfortable cabin where I opened my small travel wallet within which were all of the rail tickets that would take me variously to London, Brussels, Cologne, Warsaw, Krakow, Auschwitz, Bratislava and finally Budapest: a European Rail Journey and one I'd been thinking of, if not actively planning, for years.

The small sleeping compartment was comfortable, the bed warm and I was soon lulled to sleep by the train's movements; the clickety-clack of yesteryear now gone as a consequence of longer, smoother, welded track. Awakened upon arrival at Euston by a most attentive steward who proffered a tray containing a coffee and bacon roll, I consumed these, left and walked the short distance to 140 Gower Street wherein used to be located MI5, now given over to student accommodation. I was using the trip *inter alia* to put more colour on my then almost completed historical fiction *'Alba: Who Killed Willie McRae?'* and wanted to be able to describe accurately the former spy chief's office block referenced in the book.

Upon my arrival at St. Pancras for my train to Brussels, I visited a currency exchange outlet to ask if they'd be good enough to exchange £100 in Scottish notes. I'd fondly imagined they'd merely do a quick swap as a favour to a traveller but the cashier looked at the Clydesdale Bank notes as if they were Monopoly money, inspecting me just as suspiciously as if attempting to establish if I was Butch Cassidy before eventually telling me there'd be a £2.50 charge for their inconvenience. I took a beat but accepted since I knew I'd have problems exchanging them on the continent. When I looked at the receipt it stated 'Soiled Notes Exchange. £2.50!' *Saor Alba!*

London was sticky and humid even at seven-thirty in the morning but my short detour caused me to be slightly late for my connection to Brussels on Eurostar. I'd a few anxious moments as a large clock in front of me showed thirty-five minutes before departure and beneath it was a sign in several languages insisting that the gate would close thirty minutes before departure time. The queue moved worryingly slowly; first through the ticketing gate then Security and finally Passport Control. My mood wasn't helped by Security being staffed by two disinterested men who took their time, soporifically checking hand luggage, and passport control staff who insisted on using an automated electronic system which was so confusing they had to intervene in almost every case, doubling the time needed to get through. Finally I emerged into open space and made my way to my train seat with five minutes to spare. Phew!

I settled in to my window seat but a crying French wean one row in front of me saw me plug my ears and listen to loud music on my iPad; ('Runrig', if you must know).

As the train emerged from the Channel Tunnel at Calais, I looked around for the 'Jungle', the refugee camp which is currently the cause of much media controversy but at 150 miles per hour, the countryside was a blur and I saw nothing of import.

I'd visited Brussels many times before, to meet colleagues in The European Parliament. It's a pleasant city but as a consequence of my near miss at St. Pancras station, I stayed around the vicinity of Brussels Midi and waited for my Inter Continental Express (ICE) train to Cologne in Germany. I was tempted to visit the station's management team to point out that Intercontinental is actually one word, or is at least hyphenated and that the trains should be re-designated 'IE' trains but I decided they'd probably go with the existing sexy acronym rather than accept the accuracy I'd insist upon if I was King of the World.

I spent an hour and a half under a canopy in a Brussels' thoroughfare sipping at a Belgian beer, people-watching and avoiding the mild drizzle. Depressingly, some of the people I watched were soldiers and police officers, all armed as if they were about to invade a small nation, parading the streets following an ISIS attack on their city some weeks earlier. People went about their business but there was the merest whiff of lockdown on the streets.

Taking advantage of the much reduced fares available on the continent, I made the ICE train early and took my seat in the first class compartment while the brute of a train still smouldered at the platform awaiting release. The toilet looked much more like the thing. A normal door lock is employed whereby it's obvious from the inside that the door is secured - unlike the British Rail model which has wedded itself to the notion that toilets should have press-button, air-locked doors which slowly reveal the occupant to the world as if a prize in a TV game show. My dismay at these modern devices when on Virgin Rail isn't eased by the jocular tones of a pre-recorded announcer who prevails on users mid-pee not to place 'sanitary products, nappies or goldfish' down the toilet. Unfortunately, although secure, this high-tech WC failed to show any evidence of how to flush the toilet or dry one's hands. I left, wiping my hands on my trousers and used my constant companion, pocket alcohol-based hand sanitiser to do what a well-signed plumbing system should have taken care of.

The entire first class carriage on the Brussels-Cologne train seemed to be occupied by elderly English travellers who seemed to delight in talking loudly about the virtues of Brexit, the recent and unexpected vote by the UK to leave the European Community. I'd expected no less than traditional Scottish (when sober) reticence from all world-wide travellers. One Home Counties country squire who was clearly used to traveling on this particular ICE train stood intermittently in the aisle and pronounced loudly to the entire carriage blethering on about how borders must be protected and how the UK was making a pig's ear of it before announcing that he now lives in Hanover. It was as if I'd joined the occupants of a well-to-do care home for retired members of the right-wing 1922 Committee who'd been let out without matron on a day trip. I took refuge in my ear-plugs once more.

A brief snooze then a rail tour through a sunny Belgium and Germany. Blue skies all the way. Jesus, these countries look wealthy. Even the graffiti looked charming...*'Je Suis Charlie!'* shouted one gable end...but it was the *only* graffito, it was paint-sprayed beautifully in italics and was completely picturesque. Litter I saw none. The cities through which we passed, Ans, Liege and Aachen looked both elegant and effortlessly rich. Expensive public realm surrounded soaring buildings and houses without crumbling plasterwork or uncut grass. They seemed to want for nothing. *But does this environment produce good footballers?* I found myself wondering before remembering the recent drubbings handed Scotland in competition.

The only word I can find to describe German farms along the rail route is 'tidy'. In Scotland, fields tend to follow the contours of the land, resulting in fields the shape if not the size of Australia but in Germany it was as if a higher authority had determined that all German farmers should have farms composed of land shaped as if football pitches. 'This football pitch shall be for potatoes'. 'This football pitch shall be for wheat.' This football pitch shall be for barley.' Tidy! Golf courses I saw none. What kind of people *live* here?

I found myself initially somewhat disconcerted - although I recovered – when, having been asked by a stewardess if I'd like something to drink on board the train, responded, 'Do you have any wine?" before being asked to suggest a particular grape. I queried further whether they'd any *Sauvignon Blanc* and was rewarded by a complimentary half-bottle delivered to my plush leather seat with astonishing leg-room and upon which I benefitted from excellent air-conditioning. I'd been expecting but a glass although I managed to deal with my disappointment.

I've been used to travelling on Scotrail and British Rail where, on those few occasions where the track parallels a motorway, now and again one can witness speedy cars overtaking the train. Famously, German *autobahns* do not have any speed limits but the ICE train screamed past any and all carbon powered vehicles as if they were stationary. I hesitate to estimate the speed of the ICE train but it must have been close to a million miles per hour! *Deutschland uber alles!*

Cologne was very pleasant. Immediately outside the station stands the magnificent *Hohe Domkirche St. Petru Cathedral;* Cologne Cathedral which can accommodate some forty thousand worshippers. That's about the same capacity as Stamford Bridge, home of Chelsea Football Club although I gather that chants of *'What a load of rubbish'* sounds better when intoned in Latin by monks rather than drunken oiks from London. I'd earlier read that eighty-five per cent of Cologne had been destroyed by Allied bombing during WW2 and couldn't for the life of me understand how it could be that the cathedral, an absolutely beautiful example of ancient Gothic architecture (it's the largest Gothic construction in Europe) could have escaped untouched. As I emerged from its internal gloom, I noticed photographs of the site after the war. The cathedral had been pummelled by high explosives and had been reduced to rubble. It had taken fourteen direct hits. The twin spires had been an easily recognisable navigational landmark for Allied aircraft bombing. Only one spire had survived...but the good people of Cologne had rebuilt it and I swear had I not seen the proof, I'd have argued all day long that it was in its original state. Quite remarkable. It looked like it had been rooted there untouched since construction began in 1248.

The information Office in Cologne was not untypical of any other similar facility in any other similar city. From operatives standing outside its portals I accepted proffered leaflets announcing river cruises, affordable restaurants and hotels...and one which matter-of-factly offered information about *Pascha*, the largest legal brothel in Europe. I sat in an outdoor café and read the leaflet. It transpires that prostitution is legal in Germany and that just outside the city is located an old converted twelve storey hotel wherein each room along each corridor is occupied by a lady of the night. The brochure intimated that a five Euro admission charge would provide access

18

to the building and customers should thereafter negotiate all other details with their host or hostess. Apparently all tastes are catered for. There are gentlemen for ladies and gentlemen, ladies for gentlemen and ladies, transsexuals for...I suppose...other transsexuals, ladies with whips and probably *laddies* with whips for all I know. Every vice seems to be catered for other than bestiality, paedophilia and Radio Two disc jockeys. What impressed me about the leaflet was the Teutonic and frankly practical approach taken. There's no forced exploitation of ladies, there's free health care, they each pay tax and they all have security and somewhere to live. I well understand the arguments on the other side and I'm not looking for a matronly 'tut' or a feminist slap on the side of my head but the German approach does seem to have some merit when you consider the dangerous disbenefits to exploited ladies of streetwalking under railway bridges in darker parts of the city.

As I read the leaflets, I noticed I'd been handed one alerting visitors to a 'Hop-on, Hop-off' service for tour buses. I thought immediately that this might be a better description of the facilities available at *Pascha;* a more engaging strapline.

In Cologne, the music and the musak were all American, the taxi drivers Turkish and every second restaurant Italian but somehow it was all essentially Germanic. My fancy wristwatch which measures all of my waking and sleeping activity told me that I'd already walked for ten miles today and had climbed the equivalent of thirty-four floors. I was rank! It was hot and I was sweating. Because I enjoy eating local delicacies when I travel, I'd decided that I must eat *Wiener schnitzel* and have a German *Weiss bier* outside to cool down and walked until I found an establishment that fitted the bill. Unfortunately I was now some way distant from Cologne's *Hauptbahnhof* and decided that given my inability to shower until tomorrow given tonight's second consecutive overnight train journey, I'd better invest in some scented aftershave, paid what I felt was an extravagant amount of money and doused myself liberally hoping to disguise any malodorous effect of my continuing meanderings *sans* ablutions.

Cologne Railway Station, *Hauptbahnhof*, is massive as befits the region's largest city. It has a wonderful left-luggage facility. Small pop-up units are located all over the station. You thumb a Euro coin into a slot, a grill slides up inviting you to place your case or rucksack inside; it closes, gives you a receipt and whisks your luggage away to a bat cave somewhere near middle earth, returning it to any of the many units that populate the station when you re-enter your receipt. Brilliant! Deposit and retrieval each worked in seconds...like three or four seconds. It was as if Penn and Teller had had a hand in the backstage magic!

As night fell, I ventured out of the rear of the station looking for a coffee shop and wandered into a darker, litter-strewn space where loud drunks howled at the moon. Ah! This was the area which had been the focus of the 2015 New Year's Eve sexual assaults, with over 500 women reporting that they had been sexually assaulted by persons of African and Arab appearance. The incident had made headline news all over the world as it fed into the refugee crisis on the shores of Europe. It made the place seem a bit more like a normal city actually...not because of the sexual attacks... but because of the drunks. It was later alleged that this was an example of 'fake news' and had been fabricated. Who knows?

Ten minutes before 23.13 hrs as scheduled, the *Jan Kiepura ICE* sleeper train arrived and chaos ensued. Many of the coaches were sleepers and the designers had saved space by narrowing the corridor on each one. In consequence the long corridor in each wagon could take only one person going in one direction. Given that many people were converging on their cabin from both directions there was a lot of frustrated reversing going on.

I found my cabin and accessed it quite easily. It was roomier than the Caledonian Sleeper and very functional with sink, wardrobe, seat and bed all most acceptable. The male steward didn't speak a word of English and I couldn't communicate in German so we did a lot of smiling and miming but we both seemed to have managed to have all our questions answered.

Wow! I awoke to blue skies over Berlin as the *Jan Kiepura* powered towards Warsaw. I hadn't appreciated how hard was my mattress until I laid me down to sleep around midnight. My wife, Jean had phoned late on saying that my youngest son, Ciaran seemed to have enjoyed his second day in a row at university having commenced his criminology degree the day before so reassured and tired, l pulled the duvet over me before realising that I seemed to be sleeping on one of those absurdly named IKEA ironing boards called *Glimp* or *Skall* or something. I like a firm mattress but this was concrete. However I was soon able to ignore the absence of comfort as the chassis of the train seemed anxious to part from its shell at any moment. The noise was tremendous as metal pulled and ground against metal. Every turn in the solum seemed to threaten a parting of the ways midst much metallic squealing, groaning and creaking. I made it through to morning albeit now with what I anticipate will be lifelong spinal problems.

With Teutonic efficiency, my personal steward arrived precisely at 8.00am with coffee as he'd mimed the previous night. He folded my bed away and in doing so turned the cabin into a very comfortable and spacious office-cum-conservatory as seating sprang from the wall. I opened the accompanying food parcel he'd brought with interest but it turned out to be a small, hard loaf of sliced black bread which had the look and consistency of a discoloured half-brick. I tried a slice with some cheese but consigned it all to the dustbin. As I did so I noticed we'd pulled into a station called Rzepin before stopping again at Świebodzin. Ah, we're now in Poland.

Station platforms now exhibited weeds. Graffiti was harsher. Street lights were atop crumbling concrete pillars instead of polished and elegant steel spires and advertising hoardings were hand-painted. There were even manned (I appreciate these days I should refer to these as 'staffed'...but these were all manned) signal boxes. The land was as flat as an ironing board; no major rivers to cross other than the narrow Warta River at Poznan which helped me understand why Hitler's tanks could roll speedily across the plain to invade

Poland so comprehensively at the commencement of WW2. A Polish police officer at a station where the train paused *en route* wore all-black garb, a baseball cap instead of a hat and wore his pistol low on his thigh giving the impression of a western marshal in a frontier town in Wyoming just waiting for the James Gang to attempt to spring Jesse from the town jail.

Poland still looked picturesque but looked a wee but rougher round the edges than its more prosperous and confident neighbour to the west. Mostly arable farming here. I think I noticed only one field whereupon cattle grazed.

I noticed also that along the length of the rail track there were no fences to keep animals or people from wandering on to the line. Even in the cities: kids can just walk off the playing field to retrieve their ball on the rail line from beneath oncoming steel wheels as an Intercontinental Express barrels towards them! Instantly I realised why British Commandos had been so successful at blowing up Axis railways during WW2 whereas on mainland Britain, not one rail line was ever destroyed by sabotage. When the Germans invaded Poland and other European nations, they omitted to erect four feet high wire fences along the sides of rail tracks as was the case in the UK. Had they done so, this single act would doubtless have foxed and confounded both the Commandos and the partisans.

I ventured out from my cabin to visit the toilet. Outside a man stood in the corridor looking out of the window. He looked suspicious. He even wore a black and white thin striped vest. He may as well have been wearing a beret and carrying a bag over his shoulder marked 'Swag'. The doors of the sleeping cabins don't lock from the outside so there was nothing to prevent this obvious sneak-thief from emptying my cabin during my brief absence. I couldn't pee fast enough. I returned to see him standing at an exit door, a bulging suitcase beside him. The train slowed as it approached Poznan Gorkzwyn (I can see I'm going to have problems with the Polish language). I threw open the door to my cabin but my room contents were untouched. I returned my sneak-thief's smile and settled back down with my book, content that I'd foiled a master criminal by the simple trick of enhancing the velocity of my pee.

Aye, the old *Jan Kiepura ICE* was showing its age. Around ten o'clock, having checked that the coast was clear, and satisfied that no one saw me leave my cabin unattended, I wandered down several carriages to the restaurant wagon, more for something to do on this twelve hour train ride than because I was hungry for breakfast. Interestingly, each carriage seemed to have a different configuration from all others. They also had different ways to open the doors between coaches. Some required a push button while others stated 'automatic' but needed a handle to be pulled. Some swung open freely on hinges while others claimed automation but were clearly welded shut and required superhuman strength to prise them apart.

I managed to order a coffee but the Polish menu flummoxed me. I had to use photographs of the foodstuffs available and almost pointed to a scrumptious looking *Kielbasa Bala z Boczkiem* before reading the small print translation which told me that this delight was in fact raw sausage with horseradish and bread. I went instead for the photograph of scrambled egg.

Warsaw was bathed in warm sunlight when I arrived. I felt good about the city as soon as I arrived only to be let down when a large bejowled and unshaven taxi driver took me 'close to' my apartment. "Thurr"...he pointed..."Von hoontret maytres... Thurr". He pointed again. Had he worn a crumpled sailor's cap he'd have been the very image of Bluto, Popeye's nemesis. He pointed a third time. I lugged my travel bag from his boot and set off on what was both a voyage of discovery and a gruelling route march through Market Square until - some half a kilometre away at the bottom of a hill in Warsaw's old town - I found my apartment; an apartment whose front door he could have taken me to if he'd been bothered to circumnavigate the pedestrianised old town. My thighs were burning by the time I reached the fourth floor of the apartment block but the place was modern, clean and fit for purpose. No reception, just earlier e-mailed instructions containing eight figure codes. They all worked perfectly.

After an afternoon walk round the old town, lovingly and wonderfully restored after the Nazis had used it to imprison the city's Jewry before exterminating them and flattening their homes and businesses, I had a much-needed shower and shave, a snooze and ventured forth again in the evening to enjoy some typical Polish cuisine.

I found a beautiful restaurant called *Polka Magda Gessler* just off Market Square which must earlier have been the home of a highly successful merchant or a small hotel; lots of large, dimly lit rooms fixed with dining tables. The menu was a mystery. Some Polish words I can interpret: *Gazeta* for newspaper, *paszport* for passport, *kalendarz* for calendar. Had the menu shown *Daugz Bollokz*, I could have made a stab at it but I ordered *Pomidorowa Domowa* which turned out to be a type of tomato soup which allowed the spoon to stand unsupported and erect as if a steel lighthouse in the middle of the dish. Tasty but very filling. I could (and should) have stopped there but I was intrigued by *Kazanka na okrãglo z pieca podiana z musem z jablek i musztardy* which, upon reading the small print, turned out to be black pudding. It came in a small, cast iron skillet which itself had been placed on a wooden platter.

"Verr haat! Verr, verr haat," explained my flaxen-haired waitress urgently. I'd assumed she'd meant the food and grasped the iron handle to manoeuvre the pan. Clearly the blacksmith working alongside the chef in the kitchen had just allowed the metal handle to cool from the red hot stage of manufacture and my hand blistered and seared immediately. I permitted myself a small yelp and placed my pained hand in a nearby ice-bucket to keep my whimpering at a low ebb so as not to alarm fellow diners.

The black pudding was tasty but it wasn't the world renowned *Stornoway* Black Pudding I was used to. No, sir! More a flavoursome mince served inside a sausage skin. What I'd assumed were wedge potatoes were in fact apples which improved the dish immeasurably. One surprising addition was the placement on top of the dish of what looked like a small mound of the shaved remains of the pubic hair of a young lady who'd undergone what I understand is called a 'Brazilian'...but who'd earlier had the collection died purple. I could see no earthly reason why I might be persuaded to eat this delicacy and moved it carefully to one side.

Unlike some, I have no problem dining alone being, after all, an experienced and self-possessed traveller. Usually I take a book and tonight I had with me my trusty Kindle Fire on which I was re-reading Bill Bryson's first book in which he wrote about some of the places I was to visit. Unfortunately, he wrote so hysterically about his European adventures, I continually threatened to cough projectile *Pomidorowa Domowa* over nearby tables in suppressed laughter so I wiped my eyes and eventually had to start reading Graham Greene's '*Our Man In Havana*' to calm down and permit my chortling convulsions to ease.

Home to an early bed. As all of the television programmes were unintelligibly Polish, I watched an inspiring documentary on my iPad about Glen Campbell's uneven fight with Alzheimer's. He is a remarkable musician but has to use a teleprompter to recall all of his lyrics when performing his standards like 'Rhinestone Cowboy' and 'Galveston', songs he must have sung a thousand times. When he came to the instrumental part of the song he was singing, he read out the words on the teleprompter, '*Glen plays long guitar solo here,*' before realising his mistake and launching into a note-perfect series of riffs and licks that would have tested Eric Clapton.

It reminded me of an incident some years ago when I was flown in a small plane from Glasgow to Barrow-in-Furnace by a company called BAE Systems in order to have a look inside a nuclear submarine they were building (don't ask). There were only four seats in the cabin of the tiny aircraft; two pairs facing each other. Between them was a table which was employed only when needed at which time it was drawn upwards and out between the seats. As coffee was being served, one of my hosts, eager to reassure me that BAE Systems was not a spendthrift company, remarked that it was a second-hand plane and had been bought from some American Country and Western singer whose name was beyond his recall. As the table was put in place, I noticed that etched over its surface was a map of America with all of the states and major cities outlined. A large star, the only one on the map, depicted the position of Wichita in Kansas. "Did you buy it from Glen Campbell?" I asked. My host almost spat his coffee back into the cup. "We did! How on earth did you figure that?" He was clearly a man with an imprecise knowledge of the Glen Campbell songbook.

The following morning I stepped out on my journey around Warsaw. I walked down from the heights of the old town to the River Vistula, a slow moving body of water, hemmed in on one side by a modern quayside whilst on the other was a sandy bank, populated by the occasional fisherman. Trees grew in profusion there. I walked down to the river via the Royal Palace. *Poland has a Royal Palace*, I thought? Subsequent research in a local bar taught me that they have one no longer but that there are many dukes and princes, one of whom, Polish Prince John Zylinski challenged British Member of the European Parliament and leader of UKIP, Nigel Farage to a sword duel following his comments that it was Polish immigrants who caused traffic jams in London. Farage demurred.

I started back towards the old town through an underpass that was well-lit, graffiti-free and felt completely safe. I then had to trudge back up some twenty flights of stairs to find a coffee shop and stood, breathless and dizzy outside a Caffé Nero trying to remember whether, before patronising it, it was one of the coffee chains that didn't pay its taxes in the UK. However, I surrendered to my drouth and stood in a queue behind three burly men dressed as if labourers. They each ordered a bottle of beer (it was ten o'clock in the morning for heaven's sake) and a pastry. As they each left to sit outside and enjoy their repast. I was about to order when the first labourer returned to ask if his pastry could be heated. The harassed female barista looked at him evenly for ten clear seconds, obviously calculating whether to tell him to stick his Danish up his arse before she acceded to his request. Just as she began to heat the offending pastry, a second man appeared and made the same request. Now growling could be discerned but she snatched his croissant angrily and headed towards the microwave. As I began to order a smoothie and my own *unheated* croissant, the third man appeared, oblivious to the rising temper of the hard-pressed barista. He also asked that it be heated. I wanted to shout out, "This called for a bit of leadership, boys! A bit of forward planning...some collaboration, eh?" but restrained myself and after they'd been dispatched, took my smoothie and cold pastry from a still simmering waitress outside into the sunshine.

I sat in the warmth of the sun and enjoyed the peace and quiet which was broken when a group of Japanese tourists came along. Unnoticed by me, there was on the other side of the small green hedge marking the boundary of the *caffé*, a marble bench which, when sat upon, played Chopin's Prelude No. 4 (Opus 28 according to the legend on the seat). As the delighted tourists took turns to sit only for a few seconds, shouting with unalloyed joy that their arse could make music, the opening bars were repeated many times making me feel as if I was drinking my coffee next to a classical ice-cream van.

I started my long walk in the sun into the city centre and was now sweating copiously. I walked too far, inadvertently passed the city centre and had to return in a 'J' manoeuvre. I was knackered, needed a cool beer in a dark bar and found one (it was noon, for heaven's sake!). Opposite were located side by side, two shops; one boasting a banner above its door which said only 'Burgery'. Next to it was a second shop which advertised itself as 'Butchery and Wine', never good advice where sharp knives are in play. As I left, I passed an off-license which in Poland bears the generic name '*Alkohole*', a term I use to describe my mouth.

27

Attempting to cross the wide boulevard to the Tourist Information Office, across from *Warszawa Centralna*, the city's primary railway station, queues had formed on four corners of the intersection; perhaps upwards of thirty people on each corner. The cars and buses all stopped so I strode briskly across the road as fast as my now leaden legs would carry me. Back on the pavement no one moved. Women grasped at their necklaces in shock; men dropped briefcases in horror. The green walk-light hadn't yet come on. I read later that in Poland if such adventurism was witnessed by police, the offender would be instantly carted off to a local police cell where a wire would be attached to electrodes and an alligator clip applied painfully to a body part. However, Poland is a signatory to the European Human Rights Act, the one which currently the UK intends getting rid of. So the good news is that in Poland at present, they can attach an electrode only to one testicle at a time.

After a lunchtime beer to substitute for food, I crossed the road and jumped aboard the 'Hop-on, Hop-off' tourist bus. Unfortunately the earpieces they offered for purposes of information translation were so large they'd have tested Shrek. I held them as close to my too-small ears as possible and listened to the automated commentary. Between the (frankly) bland bletherings I was equally calmed and irritated by the constant murmurings and hummings of Enya.

I took my leave of the bus at the Polish Army Museum where I was greeted in reception by a woman with a five o'clock shadow on her chin and the scowling demeanour of a Les Dawson in drag. Towering above me, she'd obviously been allocated the job by Stalin once she'd completed her deployment as a tank commander during the period when Poland was an associate member of the Red Army. She was completely frightening and insisted that I buy a ticket (I was *going* to buy a ticket) and deposit my small rucksack in return for a token lest I smuggle one of their WW2 machine guns out in a side pocket. Other similarly crabbit women sat in silence in each of the rooms, arms folded, eyeing me suspiciously when I entered. I almost apologised for the noise of my footsteps so reverential was the atmosphere. I couldn't leave quickly enough.

Everywhere there were swords. The Poles are big on swords. Long swords, short words, curved swords, serrated swords...every statue in the city displays a man or woman wielding a sword. Even the statue of the sainted Pope and ex-goalkeeper John Paul II, humbly born Karol Józef Wojtyła in Wadowice, wielded a sword. Okay, *he* didn't, but everyone else did. The Tongs, Fleet, Crew and Cumbie gang members of my Glasgow youth would have loved it here!

I was reminded that in the Battle of Britain in 1940, twenty per cent of the airmen were Polish, flying in out-of-date aeroplanes, a fact I knew. That they also shot down fifty per cent of the enemy aircraft during that battle? Well, that I *didn't* know. Now, UKIP and the Tories would have their countrymen and women return home to Poland. How soon they forget! *And* these nationals have great skills in the plumbing and associated wet trades' areas in addition to aerial combat.

I walked back towards the old town and to the Chopin Museum. Arriving, I viewed the substantial staircase reaching upwards and upwards again to its front door and calculated whether I *really* wanted to experience all it had to offer. Wearily I climbed the stairs only to be met at the door by a large man dressed completely in black and wearing a Madonna microphone.

"Hi," he said cheerily. Things were looking up. "Has you teecket?"

"No," I replied.

"Then you mast go beck downstezz to street and buy one from teecket ouffice."

Head-butting for some in Glasgow is a common enough method of expressing frustration and I almost allowed my weegieness to overcome me but I did as he asked and trudged down, then back *up* the stairs whereupon Madonna greeted me once more. I was overheating and was about to grump but as I entered I was also met by a blast of chill air that could have come directly from the Arctic. I almost fell before him and grasped at his knees, pleading to be allowed entrance.

The museum was modern and used loads of new technology to help me understand the genius of the man; Fryderyk Chopin, that is, not Madonna the tour guide. I was much taken by authentic bill posters of the day which advertised a recital in Warsaw by 'Fred Chopin'. Somehow it made me feel he was more a man of the people offering a right good piano knees-up down the pub. If only Giuseppe Verdi had been known simply as Joe Green perhaps more people would have appreciated 'Rigoletto', 'Il Trovatore' and 'La Traviata'.

In one room a young man named Dmitry Shishkin played a televised and recorded rendition of Chopin's Nocturne No. 2. It was a masterful performance but as the camera caught his fizzog in close-up, it was clear that behind Mr. Shishkin, someone had quietly inserted a red hot poker up his bum setting his face in agony. In the next musical passage, once he'd overcome his poker problem, his eyebrows fled towards his hairline, his eyes narrowed and lips pursed as if someone had had him chew on raw onions and a lemon. This boy took his piano playing seriously.

After a refreshing shower and a snooze I walked into an area of the old town I hadn't visited before. My real purpose was to find a taxi rank for the following day's trip to the station as the old town is largely pedestrianised. I found one and just along from it, a very nice Polish restaurant advertising fish dishes. I was shown to a very comfortable table and armchair which nevertheless enabled food to be eaten without too much landing in one's lap and ordered king prawns to start and perch as a main dish. When the prawns were delivered to my table, the ceramic dish which held them crackled and spat as if it contained molten magma. I wasn't about to be fooled again and avoided the furnace in front of me, reaching instead for a bread roll, separately delivered. I swear I could hear the chef guffawing in the kitchen as my fingertips melted when I clutched the bread; straight from the baker's oven, it was searing hot. I left everything for ten minutes and concentrated on my reading at which point the fare had reduced merely to scalding hot and didn't melt the steel cutlery when I employed a fork. The perch was delicious but was again served with purple pubic hair atop. "Va*s ist das?*" I asked my Polish waitress, throwing my feeble German vocabulary at her on the basis that I was trying to be helpful and because Germany is closer to Poland than is Scotland.

"Watercress," she answered in impeccable English. So there you have it. Purple watercress is all the rage in Poland...and all over the world for all I know. However, once again I moved it carefully to the side of my plate, this time solely on the basis that she might have been lying to me.

I awoke early morning the following day and inspected the big toe on my right foot. It'd been playing up and had developed a nasty looking sore on its tip which was being aggravated when I walked. I deduced that it was pre-gangrenous and would probably require amputation (even my gynaecologist thinks I'm a hypochondriac). Still, after a shower and a clean pair of socks it didn't impede my perambulations and I walked to the taxi rank and headed for Warszawa Centralna.

When I'd earlier left the train upon arrival in Warsaw, the steward who'd been looking after me had handed me back my ticket and proffered another document which was clearly of importance. He seemed to make great play of its significance and I nodded and accepted it without having a clue as to its purpose. On the basis that it might have been the winning ticket in the Polish lottery, I asked what it was at a couple of generic information booths but they each directed me to the Intercity Bureau in the station. This morning on arrival it was just opening and some twenty people barged their way towards its doors, all clamouring for attention. I decided to go for a coffee instead of collecting my millions of Zlotys.

I'm just defeated by the Polish language. It's as if many hundreds of years ago, some drunk ruler of Poland gathered his courtiers around him and decided it would be a great laugh if they could concoct a language that only used letters K,V,W,Z,X,Y,L and. K again. I can just imagine one of this group adding, "Hey, and why not put a diagonal stroke through the letter 'l'? That would really mess them up! They'll think it's a 't'".

The beer almost came down Wojtek's nose but he recovered and countered with, "Great idea, Jareczek. And while we're at it, why not insist that we require a small 5 below an 'e'" He looked around nervously at the group each of whom returned his gaze, stony-faced. "That is...if we ever use an 'e', eh?"

Enter Bronisław.

"But to really take the biscuit, how about we extend the right leg of a capital 'A' and stick a small 'c' on as a tail? He drew a shape on the table." The drunken courtiers laughed long into the night and agreed the proposals.

I'd love to have a glass of whatever they were drinking that night. I've had obvious problems in Arab countries, Asian countries and those using the Cyrillic alphabet like Russia but here in the heart of Europe, where words occasionally suggest the merest acknowledgment of the roots of the English language, it still beats me all ends up.

Warszawa Centralna from the outside looks like a concrete manifestation of the Soviet era; a huge, grey, lumpy piece of unattractive real estate. However on the inside it was sleek and functional. Excellent illuminated signage made it hard not to find the right platform, all of which were broad and capacious. Idiosyncratically, because each platform (*Peron*) had on each side, a track (*tor*), passengers were directed to *Peron* 3, *Tor* 2. Once understood it was easy but as a first time Polish traveller it had me for a moment. The ICE bullet train arrived bang on time and whisked us from Warsaw onwards towards Kraków. It was modern, clean, had great viewing windows and was quiet, speedy and smooth. All of which counted for nothing as the air conditioning had obviously been set to deal with passengers in a stationary train, at noon in Death Valley, Nevada. It blasted a constant gale of freezing air upon my head requiring me to open my case and don the hoodie I'd carried for circumstances just like these. I think of everything! I settled back just as a light frost threatened to form on what's left of my hair.

Another sunny day. As a Scotsman, this remarkable phenomenon has to be remarked on whenever it's observed. The train route south to Kraków was pleasant, the scenery much as earlier when taking the western route from Cologne. Some of the more rural platforms we passed were grassed.

Pretty villages popped up from time to time as did stern blocks of rectangular housing, now tired, broken and depressing; their purpose in existing long gone. Mostly rural, the route nevertheless passed by one or two conurbations and zipped over a motorway. I noticed with interest that the motorway, unlike the rail tracks, had stout fences around it presumably on the basis that it'd have been funded by the European Community whose humourless Dutch officials (they're always humourless Dutch guys) would have set out exactly the conditions under which the motorway had to be built.

Somewhat worryingly, I noticed that as we zoomed across the rural landscape, a number of small sandy roads crossed the line at grade. Each had an automated barrier to stop vehicles progressing when a train was due. At each one however, it was clear by the desire paths formed by cars that these barriers were routinely ignored and cars merely steered around them. Because there are no fences, the yellow arm across the road could just be gone round! And it seemed to be common practice that this was so. I crossed my fingers and hoped that none of the local farmers felt lucky today.

Again I was taken by the apparent absence of dairy farms. In Poland there must be battery cattle ranches somewhere up north where all cows are fed and watered, milked and slaughtered in one huge shed, hidden from the public.

33

Halfway towards Kraków, at a small station, a young lady prepared to board the train with a snack trolley. There was no boarding ramp provided and she'd to manoeuvre and lift this thing up three steps onto the train. Given that this device contained not only foodstuffs but also an urn of boiling water, it looked as if this might be beyond her. I rose to assist but she'd obviously done this in many stations several times that day and lifted it aboard dismissing my offer of help. I walked the few paces to her trolley but was returned by her to my seat as she held up her hand and said, "Noh! Yoh seet! I vill drive eet toh yoh."

In heavily accented English she identified the snacks available to me. I ordered coffee and a small salami baguette. As the train gained speed and bounced giddily along the track, she handed me the coffee in an open topped cardboard container. I looked at her askance. In Glasgow's Central Station once, as I was preparing to pay a visit to Ayr Races with friends, I'd asked for a similar coffee on the concourse...on the *concourse*! The young lady serving insisted on placing the plastic cap on the cup and securing it before sliding it six inches towards me despite me saying I wanted to put sweeteners in it. "Health and safety," she murmured as I protested. Six stationary inches! Here, on a bouncing and heaving train I was handed boiling water in a cup filled so full the liquid was almost convex. There are no pussies in Poland let me tell you.

Some twenty-five minutes out from my destination, Kraków, I began to organise myself for departure, packing away my technologies and stuffing my hoodie back in the case. The Train Gods must have noticed this as the train immediately stopped at an isolated station for a full hour, and then for further periods at each subsequent station as we closed on Kraków. Eventually, the high speed, bullet-nosed intercontinental express limped in about two hours late.

I almost found my hotel in Krakow without much difficulty although to double check I was in the correct neighbourhood, I proffered my Google Map to a passing traffic warden and pointed at the address. He scratched his head several times and announced himself bemused. Shrugging his shoulders, he disappeared, presumably to lose himself in streets he walked every day. I looked up and saw that I'd been asking directions from the pavement beneath the portals of my hotel, the *Matejko*. Feeling both stupid and relieved, I got myself organised. A small, basic room met my every need.

After checking in, I crossed the road again to the railway station and looked for any information or directions for the car rental outlet from which I was to hire a car at 6.00pm. It was now 5.00pm but being early couldn't do any harm, eh? In the event it turned out to be the most cumbersome arrangement possible. It became evident that there were no car rental facilities at the station; instead I'd to phone a number which was answered in *AMERICA*! They then invited me to wait a while and phoned someone in Kraków Airport who called me and said they'd be out to the railway station by 6.00pm which of course they weren't. A few irritated calls later and a shamefaced young man clambered out of the small Ford and apologised. Some protracted paperwork later, I drove out of the station car park and into bedlam. It was now dusk.

As I'd been waiting, I noticed some redevelopment work taking place high above the station as four huge cranes towered above it moving large pieces of steel about. I figured they'd be useful landmarks if I became lost and ten minutes later they were called into action. The road network just wouldn't permit me easily to return to park my car close to my hotel only yards from the station. Still, it permitted me to suss out the motorway that the following morning would whisk me south to Auschwitz. I kept an intermittent eye on the cranes and, after a couple of illegal U-turns, was able to park at no cost only steps from my front door.

It was eight o'clock now and I wanted a light meal and a sleep so I could head off early. A nearby busy *Restauracya Jarema* seemed to fit the bill and I wanted to try their *Krupnik*, a Polish honey liqueur as a *digestif* which was lovely.

The restaurant was a fine example of classical dining in Kraków. Old furnishings, patterned tablecloths and a decor that suggested it had been in place since the war years combined to suggest that the owners had either maintained a traditional restaurant very well or had contrived a new one with an excellent eye for the past. I was impressed other than by the constant presence of small flies, harmless but ever-present.

They like their sausages in Poland. The waitress offered options as she presented the menu. It was like a variation on the Monty Python theme of beans - but they have a plenitude of sausage in Poland. My waitress intoned the options. "You ken haff sausage unt beans, sausage unt eggs, sausage unt hemm, sausage unt caviar, sausage unt sausage..."

My starter was *Burszcz Ukraiński; borscht* soup made from beetroot. It was provided blood red in quantities that would have filled an Olympic swimming pool. The large bowl I was given had a shallow end and came with a lifeguard! I couldn't finish it but it was lovely. It was followed by duck and apple accompanied by potato dumplings. The duck just fell off the fork it was so tender although the dumplings were a disappointment. I left them. They could have done with some purple pubic hair in my opinion.

The restaurant went overboard to capture an atmosphere. Waitresses, all young ladies, dressed in ankle-length, loose-fitting floral gowns even wore the same golden slippers as they served. What made the evening, however were two old timers; one playing piano, one on violin. They were probably in their eighties, certainly late seventies. They played mazurkas, ragtime, twelve bar blues, songs from the shows, waltzes, and punk (I consider Beethoven's fifth to be *quite* punkish!). They were brilliant. Each time they finished there was a deafening silence as people continued to set about their meals. Eventually as alcohol kicked in, people responded and they were rewarded by loud applause. I wanted to cheer but didn't know the Polish word for 'Bravo'. They made my night.

I take that back. The *duck* was the best I've ever eaten. *It* made my night! I whispered '*Bravo*' with every mouthful.

I rose early for breakfast as I was anxious to make an early start so I could drive to Auschwitz. Anticipating that I'd be the only one to have surfaced, I entered the breakfast room to see a group of about twenty women there before me. All either heavily breasted matrons or stick insects with zimmers, not one was under eighty. They hovered indecisively around the cold food section such that I wanted to scream, "Look, would you hurry up? I'm trying to get to a death camp, here!" I desisted and made do with some muesli and some tepid *café au lait* before departing.

In my view, when setting off on an adventure to a specific destination, the first mile can sometimes be the most important. Get it wrong and you end up in John O' Groats rather than Land's End. Fortunately, I have an inbuilt facility when driving in a strange city invariably to choose the right road; the correct junction. Well, perhaps on two occasions that's been the case...but today was almost a third.

I checked the map, trying to fix in my mind the general route from Kraków to Auschwitz and got it bang on for the first few key options. I found myself on the correct motorway heading directly there on Route 74 and made the move seamlessly onto Route 79. With no little astonishment, I managed to do this with some aplomb and there was no more to do now than to keep between the hedges and allow the motorway to take me to my destination.

Ten kilometres along the road, I came across a sign which offered Oświęcim as an option - if I left the motorway. I made an instant decision. Oświęcim was but a couple of kilometres from Auschwitz; I drove down the off-ramp realising that I had now departed from my earlier strategy and was now dependent upon letters rather than numbers.

In my experience, it's easier to remember broad directions when someone says, "Keep on keepin' on until you reach Denver," "Head south until you reach Lancaster," or "You take the high road and I'll take the low road and I'll be in Scotland before you." Easy names to remember. When you're presented with a menu of 'Brzesczcze', ' Rzczsrescz', Csbesrczcbz' and Zbrezcsezce', it's more difficult to remember which one you're aiming for. I found myself adrift in a sea of consonants.

I was headed for Oświęcim but now and again, having followed the road signs religiously, I'd come to a T junction where neither left nor right would mention my destination. Here, I'd be forced to choose the one that seemed less stupid. The Boy Scout training of my youth came into good use when I remembered their motto, 'Be Prepared!' *A map,* I thought. *That might be helpful!"* I bought a map in a garage which showed a route 77 winding its way to Oświęcim. However the road signs only mentioned route 44. I envisaged descendants of the courtiers who'd developed the language saying, "Hey boss, how about we make up road numbers for the map but when we signpost the roads, we mark them differently? That'll bugger everyone *right* up!"

My frustration was born of the fact that I needed to get there before 10.00am as after that, visitors had to join a tour group and have the camp explained to them in their own language. I'd rather swim through vomit than join any club, any association, any tour group and was driving hard to make sure I got there before ten so I could experience Auschwitz on my tod.

I accelerated but couldn't help noticing that in the middle of a ribbon development of small, pretty villages, I passed through Wieikie Drogie, which, as all footballing *aficionados* know, is a village that once played centre-forward for Chelsea.

I was only a few kilometres from Auschwitz when I noticed a large Disney-like theme park with big dippers and all the malarkey associated with the mouse. Even at that early hour in the morning, screaming kids were plummeting from heights that would have given me a nose bleed. I mused that local politicians would have had to grapple with the issue of, 'do we determine that this place has been host to such horrible experiences that we'll forever require that the local population wear sackcloth and ashes and ensure that everything here is dedicated to a sombre and respectful aspect, or do we take a load off and jazz it up a bit?' They jazzed it up a bit.

Eventually I arrived at Oświęcim but there was absolutely no mention anywhere of Auschwitz. I pressed on through the town and eventually found a sign saying 'Auschwitz 2.7 kilometres.' I drove on for miles and figured I'd missed the turn off. I returned and repeated the journey three times, going back to the first and only sign upon each occasion and measuring the distance on my car's milometer. There was *no* indication of Auschwitz. I stopped at a bus stop and waited until a teenage girl passed me. Through the open window I proffered a map and shouted questioningly, "Auschwitz?" She looked at me, horrified and ran off.

Anyway, I looked in my rear-view mirror and noticed that because I'd been driving with the windows open, my hair looked a bit like Ken Dodd's. Perhaps in a certain light, my folded map looked like a tickling stick but whatever, she obviously thought me a dangerous lunatic and left me none the wiser about my next move as she ran screaming up the street. On the other side of the road, a weather-beaten old guy sat smoking a cigarette, observing the interaction. I wasn't hopeful but asked, "Auschwitz?"

He made a circular motion with his hand and pointed to the roundabout up ahead.

"Rondo...zen leff!"

I found it in two minutes, guided by the only sign that remotely indicated Auschwitz. It said, *Muzeum* and suggested I turn left. It was still five to ten so I parked, hopped over to the queues and joined, keeping an eye on my watch. I noticed that everyone in the queue had a ticket and realised I was in the wrong line.

"Tickets?" I asked in a screech.

"Small white building," advised an American waving her ticket and pointing into the middle distance. And there, so far away I thought it a discarded shoe box...with no signage that

I could discern...was a small white structure within which lived the people who sold tickets. I ran over as fast as an unfit, sore-toed, over-weight, auld guy with a bad back can run, and waited my turn.

"Solo ticket please."

"Is naat poss'ble. You back come at sree o'clack. Zen you solo. Now only group."

I looked at my watch. Four minutes past ten.

"But I want to visit on my own. I'm a big boy now!"

She looked at me as if she'd smelled something putrid. "You Eengilsh?"

"I'm Scottish," I offered, hoping she was maybe a secret Jimmy Shand fan.

She nailed me with an incontrovertible observation. "You *spik* Eenglish!"

I resigned myself to the inevitable but decided not to make it easy for her. "Aye, hen."

"Zis iss Eenglish?"

I nodded but decided she needed to learn. "In a manner of speakin'," I said grumpily. I took my ticket and joined the group where a small, heavily-built woman of apparent Polish origin was addressing a group in English.

All kidding stops here. We toured the camp. What a sub-human, unspeakably cruel, evil species were Nazis! We visited incinerators, starvation cells, hospitals that experimented on people, hanging quarters, firing squad enclosures where kids as young as *nine* were shot, dormitories where those who'd arrived fit and well could sleep before a starvation diet and unremitting work for the Nazi cause killed them...it just went on and on.

I was impressed by our group leader who must do at least two of these tours a day. She's certainly not become inured to the experience. At one point we looked on horrified at the tonnage... that's *tonnage* of human hair on display; hair that had been shaved from women to use in textiles after their death in order to strengthen the collars of Nazi uniforms. Our guide rose on her toes in indignation, stamping her foot as she explained how this went on for years during which one and a half million Jews, gipsies, political prisoners, homosexuals, .trades unionists, Russians and anybody with a Z or K in their name was murdered. I looked at the wall of photographs taken by the camp to identify prisoners. Doctors, lawyers, farmers, shop assistants, chemists, labourers, engineers...all photographs identified beneath by name, date of birth, occupation and finally the date of entry to the camp and the date of their death. In most cases the two dates were but months apart. Those who were selected for instant death did not require to be documented in this way. They were merely stripped, told they required to have a shower, crowded into a room and gassed...on an *industrial* scale!

There was a sign in one of the early buildings saying something to the effect that those who fail to understand history are condemned to repeat it. A decent point, particularly when we reflect upon the subsequent realities of Stalinism, Vietnam, Bosnia, Iraq, Palestine, the Twin Towers, Crimea and Syria. The beat goes on. Atrocities and crimes against humanity seem to have continued unabated if not in such dramatic quantities. We have yet some distance to proceed before we can call ourselves civilised. Perhaps Scotland's national poet, Robert Burns said it best back in the late 1700's. 'Man's inhumanity to man makes countless thousands mourn.'

Aye, times a thousand, Rabbie!

After the tour, our tour guide announced that we would now be taken in a bus to Birkenau for the second phase of the visit. I'd been the only one in the group who'd asked her questions as we toured the camp. She approached me as we concluded the Auschwitz part of the tour. We'd established a respectful relationship as we'd walked round the horrors of the death camp.

"You are not Eenglish?"

"I'm Scottish." I expected her to say something about how erudite were my questions and how they were obviously based on a superior Scottish education, famed even in Poland.

"You are in wrong group. You must join other group. Zis group Eenglish."

I nodded philosophically and decided that there's only so much utter horror that a person can take in one day and drove the three kilometres on my own to Birkenau where I stayed for a short while before heading back to Kraków on route 44 that doesn't exist using that identification on the map.

Kraków's a handsome city, full of parks, tall buildings and a spaghetti-like streetscape. I became lost comprehensively upon my return and had to make several illegal U-turns. I drove deliberately up one-way streets apologising as I went, my pleading arm waving at astonished taxi drivers, drove along dedicated tram lines - a particular no-no in Kraków - and parked illegally on pavements to stop and attempt to make fruitless sense of the map I had of the city centre. Eventually I surrendered to the fact that I'd never find my way on to the agreed-upon roof of the Kraków station car park and dumped my rented car in a free space near the adjacent bus station. Hot, bothered and frustrated, I phoned the car people. "My car's in the bus station *next* to the train station. I'm in the pub." Before I'd finished my half-pint, a smiley studenty guy with Buddy Holly specs was there to relieve me of my hired car and to apologise for his city's road network. I gave him the keys and decided a second beer was required.

The evening sun was ebbing and I spent some time shuffling contentedly round the large and busy square and its environs in *Stare Miasto*, the old town. I wanted a beer desperately but establishments I came across failed my tests. I wanted a bar with no kids. A bar with no food. A pub! I wanted a bar that didn't advertise '*all-day Jazz*'! One that was dark and quiet. A pub! Eventually I found such a place. I staggered in and asked the barman for a beer...a large beer. He looked at me curiously. "A *large* beer?"

I nodded and he pursed his lips in appreciation before going into the back room and bringing out a special glass.

"This", he said, "is a *special* glass".

It was a pint tumbler; and these people call themselves civilised.

I finished it off in jig-time and now more relaxed, I returned for a second order only to be served by a comely twenty-something bartender of the female variety.

I eyed the gantry looking for a malt whisky as she addressed me.

"I heard you order earlier. You're Irish, eh?"

"Scottish."

I took account of her own accent. "You're Australian?"

"Kiwi!"

"Well. We were both close. How come you're working in Kraków?"

"I'm travelling the world. Been on the road for nearly three years."

"I'm impressed. Eh...," I pointed. "One of those beers...and, eh..."

She poured my beer as I reflected on my choice of whisky and on her world tour.

"Three years is a long time to keep yourself afloat financially."

She smiled. "Sure is. But I work to pay my way."

"Bartending in different cities?"

Her cheeks dimpled and she giggled as she wiped the foam from atop my beer. "Yeah. But I've been blessed with wanderlust, a high IQ, an outgoing personality and these puppies!" She lowered her chin, indicating her not insubstantial *décolletage*. "This is my day shift. Nights, I work in a strip club!"

I met her gaze, resisting the urge to head south in order to confirm her last assertion in regard to her assets and seeing no dogs in the vicinity, realised she was employing puppies as a metaphor. Wearily, I recognised our informal chat as but a marketing ploy and my gaze rose to the higher shelf.

"...Eh, and a wee Glenmorangie, please. I'll add the water."

I enjoyed my refreshments and wandered back towards my hotel. I was tired and decided that I'd dine again in *Restauracya Jarema* close to my hotel. Upon entering, one of the small irritating flies which'd so troubled me the previous evening recognised me and invited his pals to my table for a party.

The two old guys who played piano and violin the previous evening were back and I found it touching that the slightly younger of the two consistently deferred to the elder, the pianist at the end of each song, modestly stepping aside and offering him the greater measure of applause. Again the repertoire was catholic. 'Hava Nagila', 'Take the 'A' Train', 'Plaisir D'amour', and 'Roll Out The Barrel' were each knocked off in quick succession. Many other classical tunes I could hum but not name were also performed. I felt I was revisiting ''The Billy Cotton Bandshow' which I'd listened to on the BBC's Light Programme in my teens.

Towards the end of the recital, the elderly pianist stood, faced the diners and announced in faltering English that if anyone had watched the film, 'Schindler's List', they should know that in the scene where a pianist's hands were shown playing...he held his hands up proudly..."Zis vas zi hants playing piano for Meester Spielberg." He then proceeded to play the piece he'd performed in the film and it was such a mournful, depressing dirge of a song, I was glad we were on the ground floor lest any of my fellow diners felt compelled to throw themselves screaming from a window.

As I left, I approached the elderly pianist and thanked him for his recital (the violinist must have been visiting the men's room). Before I could finish my compliments he said, "My fee eez feefty Zloty. Vaun hour pafomanz."

I awoke the following morning not to the dawn chorus of melodically chirping finches but to what seemed to be the opening credits from Jurassic Park as kelenkens wheeled, squawked, croaked and whooped in the lane outside my hotel window. When the myriad churches in this most Catholic of cities also announced their presence by clanging their bells loudly and discordantly, I figured it was time to reach for the light switch.

I spent a leisurely hour getting organised, had breakfast and made my way to the south of the city to the factory (now a museum) used by Oscar Schindler who protected thousands of Polish Jews from the Nazis by claiming them crucial to the war work being undertaken in the factory. Compelling testimony had been captured from workers on film. They spoke of the good food, regular wages, protection from arbitrary SS and Gestapo arrest and secure accommodation provided by Schindler. He was named *Righteous Among the Nations* by Israel in 1963, died in 1974 and was buried on Mount Zion in Israel, the only Nazi to be honoured in this way.

I'd expected the tour (on my own, without the necessity of joining a tour group) to be uplifting after the horrors of Auschwitz the day previously but found that the exhibition (excellent as it was) was largely focussed upon the occupation of Kraków by the German army in 1945. An interactive map on the wall showed an account of German tanks and infantry sweeping across Poland in days, the Polish army diminishing almost hourly before their onslaught. Further stories of the excesses of the Germans were portrayed on every wall. Curiously, there were many photographs of Hitler and of Stalin portrayed but I had to wait until the exit foyer until I saw one of Schindler himself.

I left, almost as distressed as the day before. I couldn't help thinking back to the gentle and intelligent people I'd encountered in Cologne in Germany only a few days ago. Could it *be* that their grandparents or great-grandparents bayoneted babies, shot nine year old kids but produced offspring who were long-limbed, smiling, intelligent, liberal and courteous?

There are many questions which defy easy answers...but the answer to this one must be, 'yes!'

I've not yet given up on my ambition to become 'King of the World' and upon reflection decided that I'd make four rules upon achieving office;

1). No nation state is permitted to invade any other.
2). Within a nation state, everyone is required to be nice to one another.

3). Practice whichever religion you wish. It is illegal to preach your gospel in order to attempt conversions or hold other religions in disdain.

I then reflected on what might be imposed if any one of these rules were broken.

4). World powers should invade the transgressing country, bomb their facilities, decimate the population, steal their oil, replace their leadership and alienate the remaining population.

This 'King of the World' malarkey might be more complicated than at first I'd thought!

I used my ability to walk in strange cities whilst knowing *exactly* where I am at any point in time to good effect. I walked to the Vistula River then aimed to head for the Jewish Quarter only to find myself one hour later, back exactly where I'd started on the river. It was as if I had been guided by an invisible force back towards one of the many tour boats whose craft plied the river. I took a seat on one only to discover that it was the only craft which was never untethered from its berth. I was served a beer (which arrived with a straw, no less) then on to the next-door boat, a paddle-steamer which sailed in ten minutes.

Forty minutes later (a second beer helped me overlook this discrepancy) we left port. The unsheltered upstairs seating was likely to have me collapse with sunstroke so I sat in comfort downstairs where I was joined just before we set off by two families, one of whom had a one year old baby which was learning to speak Polish. Apparently screaming *Aaaaaaaaaaaaahhhhhhhh* for five minutes at a time represents an early linguistic step!

As I handed my empty glass back to the barmaid and ordered another, I pointed to the pump. I'd been drinking this local lager since I arrived in Poland. It read '*Zywiec*'. I asked the barmaid how it was pronounced to avoid the finger-pointing I usually employed in order to ask for a drink.

"*Zhikzxytizh*", she replied.

I massaged my pointing finger. It was going to have to be called into service on further occasions. As I contemplated the drinks menu while she poured, I noticed that the beer I'd been drinking was 13 per cent proof – that's the equivalent of wine! I'd just had two pints of wine and was about to enjoy a third!

The banks of the Vistula do not seem to be steeped in history (there was no running commentary, thank heavens) but we passed a number of old-looking castles which I found diverting. On its manicured grassy banks lay families with kids and courting couples; its footpath permitting cyclists out for a bit of exercise, skateboarders, walkers, tourists and locals going to church. Lovely.

As the craft docked, a burly man came downstairs, placed two empty pint glasses on the bar, lifted a child's top and walked unsteadily to the dock. Had he worn a string vest, I'd have insisted he was the *doppelgänger* of Rab.C.Nesbit. His wife lifted baby *Aaaaaaaaaaaahhhhhhhh,* corralled each of her other two under-fives, and followed him out, pushing a pram. I almost had a word with him about his need to address one or two aspects of familial obligations.

Upon disembarking myself, I had the choice of walking uphill into the Jewish Quarter or lying on the grassy bank of the river beneath Wawel Castle like scores of others.

In minutes I was asleep on the grass, doubtless as a consequence of the three glasses of 13 per cent lager. I awoke some time later, my face burned red and now, I figured, with incipient skin cancer. My liver might require attention as well.

I limped towards the old town in broiling heat. It was completely enchanting if it was possible to overlook its awful recent past under the Nazis. The heat got the better of me and I took shelter in a small dark café-bar where I ordered a coffee. I was joined in my small dark café by a tiny Japanese gentleman who spoke little

English but who ordered a baguette by pointing as had I. As I contemplated him bowing politely to the waitress, hands together in a respectful gesture then sitting patiently until his order arrived, I permitted myself the same thought I'd asked myself earlier, 'Could it *be* that his grandparents or great-grandparents bayoneted babies, shot nine year old kids but produced offspring who were long-limbed, intelligent, liberal and courteous?' Well, in his case maybe not so long-limbed.

An Irish bar, always a reliable place of refuge, allowed me to pass a diverting hour sipping at another coffee watching Swansea playing Chelsea (2-2). Next door was a super looking, inexpensive seafood restaurant called '*Destino*' where I enjoyed a meal of prawns followed by cod before walking the further distance to my hotel and collecting my case. I crossed the road to catch the 21.43hrs Intercontinental Express Train overnight to Vienna.

The train was already stationed on the platform as I arrived. I'd sauntered over to the station as I was half an hour early and the humidity had me sweating profusely. Unfortunately for me, I chose an up-ramp that took me to the far end of the train...a train, I swear, that was *fifteen miles long*! It certainly felt like that as I walked along to my carriage.

My steward showed me to my cabin...much the same as my previous Cologne-Warsaw carriage. I almost threw in my bag in relief before collapsing onto the bed. I inspected the *Deutchbahn* goodie-bag. The usual water, fruit juice, biscuit and small paper towel were in evidence. Interestingly there was also a plastic phial saying, 'Shower Gel'. As I felt like I'd just finished a two hour, five-a-side football match and was drenched in sweat, I walked hurriedly back to the platform where I asked the guard, "Shower?"

He put his hand to his mouth to suppress a laugh. "No shower. Ees trine!"

I returned defeated to my cabin and forced open the top window. After some moments the guard re-appeared and deploying both gobbledygook and sign language indicated that he expected my window to be closed between 2.00am and 6.00am. It was presently 9.30pm. I managed somehow to persuade him that I'd comply. It was like a furnace in the cabin. He then insisted that I lock my door and answer to no one until he knocked me up at around six with coffee.

As he left I thought, *if I kept the window open, how would he know?*

As the train headed towards Austria, it took a long, sweeping curve. With my window open I could look out and count the carriages in front of me; three. I looked towards the rear of the train. I couldn't see the last coach!

We pulled out slowly from Kraków *Glowny* and passed the usual grouping of car sales operators on the edge of the city. I listed them mentally as we passed; Renault, Ford, BMW, Chrysler, Daewoo, Skoda, Vauxhall, Seat; each manufactured at least in some measure in France, America, Germany, America again, South Korea, the Czech Republic, Britain and Spain. Surely with the world as interlocked economically, the horrors of Nazism can't recur? Then I picked up a paper thoughtfully left me in my cabin and read an account of Donald Trump's American Presidential campaign rhetoric, 'Send the Mexicans home'; 'Don't let any Muslins in; 'Black people are lazy scroungers'; 'Take control of our borders'; 'If someone heckles me, just punch them in the face'. And over here in the UK, we've gone down a similar path with the Leave Europe verdict in England. *Plus ça change, plus c'est la même chose.*

This was no Intercontinental *Express* Train. It stopped frequently; at Bohumin around 1.00am for the best part of an hour and for a further period around 3.00am, at Istraca-Svinov. Sleep was beyond me for long periods. I listened to the clunks and grinding which I assumed were coaches being disconnected from the *Wien* ICE. I opened my window illegally and allowed a cool night breeze to fan me while I watched the activity in the substantial railway marshalling yards around me. When we stopped in Istraca-Svinov, the train was perfectly located for me to observe a huge...I mean *huge* heavily industrialised plant outside my window. Four tall chimneys spat fire into the sky. God alone knows what was being produced there but it did seem rather a throw-back to Soviet manufacturing of the last century.

I slept fitfully and gave up the ghost entirely at 6.00am. I dressed, lowered my window again and placing my arms on the chest-level sill, watched as Austria slid past. It took me back to my youth when windows opened downwards in train carriage doors by means of loosening a leather strap and lowering it. In those days carriages were comprised of several self-contained and unsupervised compartments and if it wasn't raining, it was *de rigueur* to lean out of the window as I was doing now.

Initially the sky lightened slightly and a still mist covered the ground, awaiting the heat of the sun to burn it off. As features became discernible, it was instantly obvious that we were now in a different country. Everything was cleaner, straighter, more polished. Soil in the fields had a finer tilth. It wasn't the scrawnier scrubland I'd observed in rural Poland.

Travelling more slowly now, the train paced itself and looked like it would pull into *Wien*, Vienna at the very second it was scheduled to arrive. The sun was now orange and visible above the horizon promising yet another warm day. I looked at myself in the mirror. My hair had that careful coiffured Ken Dodd look that so frightens teenage girls and I hoped against hope that a station as large and sleek as Vienna *Hauptbahnhof* would have shower facilities. In this I was about to be disappointed.

Vienna's Central Station is huge, impressive and multi-lingual. My first stop on the way to 'Left Luggage' was at a large poster whose heading was *Verboten!* It listed, (I counted) twenty-eight behaviours that were unacceptable in *Wien Hauptbahnhof*. If you'd given me a pencil and twelve hours, I'm not sure I could list twenty-eight different ways of conducting myself that should not find a place within a station concourse. But the good people of Vienna's *Hauptbahnhof* managed it.

I wasn't particularly looking forward to seeing Vienna. I'd visited once before *en route* to Salzburg, a city I love. My previous day and a half in Vienna had found me doubled up in bed vomiting in quantities that required a regular supply of buckets such as were earlier provided by a line of people stretching from a stream in old cowboy movies in order to put out a fire in the saloon. I turned green. I lost weight. My vision blurred. I eventually made it across the road to an *Apotheke* whose pharmacist didn't speak a word of English and after my mime gave me, from memory, something to treat haemorrhoids.

Now I'm back.

Given my inability to access my hotel room until later, I decided to put my down time to good use and buy an advance onward ticket to Bratislava in the station. The ticket machine operated in English if desired but assumed that everyone using it wanted a return ticket. I didn't. The ticket office was thick with people. It was one of those egalitarian arrangements where everyone took a ticket and waited until their number was called. There were thirteen members of staff minding each of the thirteen ticket stations and they went through the requests in jig time. I bought my ticket without difficulty.

I figured that it would be more efficient to haul up to my hotel, leave my bag there until I checked in. Returning later to the station would incur a fee for the left luggage. My taxi driver took the route my google map recommended (I sat behind him monitoring every turn of the wheel). I was mildly irked, however, at his casual manner of driving. Instead of the ten-to-two hand grip on the wheel or indeed the one now popular with driving instructors these days, the push-pull, he merely laid the flat of his hand on the wheel and passed it beneath his palm, never once grasping it. I sat nervously hoping that he didn't have to manoeuvre suddenly in order to avoid a ten ton cleansing lorry or a three stone child.

My hotel, imaginatively called Hotel 1060, on *Webgasse*, was a boxy affair as were all of the other buildings in an otherwise unremarkable *Straße*. I wondered why I'd booked it back some months ago. It was the most expensive hotel of my itinerary relatively speaking, was outside the old town (I always attempt to stay in the older parts of a city) so I figured it must have been good customer reviews as location and price didn't measure up.

I walked into the town centre. One instant difference between Viennese and Polish drivers was their respective attitudes to road courtesy. In both Warsaw and Kraków, drivers of every hue invariably slowed and invited me to cross whether or not I was on a pedestrian crossing (normally I wasn't). Here, I was in danger of being mown down while drinking coffee in a café. However, I continued my practice of crossing a road at a time and place of my choosing. At one crossing at lights in the city centre when there wasn't a vehicle to be seen in either direction, an old guy with a Prussian moustache almost rugby tackled me as I stepped out.

"Aiyee, Aiyee, Aiyee!" he shouted, attempting to save my life from the approaching tram some three hundred yards away. I slithered from his grasp like a young Gareth Edwards and crossed the road deciding next to walk on the grass right next to a sign shouting *Verboten* with a large red line through a picture of feet on grass. I confess openly my problems with conformity!

I walked for miles, *five* miles according to my Fitbit wrist device, heading towards the Jewish Quarter some distance away. First of all, however, I came upon the Museum Quarter, so called because of the significant number of museums crowded into a small quarter of the city. You're way ahead of me here, aren't you?

There's no question that the buildings are ornate, admirable and deserve to be held in regard but, I don't know...maybe it's because I was ill last time I was here, or because Hitler was an Austrian, or because I was in desperate need of a shower, but they left me pretty cold. I walked on. It's just so overpowering. Massively ornate palaces jump out at you from behind lampposts, marble museums leap out from hedgerows, statues loom on all sides. It's all too much. It was as if presented with a ridiculously rich box of chocolates knowing that more than two or three would be bad for your health.

By now the sun was hot and I was tiring. I really wanted a coffee and croissant and after achieving this I wandered round then jumped on an on-off tourist bus to see as much as possible given my short stay in Vienna.

Ninety minutes later I'd *done* Vienna. My wireless-enabled wearable technology device had calculated that I'd only slept for one hour, twenty-four minutes last night and that felt about right. I'd fallen asleep intermittently on the tour bus, missing the 'Crime Museum', the one thing I wanted to have a look at; just to see if Adolph featured. We passed the Leopoldo Museum, the House of Music on *Schwartzenbergplatz*, the *Hofburg* Museum, and the State Opera House...on and on. I began to lose count and became irritated at the announcer chatting away in my earphones, preferring instead the beautiful orchestral music for which Vienna is rightly famed which punctuated his descriptions. A taxi whisked me back to my hotel where I showered and promptly fell asleep

Refreshed, I set out to explore my neighbourhood. It might best be described using the old Scots word '*douce*'; sober and sedate. Quiet apartment blocks were punctuated every so often by an electrical goods shop, a dry cleaners, a children's shoe shop, but none of these had a flashing neon finger pointing the way to their store. Indeed, none of them had any signage at all. You had to look in their window to see what they were selling. And there were no bars. No restaurants. No cafés. One shop sold lamps and lampshades for *Damen und Herren*. I paused as I passed. It had never occurred for me to go into a shop and ask for a lamp... "Could I see your women's lamp selection, please? It's for my wife."

I walked through this quiet neighbourhood downhill to the River *Wien*, clearly shown on my map as a solid blue line. Here I would find gaiety, pavement cafés with umbrellas, a cooling body of water, laughter, and *people*! The river turned out to be a shallow stream, inches deep; what in Scotland we'd call '*a wee burn*'. I could have waded across in my shoes without dampening my socks. Above and bordering it were two roads, one on each side, each enclosed by an abutment strewn with ugly graffiti. Interspersed between cartoon drawings and words in German were squiggles! No merit whatsoever. Just defacing property. Earlier when walking round the Museum District I'd heard an English-speaking guide describe to his tour group that some of the graffiti in his city were 'almost works of art'.

Depends how you define 'art', eh?

In my part of Scotland, if graffiti is seen, one quick phone call to the authorities and before you can holster your mobile phone, klaxons can be heard and a van pulls up, the smell of burning rubber assaulting your nostrils as tyres screech to a smoking halt. Two men dash from the vehicle with chemicals and a high powered water device to remove the offending defacement. And should the culpable artists be apprehended, they're taken behind a building and summarily shot behind the ear. And that's how it should be!

A thermometer on a wall showed that the afternoon had cooled now to thirty degrees. I walked back towards the old town looking for a bar using the same qualifications as earlier; no jazz, kids, food, but dark and quiet. Didn't find one. I had to compromise eventually and enjoyed a small beer in a pavement café. It did the trick.

I walked on, on toes now blistering. Another pavement cafe but with more comfortable seating took my fancy and I decided to eat more of a snack given Vienna's reputation for high prices. The waitress eventually came out to take my order during which time I'd memorised the menu backwards.

"I'll have the *Tarte Flambé Classic*, please."

"Nein! Ees nan leff!"

"The *Thunfisch auf Blattsalat* then."

"Ees feenish!"

"What *do* you have?"

"Pizza. You like pizza?"

I returned to the menu and ordered toast. And a beer. And a *schnapps*.

Some minutes later she returned with a large glass of *Schladminger* lager, two scrawny pieces of toast of which British Rail would have been proud, along with an announcement.

"*Schnapps* feenish."

I smiled at her, lifted the toast and bit into it theatrically as if it were just the sumptuous nectar of the gods and decided to go back to the hotel and raid the mini bar. She seemed pleased that I was enjoying the toast.

I was looking forward to my trip to Bratislava now even more so as a consequence of my chat with the Austrian taxi driver on the way to the railway station.

"Bratislava iss goot. Zay haff younger generation (he pronounced 'generation with a hard 'g') with more goooder Eengleesh. Zay haff more better beer, zay haff more better economy unt not so many refugees!"

I was beginning to get his drift. He proceeded to give me a history lesson.

"Zlovakia unt Austria, same country. Used to be Austria Hungaaarian Empire. Boaz on Danube. Boaz built at same time. You find Bratislava same as Vienna. Boaz same."

He continued in similar vein until we reached the station. He left me with some parting advice.

"Bratislava beer, ten, thirteen percent. Here, five percent. Be careful."

Wise counsel, if somewhat south of my experience the day before.

The rail journey between Vienna and Bratislava is a frequent, speedy and comfortable one. However, in my view, my taxi friend was wrong. Bratislava seemed more like Warsaw or Kraków than Vienna. The railway station had the feel of an older transportation hub whereas Vienna's *Hauptbahnhof* was a muscular steel and marble technological marvel. I jumped in the first taxi available whose driver drove off playing a CD of operatic tunes singing along with gusto. Seated behind him, I noted his muscular frame and his ability to sing just *slightly* off key. He screamed his way through the theme tune to 'The Godfather' word perfectly (I'd presume; he was singing in Slovak) if not *note* perfectly. I watched him in his rear view mirror and I swear that in the middle section, he teared up as he dealt with an emotional passage. As he finished, he swung the taxi into the car park of my boatel. He turned without invitation, bowed his head and nodded his presumed and anticipated applause.

"I zank you! I zank you."

He robbed me blind mind you but as I looked from the taxi window, I realised I was now on the banks of the Danube, at *Dunajský Pivovar Boatel,* a fabulously reconditioned and upgraded, centrally located barge on the river and forgot any taxi-fare grievance I had.

My room was capacious and gorgeous with a balcony overlooking the Danube; make that *on* the Danube. Above my room were a very elegant lounge-bar, a restaurant and a brewery. A small swimming pool and loungers on the deck completed the facilities. My only small reservation was the ultra-modern design of the room. Clearly at some point the architect had said to his client, "You know, so far so good...but what this room needs is a large window in the connecting wall between the bedroom and the bathroom so a sweetheart can watch their beloved taking a dump!" And so it was that each room had had placed on the wall connecting each room, a three foot wide glazed porthole where one could lie abed and watch one's partner engaged in his or her ablutions.

Maybe it's me!

Within the bathroom, the trendy toilet bowl was easily the smallest I'd ever seen; the size of a small, white deep soup bowl. Completely unnecessary given the capacious nature of the lavvy. Some larger men, in order to do the seated thing, might easily have the other thing hanging out over the edge, hovering over the floor...and military precision was necessary if standing.

I ventured up two decks to the bar and sat in the sunshine. I'd earlier promised myself that I'd be kinder to myself today and not use the day to slog round the town...that would come tomorrow. My two pained and blistered toes demanded some attention and rest. A relaxing evening in an Irish bar in the old town to watch the Celtic v Barcelona match on TV. That'd do me for the day.

I had a look at their drinks menu. The *Patrón* beer they were offering on board was advertised at a pretty spectacular thirteen percent. That's the kind of stuff they use at NASA to send rockets to Mars. I decided to order a glass of something more respectable; something less likely to have me swim the Danube while intoxicated or get arrested. It was then I noticed that *all* of the beers advertised were of similar strength. I looked out my swimming trunks just in case.

After a while I moved over to the lounge area. It was beautifully sunny and warm but I decided that no more alcohol should be taken if I was going to spend an evening in a pub. I walked towards the rooftop bar where I noticed that taxi-driving Bluto's sister must have left Warsaw and taken gainful employment in Bratislava. Standing behind the bar, her arms stretched left and right, supporting her upper body, her palms placed firmly on the bar surface she watched my approach with a scowl.

"Have you a Diet Coke," I smiled?

"Zshobrido!"

I presumed that this implied a negative and tried again. "Coka Zero?"

"Sczvinoviev!"

My smile was fading as fast as her brows were lowering. Perhaps if I explained. "Coke with no sugar?"

"Zvensti"

I tried one last time. "Pepsi Light?"

"Yah. Vee Pepsi Lat."

57

I retreated to a sun lounger at the far end of the empty sun deck and enjoyed my drink. My enjoyment wasn't entirely unalloyed however as the music blaring from the speakers was of a heavy metal type performed by the 'Dead Bats' Skulls', or something. It was obvious to me that Bluto's sister was also in charge of the music. After perhaps some fifteen minutes or so I'd downed half of my Pepsi Lat when I felt the timbers on the deck beneath me shudder rhythmically. I looked up and bearing down on me, head down, shoulders hunched and rolling, her fists balled in front of her was Bluto's sister. She came up to me, blocking out the sun.

"You vant nozzer Lat?"

"Er, no thanks. This'll do for now."

She looked at me for some moments trying either to work out what I'd just said or was contemplating throwing me overboard into the Danube. This she could have done with the flick of a finger just like Bluto used to do to Popeye before he'd taken his spinach.

Eventually the music, the heat and the service drove me back to my room where I opened my glass balcony door to the Danube and spent a very happy half-hour just watching the river run. All afternoon, small craft puttered up to a landing area on the side of the boat and passengers disembarked to enjoy the fine menu available to residents and non-residents alike. I felt very privileged as I experienced a wonderfully sunny afternoon on this great European waterway.

My large toe throbbed. A couple of years previously, I'd had to have an operation made necessary by gout which involved cutting away the painful bony toe-knuckle on my right foot (if there is such a thing...a toe-knuckle, not a foot) and inserting all manner of rods, plates and screws in repair. In recovery I'd been told I'd be able to do the Highland Fling. But in summer, my theory is that the metal swells when it's hot and causes pain and in the winter the metal contracts because it's cold and causes pain. In between times it's just painful. I should be awarded a medal just for being able to walk to the lavatory on my own. My toe goes through phases and today it didn't want to help me walk anywhere, hence my enforced (and most pleasant) rest on-board *Dunajský Pivovar.*

When gout was first diagnosed (as a consequence I was told, of too much red meat, dark spirits and red wine) it was excruciating. I narrowly avoided an earlier hospital admission at the time by explaining to my wife that gout was more painful than childbirth. The large dent in our kitchen wall where the frying pan glanced off the refrigerator remains to this day.

However, a decision had to be made to cross the SNP bridge over the Danube (its Sunday name is the *Slovenského Národného Povstania* bridge, which is why presumably everyone, even Unionists, call it the SNP Bridge) or I'd have visited Bratislava merely to record elements of my medical history. Bravely, I gathered up my small rucksack and climbed the perilously steep gang-plank to the bank of the river.

Upon reaching the final step to the walkway, I stubbed my sore toe, the very toe I was set on protecting. I sat urgently on a park bench immediately opposite and swore gutturally in broad Scots under my breath for three full minutes thereby persuading the German cyclist seated at the other end of the bench that I spoke fluent Slovakian.

I recovered eventually and walked stiffly towards the bridge. It looked great with its high pod (described by everyone, not unreasonably as a UFO) looking over the city. The two-tier bridge separating walkers from motorists surprised me in one way. It soared above a fast-running, treacherous looking Danube but the pedestrian walkway has a balcony only about three feet high. People could fall over to instant death *accidentally* never mind suicidally. Other bridges have higher sides, life belts and telephones connected at all hours to the Samaritans. Here, walkers are left to their fate or perhaps people in Bratislava are generally more chirpy.

It certainly is a lovely city. Very pretty...and nothing at all like Vienna. I couldn't think of a city less like Vienna although Reykjavik in winter does spring to mind as a possibility. I strolled up narrow lanes people-watching and enjoyed getting lost. Buildings looked elegant, classical but not as in-your-face as their pals up the road in Vienna. People were out as families, playing boule, licking ice-cream and drinking coffee. It just seemed so civilised. I chanced upon the Information Bureau and entered. The receptionist was free. She'd a sheaf of tear-off maps before her.

"Map?" I asked, indicating the pile before her.

Wordlessly she tore off the top one and handed it me.

"I'm looking for a pub called 'The Dubliner'?"

She shook her head.

"A Scottish pub called 'Loch Ness'?"

She shook her head once more.

I refrained from suggesting she should get out more and left to wander the streets.

They like their flags in Bratislava and I was encouraged by this as surely I couldn't miss the tricolour flying proudly from the Dubliner. I trudged round the pedestrianised old town but found nothing amid the zillion bars and restaurants which bore a shamrock. Just as I was about to adjust my strategy and look for a sports bar I found it; flagless. I entered, sweating from my exertions and managed to blurt out the word, 'Guinness' before depositing my rucksack on a seat awaiting the pour to complete. The bartender was clearly Slovak.

"Are you showing the Barcelona/Celtic match this evening", I asked him affably.

"No. Tonight Arsenal/PSV."

I was confused. "But this is an Irish bar!"

He smiled. "But we are Slovak bartenders. We like Arsenal."

I looked around. The bar was empty. I decided to drink my Guinness and empty the bar further.

I left the bar to darkness. In the time it had taken to drink my pint of Guinness, the sun had fled the sky.

I'd skipped breakfast and hadn't eaten all day so calories were necessary. Directly across the lane from the Dubliner was the 'Slovak Beer House' which actually looked more like a bijou café bar. It was quiet and offered a typical Slovak menu so I sat, explaining to my barman how disappointed I was that their competitor across the road wasn't showing the Celtic game. He shrugged his shoulders philosophically.

"Satellites here not show Champion League. Nowhere in Slovakia do you see this Celtic!"

Perhaps he was being diplomatic as across the way a Champions League match was about to start. I decided to eat and limp back to the boat after doing so.

I decided to avoid alcohol as I reminded myself that in order to get back home to watch a bedtime movie, I'd have to cross the SNP Bridge with its knee-high barrier. One stagger in the wrong direction...

I concentrated on eating my 'peasant bread', accompanied by cold meat and chillies, a fiery arrangement that suggests that the Slovak peasantry has asbestos mouth lining. My main meal was a fleshy white fish; *Zander*, in Scotland a slang word for pike. It was delicious and should feature more on menus. A lovely meal but bugger me if the purple pubic hair didn't make another appearance. I'd a foul taste in my mouth, whether from the chillies, the fish or the beer. It reminded me of the time I'd licked a tramp's armpit. What a night *that* was!

I walked home and crossed the SNP Bridge warily, keeping to the inside. It occurred to me as I did so that cyclists used the bridge; that winters in Bratislava often see temperatures below zero and that the slightest braking manoeuvre on slick ice would see the cyclists' centre of gravity higher than the bridge's parapet. I looked over tentatively. It didn't bear thinking about.

As I descended the stairs on the bridge to the south bank I came across the entry booth to the pod-lift, which takes passengers to the pod some ninety-five meters above me. On a whim I paid my seven Euros and was rewarded by a panoramic view of the city at night. I was informed that on a clear day, visibility of one hundred kilometres can be obtained.

I walked back along the darkened footpath along the riverbank where every twenty metres or so, people sat in ones and twos on a series of park benches. I looked along the path and noticed that in almost every case, their faces were up-lit by the screen of an electronic device. Facing the moonlit Danube, such a beautiful outlook, hardly anyone was just sitting talking; they were all diverted by the miracle of modern technology.

I was lashing with sweat when I returned and found my room like a furnace. Something had gone wrong with the air conditioning and following a mild complaint to reception I was moved instantly and with great good grace two doors down to a room which felt like an ice-box in comparison. I slept well for the first night in three.

News arrived that Barcelona had narrowly defeated Celtic at the *Camp Nou* by seven lucky breakaway goals.

I was still infatuated by the view from the window of my Boatel and lay for some time just watching the Danube slip past as Bratislava awoke to what was obviously going to be another hot day. Just upriver, the SNP bridge, majestic as it is, apparently took out two thirds of the old town when it was built; the price of progress. Photographs last night on the walls of the sky-pod showed Communist leaders in their large heavy overcoats and Homburg hats standing with trowels in their hand as the first piles were dug just a year before an unsuccessful Czechoslovak attempt to liberalise the Communist regime in 1968. This morning the city looked very smart and modern in the early sun.

I breakfasted out on deck on coffee and fruit and felt very self-satisfied with my choice until I inadvertently slipped a piece of bacon onto my plate. I could feel my left ventricle clogging as I ate it. A waitress brought me the coffee without the milk I'd asked for. Politely I asked if she'd any milk.

She pointed. "Iz on ozzer zide of boat." She walked on.

I read the morning newspapers on my iPad as I ate and noticed a small article informing readers that European Union chiefs were meeting in Bratislava the following day to discuss the UK's exit from Europe. I remembered I'd an unworn Scotland top in my case and contemplated wearing it and attending the gathering to tell them that in Scotland we'd voted to remain!

That thought passed as I wanted to climb to Bratislava Castle, high above the city, before the sun got too hot. The castle had last been occupied in 1968 when Warsaw Pact troops of the Soviet Union; Bulgaria, Hungary and Poland invaded the then Czechoslovakia and successfully halted Alexander Dubček's proposed liberalisation reforms, reinforcing the iron fist of the Communist Party. Soviet premier Leonoid Brezhnev used an unsigned request, allegedly by Communist Party of Czechoslovakia, for *'immediate assistance, including assistance with armed forces'* to justify his invasion.

The country had to wait a further twenty-one years until 1989 when an anti-Communist revolution began in Bratislava against the one-party government of the Communist Party, ending its rule and beginning a conversion to a democracy. Four years later, in 1993 a peacefully negotiated self-determined separation took place leading to today's Czech Republic and Slovakia. This place was the very stuff of history and I was anxious to find out more.

I crossed the bridge and began my ascent of the castle hill. It was quite a climb. Mountain goats would have had a hard time surviving on that gradient. I had to take a seat just as I approached the battlements as my heartbeat was approximately that of the opening drum fill of the Dave Clark Five's hit song, *'Bits and Pieces'*. A notice proclaimed that the interior of the castle would be closed to the public tomorrow as the Council of Ministers of the European Union would be hosted there. Presently, Slovakia has the presidency. I walked round to the front and watched as a camera station platform was being built for the world's press. My attempts to photograph the classically symmetrical view of the front of the palace were frustrated by two bare-chested men, smoking cigarettes, hanging over a balcony on the first floor of the castle and spoiling the shot. Either they were part of the team of roadies building the camera station or the Greek Delegation had arrived a day early.

The castle seemed to me to represent more a well-manicured five star hotel than a fortification whose history, according to legends on the escarpments, suggested a defensive structure of sorts having been on the site since the Stone Age. Nevertheless, it was very pretty with beautiful gardens and a lawn like a billiard table. I noticed as I took a short cut across it that it had actually just been laid, much in the way football pitches are these days; the joints of turf clearly visible when up close.

My habit of 'keep turning the corners' paid dividends when I chanced upon a magnificent terraced bistro built into the castle walls with great views over the city. I ordered a coffee and sipped away until noon when the bells of every church in Bratislava, and there are many, alerted everyone to the time.

It was somewhat easier walking downhill back into the city and I strolled leisurely deciding against my better judgement to have a look at the more modern part of Bratislava. It was much like every other sizeable city; charmless apartments, schools, shops and lots of on-street parking. One establishment went under the name, 'Café Depresso'. Summed it up for me.

Certainly the apparatus of the Slovakian state seems to be healthy enough as every second building seemed to sport *Slovenská Republika* above its doorway. I crossed some tramlines and entered a large concrete apartment store dominating an open space that from the outside seemed designed by Khrushchev's personal architect. Outside it proclaimed *Škola Volá*. I had no way of knowing whether this translated as *'Sale Now On'*, *'Buy One Get One Free'* or the name of the apartment store. As I walked around I saw that the clothes were branded f&f, the Tesco clothing brand. Electronics, toys and clothes seemed to be their main throughput. I wandered further around the city, got lost and emerged much further downriver than I'd anticipated.

A large shopping mall, *Euro Via*, seemed it might host the sports shop I was seeking. Whenever I'm abroad, I like to bring back a football strip from one of the countries I'm visiting for each of my two youngest. Here I found a Sports Direct retail outlet and the tops I was looking for. As I held two up for comparison, a burly security guard approached. His job, it seemed, was to watch the upper floor exit as other staff and all of the pay-tills were downstairs. He opened his empty wallet and, opening his hand, fingers raised skywards made it clear that for five Euros each top, he'd retain the coat-hangers, remove the security tags and I could just walk away with the strips. For a moment I thought of the deleterious impact this would have on the hefty wallet of owner; multi-millionaire Mike Ashley, a man who was hauled recently before Parliament and invited to discuss what some felt were his less than generous workforce pay and conditions. My second thought was, *'What if this guy isn't a real security guard but a Slovakian version of a honey trap'*. However, my third thought was, *'Nah, I'll just pay up like a civilised person should'*. My decision was made easier as another member of staff came up the escalator at precisely that moment shouting what I took to be, 'Slobberly', 'Slobberly' which I presumed to be either the real name of the security guard or the nickname his workmates had given him. He disappeared to handle a security matter downstairs and I bought the shirts legally.

I decided that fruit was necessary and sat in one of many umbrellaed bistros along the north bank of the Danube and ordered a banana smoothie from a distracted waitress. After some time she returned with a smoothie...a *red* coloured banana smoothie. I almost protested but figured it looked beneficial and would probably keep me regular. I'd also asked for a small Panini but when it came it was literally as large as a blacksmith's forearm. I ate its contents, leaving the bread and sat finishing my drink. My waitress, when not serving me, stood at the bar uttering a commentary on life to all other staff on the premises with an invective as if spat from a machine gun. I imagined her monologue was absolutely nothing to do with the business of serving customers. She had a tattoo on her shoulder of a dramatically ugly baby or a beautiful baby tattooed by a dramatically untalented tattooist. I watched the (all female) waiting staff. They were universally surly, engaged only with their own conversations and were ill-attentive to customers. They also wore tiny pelmet-esque pinnies which had an open pleat at the rear so that that part of their anatomy normally wiped tenderly by their parents when they were but months old could be seen by all. I can see that this would be much approved of by many but I just wanted to shout, "I'm eating my lunch here!"

What is it about the waiting staff of Bratislava? Everyone else I met in the city was really lovely, helpful and kind. Perhaps it's just illegal to be nice if you pull on an apron in this part of the world.

I crossed the greenish-grey river back to the boat by means of the new Old Bridge, so called because the original bridge was upgraded to its present state retaining some of its distinctive steel structure. When the authorities were casting around for a new name, they held a vote which was won (one suspects by some skulduggery) by the 'Chuck Norris Bridge'. The powers that be stepped in and named it, 'Freedom Bridge' but I gather that everyone still refers to it as the 'Old Bridge'...or possibly 'Chuck's Bridge'.

Whatever its name, it's certainly the bridge for suicides as it has a barrier that reached my shoulder so the only way you'd end up in the drink would be if you actively wanted to jump. A cycle lane sensibly hugs the interior wall and there are two lanes in the middle for a modern tram system which seems to serve the city admirably by all accounts.

I wrote for a while in my room in the late afternoon, going aloft to the deck and reading from my Kindle, transferring to my Kindle Fire as dusk fell due to the more modern device being back-lit. My eyes lifted from the page on several occasions however, as hypnotically, I watched the Danube flow, reflecting again on how privileged I was.

I'd consider idly at what speed the river ran, first deciding to calculate by estimating a walking pace of three miles per hour and deciding the river ran at perhaps nine, (about eight knots?) then reviewing this figure upwards as a swan would sail by as if turbo-charged. *Could the river run at different speeds?* I asked myself. It seemed faster in the middle. I'd certainly seen the spectacular Falls of Lora beneath Connel Bridge where it spans Loch Etive near Oban in Scotland. Here the water not only has different speeds, it also has different *levels* dependent upon the tide.

The calmness was broken by two boats, each travelling upriver at speed. I decided that one was chasing the other and that James Bond would be seen at any moment. What I *didn't* see was any evidence of industrial-commercial barge activity. I'd fondly imagined that the Danube would be a bustling waterway with barges containing all manner of goods making their way along its nearly three thousand kilometres' length. The river runs through Austria, Slovakia, Hungary, Croatia, Serbia, Romania, Bulgaria, Moldova and Ukraine before emptying into the Black Sea. I saw one barge in all the hours I walked its banks. It may have contained coal...or fairy dust for all I know. Like my native River Clyde in Glasgow, it seems a quieter river now albeit with somewhat more leisure activity on its banks. It's also the only river in Europe that runs through four European capital cities; Vienna (Austria), Bratislava (Slovakia), Budapest (Hungary) and Belgrade (Serbia).

As darkness fell I ordered a beer and felt stupid as I'd read consistently on the drinks menu that the beer was from abroad. It actually said '*aboard*' and was made in the boat's own brewery. I sampled a couple and enjoyed a small plate of *Staropražske*

Grundle; small fish perhaps one inch long, eyes and tail included and a local delicacy; probably what would be called Whitebait back home. It was a light meal and exactly what I sought as tomorrow I'm up and off early to Budapest. I amused myself by reflecting that I might see exactly the same water flow pass by the time I arrived if my calculation of nine miles per hour was near accurate.

As I left for my room, two barges passed; one going downstream, a floating hotel, the other, travelling upstream carrying tons of unidentifiable black stuff.

A sunlit Danube welcomed me to consciousness the following morning but I couldn't indulge it over much as I'd more travelling to do. I dressed and walked along to the empty restaurant where breakfast was being served and entered to the light melodic tones of Ozzy Osbourne when fronting Black Sabbath. *Oh, Jeez,* I thought. *Bluto's sister's back on duty.* She was nowhere to be seen however and must just have been undertaking early morning disc-jockeying responsibilities backstage - somewhere centrally located I deduced as the boat wasn't listing to starboard. I was to be attended to this morning by the same disinterested waitress who yesterday denied me milk for my coffee. I decided to fool her by taking a small glass of milk to my table. She then fooled *me* by talking with a friend who'd looked in while walking her dog and ignored me completely. Eventually I had to walk to the entrance of the restaurant and ask her for a coffee.

"Larch or schmall?" She asked

"Large," I replied.

After an interminable wait, she brought me a small one.

Reception ordered a taxi to take me to Bratislava *Hlavná Stanica* where I'd catch my train to Budapest. The driver charged me €5 for the three minute journey up the hill. My operatic friend who'd driven me downhill from the station took twenty minutes and charged €25.

Viewed now from the outside, I can understand why during the Cold War the railway station was one of the city's major war shelters built to protect citizens from attacks with nuclear weapons. A bit of a monstrosity but I suppose had it been called into action to provide shelter, locals would have preferred it to the sleeker but ultimately less protective shell of Vienna's *Hauptbahnhof*.

I joined a queue of one and bought a ticket for the two and a half hour journey to Budapest for exactly the same price my first taxi driver had charged to drive me downhill from the station to the boatel. I sat outside and took the air but when I re-entered, each ticket station had a queue of perhaps twenty people all supervised by six unshaven, gun-toting, bored police officers wearing poorly tailored uniforms.

I found an empty carriage of six and took a seat by the window. After a few minutes I was joined by what transpired to be a German gentleman. He sat across and away from me and placed his hand luggage on the middle seat. He then rose and sat on the same side as me, moving his hand luggage between us. Then he rose and felt for the air conditioning at the window, placed his hand luggage on the window seat across from me and sat in the middle seat. He adjusted the headrest. He re-adjusted the headrest. He adjusted the rake of the seat. He readjusted the rake of the seat. I felt like telling him that it was German indecision of this nature that allowed the Allies to escape Dunkirk.

As we approached Budapest, the train slowed and crossed surface level roads which had no barriers. I presumed there was some signalling device, invisible to me which gave motorists and cyclists a fighting chance. Graffiti reached new levels of coverage and all the way in to the city numerous, flat-roofed, high rise apartment blocks provided accommodation for the proletariat. My initial assessment was that this city offered a more poorly built public environment than any of the other cities visited on this trip.

The railway station in Budapest looked like the real thing. It soared skywards like stations used to and opened out on to a large square. I headed left to walk to my apartment along a road that suggested an earlier era and followed a long, unbroken twelve foot high brick wall on top of which were curled loops of razor wire. Puzzled at this old-fashioned approach to security I pondered its other side; a prison perhaps, a home for the criminally insane, an inner-city military facility? An opening ahead allowed me an insight. It was a cemetery. Some recent escapees, perhaps.

My apartment was in a poorer part of Buda on the east bank of the Danube. The community in which I stayed had a certain charm and evoked memories of cold war spy movies. I returned the short distance to Budapest's *Keleti Palyaudvar* station as 'The Man in Seat 69' had advised a visit to the *Baross* Restaurant on Platform six. 'The Man' runs a fabulous web site for all manner of train- related information and if he recommends something, I'm in! The restaurant was an old fashioned marble-pillared wonder that fitted well with the early-twentieth century architecture surrounding it. One could just imagine Soviet and Western spies exchanging information beneath its portals, microfilm being swapped surreptitiously at the table. I was quite taken with the place until the sandwich I'd ordered arrived completely submerged in a plate of chips. Philby, Burgess and McLean didn't have to deal with foodstuff like this. It was all *pate de foie gras* with these boys back when men were men. Smiley's People didn't eat *chips!* The beer was long and cool, though.

I went downstairs to the Metro in order to purchase a 24hr pass for all local transport and entered a ticket office which was completely empty. Two women selling tickets at the far end were deep in conversation behind a counter while a young man stood somewhat underemployed at the entrance. As I passed, he placed his hand on my shoulder and didn't look at me as he spoke.

"Teecket. You muss has teecket." So saying, he pushed a button and ticket numbered 199 popped out. He gave me this and I stepped forward into the deserted room. Each of the two ticket salespersons turned to face me, now all business. I chose the one with the smile.

The Metro was as good or as bad as anything else around. Some of the carriages had a 1960's feel to them but others were ultra-modern. I entered and long escalators took me to middle earth where I expected my ticket to be taken by a hobbit. In a few minutes I'd boarded and had made the five stops to Batthyâny on the West Bank of the Danube, in Pest. I had to smile as I exited because the escalator had quite the most stupendous rake I've ever witnessed. I'm pretty certain it wouldn't be given the green light in the UK. It was almost perpendicular. The steps once fully engaged seemed about two feet high. An Olympic hurdler might have found climbing them testing. I did as everyone else and clung to the moving handrail like grim death.

I strolled along the Danube Promenade and swore I noticed the same bobbing empty can of Coke I saw float past my window earlier that morning in Bratislava. On reaching the impressive and muscular Chain Bridge I used the funicular to transport me up to the Castle District which seemed to me to be 'aspirational Viennese.' Ever more impressive museums, churches, art galleries and castle walls vied with each other to out-ornate its neighbour. As with Vienna, a bit sickly sweet for me. Great views over a very topo-graphically flat Buda, from a mostly hilly Pest, though. Margaret Island in the centre of the Danube was clearly visible as was the view of the nation's parliament across the river, a stupendously spired Gothic building, six feet longer than the building it sought to emulate, the Houses of Parliament in London.

A ruddy-faced Englishman got into an argument with the ticket lady as we attempted to return down the funicular. She spoke at him in rapid Hungarian, shaking her head such that I worried about her subsequent ability to walk in a straight line and he responded by saying in ever-increasing decibels, "Lissssen!... Lissssen...Dahlin'...*Lisssssen, dammit,* ...FAAHKIN LISSSEN...." It was a communication between two people engaged only on transmit and I left them to their conversation.

I wanted to use the tram system delinquently, that is to say without regard to destination. I intended to board a tram, have it take me up through Buda and when the excitement waned, just cross the road and travel back eventually to where I started. Just to make sure I was headed in the broad general direction (I'd thought of having a look at the Ferenc Puskás Stadium at some point) I asked a young lady seated at the tram stop for confirmation that my intended route was there or thereabouts.

She spoke good English and gave me a full run down on the tram system *vis a vis* the underground Metro and encouraged me to use the Metro. "*Is many taams more convenient, many taams!*" I listened to her advice but realised that if I took it I'd be denied my tram trip. I thanked her, went to the other side of the tram and boarded furtively. Just as it was about to depart, she saw me seated, leapt up the three stairs and hauled me off, begging my forgiveness as obviously she hadn't made herself clear. Almost dragging me by the ear, she took me to the Metro I'd just left and escorted me to the proper station, joining me to the destination she'd presumed was my goal before leaving to catch her proper train home - in the other direction. Esther, her name was. She's studying psychology at Budapest University. She was very kind.

I had a walk round the Puskas Stadium. *Bijou*, let's call it. Yet again I was assailed, this time by an elderly woman when I crossed an empty (well, fairly empty) road when the green man hadn't given the nod. What is it about ex-communist countries? They seem yet to work on the basis that 'rules is rules'.

I walked deep into Buda. It was becoming seedy and down-at-heel and I couldn't see any sports bars (I thought I might try to catch the Manchester United match against Feyenoord but all that was ever on offer were local teams). I caught a couple of trams, each of a vintage that could have been driven by my grandfather, Hector McLeod who worked in Glasgow as a tram driver all his life. They were great but, having to share road space with other vehicles, could be slow.

I returned to my apartment where the young receptionist (who apologised for her American accent, explaining she'd learned to speak English by watching George Clooney movies - she likes George Clooney...She stood tall.... *"You're either in or you're out!"* a Clooney quote she told me was from his film, *Ocean's Eleven*), sorted a number of small domestic issues and printed my boarding cards for tomorrow's flight to Heathrow, London City Airport and home to Glasgow. Another very kind Hungarian lady.

I'd noticed a traditional if dingy Hungarian restaurant called the *Hussar* not far from my apartment, entered and was shown to my seat. I'd assumed it'd be a local community restaurant but most tables had been booked ahead and accents from all over were in evidence. I didn't turn round but I'd swear that seated behind me was ex-American President Bill Clinton. If not, it was a remarkable similarity, even down to the southern drawl and the empathic way in which he was expressing himself. Yet again I was entertained by two musicians, violin and accordion. The accordionist had fingers that were a blur as they travelled up and down the keyboard accurately but at a colossal speed. As ever I chose the local dish, in this case, *goulash*. It was delicious and had the added benefit of having eschewed any hint of hirsute accompaniment. A local brandy as a farewell to the *Hussar* and off to bed.

As I left, I glanced over at Bill Clinton. God, he's aged and put on a lot of weight; and a good foot shorter than he looked when I met and heard him talk some years ago in Glasgow.

Tomorrow I head back to the colder climes of Glasgow. I've missed my family, my friends and my dog. Everywhere I visited was fascinating although I especially found Warsaw, Auschwitz and Bratislava engaging and emotional. Some of the people I met were a credit to the human race and I hoped that I'd be as kind to a fellow traveller if I came upon a needy soul on my home turf. Others, well, were less so, 'but we're 'a' Jock Thomson's bairns' as we say in Scotland; we're all the same under the skin. Everywhere, parents loved their kids, valued education, appreciated kindness and wanted to better themselves. Sure, some nations prefer lower taxation over greater state provision, some prefer hockey to soccer, some deal with snow, some with drought but everywhere I travelled on the European mainland I hope I respected customs (with the exception of road crossing) and was a decent ambassador. I hope I've teased rather than criticised (with the exception of the purple pubic hair). I've never been in any one place long enough to have condemned.

The rail journeys themselves were great adventures and I enjoyed all of them. My trusty Fitbit tells me I've walked ninety-three miles around the cities I visited since stepping on the Caledonian Sleeper to London ten days ago. Not distances that would trouble many but enough to blister and bleed my already painful toes... toes that would now take me to America.

Adventures on the Mother Road

*Nashville, Memphis, Lubbock, Gallup, Santa Fe,
Flagstaff, Las Vegas, Los Angeles.*

My poor feet having recovered, I woke up one morning, put a red line through my list of all of the cities I'd just visited and decided that it was now time to make arrangements to drive Route 66 in America, the famous road that straddles the USA from Chicago to Los Angeles and has served countless thousands of Americans who took their families and all of their possessions to a better life in California following the dust storms of the great depression in the 1930s.

Mentioning this one night in a bar to Laurie Russell and John McManus, two of my dearest friends, they decided on the spot to accompany me on the adventure. This was to be a road trip, an adventure, an expedition. And so it was that we set off for America with great enthusiasm and some small trepidation as we'd have to navigate the best part of 2,000 miles to achieve our objective.

On arrival at Nashville - our chosen starting point - we landed in the midst of a most dramatic forked lightning storm. It was so dangerous the skycaps wouldn't operate the motorised walkway to the plane lest they were hit by lightning. After some wait, the pilot merely recommended that any passengers with an adventurous spirit 'run for it and take your chances on the apron' - or face an endless delay on board the aircraft. Well, we ran for it, got comprehensively soaked in the process and spent the next two days dealing with the effects of a weather system that left twenty-seven people dead, flooded the city and caused a state of emergency to be declared.

Laurie had earlier made arrangements for me to record a song I'd written for the occasion of our adventure on Route 66, '*The Mother Road*', in Sun Studios in Nashville where, in 1953, an eighteen year old Elvis Presley had recorded an acetate disc entitled '*My Happiness*', *but* the weather made any travelling around the city almost impossible and most places were closed. We managed, however, to hire a taxi and travelled to the famous Music Row where we spent the day playing pool, eating, visiting cowboy hat, boot and music shops, drinking in bars and listening to music until around 10.30 at night when the Sheriff arrived and told everyone to leave as the River Cumberland had burst its banks and was about to flood the place.

Reluctantly we headed for the sidewalk as requested. Shortly afterwards, the Sheriff was proved correct and the place was inundated.

The next morning, we awoke to sunshine and devastation where the river had caused carnage. We managed to hire a comfortable sedan and drove south, almost into Alabama - in doing so, travelling through Amish country - in order to find a bridge high enough to carry us over the Cumberland River safely and on to Memphis, our next port of call, in order to visit with Elvis.....

Prior to setting off, we'd devised an arrangement to ensure that we spread the task of driving evenly. One of us would take the wheel for a two hour shift with a second person doing the navigating and a third choosing all of the music we listened to. Then we rotated our roles. This system worked very well although John reckoned he was driving safely within the speed limits (I thought he was too cautious). I thought I drove confidently and briskly (John thought recklessly) and we both thought Laurie was scarily ambitious given that his poor eyesight didn't permit him to see any traffic lights at a point where John and I had both adopted the brace position and were screaming 'Reeeedddddddd...!' However, apart from each of us forgetting to drive on the right from time to time, we managed very well.

Having left a flooded Nashville in our wake, we found every day sunny and warm from then on. We had to drive hard to get to Memphis so we could make the last tour of Graceland, the erstwhile home of Elvis Presley. We were booked to stay at the Heartbreak Hotel, just across the road from Graceland - indeed, they share a car park - and in an example of supreme American commercial practicality, they'd renamed the road leading to the hotel, 'Lonely Street' so as to give life to the lyrics of the song made famous by Elvis. Being honest, the hotel was clean and functional without being impressive - but on the bright side, we had free Elvis movies 24 hours a day within the hotel and his songs were played constantly in the elevator, in the lobby, the dining rooms....everywhere.

Graceland itself was quietly impressive... a beautiful Palladian mansion within 32 acres of woodlands and meadow and it was possible to envisage a family living there. Each room was as it was when Elvis left the building and it was clear from the commentary we listened to that he was very much a family boy, constantly surrounded by friends and acolytes. His grave was also well tended and you could see in the demeanour of other visitors that many approached his final resting place with a significant measure of reverence. Us? Well by this time we'd had enough of Elvis's ubiquitous singing and were anxious to be off to explore Memphis proper - especially Beale Street, famed for the popularisation of the blues.... but first we figured we should go and see the mighty Mississippi.

The Mississippi River, the fourth longest in the world, meanders some 2,320 miles from its origins up north in Lake Itasca, Minnesota where it is responsible for draining the water from some 32 states of the union. Where we met it at Memphis it was a sluggish, brown waterway but majestic nevertheless. We gazed upon it for some time before hunger and the appeal of a cool beer took us up to nearby Beale Street - a short street comprising not much more than a couple of blocks which appeared to have little in common with its original architecture and atmosphere. But while it seemed a little gentrified and commercialised, it was done pretty well and after a reasonable meal in one of the various emporia on the street (during which we were entertained by a passable *ersatz* version of B.B. King) we wandered next door where a band - The Don Valentine Band - were wowing an appreciative audience in the open air.

Donald Valentine himself was what can only be referred to as 'American fat'. He was huge; a black giant of a man with a girth that would have defeated any hula hoop. However, he could fair carry a tune and was belting out classic after classic. As I had been wont to do in Nashville, I approached the big man and asked if he had a CD for sale (one of the characteristics we noticed about bar acts in America was that they all seemed to play only for tips and after every couple of songs either the artist themselves or an agent of theirs would come among the audience with a jug asking for tips - and they got lots of cash this way). They also (mostly) happened to have a CD of their performance available for a few bucks so we collected these enthusiastically for later use on our car journeys.

The highlight of the evening was when the drummer stepped forward to give Big Don a rest and delivered a rendition of *'Purple Rain'* that equalled that performed by 'The Artist Formerly Known As Prince' - although I gather that 'The Artist Formerly Known As Prince' is now calling himself 'Prince' again...so, Prince! Mind you, he passed away recently so perhaps we're back once more to 'The Artist Formerly Known As Prince'. We left pretty early that night by our standards as we had to be up early to deliver our rented car back at Memphis Airport and catch a flight to Lubbock, Texas.

Next morning, having been awakened by the velvet tones of our Elvis, we headed off with time to spare to return our vehicle. We arrived effortlessly (thanks to my exceptional navigational skills) at Memphis Airport only to be told that rental cars had to be returned to a pound some two miles away. Now with something approaching panic, we headed off, took the wrong turning (again thanks to my exceptional navigational skills) and found ourselves driving down a very long Interstate Highway out of town. Throwing the map to one side, we drove intuitively and by sheer luck found our way to the Alamo rental station where we caught a lift to the airport terminal to catch our plane with minutes to spare. Whew... a close shave!

When Don McLean recorded '*American Pie*', his homage to Buddy Holly in 1971, he perpetuated the legend of this remarkable *songmeister*. Holly's career was cut short due to his plane crashing *(the day the music died)* on a cold winter's night in 1959 when his small private plane took off from Clear Lake, Iowa bound for Fargo but didn't arrive. Holly hit the big time for only eighteen months but Rolling Stone Magazine still found it appropriate to include him at number 13 of the *Fifty Greatest Artists Of All Time*. We decided that visiting Lubbock would be sensible, firstly to put us back on Route 66 and secondly to say hi to Buddy. His museum - hard to find in downtown Lubbock - was actually rather a disappointment but it was adequate in its demonstration of the legacy of the man.

Lubbock itself was also something of a disappointment. Scrawny, low rise blocks of retail and housing sat along poorly paved thoroughfares. The university section of town was a bit more upmarket but all the activity centred on what the citizens of Lubbock referred to as 'Downtown' - several blocks comprising bars and restaurants. Really nothing about which to write home.

While we were there, there was a constantly strong wind in evidence although we were advised later that there was always a wind in that part of Texas as there was nothing to stop it blowing across the open plains to the city. Fortunately, this also had the effect of taking the edge off the temperature and made it quite comfortable walking around if you didn't mind sand in your eyes.

Given our evening ambition of trying always to watch some live music, we settled down on a veranda atop a bar after enjoying one of our better meals in the Triple J Restaurant. This gave us an unhindered view onto a performing area where final efforts were being made to complete arrangements for that night's band who seemed about to perform to an audience of well behaved, monied (given the high spec of the pick-up trucks in which they drove up) students. Unfortunately, although the view was fine and the beer was cool, the band was mince - just a series of cover versions which would not have done justice to a wedding band of any repute.

So, tired, we headed for bed back at our hotel and readied ourselves for a long drive the following day across Texas and New Mexico to Santa Fe.

Early the following morning, we saddled up and headed off across Texas in our comfortable Sports Utility Vehicle. Long, straight roads dotted with poorly maintained houses, rusting vehicles and occasional gas stations didn't show off the Lone Star State to best effect. The road west followed the contour of the Santa Fe Railroad for most of the journey and we bore witness to enormous freight trains - perhaps half a mile in length - hauling goods slowly across the plains. The sheer quantity of goods they must have carried was colossal and must have reduced road haulage in that part of America substantially

About half-way between Lubbock and Santa Fe lies the township of Fort Sumner, once a military fort charged with the internment of the *Navajo* and *Mescalero Apache* populations as recently as the late 1880s but more famously, as the location where Billy the Kid was shot and where his body lies buried today - despite his gravestone having twice been stolen.

We paid good dollars to visit the museum on the site but found its value only in the absolute irrelevance of anything pertinent to the history of the place. Apart from a few amateurish paintings of Billy the Kid, all that was displayed was a broken wagon wheel, part of an old plough and some Native American relics. A complete rip-off so blatant as to make us smile rather than shake our heads. The old guy who was minding the store must have been used to complaints of all designs so we decided not to bother him. The guy was making a living as best he could.

Santa Fe itself was at once a complete delight and an unending frustration. We arrived late in the afternoon and asked for directions to the hotel district. Everyone we spoke with - including a cop - told us we required to go 'downtown' - omitting to tell us that although Santa Fe is located on a mountainside, 'downtown' is actually at the top of the hill....so many miles were lost heading 'down' in the wrong direction. However, having settled in at the frankly sumptuous Inn of the Governors' Hotel, we set off to explore and could see immediately why Santa Fe is described as 'the prettiest state capital in America'. The whole place reeked of elegance, money and thoughtful design. Its *Pueblo* style architecture never rising above two floors, all properties built using rounded edges and *adobe* design brought a harmonious marriage of terracotta coloured walls, rustic beams, French doors and terraces.

Just one artistic triumph after another. Simply lovely.

Next day we drove the short distance to Albuquerque which seemed to us to represent a larger version of Santa Fe. Very beautiful in parts, if more urbanised. We shopped for some *Navajo* beads and considered buying Stetsons. As we placed cowboy hats on our heads, we'd turn to each other and invite comment. Laurie was more earnest about his purchase than either John or I. As he manoeuvred a black Stetson on his head, he obviously thought himself a real bronco-busting buckaroo. An attendant, being sociable asked him where next he was headed. The answer should have been, 'Gallup, New Mexico'. Laurie avoided her gaze, still admiring himself in the mirror, narrowed his eyes, raised his jaw the better to view a new perspective and responded, "Headin' out west, Ma'am." Had a horse been hitched to a rail outside, we wouldn't have seen Laurie for dust.

We drove to the outskirts of the town, looked over the Rio Grande and left for the town of Gallup, New Mexico, the centre of Native American culture in the United States. Still very hot.

We arrived in Gallup on the evening of the UK General Election. That evening I sat in the bar with the guys listening to a juke box and drinking beer. In acknowledgment of the election, I was wearing a T-shirt with the legend, *'I still hate Thatcher'*. The *Navajo* barman, pointing to my shirt, asked why I 'hated that guy Thatcher'. Without bothering to correct him, I answered that we viewed Thatcher as he did General Custer! "Gotcha", he replied, in immediate understanding of my antipathy.

We stayed in the famous *El Rancho* Hotel which was once the epitome of luxury in the Wild West. Used continuously as the base camp for all movie stars filming westerns due to the local countryside reflecting the west as it was always portrayed on screen, the hotel showed above the room doors, the names of every star who had stayed there...John Wayne, James Stewart, Henry Fonda...I got Elizabeth Scott, more famous, I discovered for her courtroom appearance when she sued Confidential Magazine for stating that she spent her off-work hours with "Hollywood's weird society of baritone babes" (a euphemism for lesbians). Back then, this was news! The hotel itself had great character and for once we managed to eat a hearty breakfast such as we might have enjoyed back in Scotland.

We dined that night in the Coal Street Bar having been taken there by a *Navajo* taxi driver who warned us away from all of the bars frequented by Yankees. In fact the restaurant was great fun - if a bit tawdry. We conversed freely with a young Native American waitress who couldn't wait to get out of Gallup and become a zoologist in a large city.

Next day we visited the Electric Shoe Shop (sic) where the taxi driver told us we could buy great leather cowboy boots - one of my 'must do's'. Again as elsewhere, all of the shop workers were *Navajo* and were most helpful, other than speaking to one another in their native tongue when in front of us. I decided to respond in kind and having tried one boot on, asked the assistant "Have you the neebour of this wan, Hen?" In the event I bought a lovely pair of black polished leather cowboy boots which proceeded to cripple me for the next few days until I admitted defeat - but by which time my feet were blistered and cut.

As with most towns we encountered in this part of the journey, Route 66 was actually the main street of the town, but over the years it had fallen into disrepair and it was difficult to see how Gallup faced anything other than a slow, downward decline without the infusion of new funds or a revitalisation of cowboy films.

Next morning we rose, digested more election results and set off in sombre mood towards Arizona - where we promptly got lost trying to follow the actual route of Route 66. Across America, the road is now overgrown, has been overlaid by tarmac and is now the new Interstate Highway. It remains only as a feeder road or as a main street in a township. There is actually no way physically that anyone could navigate the entire Mother Road these days but when we visited the Petrified Forest National Park to see 'The Painted Desert', we could appreciate the trials of trying to walk or drive Route 66 all the way to the coast in blistering heat.

As well as visiting the National Park - hugely impressive - we also visited 'The Meteor Crater' - a hole punched in the earth when a meteor struck some 50,000 years previously creating an indentation some 4,000 ft. in diameter and 570 ft. deep. We spent good beer money climbing up to the top before peering over and seeing....a big hole! Big mistake.

Much more to our taste was our next stop, in Winslow Arizona, made famous due to the Eagles' line in their song *'Take It Easy'* ..."*Well I'm standin' on a corner in Winslow, Arizona, such a fine sight to see...*" We spent ages photographing ourselves with a statue of an 'Eagle' on the aforementioned corner and applauded the entrepreneurialism of the locals who now saw group after group drape themselves around the statue for photographs as we did before filing in to the coffee houses, bars and shops to spend their tourist dollars. Well done, Winslow.

Having left Winslow, we arrived in Flagstaff late in the afternoon but found difficulty getting accommodation. We settled on a motel just on the edge of downtown and as I entered reception to book it, John and Laurie looked round, realised it was a dump and made to call off the deal - but too late, we were in. With a gun shop across the street and dreadfully flimsy doors in our rooms, we didn't feel very safe. So much so, that John wore most of his personal wardrobe that evening as we went in search of food. If he'd had a dog on a string and a cup, people would certainly have mistaken him for a panhandler and given him money!

Leaving for the sunny town centre in shirt sleeves, I was encouraged by John and Laurie to wear a sweater as they figured that wee places like Flagstaff out in the boondocks could get cold at night. I rubbished this suggestion with the same strength of feeling I used an hour later as the sun set and the rapidly cooling evening had me hustle away to buy a plaid shirt, which when worn along with my *Navajo* beads and Stetson, made me look even more like a cowboy - or an eegit, as Laurie and John thought!

Flagstaff is a university town and houses an observatory due to its clean air and heightened elevation. More than once one of us would feel nauseous before realising that imperceptibly, we had been climbing to six or seven thousand feet and were quite unprepared for the effects of altitude sickness.

Pretty and with a student feel to it, Flagstaff was a most enjoyable stop-off. We dined outside that night on a sidewalk where the waiting staff seemed to delight in taking ages to serve or clean up. We were in no rush so it was pleasant watching the world go by until the evening chill hastened us into a local sports bar where unaccountably we ended up playing a basketball game following my initial high score until we realised that the illuminated digits didn't reflect any prowess on my part but the number of games played on the machine. The machine hadn't been keeping score which was probably just as well as we were no match for the local students who knew how to score baskets alright.

A poor night's sleep following some fellow guests shouting at each other and knowing that we'd have to face the same sticky carpets and stained bedclothes on rising the following morning. Alcohol taken on board at an Irish Bar before bedtime didn't help either. Up early and away before the world awoke. This time to Las Vegas.

Another beautiful, warm and sunny day greeted us as we left the wooded mountain wonderland of Flagstaff and headed towards Las Vegas. John had half a driving shift to complete so we pulled in after an hour to the township of Seligman which, as well as a stopping point on Route 66, serves the various needs of the nearby *Hualapai* Indian Reservation. Seligman was another small town which had clung to survival using Route 66 as its economic bolster. We pulled in at a cafe and tourist shop on the main drag and were Tony's first customers that morning. He was friendly and solicitous but wanted to get on with business as he had two large German tour buses coming in shortly and had pre-booked breakfasts to prepare for them. In between times he had to sell his trinkets as well as the bootleg music he played in the background. We ate well and, as Tony had predicted, our quiet backwater was soon swamped by German tourists all milling around the shop buying up Route 66 memorabilia. Seligman's fortunes, such as they were, were predicated upon its distance from Vegas, allowing bus operators to accomplish some distance towards the Grand Canyon yet providing a pit stop for food, washrooms and gifts. God only knows how this was accomplished as he only had one toilet stall to accommodate perhaps 100 tourists at one time.

Thirty miles out from Las Vegas we stopped at the Hoover Dam, once known as Boulder Dam, a concrete arch-gravity dam in the Black Canyon of the Colorado River on the border between the U.S. states of Arizona and Nevada. Security was tight and each and every vehicle was stopped and some searched lest one of us were attempting to explode the structure. It was such a massive edifice that one could only imagine the size of explosive charge that would be necessary to do damage - but if one were to be discharged successfully, there's no doubt as to the damage it would cause the economy of the USA as entire cities, like Phoenix, Arizona and Las Vegas, Nevada depend entirely on its gifts. Lake Mead, which it impounds, was noticeably reduced in its capacity - a consequence some said, of global warming affecting rainfall in the Rocky Mountains which drain into the Colorado. It was a magnificently impressive undertaking, even more so as a Federal decision had been taken to build a freeway over the tops of nearby mountains so as to ease transport difficulties and exclude the public in the near future further to safeguard this national asset from attack.

We drove on to Vegas and entered it from the northern end of the Strip because John couldn't follow my easily understandable directions - but it permitted us to view that more tawdry and down at heel part of the four-mile Boulevard to which we didn't intend to return.

Nineteen of the world's twenty-five largest hotels by bed count are on the Strip - each abutting the other, each attempting to out-rival the others in their ostentatious design, each seeking to lure those who would bet on beating the house in a game of chance. Some chance!

We stayed at the southern end of the Strip, at the Luxor Hotel, shaped as a pyramid within which is the largest atrium in the world as the hotel rooms are all affixed to an external wall. This provides a most unsettling experience upon arrival as on entering an elevator, guests are transported both upwards and to one side as it follows the contour of an edge of the pyramid.

Vegas came as something of a culture shock following our earlier visits to small desert townships but it was an interesting place nevertheless.

There was a more vacational feel to the Vegas stay and we went to shows, sunbathed and shopped in some of the very elegant shopping malls which had been crafted to represent Venetian canals, Roman temples - and surprisingly effectively too. We saw a passable Elvis (you can't have too much Elvis) and lost a couple of dollars on the tables - but only a couple as none of us were really tempted by the built-in advantage to the house.

Collected early in the morning from our hotel by our guide, Amie in a large SUV, we managed to reduce her to helpless laughter on the way to Boulder Airport where we were to pick up the helicopter along with Marcie and Bill, our two fellow passengers.

The Grand Canyon can only be described as simply stunning. Its jaw-dropping grandeur just took our breath away - especially as we entered the Canyon from the air and descended its depth of one mile. At 277 miles long we could only see the first few miles but it was sufficient to appreciate the real beauty of the place. Our pilot landed at a government licensed outcrop and we stepped out onto the two billion year-old rock that forms the floor of the canyon. A *very* civilised glass of Champagne and a sandwich breakfast awaited as and we took photographs and wandered around taking in the astonishing structures that surrounded us.

John scratched his leg badly on some cactus and I stole a rock from the Canyon floor for my collection as they seemed to have a surfeit. Heading back, our pilot pointed out some Hippy encampments below leaving us in little doubt that were he still to be flying the gunship he did in Vietnam, he'd 'machine gun them bead-wearing Hippies'. Worried, I clutched my own *Navajo* beads closer to my chest and hoped he wouldn't notice.

The following morning, we collected our car from the Luxor valet and drove off in search of the Beverly Garland Hotel complex in North Hollywood, Los Angeles. First we had to cross the Rockies but road engineers had flattened the contours so much that apart from a couple of long haul drags ascending and then descending all the way, we had no trouble. We left early as was our practice, got lost immediately, but eventually found ourselves on Interstate 15 to L.A. Breakfast was called for so we stopped at a most unusually situated restaurant billing itself for miles beforehand on the Interstate as 'The Mad Greek's'. It was located in a hamlet called

Baker in the Mojave Desert at the junction of Interstate 15 and Death Valley Road. Its claim to fame was that it hosted the world's largest thermometer and because of its proximity to Death Valley, which features the lowest, driest, and hottest temperatures in North America, it attracts tourists who like to photograph its totem pole thermometer showing some outrageously scorching scores. The restaurant itself was as if we had entered a fast food Greek *taverna*... all Greek flags and photographs of the owners' homeland. I can just imagine the face of the bank manager when Mr Papadopoulos first told him of his business plan to open a large Greek restaurant for truckers in the middle of the Mojave Desert!

We stopped off again to visit the 'ghost town' of Calico. We figured this would be a real-life abandoned town but upon arrival we were asked to pay $8 to park and realised once again how entrepreneurial are our colonial friends the Americans; any chance to turn a dollar. From the outside, the various wooden structures look like Wyatt Earp might step out of one at any moment but upon entering, there were trinkets a-plenty and modern washrooms to boot.

Mid-afternoon we entered Los Angeles but hadn't adequately prepared ourselves for the eight lane highways - each of which carried traffic travelling at full speed - and the distance...the distance. Los Angeles sprawls over some 500 square miles and hosts a population of 3.8 million and counting. It was nerve shredding but we found our way surprisingly easily to the hotel, located next to Hollywood Bowl, Mulholland Avenue, Sunset Strip, Universal Studios and Beverly Hills. Perfect!

After settling in we headed off for dinner but instead of heading to the Strip, we set off up Mulholland Drive to have a look at sunset over L.A. Taking the obligatory photographs with the Hollywood sign in the background we parked the car at the hotel and took a taxi to a local bar where we'd been told that live music was on the agenda. We duly found Joe's All American Bar and had a blast eating, drinking and listening to The Smokin' Cobras - surely the worst band in the world...but great fun!

On the Hollywood Walk of Fame, I was photographed in front of the star inscribed 'Spencer Tracey'...my favourite actor. Next to it was a star devoted, it said, to 'Jose Jose'. We liked to think that this was a typing error and it was really intended to honour '*Francie* and Jose'.

On Wednesday 12th May, less than two weeks after we arrived in Nashville, we drove onto the car park at Santa Monica Pier - the end of Route 66. We'd covered the guts of 2,000 miles and seen parts of America that most *Americans* have only read about or seen on television. We'd shared time together in friendship and not a harsh word had been spoken. We'd laughed a lot and learned a lot too.

America is a conundrum. 'Give me your tired, your poor, your huddled masses', is the inscription on the Statue of Liberty. The authors might also have added.... "and if you have any loud, fat-arsed people who nick about with the aid of sticks and who prefer eating and drinking anything just so long as the container is made of cardboard....well, we're the very destination you're looking for!" America elected Donald Trump and George Bush; in fact, two Bushes. But they also have the Hoover Dam, the Grand Canyon, lovely people, Disney, Elvis and Coors Lite. But then again, they can't spell 'Light'.

The three of us journeyed west - broadly along the route taken by those dispossessed in the 1930s. They walked and spluttered along in their old jalopies where we purred through the desert in our all-terrain vehicle and slept in an air-conditioned bedroom every night. But it felt like an adventure. It felt like a road trip. We'd managed it safely and had lived to tell the tale.

The Rhythm Road

New York, Chicago, Lexington, Birmingham,
New Orleans.

aving successfully travelled Route 66 with Laurie and
John, it was agreed that an early attempt should be made
to continue our adventures and follow 'The Rhythm
Road', so-called because it takes in the musical cities of Chicago
(Blues) in the north, Nashville (Country & Western) in the mid-
west and New Orleans (Jazz and Boogie-woogie)in the south.

Our itinerary was adjusted slightly as travel arrangements required
that we pass through New York so we figured we may as well
make the most of it and see what the Big Apple had to offer before
beginning our adventure proper.

We left Glasgow on a beautiful spring morning, John collecting
me at 6.15am in his car. We arrived at Glasgow airport almost
simultaneously with Laurie (who regaled us with his story of how
he'd saved £60 on a £600 dollar purchase due to his Travelex
currency exchange vendor having a 'Happy Hour!')

Our flight south was uneventful and upon arrival in London, I
persuaded the guys to join me in the Fortnum and Mason's Cocktail
Bar at the end of Terminal 5 at Heathrow...very peaceful midst the
maelstrom of activity surrounding it...and little wonder given their
prices! We eventually paid £33 for a bottle of rather fine *Piedmont*
wine which we rather slugged in order to make a timeous connection
to JFK...and all at 10.30 in the morning! Such debauchery!

A lengthy limo drive into New York, a shower and then a walk to
Strawberry Fields in Central Park where we paid homage to John

Lennon before jumping in a taxi to Times Square where, flagging, we enjoyed a meal in The View Revolving Restaurant. The views as ever were spectacular - particularly as it was dusk and we watched New York transform from a sunny metropolis to a twinkling electric symphony of light and shade. We shifted uneasily in our seats, however upon the arrival of the bill which was approximately the price of an air-ticket from Heathrow to New York!

We were by now quite weary after a long day (New York is five hours behind Glasgow). In reality our ten o'clock pm return to our hotel was actually three o'clock am - a twenty-two hour shift.

A poor sleep last night but I emerged quite buoyant and keen to explore the Big Apple. However, due to my body harbouring the herpes simplex virus, every time I come across the first of summer sunshine, I get a sore lip. This one threatened to light up like a beacon.

We navigated the New York Subway system without erring and caught the ferry to Staten Island. The view of the iconic Manhattan skyline as the ferry pulls out into Upper New York Bay is always impressive and numerous photographs were taken. One surprise was that on an island that is so committed to commerce and making a buck, the ferry ride was free for all passengers. We walked hurriedly upon arrival and caught the next ferry back; our time on Staten Island being approximately thirty seconds. We even found time to advise a travelling family from Japan on directions although it took a while to understand that *Balloakalan Bleach* was an enquiry asking the way to Brooklyn Bridge.

We walked in pretty sunny weather past Wall Street, through SoHo, up to China Town and into Little Italy where we shared a light pizza before continuing our walk through Greenwich Village admiring the cast iron buildings, sidewalk stoops and fascinating architecture so typical of that part of Manhattan. I'd earlier persuaded John and Laurie of the pearl that is the sawdust-strewn floor of McSorley's Old Ale House, an ancient bar in the East

Village frequented by most American Presidents including Abraham Lincoln and Teddy Roosevelt as well as playwrights like Brendan Behan. Musicians from John Lennon to Woody Guthrie – who inspired the union movement from atop one of the bar's sturdy tables - have enjoyed a beer here. The pub only sells dark ale, light ale and raw onions! They serve their beer in small glasses that hold about a half pint and provide every purchaser with two of each on every order. We blanched at the raw onions offer. At our table we met and chatted with three locals called Sean, Desiré, a nurse and John, a pharmacy student. Five rounds later we stumbled out into the light and found a restaurant in the Village before being given directions to a 'music bar' that turned out to be a haven for jazz enthusiasts. The performer on the night was singing 'scat' (using wordless vocables) and I'm afraid I got a fit of the giggles as she do-wahed and diddy-boo-hooed her way through songs. A tiring day and too much alcohol. I went to bed woozy.

We each rose early to catch an early morning flight to Chicago but upon arrival at the hotel's Reception where we were due to meet, I took a call from our tour operators, Trailfinders who advised me that American Airlines had cancelled the flight we were scheduled to take from Newark and had instead booked us on the 16.16 flight from La Guardia. Being seasoned adventurers, we took this in our stride and used our free morning by going to Union Station for breakfast and visited the High Line in the Meatpackers District - a most impressive community development which repurposed an old railway solum some twenty feet from the ground. It's a boardwalk in the sky, populated by trees and plants and dotted throughout with small market stalls and outdoor cafés. All along its length there are views of the River Hudson and myriad examples of the gentrification of a once run-down part of New York. Imaginative and a great environmental asset for locals and tourists both.

After arriving at Chicago and checking in at the Essex Inn on Michigan Avenue, we walked to Navy Pier - a visit I'd recommended but I misread the Google Map and told the guys it was a twelve minute walk but it transpired that it was a twelve minute *drive*! Much grumbling and when we got there everything was either closed or had no custom. Frustrated, we jumped in a taxi and headed to Rush Street where we'd been told there were many bars and restaurants. None of us were feeling particularly in party mode following the previous evening's excesses but we settled upon a Mexican restaurant where I ordered a diet coke. Feeling quite proud of my more measured selection of drink, I scanned the unfamiliar menu and ordered a dish which proudly boasted that it would arrive at the table in a lava bowl heated to 400 degrees. Not only did it live up to its claim, the food bubbling and frothing before me, but it also made use of spicy chillies which seared the roof of my mouth and left my tongue resembling a slice of crispy bacon. My Diet Coke was consumed almost in one gulp as I tried to recover from the assault on my taste buds. Sweating, my nose and eyes running like a burst gutter, I staggered from the place swearing to stick to fish and chips in the future.

My upper lip now has an inflamed red sore, making drinking from a glass problematic.

Chicago transit relies in some measure on its 'L'...its Loop Rail system. It circumnavigates Downtown Chicago and although completely antiquated, running on rusty rails supported by even more rusty supports which hold it aloft, it is quite the perfect way to get around much of the city. We each bought a day pass and headed into the Windy City on a gloriously sunny day looking for a bar in which to watch the Kentucky Derby, intent upon finding one adjacent to a bookie's in which we might place a small wager on its outcome. You could have bowled us over with a small betting slip when we were advised by a waitress that gambling was illegal in the state of Illinois. Our ambitions thwarted, we walked round the city and took front seats in a boat tour through the city along the River Chicago. It was very interesting but we'd been unprepared for the strong sun and as John would have it, were well and truly 'skelped ' by the blazing Chicago sunshine.

In the evening, having researched blues bars in the city, we plumped for B.L.U.E.S. in Lincoln Park, a suburb of the city. John was mildly anxious about our safety as he'd read that the previous day - a normal day in Chicago - there had been twenty-six shootings, five of which had been mortal. I had immediate cause to remonstrate with him as while Laurie and I turned up for our visit to a hot and sweaty blues bar in 'street clothes' John chose to wear his blazer, dressing as if he was going to watch a cricket match at Lords! I thought it made him being shot more likely, and encouraged a change of attire solely on the basis that I might be hit by the ricochet.

The evening's entertainment was provided by Carlos Johnston and the Serious Blues Band who were simply magnificent. Carlos's mastery of his fender guitar (played upside down and left-handed) was astonishingly impressive, his lavish guitar licks sending the audience into regular frenzies. The small bar was crowded, beer flowed and we had a great time although, mindful of the need to drive the following morning, I drank but Diet Coke for the second half of the evening.

We collected our Ford Escape Sports Utility Vehicle from Alamo having checked out of the hotel and made our way south. Being Sunday, the roads were quite quiet but we still managed to lose our way a couple of times. With no fixed destination, we changed our minds several times on the most propitious location for the evening. Indianapolis, Lexington, St Louis, Cincinnati, Louisville and nearby Bloomingdale were all considered - the last because John mentioned that as a young man he'd had an eight year distant relationship with a pen-pal called Becky who hailed from there. We had good fun at his expense as I had the wheel and John was concerned that I'd just turn right to Bloomingdale, find a phone book and look up her name as I threatened to do.

Laurie also drove and did well despite his vision not being as good as once it was. We had a coffee in a Wendy's in a small township called Frankfort and I complimented Laurie on his visual acuity when driving. He accepted my compliment graciously, told me he needed to go to the toilet and promptly disappeared into a cleaners' cupboard. I revised my opinion of his ability to drive accordingly.

Into Lexington, Kentucky where we took rooms in Quality Inns - a double-decker motel just outside the town. Both John and Laurie were apprehensive as it was a rather down-at-heel motel prompting John to speak with the front desk guy and ask for reassurances that the place was clean and safe; like the motel guy was going to tell him that there was a percentage chance he'd be shot if he laid his head on one of the motel's pillows! In fact Mike at the front desk was helpful to the point of being unctuous.

A quick turn around and off in a taxi driven by an informative and entertaining Martin, a Dutch *émigré* to a simply charming Lexington to sample a couple of beers then back home to our gangster's hideaway.

I awoke the following morning and looked in the mirror where I noticed that the sore on my upper lip now resembles the red tail light on a bicycle.

Lexington is famous for battles and skirmishes during the Civil War - but these days more for bourbon manufacture, horse breeding and racing. We walked round the town for a while then drove the few miles to Keeneland Racetrack where we breakfasted for $5 and wandered round a most impressive racing campus in glorious sunshine. Off next to see the Four Roses Distillery up in Bluegrass Country where a tours guide let us into the secrets of their processes. At the end of the tour we were all given three glasses of three neat Bourbons in order of their greater maturation. Where everyone sipped at the nectar and nodded their approval, John's face conveyed utter horror at being asked to drink what he obviously thought was vomit distilled through a shitey cloot. His mouth pursed as though he'd eaten a lemon raw and finding nowhere to spit the contents of his mouth was compelled to swallow before handing me his glass, shaking his head violently to rid himself of both the taste and memory. At no point did we see grass that was blue!

Later coming upon a massive traffic jam, we took the opportunity to exit the freeway, make a left onto smaller country roads - and were rewarded beyond anything we might have expected. Stopping at the Longbranch Saloon in a small town called New Haven, well off the beaten path, it seemed a bit of a roughneck establishment but the owners couldn't have been nicer. We enjoyed a sandwich and a beer in a completely empty saloon and contemplated the likelihood of it ever being full. However, the owner joined us at our table and told us how it was home to three hundred revellers of an evening. As we drank our coffee, he told us that below the saloon, running from the nearby river to a train stop in the town was a man-made tunnel built by slaves escaping north. I'd seen a documentary about this some months before and found the coincidence remarkable. We travelled onwards to Hodgenville, the birthplace of Abraham Lincoln, visiting the local Lincoln Memorial within which was reproduced the small hut in which he was born. A few miles further on we stopped momentarily at the township called Glasgow to photograph ourselves in front of the town sign.

Kentucky is bucolic; a green and pleasant land, well-manicured and our route kept such poverty as it may have well hidden. Long, sun-lit country roads were populated on each side by wealthy looking cattle farms and small holdings punctuated now and again by a shabby looking trailer with a rusty Oldsmobile out front. Travelling along the narrow E31 towards Nashville, every second establishment was of a religious nature. We were well and truly in the Bible Belt; *The Church of the Latter Day Saints, The Church of God of Prophecy, The Baptist Church of Kentucky, The Church of Christ The Redeemer* and most memorably, *the Church of Bikers for Jesus* midst many others each competed for the souls of local Kentuckians. People are unfailingly polite but they vote Republican, celebrate their right to bear arms and pray for their family out here!

After some poor navigational advice on my part, we eventually arrived in Nashville and settled in to our hotel, the Holiday Inn Express up the hill from Broadway. We'd stayed there on our last visit when driving Route 66.

In the evening we went down to Broadway to sample again the ubiquitous bars, restaurants and boot shops - each bar belting out country music like there was no tomorrow. In Second Fiddle we listened to Moulton Steel, a C&W band which majored in George Jones songs. They were great and had a guy called 'Chief' on pedal steel guitar. He was an older guy, bedenimed, long straggly beard, unkempt hair, crumpled trousers and looked like he'd sleep in a shop doorway after he'd finished the gig but boy could he play guitar! I fell into conversation with him and as ever, the conversation turned to my accent.

"You from Scotland?"

"Aye."

"I've always wanted to go see Scotland ever since Paul McCartney sang that song about...Campbellville."

"Campbeltown?"

"That's it! Campbeltown."

We moved on to Printers Alley, a small, narrow lane populated by bars and places to eat...I wouldn't bestow the description '*restaurant*' on any of them...and took seats in a blues bar where bands and guitarists would just turn up and jam on stage. I spoke to one act who told me he'd never met any of his fellow musicians until he struck the first chord on stage. Remarkable; although with blues, there's such a fixed and solid format to the songs that it's easy to anticipate the chord progression. These guys were one and all superb guitarists - much better than the country guys we'd seen down on Broadway - but didn't have the stage presence. A great night.

Next morning, Tennessee was again resplendent in glorious sunshine so we decided to walk to Antiques Archaeology, the Nashville store location of the popular American Pickers TV show. Gargantuan construction sites blocked our way so we wandered through the city's sizeable civic centre and down to the River Cumberland which on our last visit to Nashville five years ago had burst its banks and flooded downtown, killing some twenty-seven people. We'd a beer in a bar on Broadway to hide from the sun then, looking for a taxi to take us over to Antique Archaeology, happened upon a pony-tailed guy driving a six-seater golf buggy with a hand-written taxi sign on his windscreen. Once we'd established that he was for hire, I asked for an estimate of the fare.

"It's free, man. I just work for tips!"

Our taxi driver was a totally laid-back guy and failed guitarist called Mike who worked for a local company called Joyride. This was indeed a business model I hadn't come across before but he drove us (slowly) out to our destination, giving us a guided tour all the way and took us to the Musicians' Hall of Fame. Interesting. We gave him tips of $30 then a further $10; more than we'd have given a regular, metered taxi driver but it was worth it for the open air, the education and the banter.

After a couple of hours' break in our hotel we walked down to Broadway, to Second Fiddle and watched a band which resembled the Marx Brothers playing C&W. They clowned around, irritating me and intermittently would stop proceedings to fine-tune the mix. A shame as they were brilliant musicians.

We left and stumbled serendipitously across the newly opened George Jones Museum on the banks of the Cumberland River. Although downstairs was a shop and museum, two elderly, diminutive identical twins wearing large Stetsons and called the 'Bang This Twins' cornered us and persuaded us up to its rooftop bar and restaurant where tonight two beers could be had for the price of one. The entertainment was provided by a talented band of musicians whose purpose was to back the lead singer, Jimmy Charles. In truth, they were far more gifted than was he.

We enjoyed a couple of hours in their company. I couldn't help but reflect that upon our last trip all musicians wore cowboy hats and boots. On this visit it was baseball caps and trainers that predominated. So much for my bringing my black leather Stetson. I looked like yesterday's cowboy; as if John Wayne had turned up at an Apple convention!

To bed via another bar where we listened to Paula-Jo Taylor and her family play. Mum, Paula was the star turn, playing brilliant guitar like the veteran she was. Back at the hotel, it was difficult falling asleep as during the night the rail authorities obviously decided to send a few of the mile-long coal trains through the city. Every so often they'd blow their horns and hold the note a couple of blocks away, awakening the city.

We'd a frustrating morning as the Holiday Inn Hotel's wi-fi crashed, followed by the computers in their business centre going down so trying to book a place to sleep on-line in Birmingham, Alabama proved problematic. Eventually we managed to get something inexpensive and after a long drive and a confusing final few miles, we eventually found the Days Inn in West Birmingham. However, in doing so we had to travel (slowly) through some pretty insalubrious areas of the city. One garage we passed at a crossroads had someone standing guard at each entry point and it looked for all the world that fuel wasn't perhaps the main product being sold there.

The hotel didn't look very safe either so we decided to play the odds and use it only for a few hours' sleep. The windows were all barred by steel protectors and my door at least, was flimsy and looked as it had been kicked in a few times. We phoned a taxi and went downtown where we visited a most impressive Birmingham Civil Rights Institute across the road from the 16th Baptist Church which had been bombed back in 1963 killing four young girls.

Visiting the Institute was a very moving experience and helped me understand the emotional impact of a song I'd sung innumerable times when in folk clubs as a youth without understanding much of its potency.

During a strike by black women who worked on a tobacco plantation in South Carolina just after the Second World War, one of them started singing, 'We shall overcome', a song borrowed from a rich black church heritage. Shortly thereafter when Deputy Sheriffs with dogs raided a school and forced black students to sit on the floor while they smashed the place up looking for 'subversive' material, a student added another verse as they sang their defiance... 'We are not afraid'. As the civil rights movement gathered force in the South in general and in Birmingham in particular, activists would cross their arms and hold the hand of the person on either side of them and sing a further verse, 'We'll walk hand in hand' and as more Anglo-Saxon supporters joined the cause a penultimate verse was intoned, 'Black and white together'. That they could sing this song in common cause with hundreds of others as officers of the law, beat them and set dogs on them humbled me. As the song gained in popularity, a final verse, 'We shall live in peace' rang out.

The city is now 84% black but progress has been made since the days of cynical segregation and brutal repression. That said, when we went to Lakeview for food and then some drink, we couldn't help but notice that it was still the blacks who were serving and the whites who were relaxing over a glass of chilled Chardonnay... as were we! Laurie came up with the quote of the trip after I'd said I didn't like Chardonnay wine. He remonstrated with me, shaking his head sadly at my ignorance and explaining. 'You canny write aff the hale grape, Ron!'

An experienced *sommelier* is our Laurie!

We chatted at length to Ben Snieder, the owner of the Good People Bar where we had been drinking who told us much about the aspirations of the new Birmingham and his role as an entrepreneur within it. He called his friend, Mike Micinzi, a taxi driver, to take us downtown but when we got there, he refused all offers of payment. A very nice man. We had some Mexican food in Babalu's - this time a rather more bland repast that my previous experience - and then sat outside a dive bar and listened to Logan Mize, an 'up and coming' C&W singer/songwriter from Kansas. He was very good and certainly one to watch out for in the future. We phoned our favourite taxi driver Mike and he collected us from the Tin Roof bar and took us back to the hotel, waiting until we'd entered before driving off. Not a safe area. We agreed that we'd rise early and head off to minimise any likelihood of problems. A second night listening to long wailing train horns from the nearby freight rail terminal hindered my falling asleep.

As I lay awake, I recalled that it was another Election Day back home ...and we're 4,000 miles on the other side of the Atlantic. My wife, Jean has my proxy vote and John and Laurie have used a postal vote.

I rose early, preoccupied by the election and mildly anxious about the general safety of our motel. Ready to leave by 06.00am, I sat in an armchair and watched re-runs of *I Love Lucy* with the volume turned down until it was time to grab a banana for breakfast and head off to New Orleans via Selma...another location which was a centre of civil unrest during the 60's. With John at the wheel we set off, wheels spinning, heading south through Birmingham and onwards towards Selma looking for the iconic arched bridge which played a material role in bringing civil rights to black Americans in the South.

On three occasions in March 1965, protest marches in pursuit of civil rights from Selma to Montgomery were held along the 54-mile highway that connects the two. The marches were organised by non-violent activists and the Edmund Pettus Bridge carried repeated lines of black people marching peaceably towards serried ranks of state troopers who were wearing gas masks, helmets and body armour. Repeatedly during the marches, police on horseback whipped those walking as their colleagues on foot assaulted them with clubs while tear-gas canisters were thrown. On the banks of the river, white onlookers shouted their support of the forces of law and order. The leadership of the black protesters, mainly clergymen, were clubbed to the ground, their skulls cracked. Wounded and beaten, they rose and made the same journey on the next march. Incidents such as this were commonplace in the racist South but what made a difference this time was that the nation watched on in horror as newsreels nightly brought the beatings into their living rooms. History was made on that bridge as President Lyndon Baines Johnston, himself a southerner – indeed one who had in the past voted against legislation outlawing *lynching* - reacted to public outrage and made a speech in Congress intimating that he intended bringing forward a bill which would guarantee the rights of black people to vote in American elections. Completing his oration to legislators, he finished with the sentence, 'We shall overcome'. Martin Luther King Jr. cried upon hearing the President's words.

I very much wanted to see the bridge but John who was driving 'couldn't find somewhere safe to pull over' so we passed it by and settled instead for stopping for a coffee somewhere. So much for our liberal credentials!

The town of Selma is a ribbon development sprawling out along the 80 West. KFCs, Burger Kings, MacDonald's and Wendy's crowded the sidewalk. 'Trying to find somewhere safe to pull over', we had reached the extremity of the town limits and were continuing along the country road to Uniontown, described as the most polluted town in America. Certainly there was a distinctive aroma in the air redolent of a chemical factory and the town itself was very obviously poor and unkempt. A quick keek on my laptop revealed that the town had a *per capita* income of $8,268 and that 47.4% of the population were below the poverty line. It's also home to millions of tons of toxic coal ash-contaminated soil, brought in by rail from Harrison, Tennessee. I was advised that blowing ash can cover automobiles - taking paint off the roofs of vehicles. My laptop advised that at certain times of day, the place has an acrid smell that is horrendous. Well, we figured that last bit out ourselves.

By now, John had had three hours behind the wheel so we pulled over for a coffee in Kathleen's Korner Kitchen, (KKK eh?) a pretty shabby looking roadside café in a forlorn looking part of a poor town. It was popular with blue collar workers; both black and white, and resembled an old fashioned transport café back home. People were polite and helpful.

John has a general discomfort about driving over bridges so, as the group navigator, I arranged that we entered the city of New Orleans with him at the wheel and advised him too late for counter-action to be taken that we were about to cross the Lake Pontchartrain Bridge, which is some twenty-four miles across. Oh, how we laughed!

We arrived, organised ourselves and dined in New Orleans before settling in a comfortable bar with wi-fi so we could watch the UK General Election results coming in. My then local MP, Jim Murphy, Leader of the Labour Party in Scotland was defeated and result after result was called for the SNP. Eventually drink forced us to stow our technologies and head for bed, satisfied that a seismic political shift had taken place in Scotland and with the Tories in power down south, who knows what'll happen next. For the Labour Party, well, it seems that presently it's too right-wing for Scotland and too left-wing for England.

Up and out for breakfast before walking around the French Quarter (very beautiful...other than a surprising number of drunks who were laid out in the streets and doorways and who were ignored completely by those who walked past...including us.)

The sun was hot again so we decided upon a cruise up the Mississippi but shade wasn't available where we sat so my head was burned as somehow the strong sun had found its way through my thinning locks. Upon alighting from the ship we headed back to the French Quarter, to a balcony restaurant, and enjoyed (in my case) a tasty dish of Jambalaya for lunch before going back downstairs to a bar which had an astonishingly accomplished young jazz band playing. The teenage girl playing bass guitar...'Bass Girl' as she was called by the band leader...was extremely talented.

New Orleans, particularly Bourbon Street in the French Quarter, is quite a place. Drunks lie unconscious and unattended on the pavement, music blasts out from every bar doorway, street entertainers juggle, sing, dance, pose and generally bring a vibrancy to the area. One rather plump young lady wearing only a 'G' string and painted from head to toe in silver, pirouetted along the sidewalk hoping for tips. Another, skinny and topless but for a pastie on either breast, each with a tassel, doused them (the tassels) in petrol, lit them and gyrated and birlled so that the flames formed a fiery circle...and they say that entertainment is dead!

In the evening we attended Preservation Hall to listen to traditional jazz played by five old stagers, The 'Joint Chiefs of Jazz', who ambled on to a stage area, each wearing a white shirt and black trousers. Drums, piano, trumpet, double-bass and clarinet. Obviously at complete ease with their music, they laid into standards such as '*When The Saints Go Marching In*', '*The Maple Leaf Rag*' *and* '*Careless Love*'. The building was an original playhouse for jazz musicians and is merely a large room off an entry. It reeked of age and tradition and the musical experience was wondrous.

Back at the hotel, I read the Scottish and UK morning papers on-line before turning in as they come out six hours in advance of New Orleans time. I also checked my Junk Mail and found an email from my friend Alan (Murray's) daughter, Helen who wrote that Alan had been diagnosed with pancreatic cancer and further that it had progressed into his lungs so no operation is possible. Things look bleak. I wrote back immediately telling Helen I'd visit as soon as I returned to Scotland. It's all very, very sad. My second emotion, however, was one of angry frustration as I'd spoken with Alan some time ago about his health, had suggested that his symptoms suggested one of four possibilities, including pancreatic cancer but Alan was a bit phlegmatic. Had he been diagnosed earlier, before it had spread, he might have had a better chance of recovery. Sometimes it pays to be even slightly hypochondriacal.

I had an unsettled night thinking about poor Alan. Upon awakening I received a response to my email from his daughter, Helen confirming that his condition wasn't curable.

We retrieved the Ford Escape SUV from the valet and drove uncertainly towards the Louisiana swamps. My navigational abilities were lousy today and we ended up in another poor area miles from where we intended but we decided to go in for breakfast and again were treated like royalty. We were fed, watered and set on the correct route by a very attentive elderly waitress called Jodie. $25 each bought us tickets on a barge-like boat which drove us entertainingly and occasionally at some considerable pace through the sleepy bayous and waterways of the Pearl River. Over two hours, we became acquainted with the alligators, hogs, turtles, raccoons, snakes and bird life of this fascinating area of southern Louisiana. As we bobbed along the river listening to the Captain tell us stories of the Katrina disaster, he pointed to an upturned houseboat, now broken and languishing atop the Bald Cypress trees that edged the waterway. "That boat started twenty-five miles away. Katrina lifted it up and dropped it here."

One interesting facet of our unintended circuitous journey was that we were able to drive through the areas inundated when Hurricane Katrina hit in 2005. Many of the homes were flimsy to start with, others were trailers and they'd have stood no chance against the twenty-five foot surge and one hundred and thirty mph winds. Some 90,000 square miles were affected and 80% of New Orleans flooded. Given that the city is substantially below sea level, the levies are perhaps the most important investment New Orleans makes in its future.

Our last evening in New Orleans was spent on Frenchman Street. It's a lot more sophisticated than Bourbon Street, although that's like saying Loch Lomond's more scenic than Wishaw! We listened to the New Orleans Swamp Donkey Band in the Spotted Cat Music Club where they played standards like the 'Saint James Infirmary' and 'After I've Gone'. Excellent traditional jazz.

After some dinner we ventured further down Frenchman Street and watched a group called the Dana Abbott Band. They were tight and efficient but Dana herself was clearly a star of the future. She could be up there with guitar singer/songwriters like Joan Jett, Bonnie Rait and Joni Mitchell...although she might find that her song writing requires to become rather more commercial. Her self-penned songs, to my ears, were slightly lounge bar. But she could rock when she chose to!

My sore lip has almost cleared up, just in time for me to show my face in public back in Glasgow.

Tomorrow we return to Scotland after a wonderfully interesting and enjoyable road trip. However, I won't miss American television. They can produce some great movies and snappy comedies but the news programmes are infantile, biased, everything's dramatic and the ubiquitous and execrable adverts came almost as a relief.

We decided on a relaxed start to the day as our flight wasn't until after 4.00pm. Breakfast in a café in Royal Street then off to Destrehan Plantation where we toured the Palladian mansion of the local slave owner. The tour guide guy was obviously suffering from some kind of emotional ailment as although very knowledgeable about the history of the house and plantation, he had a very curious manner about him...a *very* curious manner about him! His attempt at jokes was decidedly unfunny and the history of the plantation, although very detailed, wasn't that interesting.

We handed the car back at the airport and flew home to Glasgow, tired but content at having completed another very successful road trip.

Over the years I've developed a love/hate relationship with the United States. In my younger days, as with most people I was enthralled by the scale and excitement of the place. My first visit was to New York *en route* to work in a Summer Camp up in Maine and just loved the idea that the sun shone most days but that when it rained it poured just like in the movies, that buildings were gigantic, that in Tad's Steak House you could see your steak being barbecued in the window while you queued in the street for lunch at little cost, that newspapers were the size of doorsteps and that they used funny words like sidewalk and elevator.

When up in Maine, I genuinely found the people to be naturally friendly, less distant than their New York cousins although almost to a man and woman they assumed that I was Irish and frequently complemented me on my rich Irish brogue although when I corrected them they found my Scots heritage just as charming and romantic.

However, it was also the time when almost from the outset, my schizophrenic American feelings surfaced. Richard Nixon was in the White House and the Vietnam War was at its height. Back home in Scotland I could watch dispassionately in the sense that while I was opposed to the war and was delighted when Harold Wilson rejected LBJ's overtures and refused to commit British troops, it was still a war that affected two other peoples. But it was the first 'TV war' which nightly brought home the horrors of warfare to millions of people and it was easy to side with the Vietnamese people and be critical of American foreign policy and their military might. Power in those days was measured in what a nation could destroy rather than what it could build. *Plus ca change, plus c'est la meme chose!*

But back then, sitting in a Greyhound bus talking with other students or on a camp bus on the way to some destination with the kids at the camp, it was confusing speaking to people my age with whom I'd become friendly, knowing that I'd be heading back to a lecture theatre after the summer and they'd be off to serve in Vietnam as many of them had been selected for the draft. Higher education provided deferment from the draft – but it merely postponed the inevitable rather than avoided it. In the years 1968 – 70, some 25% of American males about my age were in the armed forces. My subsequent visit to Vietnam further enhanced my discomfort about that particular episode of American adventurism.

Not one of my fellow staffers then agreed with the war – except Mike, a large, intelligent, right-wing educationalist who passionately supported the war but who had thus far escaped the draft and would sit and pronounce upon the need to do one's duty. There was a terrible sense of resignation and resentment amongst them. Nothing could be done. Nothing could be changed. I remember very clearly one trip on the bus back from the coast on the 17th of June 1972 the when the conversation was all about Nixon and the hate figure he'd become. There were real feelings of impotence held by my friends as there was no way he'd be influenced while in office. I was naively blustering away about how eventually the American people would see him off but my appraisal was met with derision. Little did we know that almost literally as we spoke that evening (as I calculated some months later), five burglars were breaking in to the Democratic headquarters in the Watergate Building in Washington paid for by money gathered to re-elect Richard Nixon and that the clock had begun ticking on his unceremonious helicopter departure on the 9th of August 1974 from the White House lawn in order to avoid impeachment charges.

Following my return to Scotland, I watched the Senate Hearings chaired by the elderly but completely charismatic Senator Sam Ervin each night and bored anyone within earshot the following day. It completely consumed me. I was watching history being made. Seeing a mendacious American President gradually having to reveal his venal coarseness, his duplicity, his inarticulacy, was riveting television and I felt part of it. Every so often when in my own life if I can't see a way out of a predicament, I reflect upon the circumstances pertaining to Nixon's domination of the White House and tell myself, *you never know. Expect the unexpected... things change...*

I've now visited twenty-six of the contiguous states of America. Now, as I contemplate a United States with Donald. J. Trump as President, I fall to wondering whether I'll ever return.

Fire and Ice

Oslo, Tromsø, Reykjavik

I'd always wanted to travel to the Arctic Circle and in fulfilling this ambition, I'd booked a stay in Tromsø, in northern Norway. This required a particularly early morning take-off from Glasgow Airport - flying out of the city in darkness; an amber-lit bejewelled city slumbering below. Still early when I arrived at Heathrow and with a two hour wait until my flight to Oslo, I took to walking the length of Terminal Five to get some mild exercise in between the lumps of time when all I was doing was sitting.

It was Sheryl Crow, I think, who first croaked the lyrics, '*I like a good beer buzz early in the morning...and Billy likes to peel the labels from his bottle of Bud....*' from her song, '*All I wanna do*'. For whatever reason, one end of Terminal Five was absolutely jam-packed whilst the other - perhaps incorporating waiting areas for more esoteric destinations - was quiet and was possessed of more sophisticated refreshment outlets. I chose to spend some time at the otherwise deserted Fortnum & Mason's cocktail and pastry bar, the only debate being whether to order a high calorie pastry and coffee or a delicious glass of chilled *Chablis*. I wrestled with this for some time given the unbreakable protocol of never drinking alcohol until the sun was over the yardarm - unless on my friend Bob's boat when drinking alcohol commences when the yardarm still casts a long angular shadow - and settled for a good *wine* buzz early in the morning; the quiet, somnolent atmosphere being in sharp counterpoint to the crowded melee of the section occupied by the varletry and proletariat. I read Scotland's newest newspaper, *The National* on my iPad in some small contentment thanks to a decent and free wi-fi link throughout the terminal.

A second, sipped chilled *Chablis* saw me on to the Airbus A320 to Oslo without a furrow on my brow.

On arrival at Oslo Airport, I took advantage of the five hour hiatus to jump on the express train into town and revisit the streets I'd come to know so well on my several earlier visits when I'd been invited to attend the annual Nobel Peace Prize Concert. The buildings in Oslo are substantial, handsome affairs and all seem to conform to classic rules of symmetry. *Sentralstasjon* (Central Station) in Oslo is a hell of a size. I arrived during a blizzard but the streets and pavements were all free of snow, the people seemed better dressed, fitter and wealthier than in my Glasgow - so maybe a nation of some five million *can* make a fair stab at economic and social well-being.

My earlier visits to Norway had been to attend an annual information technology conference which always coincided with the Nobel Peace Prize event in Oslo sponsored by a large technology company. Typically we were invited to the conference in Stockholm for the most part of the week where we listened to debates between the various winners of the Nobel Scientists about the 'next big thing' in science (the brain, in 2004 for example). I was completely taken by our access to these giant intellects.

Once when in Oslo attending the Nobel malarkey, I struck out on my own one afternoon in order to listen to a debate that was being broadcast by the BBC Home Service. In front of eight Nobel scientists, I was struck by two things. First, these people really were not only extraordinarily bright and articulate, they were often *witty*...not the caricature of the absent-minded, one-dimensional professor often presented. Secondly, though I was confronted by Nobel winners that included an Egyptian, an Englishman, a Pole, two Americans, a Canadian, a Russian and a Japanese chap, I noted three things. First, all were men. Secondly, with the exception of the big guy from Japan, they all spoke English (and with the exception of the Englishman from Cambridge, all spoke with an American tinge to their accent) and finally, again with the exception of the Englishman, their research had all been funded by the mighty dollar.

I enjoyed the 2003 conference whose special guest speaker was Al Gore. Defeated only three years earlier in the American Presidential race, Gore had been building a reputation as 'the best President we never had'. Having stepped out from Clinton's shadow, he had been defeated in the November 2000 election by George W Bush in an infamous, close-run election where he won the popular vote but because of the peculiarities of the American election system, had had to await the final results from Florida. After several recounts considering the acceptability of 'hanging chads'; voting preferences where the machine hadn't sufficiently punctured the voting slip, Gore was declared the loser. The vote was certified by Katherine Harris, the Floridian Secretary of State and a Republican who had publicly supported Bush during the campaign. Additionally, Bush's younger brother Jeb, was Governor of Florida and this led to allegations that Harris and Bush had somehow manipulated the election to favour the Governor's brother. Bush's margin of victory in Florida was officially decided at 537 votes (out of more than almost six million cast), making it the closest presidential election in the history of the state. Despite an appeal to the Supreme Court, also populated by conservative appointees, he lost and took the decision gracefully rather than drag America into a constitutional conflict.

Gore spoke to us about the World Wide Web – as he had been credited in many circles for having been its progenitor. Gore side-stepped this effortlessly, with many 'shucks' and self-effacing deprecations but somehow managed through his explanations to convince his audience that although he hadn't *invented* the WWW; *'Of course not!'* he had been there or thereabouts at its birth. On stage he was warm, witty and charming – everything he hadn't been during the election where he came across as wooden. The thought bubbles from the audience, had they been able to have been read, would all have said the same thing...
"If only...."

Gore gave a spellbinding performance...a *tour de force*. Question time followed and I found my arm raised and was allocated the second question. That morning, according to the newspapers, Gore had announced for Howard Dean as his preferred Democratic candidate in the upcoming American Primaries. I wanted to ask if Dean or Republican Presidential nominee George W Bush would give America the leadership Gore argued it now needed after three years of a first Bush administration. The first question was from a Mexican delegate who asked Gore if he could list three mistakes he made whilst in office as Vice President. The confident, articulate, witty Gore stumbled and mumbled and couldn't form a complete sentence. It became evident that politicians – no matter how accomplished - just aren't programmed to deal with a question inviting them to admit mistakes. He rambled for a while and asked for the next question. Realising his predicament, when my turn came, I abandoned my original question, gave my name and nationality as requested and asked...."Can you give us *another* three?"

Big laugh... including from Gore, and I went on to ask my rehearsed question. Gore laughed, took the joke on the chin, used my name throughout his answer, held eye contact and asked at the end if he'd answered my question to my satisfaction. My friend Jim, a media-savvy PR supremo, seated beside me, was impressed by the man's technical abilities as afterwards we all articulated our thoughts over coffee, impressed by a very able and assured politician. The world would have been a very different place had Gore presented that persona on television during the election. Five hundred and thirty-seven votes out of one hundred and one million!

The tradition was that when the technological Stockholm conference had been completed, the entire conference membership joined the Swedish Royal Train at Stockholm Railway Station (via the special royal entrance; just a door set aside from the others) and were transported across a winter wonderland to Oslo where were gathered some of the world's greatest entertainers in front of the Danish royal family – reassuringly normal people who had forsaken most of the trappings of privilege enjoyed by their cousins in the UK.

Over the years, the concert highlights included Paul McCartney, Andrea Bocelli, the Chieftains and Willie Nelson. The tradition was also that that year's Nobel Peace Prize winner took to the stage just before the interval and said a few words. Perhaps the most exhilarating year was when the best ever *ex*-American President, Jimmy Carter was introduced to the audience and received a great reception. The previous act had been Willie Nelson and his band. As the cheers ebbed after Carter's speech, Willie Nelson, still on stage, struck up the opening bars to *'Georgia'*, a song referencing Jimmy Carter's home state. The place erupted and I don't mind admitting that it was a performance that brought tears to my eyes. Simply magnificent.

Another memorable year was the event celebrating not only the achievements of that year's Nobel Peace Prize Laureate, United Nations Secretary-General, Kofi Annan, but also the one hundredth anniversary of the Nobel Prize. Paul McCartney appeared with Wyclef John, Natalie Imbruglia, '80s favourites A-Ha, world-beat leader Youssou N'Dour and opera singer Russell Watson. Actors Meryl Streep and Liam Neeson hosted the event.

Over the years, another delegate, Damien and I had had an amicable argument as to who was the more talented Beatle – John Lennon or Paul McCartney. I was for Paul and he for John. Damien's position was that he accepted that the four Beatles had each to die eventually – it was just that they were dying in the wrong order!

I couldn't wait to hear Paul perform his new song *'Freedom'*, dedicated to those who died at the 9/11 destruction of the Twin Towers in New York. I'd misread the invitation details and was the first to arrive, half an hour early at the Champagne banquet laid on by Cisco. It was deadly quiet as I entered the hall and I became aware that in the main auditorium through the wall, I could hear Paul McCartney practising. Armed only with the VIP badge given to all of those at the Cisco reception, I marched confidently past the machine-gun toting guards barring the way backstage. As I'd got past them, the next set of guards figured I must have had approval so I passed by all security until I reached the empty, vast hall in which the show would be performed. There on the stage right in front of me, talking to the stage director was my musical hero – Beatle, Paul McCartney. I could hardly speak. Just then I felt a tap on my shoulder. It was Damien. He'd seen me leaving and had followed me to the theatre across the road from the hotel. He too had marched confidently past the guards who had also been deceived by his badge.

Quickly, I saw my opportunity to capture the moment. I had a disposable camera in my pocket. Confidently, I called over to Paul – no more than five paces away.

"Hey, Paul, a quick photograph? I shouted.

Paul responded immediately, gave me his traditional thumbs up sign and stepped forward.

"No problem."

I pulled Damien's sleeve, positioned him next to Paul and fired off three or four shots before handing the camera to him and replacing him next to McCartney. Damien looked through the eyepiece and was just ready to push the button when a besuited security man came up from behind him and said, "I think you've taken enough shots, sir." Instead of just pushing the button, unaccountably, he acquiesced and put the camera down. I was beside myself in frustration as we were escorted back to the Champagne

"You don't even like him! You just needed to push the button."

"Did you see the size of him?" he countered, referring to the security guard who, I might say, spoke with what sounded very much like a Glaswegian accent. We could have negotiated! And so history will recall that there's now no proof that I met Paul McCartney face to face while Damien gets to glory in a story about meeting a man he doesn't even like!

My friend Laurie and I had often travelled to the conference in Oslo. One year, we left a calm but cold Oslo airport but as we closed on Glasgow the weather became very rough indeed. Everyone was strapped in as the plane bucked and dropped, rose and flailed. I was listening to music on my iPod when a most frightening, loud crash of an explosion took place. Everyone screamed and I looked out to see if a wing had been blown off or if a bird had entered the engine causing the aeroplane to plummet earthwards. Nothing was apparent and the plane continued to buck in the storm as it approached Glasgow Airport.

After a couple of minutes a very composed co-pilot spoke on the intercom to tell us that the plane had just been hit by lightning, but that these days, electronics were very sophisticated and plane structures were designed to deal with this kind of thing. Something in the order of one hundred million volts had struck the plane. I was very relieved as were all of my fellow passengers. At that point, a stewardess approached me and asked if I'd turn off my iPod as we were about to land! Amazing how technology can handle forked lightning but can't deal with a battery the size of a fingernail.

Anyway, enough of Oslo's Nobel...back to my Arctic Circle trip. The notion that all Norwegian women look like a younger Agnetha Fältskog (her out of Abba...although, she's Swedish) is a myth - but a good 30% of them do! The men look like supermen but I did notice a goodly number of street beggars. Don't know why this would be as Norway is famed for having a very obliging and generous welfare system. It was cold in Oslo, but only *Glasgow* cold. I see that Tromsø was seven degrees below zero so I figured I'd soon see how I coped with more Arctic temperatures all too soon.

My return to Oslo Airport station was fraught as the platform at Central Station was crowded and I began to wonder if everyone would find a place on the express. I needn't have worried as the train must have had more than twenty coaches, all fitted out to a very high standard. It filled up but it was all very civilised - more than could be said of Oslo Airport as they'd decided to go self-service, even down to checking in one's own case! I managed to organise a boarding pass but the thought of me sending my case inadvertently to Prague had me heading to a short queue where I spoke with a real person who tagged my case and who seemed to know what she was doing.

The Boeing 737 to Tromsø was interesting if only because instead of the usual warnings of dire consequences if I read my Kindle while the plane was taking off, the stewardess advised that there was free wi-fi on board - so wire in and switch on! Technology has advanced sufficiently that people checking their on-line diary no longer need fear crashing their plane into the side of a mountain as a consequence of their delinquency. That said, the wi-fi didn't work very well but humankind has made a start! On the runway, as we prepared to lift off at 17.15, I even received a text on my iPad telling me that 'Norwegian Air regret to inform that flight DY382 due to depart at 17.10 from Gard - Tromsø will not now leave until a new estimated time of 17:30.' A bit late but we're getting there.

Well, I *got* there....and I wondered if I hadn't bitten off a bit more than I could chew!

As the plane banked to land at *Tromsø* Airport, I noticed that the runways were deep in snow. As we closed on the airport, I could see snow machines fountaining snow up and away from the runway but without much success. We landed perfectly without a hitch! As I walked from the Boeing, it was snowing heavily and I could see snow lying four inches deep on the runway - and this after the energetic ministrations of gigantic snow machines!

The taxi journey to my hotel was equally worrying as the snow was sufficiently deep...knee deep... that it obliterated any differential between road and pavement, it covered all signage and was coming down so fast, the driver's windscreen wipers couldn't brush it off quickly enough...and it was completely dark. I'd hired a car for two days, hoping to drive to Finland. I began to appreciate the fact that it's dark other than for two hours each day and the forecast was for more snow until Monday (at which point the sky might be clear enough to see the *Aurora Borealis.*)

We'll see.

My hotel, *Smarthotel*, in *Vestregatta*, *Tromsø* town centre, was perfectly designed for my needs. It resembled a monk's cell but with a TV showing BBC News and a Nordic Channel 'Dave' among other Norwegian (and subtitled) channels. It had a warm bed and a serviceable toilet and shower. A small table and chair allowed me to spend time writing as I suspected that conditions outside in this Arctic winter might see me hotel-bound...or pub-bound if I was able to afford the drink.

My friend John phoned to check on my situation as I was about to step out and, when he heard my description of conditions, implored me to write off the cost of the car hire and avoid driving lest I end up writing *myself* off. I promised him I'd be careful.

The huge, eight feet high mounds of snow that punctuated the road outside at regular intervals, it transpired, were snow-bound parked cars! However, I headed out into the white night to a pizza place and found it buzzing with the university crowd (it's a university town) that I suspect makes up much of the purchasing power in *Tromsø*. Everyone sat around in the restaurant chewing on pizza, wearing T-shirts and lighter garments. It was only when I looked at their feet and their substantial booted footwear as well as the fur-lined parkas hanging on the back of their chairs that diners could be observed as being different from students eating pizza in Glasgow and that our position on the globe could be appreciated. I bought a small pizza and asked for a beer. I was offered a 0.4 or a 0.6 Pilsner (interestingly, that's how seriously they take their alcohol consumption here...they marketed it not by its brand but by its alcohol content!)...and *everyone* spoke English as well as I did, if with a mid-Atlantic accent. It was also freezing but I was dressed for that and didn't mind it a bit.

The following day it was knee-deep snow outside but I dressed warmly and headed off to see what the Arctic Circle had to offer. I walked for miles in driving snow, across a long, elevated bridge from Tromsø to the next island but had earlier decided I wouldn't need my thermal trousers. Result; a major case of ball-freeze! I had to walk back to the hotel, dry out and warm up. The Receptionist in the hotel had earlier refused a resident a car hire on the grounds that it was 'too snowy'. I just hope that it's not a harbinger of my fortunes tomorrow as although the travel conditions were crazy, I was keen to have a go. I've always enjoyed driving in snow but had never experienced anything like this. In town the snow is hard packed and there's a constant convoy of bulldozers and snow ploughs shovelling it to the side - but as it seems to snow continuously, everything blown or lifted from the roadway is replaced moments later...a bit like painting the Forth Bridge. However, out of town, the signage is obscured by snow, as are pedestrian crossings and road markings showing 'No Overtaking', 'Give Way', 'Stop'! One discovery was that although they advertise only two hours of daylight between 11.00am and 1.00pm, there's a languid period of dawn and twilight that's actually pretty decent...and daylight comes five minutes early each morning and darkens five minutes later each afternoon at present so there's ten minutes more light each day. Spring weather comes pretty quickly from about February on.

I'd imagined that life up here would be pretty ascetic; that people would lead lives comparable to Trappist monks - but they've a fabulous and sizeable library, loads of great pubs and restaurants, a six-screen cinema, high-fashion stores and a pretty substantial university. All they have to defeat is the weather and they do that well. Road conditions are dealt with admirably, if not altogether conquered, buildings are all insulated and warm; it's all super. Even the language is no problem as everyone speaks excellent English and where they don't and sense has to be made of the printed word, it's not too difficult to work out...as I looked out of the pub window (while watching West Brom beat West Ham 4-0) in O'Leary's pub, I observed signs which read; *Metodistkirk,*

Auto-elektriker, Parkering Forbudt, Bokhandler and *Erotikkhuset (a Nordic Anne Summers).*

One cultural imperative up here seems to be that all cars slow and stop in all snowy circumstances if someone's crossing a road. It's as if the road was one big Zebra Crossing. It's delightful and gives a sense of everything being very civilised.

On a health kick today. Guinness and free pub popcorn for lunch. I'd earlier been advised that in Norway, Guinness was £10 a pint. Myth! It's £7.35 a pint.

In the evening, I went to the cinema to escape the cold. Writing in pubs is all very well but eventually - even if sipping slowly - one becomes inebriated so I took an evening off.

I'm increasingly impressed by our Nordic cousins. They put us to shame in many ways - not just in their more communal approach to matters to do with welfare - but in their green tendencies. There's no waste paper basket in my hotel room, but three trendy recycling bins in the hall outside. At the cinema, I had a bottle of diet coke - and left the empty carton in its place on the arm rest as one does in Scotland. Here, everyone gathered up their detritus as they left and placed it appropriately in recycling bins in the foyer. Impressive...and shaming!

I took possession of a hired car today - a four wheeled drive, VW Golf with snow tyres. I headed directly for the mountain that overlooks *Tromsø* and in the process had to drive up narrow, precipitous snowbound roads that would pose problems for someone walking. The Golf took it without breaking car-sweat, even though it was like driving *up* a toboggan run. The snow was piled high on either side of what seemed like a narrow tunnel without a roof.

Taking the cable car to the top of Mount *Storsteinen* was quick and efficient but once I'd arrived, left the safety of the upper wheelhouse and started walking, I entered a different world - one in which I felt the full force of Arctic weather. The wind howled, the snow drove and every footstep upwards was a challenge as the snow deepened to my thighs. I shake my head now at how stupid I can be! As yesterday, I'd forgotten my waterproof leggings and before very long my corduroy trousers were soaked through. I wanted to reach the edge of a cliff some distance away in order to take photographs of *Tromsø* which lay down below and across the *fjord* but it took much longer than I'd anticipated. When I eventually reached my vantage point, wind-chill compounded the low temperature, I was freezing from the waist down, my legs were covered in snow which was melting and refrigerating my legs so I quickly took the photographs I wanted with some small measure of alacrity and trudged back slowly to the distant safety of the wheelhouse. I had to warm myself in front of a very welcome log fire before my descent - and rebuked myself quietly for not anticipating the likely conditions atop a mountain inside the Arctic Circle. It really shouldn't have been rocket science! Any time spent in those conditions without the proper clothing could easily be fatal - and quite quickly. When I arrived back down at the car, it was eight degrees below zero - but felt positively balmy, so God alone knows the depths to which the mercury had plummeted atop the positively Arctic Mount *Storsteinen*.

After returning to the hotel and gathering myself, I set off for *Skibotn*, a small village two hours' drive from *Tromsø* which is apparently possessed of the best dry, cloudless conditions on the Norwegian land mass in which to view *Aurora Borealis*, the 'Northern Lights'. The hotel had posted a notice in Reception saying that the *Aurora Borealis* was active so I figured I'd a good chance of at last seeing this amazing phenomenon. The two hour journey was pretty tense as the roads were snow-covered and initially I didn't trust the car to cope but it held the road admirably as if I were driving on dry tarmac. Cars driving ahead disturbed whiffs of snow crystals which hovered above the road surface like dry ice at a rock concert. Upon arrival at *Skibotn*, I drove around looking for dark sky. Even the distant lights of small communes across the *fjord* interfered with this and to find the conditions I sought I found myself on a narrow track deep inside a forest, the car ploughing its way slowly through wheel-deep snow. I parked and waited an hour with no sign of celestial shimmerings and silently rebuked myself; an old eegit in the middle of nowhere. If I'd slipped and fallen, injuring myself while trying (unsuccessfully, despite my son, Ron's tuition) to set up my camera, I'd have been a goner. Probably sensibly, I packed up my gear and headed back to *Tromsø*. When I got back, I was looking forward to a Cesar Salad and a Guinness only to find that the Irish pub I'd adopted was out of Guinness, out of lager...and the kitchens were shut! It was just like being back in Scotland!

The following day, I drove to a *fjord* due west of *Tromsø* where during the Second World War, British bombers sank the German battleship, *Tirpitz*, which had threatened the North Atlantic convoys with such menace. Nothing to see now other than the waves that enveloped her but with a cloudless blue sky framing brilliantly white snowy mountains, the scenery was spectacular and I took a number of what I hoped would be pretty impressive photographs.

I'd decided to retrace my steps of the previous night, but this time to go beyond *Skibotn* and drive on to Finland, to *Kilpisjärvi*, skirting the tip of Sweden on the way. The day had been predicted to be sunny if not warm and so it was...freezing, that is. The three hour journey was uneventful although I did notice that in the daylight, the road twisted and turned, rose and fell, narrowed and widened in ways that I hadn't appreciated the previous night when I'd driven back from *Skibotn*...in the dark and at pace, it must be said. I could now witness what I missed in the night drive; simply magnificent scenery. Huge ivory mountains leapt skywards. Lakes, frozen over, now provided new thoroughfares for skis, bobsleighs, snowshoes and snowmobiles. Iced waterfalls hung static and immobile from roadside overhangs and people went nonchalantly about their daily business in the hamlets that dotted the road south-east to Finland.

As the road nears the Finish border, it rises and the snow deepens. Progress is slower and my driving was more cautious. Nearing the national boundary, I stopped and took photographs then drove on *larghetto* past the border post to *Kilpisjärvi*. I travelled yet further on and parked in a snow-bound lay-by in order to wait for darkness and the possibility of seeing the northern lights. Given that I'd been seated all day, I decided to walk back perhaps a mile to the staffed but disinterested customs post just to keep my circulation going. Before leaving, my car's 'infotainment system' informed me that it was now fifteen below outside and once I started walking, I could vouch for its accuracy. In order to experiment, I purposefully left half a bottle of diet Pepsi outside the car. When I returned an hour later, it was frozen. I'd a full tank of fuel so could afford to keep the engine running every half hour or so to warm up the car. As night fell, the temperature dropped to eighteen...and then to twenty degrees below zero. But the skies were clear and that heralded good conditions for the northern lights so I persevered. Of course, in my earlier efforts to remain hydrated, I discovered that I needed to pee, so at twenty below, I stepped out behind the car and coaxed a stream into the snow as quickly as possible before anything important fell off...and it *does* turn yellow, the snow that is, hence the old adage.

Well, so much for the northern lights...the *Aurora Borealis*...I sat for three hours in the car in complete darkness watching the sky. During this time, I used my iPad to write then shut it down and gave it five minutes to allow my eyes to become accustomed to the darkness which enveloped me before stepping out of the car. The night sky was magnificent. Because of light pollution we don't often see the stars as majestically as is possible in Scotland. But when they're on display in the heavens, it's a pretty impressive sight. That said, the cold was actually painful to experience. I'd step out of the car at twenty below and could take no more than a few minutes before retreating. However, after three hours I decided that although the experts had advised that tonight was the best night to see the northern lights, despite me being in the best valley, at the best time, in the best conditions, in the best country in the world.... nothing! I headed home.

Upon arriving back in Tromsø and after parking the car, I slid, skidded and slalomed down the road the short distance to O'Leary's to catch the Manchester United match against Preston North End in the FA Cup at Preston. The temperature had risen and was now merely zero in the town where a slight thaw had made the pavement ice slick and unwalkable. I slipped more in the few yards to the hotel than I'd done all day walking in seriously sub-zero temperatures in Finland. And when I got to O'Leary's, to be honest, the only thing that impressed me about the football was Preston North End's stadium which was the equal of anything in the English Premiership. Still, it was interesting listening to the Norwegian commentary....'Hoordy goordy, hoordy goordy, Whhennn Hhhrooooooney... Goaaaal!' At least that was authentic. I realised I was eating a Mexican (yes, Mexican) Caesar Salad, drinking Irish stout, French Brandy and as soon as the full-time whistle blew, I found myself listening to Americans Hall & Oates singing 'Every Time You Go Away' before Springsteen continued the Norwegian experience.

And Manchester United were mince...complete mince! They won 3-1 as a consequence of a Wayne Rooney dive in the penalty box and his subsequent conversion.

I sat awhile in the pub listening to two Norwegian guys at the table next to me spending their evening clearing their throats and snuffling phlegm so far back it must have congealed around their cerebral cortex. They shifted their drinks back and forth on the table and, each lost in their own thoughts, spoke about two words to each other all night. Now that's friendship!

I asked for one of my common tipples when back home in Scotland...a half pint of Guinness and a brandy and diet coke with no ice. The barman looked confused but I explained that 'a hauf and a hauf pint' was a Scottish custom. I was subsequently served...in a single pint glass, a half pint of Guinness topped up with a brandy and diet coke, no ice. As it was served, it took me a moment to realise what had been provided me....but I had the presence of mind to take a wee sip to see what it tasted like before returning said drink to the bar and having it replaced.

I think it might catch on!

Walked back up to the hotel without breaking a hip...but it was a close-run thing.

For my last morning in Tromsø, I decided to take in the city environs to see how the people of Tromsø live. I was impressed. Behind and above the town there are timber houses; bungalows we'd call them. Wood is obviously the preferred material for building here. Every house was made of the stuff. Hardly surprising in a country which is afforested as much as is Norway. The houses were all well-kept, spacious and even where they were apartments, the building was still wood panelled. The houses were all in neighbourhoods with narrow, hilly, twisting snowbound roads wending their way through the commune within which schools, crèches, churches and parks abounded. The roads had all been semi-cleared of snow to make them almost drivable but this meant that each house was walled in by a bank of snow. People coped admirably with this impediment merely by fashioning a small doorway exit through the snow. I also drove round the university again given that it was now open for business. Very impressive. The main focus of the University's activities is on the Auroral light research, Space science, Fishery science, Biotechnology, Linguistics, Multicultural societies, *Saami* culture, Telemedicine, epidemiology and a wide spectrum of Arctic research projects. Many of the courses are taught in English... and there are no tuition fees for Norwegian students...or for international students following overtures made by indigenous students who figured that if fees were imposed on foreign students, they'd be next!

I returned the car to Tromsø airport. When I went through security and again after I used the toilet facilities, I was faced with a small stand on which was located a computer screen. On each screen was a green smiley face, a pink non-smiley face and a red face with a sad expression. I was being asked to provide instant feedback on the experience; which I did. I pressed the green button each time.

I suppose in assessing my trip driving around northern Norway, I was most struck by the ubiquitous and cavernous tunnels burrowing through mountains, the arched bridges sweeping over *fjords* and the muscular ferries that ply the waters of the Norwegian Sea in order that the inhabitants of the nation's 50,000 islands can remain in easy touch with the mainland. In urban settings, pigeons looking for a toilet are spoiled for choice as public art dominates street corners and city squares. Libraries, nurseries, schools, hospitals and parks all abound and when they create car parks in cities, they do so by gouging huge underground vaults that would serve perfectly as the *Smersh* hideaway at the *denouement* of any James Bond movie.

Now, these public goods come at a cost. So how does Norway afford and maintain this standard of living? Well, for a kick-off, it tends not to war with other countries as much as the UK. It doesn't have a costly nuclear deterrent. Indeed, if anything, it now has something of a world reputation for offering peace facilitation. During the past thirty years Norway has become synonymous with peace brokering, reaching its high-point in 1996 when Bjorn Tore Godal, then minister of foreign affairs, concluded his foreign policy address to the Norwegian Parliament with a clear statement of intent: "To build the road or roads to peace is the top task of our foreign policy."

Perhaps because Norway doesn't have a colonial past, it doesn't carry the baggage that some other interventionists might and in consequence, as well as pronouncing on peace activism each year since 1901 via its Nobel Peace Prize, it has also assisted in peace negotiations in Palestine, Mali, Guatemala, Sri Lanka, Afghanistan, Colombia, Myanmar, the Philippines, and Sudan-South Sudan. And even this list is incomplete, as some of the peace processes Norway has been part of are bound by secrecy. The country has also provided financial and technical support to several other peace processes, such as the ones in Aceh, Burundi, the Democratic Republic of the Congo, Kenya, the Philippines, Syria and Uganda.

With peace high on the agenda, and with costs associated with each of these interventions, it is indeed fortunate that according to the Global Peace Index, Norway is one of the world's most wealthy nations as it's richly endowed with natural resources such as hydropower, fish, forests, and minerals – but then, so is Britain.

Perhaps most importantly, it has to be said that Norway has dealt with the bounty that is oil and gas much more wisely that has Britain. When oil was discovered off the coast of each country back in the sixties, subsequent UK governments of both stripes couldn't spend it quickly enough once they figured out how to suck it up from beneath the sea-bed. A common perception is that Thatcher splurged the windfall on breaking the trades unions – especially the miners - and Blair on overseas militarism. However, academic research suggests a different analysis, arguing that Thatcher's Chancellor, Nigel Lawson used it to cut taxes from 60% to 40% by 1988 and the wealthy, now with even more money in their pockets, used it to buy property. Everyone now knows where that ever-increasing upward spiral of house prices left us.

But Norway decided upon a different approach. They set up an Oil Fund and invested the income from its oil and gas reserves so wisely that it now has what most economists consider to be the world's largest sovereign wealth fund which will by some estimates be worth $1trillion by 2020. Indeed, last year, everyone in Norway became a theoretical *krone* millionaire due to its performance. Set up in 1990, the fund now owns around one percent of the world's stocks, and in consequence, Norway is exceptionally well-off at a time when Britain organises a network of food-banks for its poor. That said, perhaps a new future is opening as a consequence of claims of the discovery of a £300 billion oil field near Gatwick Airport in West Sussex...however, I wouldn't hold my breath. I'd fully expect it to be squandered just like existing revenues derived from current reserves.

But despite marshalling the financial resources derived from oil and gas with such aplomb, Norway is still a highly taxed country. Its economic system is about as social democratic as it gets. The Norwegian tax authority's own website states, "The Norwegian tax system is based on the principle that everybody should pay tax according to their means and receive services according to their needs." Down Highgate Cemetery way, a certain Mr. Karl Marx must be nodding his head in quiet satisfaction although Norway's robust and vibrant private sector must also give him pause for thought.

And they're a happy bunch too! According to the Legatum Institute's Prosperity Index of the world's happiest countries, Norway topped a poll at number one where 95% of those surveyed were happy with the freedom to choose the direction of their lives. The UK charted at number thirty-eight.

But despite being wealthy, healthy and happy, they're not one of the great sporting nations – although with a population of only some five million, about the same as Scotland's - they probably achieve their potential. Perhaps their most memorable footballing achievement came in 1981 when Norway defeated England 2-1 in a World Cup Qualifier at London's old Wembley causing commentator Bjorge Lillelien to issue his famous exuberant summary at the final whistle, taunting a roll call of English warriors, statesmen, a boxer and a royal princess, usually quoted in an edited, English-only form as follows:

"Lord Nelson, Lord Beaverbrook, Sir Winston Churchill, Sir Anthony Eden, Clement Attlee, Henry Cooper! Lady Diana! Maggie Thatcher! - can you hear me, Maggie Thatcher! Your boys took one hell of a beating! Your boys took one hell of a beating!"

The barman in O'Leary's pub in Tromsø was in no doubt as to the benefit that oil, when administered as it has been by the Norwegian Government, has brought him.

"I've been educated, my kids are looked after, my family's health needs are taken care of and I know that in old age, my country will look after me. As a nation, we have saved for the future. It's not rocket science."

I later recounted Bjorge Lillelien's commentary to him.

He replied, "You English (sic) boys are still taking a hell of a beating." He smiled, "But this time economically.

I needed to visit Iceland in order to undertake research I was doing in support of a book I was writing about big oil' called 'A Confusion Of Mandarins', and had booked an onwards flight. It was a February visit, deliberately timed as I saw little interest in visiting the island when it did not display the wintry weather with which it is most associated.

Well, *that* worked! It was absolutely freezing upon arrival and the entire island was blanketed in deep snow. Huge snow-moving machines patrolled the runway issuing massive blasts of snow skywards and sideways as they cleared pathways for airplanes. Keflavik International Airport where I landed, is sited thirty miles out of town and deals with other than domestic flights, catered for by the smaller Reykjavik Airport which I discovered was located but a few yards from my accommodation at the confluence of Filkirkjuvegur and Skalholtsstigur, just across the road from a lake called Reykjavikurtjirn. Having determined that weather conditions might take a bit of getting used to, I reflected that language might come a close second.

I'd booked into an inexpensive self-catering apartment across the road from the lake and was pleased at its simple function and open aspect. Its location, only a short walk from the city centre proved too enticing and I quickly deposited my rucksack, supplemented my traveling garb in view of the snowstorm outside and headed off to see what Reykjavik was like.

I loved it. As is often the case in more northerly Arctic and Nordic buildings, much use is made of toughened corrugated steel roofs, suitably insulated. Easily painted, the roofs of buildings in this small city present a blissful wonder of colourful pastel shades providing delightful contrast to the all-enveloping whiteness of the snow.

The population of the city-region of Reykjavik is some two-hundred thousand. While earlier awaiting the mini-bus from the airport into the city, I'd picked up some bumff from the tourist board which proclaimed that Reykjavik was the cleanest, greenest, and safest capital city in the world. A proud claim and I was keen to find out the extent to which it was accurate. I didn't notice any particular preference for electric vehicles over carbon-based but given the scarcity of motor vehicles relative to the land mass of Iceland I suppose it's reasonable for them to claim clean air. In terms of clean energy, they win hands-down. The geothermal conditions on the island are remarkable due to its advantageous geological location over a rift in continental plates. The high concentration of volcanoes on the island provides for the generation of geothermal energy, heating and electricity. The pavements upon which I was walking were heated underfoot due to this phenomenon. Impressive.

The five geothermal power plants that serve the needs of Iceland, produce approximately a quarter of the nation's electricity. In addition, geothermal power meets the heating and hot water requirements of approximately 90% of all buildings and beyond geothermal energy, three-quarters of the nation's electricity is generated by hydro power. Less than one percent of the nation's needs are served by fossil fuels. Sheesh!

In terms of crime and safety, the population of Iceland takes the biscuit and remarkably, one of the features of their sociology pointed to by criminologists is the fact that there is virtually no perceived difference among upper, middle and lower classes in the country. In consequence the usual tensions between economic classes is pretty much non-existent. In a study undertaken by the University of Missouri, it was discovered that in Iceland, only 1.1% of participants identified themselves as upper class, while

1.5% saw themselves as lower class. The remaining 97% identified themselves as some kind of homogenous middle class.

In 2009 there were over 43,000 murders in Brazil, 15,000 in the USA, just over 700 in the UK and one in Iceland. *GunPolicy.org,* arguably the world's most comprehensive and accessible source for published evidence on armed violence, firearm law and gun control (hosted by the Sydney School of Public Health), estimates there are approximately 90,000 guns in Iceland, in a country with just over 300,000 people. It ranks Iceland as 15th in the world in terms of legal *per capita* gun ownership. However, acquiring a gun is not an easy process on the island as applicants have to undergo a medical examination as well as a written test. In consequence, it would appear that the country has come upon an approach that keeps deadly weapons from the nutters. So...awash with guns but no violence to speak of. Perhaps their claims of a safe society hold water.

I returned to my apartment via a store wherein I purchased easy to cook food. I'd intended to buy some liquor as I'd been told tales of punitive prices for beer in the country but decided first to test this tale and after a warm meal, edged out into the cauld blast and walked the short distance to the centre of town where a few pubs were open for business. I stepped into a somewhat tawdry and deserted bar, enjoyed a pint of Guinness and read a book in front of a blazing log fire. Sleepy after a couple of beers and a long day, I retired the short distance to my apartment and planned my next day's itinerary.

I'd long read of the Blue Lagoon, a man-made body of water which is fed by the output of the nearby geothermal power plant at nearby Svartsengi. Situated only twelve miles from Reykjavik, I decided to drive using a hire from a cheap car hire firm called 'SadCars' - well named as they offered 'used cars with experience'! I'd hired a bit of a bargain basement rust-bucket but it was equipped with snow tyres so I figured it'd meet my needs adequately.

I set off and arrived at the Blue Lagoon where I was instructed to shower before dipping myself in the lake (very big on hygiene here) and dressed in only my swimming trunks, stepped out into a freezing hail storm and walked the ten yards or so to the inviting waters of the Lagoon, asking myself with each step what I thought I was doing walking around almost naked in sub-zero temperatures.

My considerable discomfort eased immediately I lowered myself into the one hundred degrees Fahrenheit pool whose warm waters are rich in minerals like silica and sulphur, presumed by many to have medicament properties.

The pool functions as it does due to super-heated water being vented from a lava flow and used to run turbines that generate electricity before providing heat for a municipal water heating system in which recreational and medicinal users can bathe. It was a very relaxing experience. Perhaps only four feet deep with a sandy floor, I luxuriated from the neck down while my face was sand-blasted by a freezing hail storm. An unusual experience I'll grant you.

I'd asked for a massage in the pool largely because I couldn't help but imagine that drowning might require to be a constituent part of the process and was interested in how this might be avoided. After swimming around for a while, a large, bearded Viking-looking guy approached with a couple of blue mats. He invited me to swim towards him and position myself on top of one before pulling the second one over me as if a duvet. This acted as a wick and drew the warm waters over me, keeping me afloat while he administered to my back and neck. Again, an unusual experience but I slept well that night.

I wanted to visit the Athling, the oldest seat of democratic governance in the world although this is contested by the Greeks and by the Iroquois, the Native American people of the Six Nations. Established in the year 930, the Athling is located in Þingvellir some thirty-five miles from Reykjavik and was in continuous operation until 1798 when it moved to its present building in the capital city (a square building which is but two stories high and seven windows wide) Built in sandstone, it resembles an old Glasgow Primary School.

Again the weather was horrendous, a snow blizzard made it difficult to see much before me and the wipers struggled to clear the windscreen but I figured that these were the conditions I'd to expect in a place called Iceland and pressed on.

As I drove inland I came across the geological frailty that defines the continental drift between the North American and Eurasian Plates. *Pingvellir* lies in the concomitant rift valley and as the car proceeded along the lonely, cambered single track road, slick with ice, the windscreen wipers fighting off the snow, I experienced some minor apprehension as on each side of the road was clear green, iced water. If I made the slightest mistake and slid, I'd drift sideways into oblivion, never to be discovered. I eased back on the peddle and proceeded with extreme caution.

There's nothing now to see of the original parliament but I drove for miles along the rift valley which seemed almost like an inverted Great Wall of China. It was as dramatic as it was dangerous but my senses were alive as I attempted carefully to keep the car on the road. I didn't pass a car all morning. A couple that I passed, parked outside remote houses were simply gigantic. Their *wheels* were significantly higher than my car. The entire area was made a World Heritage Site in 2004 and I can understand why. It was simply magnificent topography.

It took me all day to return to Reykjavik and I hadn't eaten so I heated some beans and made toast in the apartment - the extent of my culinary prowess - and ventured out to a local sports bar. Scotland was playing Northern Ireland in a game that had the footballing world on the edge of its seat (not) but I asked if one of the six screens might be tuned to the match. There were perhaps a total of seven people in the bar but the barman was reticent for some reason. I deployed the 'broken record' technique I'd learned in assertive training many years before and merely repeated my request; "One screen?...One screen, eh? C'mon...one screen?" until at last the remote was called into service and I watched my team win 3-0 in a match that was comprehensively boring. There was no one around to celebrate our scintillating performance however, so I had to make do with a solo celebratory malt whisky before heading homewards.

I was also keen to visit Geysir, some seventy miles north east of Reykjavik and the place which gave its name to the geological phenomena we now know as geysers. Again the weather was awful but I calculated that I could make it in perhaps three hours if I drove carefully. The road surface was markedly better than the one I'd experienced the day before but any deviation from the main road took traffic on to ash roads, easily constructed and maintained and perfectly acceptable if one's car was, well, in better nick than the one supplied me by SadCars.

En route I wanted to visit a glacier and chose Eyjafjallajökull which is one of the smaller ice caps of Iceland but this would add considerably to my journey time so I left early in darkness and drove until I came to the side road I calculated would take me to the glacier. I drove for perhaps a mile until the steep ash road became impassable to all but the monster vehicles I noticed increasingly were the transport of choice for those living at distance from the capital.

I parked and suitably attired, set off on a walk to the glacier. It was a rough climb through deep snow but I managed to take photographs of what was effectively a static scene. I didn't venture on to the glacier itself as I'd too many images in my head of falling down a crevasse and never being seen again so I returned to my car where, in the middle of nowhere, without a signal on my phone, in a snow blizzard, I noticed that the front off-side tyre was flat.

Cursing my luck (or poor judgement more likely) I decided that I wouldn't attempt to change the wheel in case my technical skills let me down and I found myself stranded with only three wheels on my wagon and so reversed the car tentatively and travelled bumpily at snail's pace to the main road where I puttered along until I reached a garage where I inflated the tyre sufficiently to reach another garage where a swift repair was carried out. The trip didn't do a lot of good for the car wheel but by the time I'd reflated it just seemed to be in keeping with the general run-down condition of the vehicle. (Certainly, when I returned the vehicle to SadCars at the end of my visit there was none of the usual inspection checking for damage. They seemed to be satisfied that the roof was still attached and waved me cheerily on my way.)

Now concerned about time, I decided to adjust my arrangements and visit instead the closer geyser called Strokkur which, in any event erupts much more frequently than Geysir, reaching heights of up to 30 metres every few minutes. The smell of sulphur, never far away in Iceland, was overpowering but I'd become used to the smell of rotten eggs and watched in some amazement as the hot spring gushed upwards at super-heated temperatures, spattering on and melting the surrounding ice, just missing some tourists more adventurous (or stupid) than the others.

As I made my way home along the coast road, I pulled onto another ash road and drove closer to a massive waterfall I'd seen through the blizzard subsequently discovering that it was called Skogafoss. A couple of cars had made the journey before me and as I approached they seemed completely dwarfed by the huge torrent of water that deluged from a cliff edge. I suppose there's nothing particularly magical about water following the laws of gravity but when it's witnessed in such a powerful descent, it does invite the accurate use of the word 'awesome'; a word stripped of all precise meaning by today's youth!

My final day was spent heading somewhat aimlessly in a northerly direction. I began by visiting the house in which Ronald Reagan had met Mikhail Gorbachov in one of the occasional summits that American and Russian Presidents are wont to have. A former

French Consulate, the large white house seemed deserted as I arrived. It had hosted the meeting in 1986 at which Gorbachev, to the surprise of the Americans, had proposed banning all ballistic missiles. Reagan, however, wanted to continue research on his Strategic Defence Initiative, which involved the militarisation of outer space. The talks didn't go well.

On a more optimistic note, I drove the short distance along the waterfront to a house I'd been told by a guy in a pub was owned by Bjork, the pishy Icelandic singer and general nut-case. At first glance, it suited her chaotic personality very well. Made from recycled everything, it sported second-hand doors as walls, flotsam of all types, walls of empty bottles, old tyres and, frankly, looked great! I was much taken with the thought that had gone into its construction and impressed by the principles of conservation that lay behind it. I subsequently discovered that Bjork was living in an isolated cottage on an islet just off the coast and that I'd been misinformed as the recycled house had been built and occupied by an elderly, eccentric Icelandic film director.

I drove north through long dark tunnels under the fjords that would otherwise have required a substantial journey following the contour of the coastline. They must have cost a princely sum to build and I was impressed that a country of only some 320,000 could afford such infrastructure. This time the weather defeated me. I could hardly see anything in front of me so fierce was the snowstorm and I decided that driving deeper into a blanket of white didn't seem sensible. Not long after I manoeuvred my car to face homewards, the sun broke through and I was presented with simply wonderful views of rural Iceland, tall mountains with sheer cliffs and occasional brightly painted farmhouses, steam issuing from their back yard as they tapped into their own power source not too far below the ground on which the house stood.

Reykjavik was a lovely, modest city. On my last afternoon before departing the following day, I decided to have a haircut (for a while there it was my standard practice when visiting a foreign city) on the basis that it provided me with an opportunity to speak with a local for perhaps twenty minutes. As the years have passed, the twenty minutes has reduced as my hair has thinned so it's hardly worth my while now.

Anyway, I sat in a short queue and was ushered into a leather chair and was spoken to in what I presumed was Icelandic.

"Sorry, do you speak English?"

"Yes," replied my young coiffeuse. "And German, Danish and a small amount of Gaelic!"

She spoke English as perfectly as had she lived all her days in Glasgow; but perhaps with a better grasp of grammar.

In Iceland, a remote and isolated island nation, the national language is Icelandic, a tongue that has been spoken there since the place was settled way back when. However, my hairdresser was required to take either English or another Scandinavian language at school, enjoyed it and also took German. Gaelic, which surprised me, was learned at the knee of her grandmother. Hardly anyone speaks it now but it was a language that was native to the early settlers and there remain smatterings here and there in the island. She showed off by speaking a few stock sentences in Gaelic but I could only nod my approval and favourable impression whilst being completely ignorant of her meaning. She could have been calling me a complete eegit and I'd have been grinning away incomprehensibly.

Still, it's been a while since I've had my hair cut in Glasgow by a multi-lingual barber, so hats off to Reykjavik. It was brilliant.

East of Suez

New Delhi, Patiala, Kathmandu,
Ho Chi Minh City, Hanoi

Whilst planning a trip to the Punjab in India to attend the wedding of a friend, I received an invitation to assist in writing an economic development strategy for the mid-West region of Nepal. Given its location as India's next door neighbour on its eastern border, I managed to organise dates so that I might visit both countries during a single visit without the need for separate long-haul flights or a discrete series of inoculations and medications.

I've always enjoyed visiting India. It's just such a separate culture; quite unlike anything experienced in Europe. My wedding invitation had come from my Glaswegian friend, Sohan Singh Randhawa whose son, Amitoj (known to all as Bobby) was to marry his bride Navseerat in Patiala, a city in south-eastern Punjab, in northern India. I was collected at the airport just outside New Delhi and taken in a lengthy journey by car to The Baradari Palace, a white, colonnaded twelve door pavilion or *baradari* which is possessed of a splendid garden commissioned by the then ruler Maharaja Rajinder Singh. It was designed in 1876 by Kaur Sahib Ranbir Singh, the younger brother of the Maharaja...and well played that man as it was completely delightful.

Its website suggested that it was not as ostentatious as the other palaces of Patiala, but God alone knows what *they* must have been like as to my eyes it was a veritable feast and a significant piece of Colonial architecture. I was to stay the night and was allocated the Maharajah's room wherein was located the Royal

Bed. My bedroom could have accommodated a tennis match...
actually; my *bed* could have accommodated a tennis match!

The Royal Bed was raised, requiring me to walk up three steps to
reach the mattress. The en-suite bathroom was vast and the ceiling
from which hung a splendid chandelier, was almost out of sight...and
that's 'out of sight' in the literal sense and, well, I suppose also 'out of
sight' in the Californian hippy sense as well! It must have been thirty
feet from floor to ceiling. I was tired after a long flight from Glasgow
and a subsequent long drive from New Delhi and was eyeing the
drinks menu prior to a visit to the bar when the phone rang. It was
Sohan. Now, our Sohan, a successful entrepreneur, property tycoon
and hotelier in Glasgow is also a bit of a big noise in the Punjab and
in consequence is well acquainted with the top dogs in that part of
the world.

"My brother. You must prepare at once!"

"I was just thinking of heading to the bar for a nightcap,
Sohan...then to bed!"

"No, my brother. You must wear your best clothes. I have
sent a car. You are to meet with the Maharaja. This is very
important. It is like meeting the Queen!"

"I'm a left of centre, nationalistic, social democratic, atheistic,
republican. Not big on Queenie!"

"This is different, Ron...and wear your kilt! He'll love that!"

I replaced the phone and changed into my kilt (all Scottish
guests had been brow-beaten over previous weeks by Sohan into
wearing the kilt. I was one of the few who'd succumbed).

After a short drive in darkness, the car swept into a driveway and
my fellow wedding guests and I were ushered into a reception
room which was already full of turban-wearing dignitaries. Trays
of drinks were being carried around by white-jacketed waiters so
my earlier disappointment of missing out on a nightcap dissipated
instantly I collected a glass from the salver. I circulated dutifully
and was rewarded in spades as the other guests were entirely
delightful. My favourite was Ramesh Chander who was a retired
ambassador who'd been educated in Cambridge. He and I fell into

a discussion about Scottish Independence which he opposed and I took great delight in teasing him about how it was okay for India to declare independence from the Crown, but not Scotland? I don't mean this disparagingly...perhaps I do; actually, *certainly* I do, but while he was completely enjoyable company, he was also slightly rather a snob. He was one of the very few Indian civil servants who'd made his way to the very top of the English system of elite, establishment, Daily Mail reading, Conservative beneficiaries and he'd wrapped himself in the flag...the Union Flag, that is, not the Indian Flag and he wasn't about to let those advantages diminish. He spoke with a refined English accent and when I suggested that Britain's colonialist, imperialist past in India was now an embarrassment to people like me, he demurred.

"Not at all," he argued. "The British Crown had a civilising mission! It gave us the English language. It gave us an education system. And it gave us a railroad!"

I could see his point but he wouldn't agree my subsequent premise that it'd have been better had India chosen to pursue those advantages without the massacres, partitioning and theft of natural resources that had ensued under the paramountcy (as it was called by Queen Victoria) of the British Crown between 1858 and 1947. I argued that whilst I acknowledged his point that under the British Raj, various economic developments in India and in other parts of the world it controlled were advanced, it was also necessary to point out the massacres, famines and the use of concentration camps by the British Empire.

He shook his head in dissent. "Not at all, sir. Not at all!"

I counted them off on my fingers. "The Amritsar massacre where soldiers, British soldiers, kept firing at peaceful protesters until they ran out of ammunition, killing and wounding some 2,000?"

He shook his head dismissively.

"What about the many millions of Indians who died of starvation while it was under the control of the British Empire because millions of tons of wheat were exported to Britain as famine raged in India or the four million Bengali Indians who starved to death when Winston Churchill diverted food to British soldiers and countries such as Greece while a deadly famine swept through Bengal?"

His head maintained its pendulum motion, his smile never leaving his lips. He wouldn't acknowledge my argument.

Aye, well...

The following morning I rose early and walked round the magnificent gardens watching a milky sun rise over the palace, only slightly perturbed at being followed each step of the way by a security guard carrying an automatic weapon. I felt perfectly safe, however and after a late breakfast, attended the wedding proper. It was a lavish affair which mixed droned photography, ear-splitting music and garishly bright attire with solemn ceremony. For much of the wedding I was seated cross-legged on the floor. Be-kilted, (and a true Scotsman if you follow my drift) I found the requirement to sit in that position for any time extremely uncomfortable and writhed around cursing my decision not to wear any undergarments below the kilt as I tried to protect my modesty whilst finding a modicum of comfort sitting on the floor.

Bobby was a handsome groom and - normally clean shaven - had grown a beard for his nuptials as Sikh tradition demanded. He wore a turban, carried a sword and as a tall, lean and muscular man, looked exceedingly fierce. His bride, Navseerat was beautiful and was dressed extravagantly in traditional garb. It was a very moving ceremony involving many floral garlands being exchanged and all with no little humour. Lots of smiley faces and good-hearted ribbing.

Beyond the bride and groom, Sohan effortlessly commanded attention, even given the attendance of guest, Punjab Governor (and adopted Scot, ex Member of Parliament for Glasgow Govan) Mohammad Sarwar who brought with him a veritable army of machine-gun-toting security guards. A tall, good-looking man, Sohan certainly had charisma and presence. A Communist in his university years, he came from a family steeped in politics.

On a previous sojourn to New Delhi, I had been invited to visit his nephew, Sonu's home in the Government quarter which was located in an area of tight military security. The home had been allocated to Harkishan Singh Surjeet, the leader of the Communist Party in India and backed on to the Prime Minister's residence. All of the party leaders and senior Indian figures were housed in the campus and it must have made for interesting barbecues. Although Communist leader, Surjeet had died in 2008, his presence was everywhere in the home. Pictures of him with Gandhi, Nelson Mandela and Castro were hung throughout his house and Sonu told a story of how when Surjeet was fourteen, the British Raj had instructed the raising of the Union flag at the court in Hoshiarpur, proclaiming that if any person obstructed this act, they would be shot. The elders were incensed by this but no one wanted to test their resolve until young Surjeet slipped into the building, shimmied up the flag pole, took down the Union Flag and raised the Indian Tricolour. He was shot twice and wounded for his efforts then jailed for three years. In court he stated his name as *London Tod Singh* (one who breaks London). In 1936, Surjeet joined the Communist Party of India and became a co-founder of the *Kisan Sabha* (Peasants Union) in the Punjab and during the Second World War he was imprisoned by the colonial authorities. When India became independent and partitioned in 1947, Surjeet was the Secretary of CPI in Punjab and over a long political career became the conscience of the nation. He always refused offers of political leadership but was the king-maker in innumerable Indian elections in the sixty years after his nation's independence. It was a very moving experience listening to Sohan and Sonu explain their journey through Communism and, in Sohan's case, to the Labour Party in Glasgow where he'd become a Councillor.

Back at the wedding, the evening's ceremony was lavish in the extreme. It took place at a distant, purpose-built entertainment complex where lorry loads of food had been made available and a free bar catered for the many western guests. Sikhs being Sikhs, there was also a contingent which took alcohol as they're not as enthusiastic about prohibition and abstinence as those guests of the Muslim persuasion who were in attendance; most of whom had crossed the border from Pakistan.

An ear-splitting disco saw me rush from the vicinity and take refuge near an outlying bar but jet-lag had caught up with me and after a respectful interval, I decided to remove myself back to the hotel. However, to my immense frustration, no vehicle would move (or was permitted to move) until Pakistan Punjabi Governor Mohammad Sarwar had left with his private army...and he was having a whale of a time. I nursed a glass of beer and simmered.

Next morning I went for a walk in the countryside in the warm sunshine. It really is a beautiful part of the country. The route I took was completely flat, being part of the great fertile, irrigated plain that distinguishes the area. The entire locality was under cultivation and I passed by orchards wherein were grown mangoes, oranges, apples and figs. Children played happily and cycled past me mildly surprised at seeing a European face in their rural playground.

I returned and was driven back to New Delhi where I was to catch a plane to my next port of call, Kathmandu in Nepal. Journeying in India excited the visual, aural, gustatory and olfactory senses. Roads, in part, are often of poor quality and so the ride tended to be interesting; either because the driver routinely ploughed headlong into potholes with deep, cavernous sides, or attempted to avoid them by careering all over the road, missing on-coming traffic by a whisker. The use of the air horn was ubiquitous and seemed to be used whenever a driver decided to manoeuvre or to breathe, whichever occurred more frequently. Often, these lavishly decorated lorries carry goods which are laden in a way that defied the laws of physics but which yet permitted them to barrel down the road at speeds which I viewed as less than wise.

My driver, Santa (I challenged him about his name and he giggled happily, having surprised yet another Westerner by his genuine Indian forename) explained that the trucks tend to be owned by families and represent that family's main source of income so attention is lavished upon them. And so we travelled on to New Delhi, a four hour drive that felt as if I was a participant in a crazed fairground ride sponsored by the CEO of Dulux Paint whilst under the influence of a particularly powerful psychedelic drug.

My hotel was close to India Gate, an enormous war memorial dedicated to the soldiers of the undivided Indian Army who died in the period 1914–21 in the First World War, in France, Flanders, Mesopotamia, Persia, East Africa, Gallipoli, elsewhere in the Near and the Far East, and the Third Anglo-Afghan War. To the disinterested observer, it would appear that Indians like a rammy... or were perhaps too involved with imperialist forces for their own good.

India has a peculiar misty light of a morning and although there can be little doubt that at least in New Delhi, pollution plays its part in this phenomenon, it somehow presents the place as romantic and peaceful even if it engenders coughing fits. I loved it but it was time to move on to Nepal.

Airport queues in some far-flung airports are not the efficient, smooth, systematised experience I'm used to when travelling in Europe or North America. New Delhi was a case in point. The queue was more hinted at than orderly and people merely took opportunities to move forward as and when an opportunity presented itself. My initial good manners and inhibitions borne of decades of queuing properly were tested and eventually disposed with in order to ensure that I reached one of the two desks that purported to administer boarding to Kathmandu in Nepal. Families of six or seven tended to surround the airport ticketing clerk, all members speaking and gesticulating at once. Over the years in order to survive the attentions of such assailants, the clerk had obviously learned to adopt a rather haughty and dismissive attitude which merely served to slow the process and increase not only his facing customers' frustrations but send mine into overdrive. When eventually I was thrust before the man, I handed over my passport and was immediately issued with a ticket and sent on my way to security. Why can't *everyone* be as effortlessly debonair, patient and polite as me?

Only a couple of weeks prior to my plane journey, the same scheduled flight I was taking had caught fire on landing in Kathmandu. This, perversely, gave me some confidence on the basis that lightening doesn't strike twice. However as we flew towards Kathmandu airport, surrounded as it is by the majestic Himalayas, I did experience the mildest of sweaty palms.

The taxi to my hotel was surprisingly efficient as I was to be accommodated in a small hotel situated in the midst of Thamel, the old part of the city which was comprised of a spaghetti warren of small alleys - none of which had street signs. How the driver found the Mums Hotel (three stars, bijou, basic and no apostrophe) was beyond me. However, my room, although small...very small... provided everything I needed - a lockable door, a bed, a toilet and a shower. And at £12 a night I could hardly complain.

It was approaching dusk when I'd organised myself and I ventured out, mapless and gormless! I lost myself immediately in the tumult and confusion of tiny lanes although I had the presence of mind taught me by Robert Baden-Powell, founder of the scouting movement who recommended turning around when making a trip so as to recognise the place you'd just come from in order to return safely. I took note of a larger hotel on my corner called the Friends Hotel and walked on.

The receptionist at Mums Hotel had warned me that in certain parts of the old city, the power is unreliable and in any event street lights shut off around 9.00pm. I thought little of this as I'd anticipated being back for dinner (costing around £1.80) in my small hotel before then. However, I was soon hopelessly lost and found myself coming across the same corner time and again. No one spoke English and such signage as was evident was indecipherable. The lights went out as predicted and were then supplemented by each shopkeeper in the puddle-strewn narrow lanes making use of their own petrol-driven generator. The toxic fug thereby created had me walk with my scarf over my mouth and nose leaving my eyes to water copiously. You could almost *see* the atmosphere thereby created although once I'd moved beyond the immediate light of a particular shopkeeper, I'd walk through muddy puddles in complete darkness until I stumbled across the next generator-powered illumination.

I came across no roads or streets that looked like they might lead somewhere which might accommodate an official or a hotel where someone might give me directions in English. I was completely disorientated, now tired and beginning to imagine that I might walk all night when momentarily reversing my step, out of the corner of my eye, I recognised the Friends Hotel at the end of an alley. Gratefully I splashed through more puddles to reach safety, dinner and bed.

Next morning I had to spend some time tweaking a report I'd written on the Karnali Employment Programme and the activities of the nascent Karnali Development Corporation. Those who live at distance from the capital of Nepal lead difficult lives. Programmes are in place, some (as was this) funded by the UK Department for International Development (DfID) and focus upon interventions such as rural road construction, micro-hydro canal and electrification, wooden bridge construction, school and health initiatives, water supply improvements and skills training. Every year an exodus of males to India or the more distant Emirates for remunerative employment leave women as sole breadwinners and family managers due to an absence of work on the steep hillsides of Nepal. I ticked off the problems I saw and looked through solutions I'd offered, all the while acutely aware of the inappropriateness of someone like me suggesting interventions I'd propose about a culture I didn't understand.

I satisfied myself that my analysis would stand some small measure of scrutiny and left to meet with my three colleagues, Shuva Sharma, Basu Dev Neoprane and Sanjaya Acharya. My friend, Kevin who was project leader had advised prior to my departure from Scotland of the high level of ability of my cohorts. He was absolutely correct on that point. We enjoyed a most informative and relaxed meeting at the end of which I found myself asking why on earth DfID required UK input to projects such as these when it was obvious that these guys were intellectually right on the money and had local knowledge that dwarfed anything I could bring to the table. To my relief they never mentioned my frailties on this and were unfailingly polite and affirming.

My economic development obligations apart, I managed to set aside time to see more of Kathmandu and its environs. I hired a car and driver to take me to the foothills of the Himalayas and was deposited alone at a roadside at 04.00am where following a steep solo climb in complete darkness, my torch guiding my path, I found myself atop a platform above the jaw-droppingly beautiful village of Nagarkot which commands one of the broadest views of the Himalayas in the Kathmandu valley. As the sun rose, I noticed that I wasn't alone and that half-a-dozen other early birds had gathered in the blackness to photograph the sun rising over Mount Everest. Well, it was emotional, man! A clear sky allowed an unimpaired view and gradually the outline of the highest mountain in the world made itself apparent. First grey then red then amber, the light improved until there, in all its majesty, glistening and shimmering white, was Everest. But in all truth, the setting allowed a proper appreciation of the sheer scale of the majesty as all around was the preposterously magnificent Himalayan mountain range. I stood for some time, sometimes just watching the rising sun change the appearance of the range, sometimes prompted to take a photograph.

I spent a week in Kathmandu and for most meals chose *dal bhat* which consists of rice and lentil soup, generally served with vegetable curries and sometimes chutney. *Momo*, a type of Nepali dumpling, was also a food of choice with many street vendors and restaurants selling it. My free time was spent walking the streets of this astonishing city. I was fortunate to have visited one year before an earthquake reduced to dust many of the sights over which I'd drooled....and they say there's a God! Durbar Square, for example was one of the most enchanting architectural showpieces I'd ever seen. It highlights the ancient arts of Nepal.

Before the quake, there were ninety-nine courtyards attached to the square but now only six are left.

I visited the Narayanhiti Palace, the home of the Nepalese Royal family until 2001 where the scene of the 2001 Nepalese Royal Massacre took place. I completely misunderstood the story as it was revealed on my visit via a number of small signs throughout the ground floor which stated, 'This is where King Birendra was shot. 'This is where Princess Shruti was shot'. 'This is where Princess Shahi was shot'. Due to my disinclination to join groups but to find things out for myself, I'd assumed that this was a palace revolt undertaken by the Nepalese people when in fact back at my lodgings, I discovered a far more fascinating story.

Apparently, dinner was being served in the Narayanhity Royal Palace and according to reports, prior to the dinner Crown Prince Dipendra had been drinking heavily, had smoked large quantities of hashish and had then behaved in a way which had resulted in his father, King Birendra telling him to leave the diner party. The Crown Prince was escorted to his room by his brother Prince Nirajan and his cousin Prince Paras. I mean this kind of thing happens in the best of families. What doesn't *usually* follow is the subsequent murder of ten family members by the one asked to leave the dining room!

In the space of some few minutes, Dipendra committed fratricide, patricide, sororicide, regicide, matricide, avunculicide and suicide having calmly taken possession of a Heckler & Koch MP5 sub-machine gun, returned to the dinner table and riddled his family with a barrage of 9mm bullets. Ten died and five were badly wounded. Jeeeez, he must have been seriously pissed off at not being allowed to finish his starter.

After the monarchy was abolished through a subsequent populist uprising there have been a number of claims refuting the official report on the massacre. It is being alleged that two masked men fired the shots that led to the massacre. This story is given a certain measure of credence as the alleged perpetrator, Crown Prince Dipendra, committed suicide after the killings by the simple expedient of shooting himself in the back six times!

The Royal Family limped on until a Maoist insurgency supported by pro-democracy activists forced the new King to restore Nepal's House of Representatives which promptly restricted then abolished the monarchy. If only the King had allowed Crown Prince Dipendra to finish his greens!

The royal palace is now a public museum. It largely survived the 2015 violent 7.8 MMS earthquake (Moment Magnitude Scale is now used by seismologists to measure the size of earthquakes in terms of the energy released, replacing the more usual Richter Scale). However, many other ancient monuments were lost. Indeed, Kasthamandap, a three-storied public shelter and temple, the very building that gave Kathmandu its name was destroyed and will have to be completely rebuilt. There was a plaque inside it that dates to 1048 which made it one of the oldest buildings in Nepal. Utterly lost. The Dharahara, a 60-metre white minaret tower built in in 1832 has been destroyed. Four of the seven Unesco world heritage sites in the valley were severely damaged. I was hugely fortunate to have managed to visit these places before they were lost to the world.

I also visited the crematoria at Pashupatinath Temple. I'd anticipated beforehand the culture clash I might expect but upon finding the crematoria on the Bagmati River which is considered holy by both Hindus and Buddhists, I was too squeamish to ask what the 'Cornea Excision Centre' was all about as some things are better left to the imagination...or not! I watched in fascination as elaborate preparations were made on the stoop below me for the cremation of an elderly woman. Her body was laid out on an elevated raft of logs beneath which was a generous supply of kindling. Once organised, mourners gathered and circled the corpse several times bestowing it with floral tributes prior to the kindling and straw, overlaid on the body, being set alight.

In short measure the fire gathered momentum but it took a while before the flames licked at the demised. It was as if the conflagration was designed for eventual consumptive power rather than early toasting; a marathon rather than a sprint. Similar funeral pyres were located yards apart on each side of the Bagmati and across the way officials were busily brushing the remains of an earlier cremation into the stream below. What made this experience somewhat less than dignified was the fact that the course of water into which the remains were swept was, despite it being a holy river, little more than a slow-moving, toxic, litter-strewn body of polluted effluence.

Perhaps my most interesting visit, however, was to the Royal City of Bhaktapur. Only a short distance from Kathmandu, the place just drips with splendour, history and astonishing architecture. It is filled with Hindu and Buddhist religious sites and although the population is primarily Hindu, there are nineteen Buddhist monasteries. Only thirty miles from the epicentre of the 2015 earthquake, the place was badly damaged, the delicate brickwork proving to be particularly fragile. But when I visited it was a sumptuous feast for the eyes.

Bhaktapur remains refreshingly devoid of the traffic, bustle and pollution of neighbouring Kathmandu, its temple-studded medieval squares and tight, narrow lanes allowing me to become hopelessly lost in minutes. I enjoyed a soft drink and listened to Buddhist chants, caring little about my disorientation. Carefully constructed wells, still used by locals for washing, small courtyards and everywhere statues and buildings that have stood there since medieval times completely entranced me.

But at the end of the day, it was Kathmandu and its people that captured my heart. I returned to Scotland humbled at the resourcefulness, dignity and cheerfulness of the Nepalese people, fascinated and awe-struck at the venerable and ancient architecture and filled with a determination to return.

I flew back to Glasgow but it wasn't long before I was headed back to Asia, this time to Vietnam.

D'you know for someone who professes to enjoy few things more than international travel, I have reluctantly to confess an intermittent deep and abiding loathing for my fellow travellers. As I set off from Giffnock to Vietnam via Abu Dhabi I first had to catch a bus! A *bus*! Recent storms had damaged a rail bridge near Lamington in the Scottish Borders and cut the rail link south so a bus to Carlisle it was. My wife, Jean drove me into town to start my adventure and my mood darkened almost immediately as I hoisted for the first time my bargain £5 backpack bought via eBay from a very respectable sales outlet in Hong Kong only for the two shoulder-straps to uncouple themselves from the pack they were meant to hold tight to my back. I inspected the damage and realised that a couple of kirby grips would have held them more securely than the flimsy stitching with which they'd been attached. I had little alternative but to carry my belongings as if they were contained in a hessian sack holding potatoes.

But my fellow travellers take the biscuit. They were to a man and to a woman, complete eegits! In Manchester Airport at any rate, they couldn't find things at the precise moment they needed them, they joined the wrong queue, they dressed in flimsy T-shirts for their destination thereby braving sub-zero temperatures *en route*, they felt able to begin a long, chirpy social chit-chat with ticketing staff once they, *themselves* had completed their check-in, completely ignoring the fact that behind them stood a queue like an execution! In the adjoining queue a man tried to persuade the desk clerk that the item he was attempting to have them carry in the hold was a regular case - but was in fact a box of industrial character approximately the size of a prefab. In front of me in the queue, an old guy (defined as someone who looked at least six months older than me) decided that modern travel dress required that he wear a pair of baggy training breeks that resembled something Jock Stein might have worn when training the Lisbon Lions back in 1967; whereas I wore an elegant pair of light denim trousers, a light micro-weave jumper, a shirt in contrasting colour and a dark coloured blouson jacket. Ian Fleming couldn't have described a more debonair outfit when introducing James Bond to his public in *Casino Royale*. That said the fact that this debonair traveller had to lug his belongings around as if carrying a sandbag, did dent the image somewhat.

Landing at Saigon, I first approached a currency exchange outlet and asked to convert fifty US Dollars to Vietnamese Dong so I could pay the taxi driver. I handed over my fifty bucks and was passed one million two hundred thousand Dong!

Passport Control was more of a challenge. I'd researched the requirement for a visa and had an email from the Vietnamese Embassy reassuring me that I did not need one. Everyone in the queue before me was ushered through but the officer of the watch changed just as it was my turn. A lot of Vietnamese verbals were shouted in my direction, the only word I recognised being 'visa'. I calmly explained a number of times about my email, taken by my customs officer as an aggressive provocation which threatened physical assault. Just as I imagined I was about to be taken to a cell somewhere or escorted on to the next plane home, the uniformed officer stopped shouting and abruptly stamped my passport, gesturing for me to accept his welcome to his fine country. It was only later as I perused a guide book I realised that the expected protocol was to have placed a few quid in the palm of his hand. I was delighted. I'd beaten the system...however unwittingly.

I arrived blinking from the airport into the darkness and took a taxi. After unpacking, I discovered a Ho Chi Minh City that was a dimly-lit, maelstrom of honking scooters and back alleys. I was too knackered to do other than walk from my hotel, Ngoc Linh round a noisy block before bed. I stopped off in a nearby bar and ordered a bottle of beer. Yet unaccustomed to the currency, I offered the largest note in my wallet and gave it to my waitress who took it smiling and returned a fistful of Dong notes along with my beer. Grateful, I peeled off the top note and tipped her. She accepted graciously but when I returned to my small hotel room I checked the transaction on my trusty currency exchange calculator and realised I'd given her the equivalent of one pence!

I rose the following morning refreshed. That lasted until roughly 9.30am when my trusty cotton sweat-cloth made its first appearance as it was 35 degrees and rising...and I'm not good in the warm! I visited first the old Presidential Palace of Nguyễn Văn Thiệu which was opulent although it probably pales into insignificance compared with the royal households and political hideaways that we have in Britain. I then took the short walk to the War Museum which was hard to stomach. French colonialism and, following them, the Vietnamese Army (supported all the way by American 'advisers') behaved appallingly and cruelly towards the Viet Cong insurgents. Photographs showing the effect of 'Agent Orange' used by the Americans to deforest huge tracts of land (to remove cover from the Vietcong) but which to this day produces babies with no arms and other disfigurements) were on display. Tanks and weapons used in the 'American War'...unsurprisingly, nationals don't refer to it as the 'Vietnamese War'...along with other ordinance and the canons they used to fire them were all on show along with the hideously perfunctory notice boards showing figures which listed quite matter-of-factly the extent of their kill range (lethal for everyone within 300 meters of the blast!) A regular football pitch is between 90 - 120 meters. This was a Howitzer shell.

I was out on my feet by noon so accepted an offer from a cycle taxi ("Happy New Year, Boss. You need lift?" It turned out it was recently the *Tet* New Year just over a week previously). He took me leisurely to the Rex Hotel whose fifth floor, roof-top bar was a favourite for American brass during the Vietnam War (it was said that four star generals could drink their Dry Martinis and watch the war being conducted on the other side of the Saigon River from their vantage point). In a nearby currency exchange I converted $100 into Vietnamese Dong and was given 2.4 million of them. A millionaire at last!

A bottle of beer is about £1 and 100,000 Dong is about £3 so when I scrabbled about convinced I was being ripped off when trying to buy a cheap pen having been asked for 5,000 Dong, I had to check my currency converter app to see that this amounted to 17 pence. The rooftop bar was both elegant and airy so I spent some time writing postcards (remember them?) and enjoying a cocktail (a second *Mojito*) and some *phu* (chicken noodle soup...a

Vietnamese specialty). I asked the waiter how to pronounce it (the guide book suggested 'fur') and was offered what sounded like a yodel in return so I just pointed silently at its photograph and subsequently enjoyed it. It was superb! I'd never been one for cocktails preferring beer, whisky or brandy but cocktails were incredibly inexpensive and tasted delicious so I decided to get to know this approach to alcohol consumption better while in Vietnam...and boy, did I get to know cocktails!

The topography of Ho Chi Minh City is basically flat. I attempted to walk back to my small, one star hotel in District 1 but gave up the ghost when my feet started blistering. I decided a haircut was in order and stepped into a hairdressers'. I'd read that in Vietnam, customers are attended to by nubile young ladies who massaged your shoulders and painted your nails as your hair is cut. I'd already decided to refuse such offers were they to be offered. My nails are *my* business. In the event I was attended to by an elderly gentleman who seemed possessed of great dignity. His face was comprehensively pock-marked, either as a result of devastating childhood acne or because someone had set his face on fire and had extinguished it by beating it out with a golf shoe. He cut my hair as if every snip was a carefully considered work of art. I noticed as he finished that my sideburns were uneven and my right side was half an inch higher than the left but decided that assertiveness was not in order on the basis that never in my life have I thought to challenge someone on the basis that their sideburns seemed skew-whiff. He asked if I needed a shave and I said, 'no' but witnessing his disappointment, then agreed. Again he set to as if painting a masterpiece but merely succeeded in leaving my face feeling as if it had been sandpapered. He asked for 200,000 Dong and I gave him 300,000 (£9) and bowed and scraped in gratitude, attempting to make clear that I respected his work. He was clearly of an age to have been required to have taken part in the Vietnam War - but on whose side? Little matter, he's a Communist now!

I left and limped back to my hotel with my hair lopsided and my chin on fire.

At twilight I was wheeched up the ultra-fast lift to the 52nd floor of Saigon's tallest building, the Bitexo Financial Tower, to the Skybar where I watched the city light up at sunset. Any city looks more ordered from height and when illuminated and Ho Chi Minh City is no different. The manic rush of traffic at ground zero is made invisible and a radiant, symmetrical pattern of light emerges. Very pretty (although that might have been flavoured by the three D.O.M cocktails (Diamo, Optimo, Maximo)...sounds like they figure it's the tops!) I'd enjoyed while waiting for this miracle of radiance to occur. (The bar sold a cocktail, 'Oceans Eight' which cost two million Dong! (£62).) I wasn't tempted). Wrote more of my book, 'Alba' in the process being entertained by an American duo warbling cover-songs of someone called 'Adele' and in the process annoying me with their hippy-pish unfunny, contrived, shitey patter between songs 'Hey there...welcome to ground zero!' (I'm easily annoyed with three D.O.M.s in me!)

I was collected the following morning at 7.30am by a Vietnamese woman, 'Call me Moon!' who drove me to a motor launch on the river where I joined three couples; two American, one Singaporean. It transpired that upon informing everyone that I was from Scotland, one of the women told me she'd just returned from three months in Largs, one had stayed in Cumbernauld for a year some time before and the other had last year visited the Edinburgh Festival. Go figure! Today, in their company, I sped up the Saigon River at some considerable speed, the Captain winding his way through the thick blanket of Water Hyacinths which, from time to time wrapped themselves around his propeller and required that he reverse in order to free the boat. We visited the military tunnel complex at *Cu Chi,* some seventy kilometres up the River Saigon.

The Vietcong were an impressive fighting force. Perhaps inevitably, their opposing forces, the American and South Vietnamese Armies, dehumanised them, calling them 'Gooks' and possibly less disparagingly, 'Charlie'. They lived below ground on three ever-deepening levels whereby they'd rest, cook, strategise and recover before sneaking out and warring with the invading American soldiers. There were 250 kilometres of these tunnels in the strategically important area of *Cu Chi* north of Saigon. We were shown the booby traps they made which were at once horrifying, imaginative and very effective; disguised holes in the ground which, when stepped on, dropped the soldier onto spikes of tremendous lethality. Interestingly, some of the traps were specifically designed not to kill but to maim and poison in order to consume American resources in treating the soldier for a long time and to permit him to spread his tale, lowering morale. We were shown the entrance to a tunnel. Covered by leaves it was completely invisible. We were also shown how they made sandals from rubber tyres...and fabulously, how they reverse-designed them with the smaller heel part forming the front of the foot and the sole facing the rear so that in the rainy season, when GIs followed footprints, they'd track in the opposite direction to the Vietcong soldier!

We were asked if anyone would volunteer to go down the tunnel and, eager to experience all that Vietnam had to offer, I raised my arm. What Moon went on to explain as I prepared to drop into the entrance was that this was an *actual* tunnel opening for Vietnamese soldiers (who were tiny compared to Westerners). Other larger touristic holes were available later on to suit the build of 5'11" Scotsmen. Too late...as I squeezed into the small opening, I realised I was stuck fast and no amount of manoeuvring would allow me to get down...or back out. My feet couldn't touch the ground of the larger chamber beneath and I was stuck firmly at the hips. Ten minutes passed as if it was an hour and I wearied of ever seeing my loved ones again. Three, four and eventually, five strong men couldn't lift me from my predicament. Eventually a large American arrived in one of the tour groups (I was by now holding up hundreds of people, all of whom had gathered in a large circle to see this car crash. Had it taken place in America, helicopters hovering overhead would have carried a live video link back to CNN or whatever). One smart-arsed tourist shouted "You'll just have to take your pants off, buddy," to which I replied, "No good, pal. I have an erection!" BIG laugh followed by a rippled series of lesser titters as tour guides explained my retort to those who didn't speak English! My big American pal placed his arms under my arms...the other five still had a piece of me...and as if I were a Champagne cork, out I popped to a loud cheer and the popping of scores of flashbulbs which had been waiting to capture the moment in order to allow the folks back home to laugh at my stupidity. Each of my hips were cut and badly grazed by the wooden sides of the tunnel hole but I pretended I was uninjured until no one was looking and I could whimper and apply some sunscreen (the closest I had to balm). My main injuries, however, were to my dignity and my bruised upper arms which had taken the brunt of the pull.

We moved on through the jungle and I paid 400,000 Dong (£12) to fire twenty rounds of live ammo at a target using an AK47, the Soviet rifle used by the Vietcong. I could have used the American rifle, the M16 Carbine, but my Vietnam loyalties lay with the Russian rifle. Surprising myself, I hit the target some further 100 yards away dead centre on each shot. I even shot at angled, more distant targets to see if I was as devastating a sniper as I'd imagined as I thought it would be more difficult. Bullseye! What surprised me most was the noise of the shot as I fired; I was required to wear earmuffs. But there wasn't much recoil.

Upon arrival back in the city, a visit to the rooftop bar of the Caravelle Hotel, the historic *Saigon, Saigon* bar was a welcome, elegant and chilled atmosphere in which to recover what was left of my dignity. I was joined three martinis in by a retired couple from Quebec and enjoyed a spirited, light-hearted conversation. Jacques was more impressed by my choice of cocktail when I drained a Cosmopolitan and ordered a Dry Martini (one I didn't fancy but wanted to try...in the event it was more than passable!) Great *craic*!

The following day was one of mixed experiences. I was collected by *Thanh* and *Tuan*, respectively 21year old male and female students, who drove me round Saigon on *Thanh's* pillion. (*Tuan*, the female, was present on her scooter, riding shotgun in case of trouble. She was the back-up driver.) We visited seven of Saigon's districts and saw the Chinese Quarter, the Korean Quarter (much wealthier) and the silk, furniture, pet, fruit, flower, wholesale, chemical and spice markets. Over coffee and a chat I found out more about Vietnam. Thanh explained to me that if you want to become a policeman, your family had to have had a Communist past. People from South Vietnam, as was, don't have much of a chance of civil office. Even a top Communist, if he marries a Roman Catholic (which religion is prevalent in Vietnam in appreciable numbers), is considered too Western and subsequently denied advancement. You pay one million Dong (£31) to a senior police officer and expect to make this back in bribes collected from potential arrestees in your first year. You pay for all education - but it is the only way you can have a future. You pay for all health care unless you have insurance. If you are poor and have an accident, your relatives are phoned to ask if they'll pay for your treatment...if not, the leg stays broken. It's kinda like America! If you want to travel abroad you have to have £10,000 in your bank account (a forbidding sum) and pass an interview so the Communist Party is confident you'll return...but there are companies which will provide you with a false credit score so you can apply and then you need only depend on the interview. Each of my escorts took the view that the days of the Communist Government were numbered ... young people won't accept this form of totalitarian administration, they reckoned.

On the River Saigon, an entire bank is given over to hundreds of neatly organised large golf umbrellas beneath which are two-seater deckchairs. This is for courting couples as most households have large families and there's no privacy for snogging. There are eleven million people in Saigon and five million of them have scooters which results in the most chaotic transport confusion. It's a miracle that no one is injured as solid walls of motorcyclists lace their way through each other left and right with relaxed impunity. Compounding this is the fact that many other citizens are trying to walk across the road. It all amounts to what Strathclyde University lecturer, Professor Lewis Gunn described to me once as 'Partisan Mutual Adjustment'...somehow muddling through; accommodating the needs of others while looking after your own ambitions. I didn't see one accident or near miss!

I mentioned that I hadn't seen any dogs. It was explained to me that dogs are valued. Either they are kidnapped and held to ransom if they're pedigree or they end up in a curry. 80% of dogs are eaten...I wondered what that chewy stew was last night!

Dropped off at lunchtime, I changed clothes and took a taxi to a part of the city not visited by tourists. I wanted to buy a couple of shirts as I'd been required to change three times a day because it has been so hot and humid. Immediately, I realised my error as all of the shirts available were designed not unreasonably to fit Vietnamese men who tend to be much smaller (see earlier comments about the tunnel entrance!)

After checking out a few (pretty scabby) shops and realising that they only sold shirts that would fit ten year old male Scots children, I took a taxi back to the city centre and found a shopping mall (equally comparable to any UK mall) wherein Marks and Spencer had a store. I wandered round and discovered that they only sold sizes small and medium. Not for me. I decided to check whether there was a Black's of Greenock, a famed tent manufacturer and outdoors' store, in Saigon wherein they might have a stock sufficient to sell the size of garment necessary to clad a sensibly-sized Scotsman.

In the afternoon, I walked about the downtown area in District One for a while but it was so hot I eventually decided upon refreshment and noticed a modern, tall hotel with what from a distance looked like a sky-bar (my new hobby in Saigon). It transpired that this was the *Hotel des Arts* and it was probably the most opulent hotel and bar I've ever visited since Beijing...the *last* Communist country I was in! (Commies seem to do opulence much better than Capitalists!)

The rooftop bar had a very inviting infinity pool but had no cover from the sun so I quaffed a beer and a Bramble Cocktail and left after about fifteen minutes as the temperature must have been over forty degrees and the sun was unremitting. A taxi to the breezier, cooler and much more famous Majestic Hotel (where Graham Greene used to write novels such as 'Our Man In Havana') and I was up only five floors, this time to the Breeze Sky Bar (where the sunset view over the River Saigon was unparalleled). One of the grand old Colonial hotels from the days when the French ruled in Indochina, it was built in 1925. I enjoyed a Brandy Alexander and a Happy Saigon (importantly, according to the drinks' menu, a cocktail dedicated to peace). There can't be too many cocktails dedicated to peace... but I'm prepared to try them all! These when combined allowed me to reminisce quietly through drink how luck favours us in Scotland as opposed to those in Vietnam. (Basic social care, free education and health care, protected egalitarian rights, no drafted wars for four generations, legal guarantees, freedom of expression and of travel, sensible weather....I could go on but the Brandy Alexander was kicking in!

Interesting lavvies here in the Majestic! All rich dark wood, elegant art deco and stained glass. A saloon-style swing door separates the men from the women but the configuration is such that any gentleman pointing Percy at porcelain would be entirely in view of the fairer sex as they sought a cubicle upon their own entry. Note to self... Must read 'Our Man In Havana' to see if there's any reference to controversial lavvie confrontations!

A Singapore Sling and then home to bed. Tomorrow I fly to Hanoi!

As I slurped the final drains of the Sling, it occurred to me that there hadn't been a cocktail I hadn't enjoyed since arrival.

I packed, paid, said farewell to the Ngoc Linh Hotel and walked from District 1 to District 3 in ever-increasing morning heat. The traffic, as ever, was crazy busy. Pedestrians have to cross a constant flow of motorcycles and cars...perhaps twelve abreast and a hundred yards deep...then face a similar crush of traffic coming in the opposite direction upon reaching the middle of the road. Almost unbelievably, there are, in each passage of play, one or two deranged motorcyclists who travel in the gutter *against* the flow of traffic. Compounding all of this is the fact that most pavements don't fall to the road at a ninety degree angle; they're sloped to permit easy access for wheeled vehicles so many take advantage of this to take a shortcut or to park. However, I've now become quite adept at crossing wherever and whenever I want now that I've worked out the rule, which seems to be 'cross as you choose and we'll do our best to avoid hitting you'. It seems to work! When I think of it, it's pretty much how I conduct myself in Glasgow... without the implied understanding of motorists.

I was advised yesterday that parking in Saigon is simple. You pull on to the pavement and a wee guy approaches and takes a few Dong in exchange for parking your bike neatly against a wall. At some point in the day, the local beat bobby wanders by and takes his cut of the dosh. Seems a decent job creation scheme.

Bewitched, bothered and bewildered by the traffic, I took refuge in a Vietnamese cafe somewhat off the tourist track. Now that I'm fluent in Vietnamese sign language, I managed to ask for a milky coffee and a fruit smoothie and was delivered of an iced, unsweetened coffee which had the consistency of tar, and a knickerbocker glory. Still, their consumption kept me off the hot streets for a while.

Flying north to Hanoi at noon and in bright sunshine, I was able to view the lush green carpet of Vietnam's mountainous hinterland now recovering from the 7,662,000 tons of explosives dropped (compared to a grand total of 2,150,000 tons dropped by all of the belligerents in the WW2 conflict - world-wide!) as well as the Agent Orange which defoliated much of the greenery to deny the Vietcong the cover of the treetop canopy. As Robert Burns said, '' *Oh, why has man the will and pow'r to make his fellow mourn?'* Not half! But my experience of the Vietnamese people thus far has been comprehensively positive. They seem intelligent, humble, kind and optimistic. That American geopolitical priorities required that they be bombed into the Stone Age remains, even now, a bewildering act (understandable only by appreciating the might and influence of the American military-industrial machine which requires constant wars to feed its appetite!).

Some 58,000 US soldiers were killed in action in Vietnam...and their *average* age was nineteen! The total Communist losses were 666,000 and in addition, two million Vietnamese civilians lost their lives - a statistic only revealed reluctantly by the Pentagon after persistent questioning by Senator Edward Kennedy. Air Force Captain Brian Wilson, who carried out bomb-damage assessments in free-fire zones throughout the delta, saw the results of American shoot to kill policy at first-hand. "It was the epitome of immorality... One of the times I counted bodies after an air strike—which always ended with two napalm bombs which would just fry everything that was left—I counted sixty-two bodies. In my report I described them as so many women between fifteen and twenty-five and so many children—usually in their mothers' arms or very close to them—and so many old people." When he later read the official tally of dead, he found that it listed them as 130 Vietcong killed. So who knows *how* many Vietnamese people were killed!

(1) Source, Turse, Nick (2013). Kill Anything That Moves: The Real American War in Vietnam.

And that's not all, the American body politic takes some beating. Of the twenty-seven million draft-age men between 1964 and 1973, 40% were drafted into military service, and only 10% were actually sent to Vietnam. This group was made up almost entirely of either working class or rural youth. University students who did not avoid the draft were generally sent to non-combat and service roles or made officers, while high school drop-outs and the working class were sent into combat roles. Blacks made up a disproportionate 25% or more of combat units, while constituting only 12% of the military.

Perhaps the saddest statistic I read is that a number greater than the 58,000 Americans killed in combat have subsequently committed suicide.

What seems even more astonishing given that history is that the failure of the American military to defeat these small, brave souls has pointed up the irony of social and cultural change. My two Vietnamese tour guides yesterday talked of the admiration they had for 'American culture' and each intimated that they'd love to live and work in the States were they ever to be allowed to leave. Tim Berners-Lee and John Logie Baird have simply changed the dynamic! Steve Jobs and Bill Gates have helped. Everywhere, adverts are for Western products. Coca Cola and Pepsi have conquered the world in a way that B52 Bombers failed to do. Characters in Vietnamese television adverts are usually dressed in smart Western attire (if still exhibiting the smouldering looks and over-dramatic gestures normally found in Bollywood). The citizens of Saigon and Hanoi - especially the young - are adorned with T-shirts depicting Taylor Swift and Manchester United. Adidas and Nike footwear are ubiquitous and the music in almost every bar I entered was C&W, rap or rock. In school, kids are now required to learn English as a core part of their curriculum. In one relaxed cocktail bar I listened to some Vietnamese music. Entirely listenable....still four beats to a bar...but in the midst of this musical confection they played 'My Love Is Like A Red Red Rose', 'Carrickfergus' and 'Over The Sea To Sky' played on a *clàirseach* ...they obviously saw my Scottish wristband!

It was cold and miserable in Hanoi but my hotel, the Symphony Hotel in *Hang Hom* Street was entirely acceptable. Two stars, but completely fine although the street outside seems to have been given over to the sale, repair and maintenance of motorbikes. It was noisy and the smell of gasoline was all pervasive. Most worrying as I left for a stroll in the evening was the fact that many of the stalls, in their mechanical ministrations, seemed to act as unofficial refuelling stops for motorbikes (my hotel is five storeys high, two rooms per storey and with no obvious fire exits). Compounding the felony was the fact that many shopkeepers in Hanoi (and this street was no exception) lit small charcoal fires for cooking or warmth in metal boxes on the pavement. In addition, small men squatted and worked with focused concentration on an errant gearbox, firing welding sparks in great profusion all over the pavement. One wee accident and we'd all go up in a big bang with no means of escape! Health and Safety would have a field day over here.

I awoke the following morning to a misty *smir* which enveloped Hanoi today. It was mild enough but the dampness was something of a distraction especially since having come from sunny Saigon. I walked out and traipsed round the central city area. I visited the British Embassy which was located on the fourth floor of an office building as I wanted to discover whether the embassy was located there during the administration of Sir Michael Pike ('82-'85) as this fact will figure in my novel, '*Alba*'. Perhaps unsurprisingly, this wasn't the kind of question they were used to and I was asked to e-mail them. (Interestingly, I noticed that the Australian Embassy is located within its own huge edifice surrounded by substantial grounds. The U.K. has a few offices on the fourth floor above Brookes Brothers!)

I walked on to the infamous 'Hanoi Hilton', the *Hoa Lo* Prison which incarcerated among others ex-Republican Presidential candidate Senator John McCain during the American War. The flying gear in which he was captured was on display as were many photographs showing how well treated were American prisoners of war although given that John McCain cannot lift his arms above his head these days suggests that it wasn't an unalloyed curriculum of basketball and board games that was the order of the day in the prison. Of equal concern was the obviously cruel way in which the French colonialists treated the Vietnamese people. Back in the day, subjugation seemed to require the most appalling behaviour. *Madame la Guillotine* was prominently displayed (and was used enthusiastically) as a means of encouraging the locals to accept French rule.

The railway station was my next stop but an officious woman guard stopped me taking photographs of trains so I wandered along to the next entrance and did so there. An unremarkable transport hub. A *cappuccino* coffee in a really nice coffee shop cost me fourteen pence. I left *circa* six pence as a tip.

Further walking in the rain took me back to the *Hoan Kiem* Lake where I crossed the famous red bridge and looked around the *Ngoc Son* Temple. Interesting and photogenic but what took me most was a large charcoal pit on its island periphery where a young couple took a wad of American Dollars (there must have been seventy or eighty Dollars in the man's fist) and threw them on the fire, stoking it and turning them to ash. I took a photograph. Seventy Dollars is a not insubstantial sum in Vietnam. Curious! I didn't have the ability to communicate with them to ask the motivation that lay behind this.

Hanoi is *much* colder than Saigon, a good twenty degrees colder; wetter and windier. There are proportionately more cars although motor scooters still predominate. Because the pavements in the city centre are somewhat wider, it makes common sense for motorcyclists to use them as well, so it's the efficiency principle in action. Many more uniforms are in evidence; police, soldiers, security and people in ill-fitting garb who seem merely to stand beside or sit on one of the city's ubiquitous small stools outside a shop or business and just look at things! As Yogi Berra said, 'You can observe a lot by just watching.' The buildings are more substantial courtesy of the French occupation of Indochina and to my eyes, there were fewer bars than in Saigon. Everywhere, women swept. Less of a party town in the Communist north. I had to find sustenance in the occasional hotel. But find it I did!

After further walking in the mist and a visit to the War Museum (where I'd been told by my guide book there'd be a B52 aeroplane to view upon arrival...but I couldn't find it and it's the size of a football field) I returned to the hotel via the services of a taxi driver who ripped me off. I'd been advised that only three cab firms could be trusted, *Mai Linh,* Taxi Group and ABC and I flagged down an ABC taxi but rather than the 40,000 Dong I'd come to expect, this boyo wanted 150,000 Dong. I stopped him and remonstrated, deciding I'd rather walk. The difference was about £1 but it was the principle that upset me so I walked the last two hundred yards growling my displeasure to make a point. I'm almost certain he'll never do it again!

After booking tomorrow's trip to *Duomg Lam* village via my hotelier, I set off in a *Mai Linh* taxi to the Metropole Hotel, the very epitome of colonial elegance in this part of the world. It's where 'Hanoi Jane' Fonda stayed when, sitting on a North Vietnamese anti-aircraft battery in 1972, she denounced the American invasion of Vietnam (before renouncing much of what she said upon her return to America). Not only did Charlie Chaplin stay in the Metropole, they named a cocktail after him - and so I had a go. It was quite nice; Gin, Apricot Brandy and Lime Juice. The entire hotel was draped in visiting Americans and I couldn't find a seat in their spacious cocktail bar. A helpful *concierge* found me a seat in their *'Le Club'* Brasserie but it was open to the elements at one side and drove me from the premises after my Charlie Chaplin. It was a chill wind.

I figured out that I couldn't be far from O'Leary's Sports Bar and found it right where I'd expected it to be (actually pretty impressive when account is taken of the complex local maze of small streets). Warmth, at this point, was more important than authenticity but all of the Irish staff seemed Vietnamese. I entered and the Scottish band, Deacon Blue were playing *'Your Swaying Arms';* nice touch. I ordered (as I always do here) a bottle of Saigon Beer and on this occasion, a glass of *nep-cam* (local rice wine). It tasted like poor quality brandy but the bar was warm and cosy so I persevered. For dinner, I ordered a Vietnamese dish by pointing at a picture but couldn't quite determine the meat content...but it reminded me of Spaniel or Beagle.

Earlier, when I visited the War Museum I'd had to furrow my brow to work out which was the gent's toilet as the signage was only in Vietnamese...*Nam* or *Nu*...In O'Leary's, it was more prosaic... Willies or Fannies! And as I walked back to the Symphony Hotel, I noticed again that on every second building, golden, ornate writing wished everyone a Happy New Year (Tet). However, to my eyes, the lush, swirling Vietnamese scroll seemed to say, 'Chick Murray'. I'd bet he'd have found it hilarious that he was apparently being celebrated so enthusiastically in Indochina. I also anglicised in my mind a number of other signs I noticed to help me remember them; *Chic Mury* as I mentioned, *Le Lang Chuc, Bahn My Gas, Ca Alam, Bang Thi Gong* and my favourite, *Phuc Dat!*

While downing my *nep-cam*, I phoned my local surgery in Glasgow and made appointments to see Ruby, the Practice Nurse and Dr. Gaw, my GP, following my return next week marvelling all the while that I could do this as easily from the other side of the world than I could from home in Glasgow. It occurred to me later that the receptionist might choose to have a word with my doctor telling him that I'd phoned that morning at 10.30am (GMT) (actually 5.30pm Vietnam time) and it had seemed as if I'd had a few!

I awoke the following morning to a gey dreich, grey, misty, Glasgow day in Hanoi. Fifteen degrees but it felt chilly. My hotelier *Hing* had attempted to book me on a tour bus going to *Duong Lam*, an ancient UNESCO village south of the city but had had a better idea...he'd have his pal *Tang* drive me instead. Same price. Hmmm... but it worked out perfectly in that we drove straight there, no hanging around, no traipsing round everyone else's hotel to collect them. Nice car too; a wee Honda, and quite new. *Tang's* English was pretty basic...if somewhat better than my Vietnamese...so my questions were usually answered quite perfunctorily.

Vietnam has a population at present of some ninety million, seven and a half million of whom live in Hanoi, a city which is as flat as Amsterdam but where few properties reach higher than three storeys. In consequence, the city spreads out comfortably and it took us an hour and a half's drive to reach anything approaching the countryside.

Duong Lam was fascinating and worth the drive. The village has been continuously occupied for three millennia. I visited homes which had been continuously occupied for four hundred years. I took my time walking around the village until my back began to play up and I stopped for a coffee in a pretty rudimentary wee gaff, empty apart from the old lady who looked like she'd been there continuously for the same four hundred years. Again I slipped up by ordering milky coffee and getting a glass of iced, glutinous stuff straight from the black lagoon. When will I ever learn? It was tasty enough, mind you.

One surprise was a framed picture of 'The Last Supper' featuring prominently in one of the ancient houses I visited. I'd assumed that the dominant religion - acknowledging Communism isn't one of them - would have been Confucianism, Taoism or Buddhism - but I checked and some 6% are Roman Catholic, a circumstance which predates the French colonial period.

Some of the homes were truly remarkable and looked both elegant and aged. No one seemed to mind being photographed (there was a 20,000 Dong entry fee to the village so I suppose they're all signed up). I did notice that discretely, some of the homes had satellite dishes and most had a sizeable liquid gas container strapped to their roof somewhere. I also noticed a dog. Perhaps only the second dog I'd seen since my arrival in Vietnam. Still haven't seen a cat! Delightfully, I've not seen a single mosquito either, an earlier fear! Nor have I seen a drunk, a beggar or a car crash...despite their idiosyncratic driving over here.

Perhaps because I was on my own and hadn't a deadline, I wandered off down alleys and onto paths that took me to the paddy fields that surrounded the village, in the process becoming completely lost. My navigational abilities deserted me due to my inclination to take what I now laughably call shortcuts. The village was much larger than I'd anticipated and was a maze of small vennels. In one such, the village school emptied for lunch and lots of ten year old kids cycled down towards me. Each of them smiled, waved, said, 'Hello' and were dressed exactly as would their counterparts in Glasgow; trainers, denim trousers and track suit top...but they all seemed happy, respectful and confident enough to address a stranger in his own language. I responded by saying, xin chào (hello) which amused them. My Saigon student tour guides Thanh and Tuan had earlier taught me a few words but I'm disinclined to attempt them largely because they explained that *cam on* (which I figured I could remember) means 'thank you' but when the two words are pronounced as one, *(camon)* it means 'shut up'!

I suppose I was most taken by the village square where a dozen elderly men sat drinking tea, playing a table-top game I didn't recognise, and laughing a lot. A very detailed sheet of paper pinned to a board next to them seemed to record the various fortunes of the gamers. Gambling is illegal in Vietnam but their nearby cousins, the Chinese, love a punt and it occurred to me that this might be an illegal record of gambling debts. They also gobbed like there was no tomorrow. The Vietnamese are lovely people but (also like the Chinese) they're never happier than when they're summoning up a few fluid ounces of gunge from somewhere near their left lung to bestow upon the pavement. They're big on the coughing too, usually as a preamble to the gobbing!

The younger men and women all worked the fields or busied themselves in one of the many small (and ancient) units that were to be found from time to time along the labyrinth of lanes within the village. I found it quaint that the adverts denoting the presence of the village mechanic were such as the now defunct *'Benzole'* hung from his wall. I figured that the only way I'd find the entry point to the village was to show this guy a photograph I'd taken of the gated entrance and gesture something to the effect that I was lost and would welcome directions. He looked at the photograph, nodded sagely and indicated his agreement when I suggested that perhaps I go left. However, he also nodded enthusiastically when I suggested I go right and when he agreed that I could also go down the hill towards the dead end from which I'd just emerged I decided that against all my inclinations, I'd better just retrace my steps. I found my way nae bother having taken this course of action.

Duong Lam is well worthy of its recognition by UNESCO.

Today was my last day in Hanoi so I rose early to pay a visit to Uncle Ho...*Ho Chi Minh*, President of North Vietnam (more accurately, Chairman of the Central Committee of the Communist Party of Vietnam) and the person who most embodied his peoples' struggle against the American invaders. I checked out of the hotel leaving my suitcase for later collection and joined the queues at the Mausoleum which is located in the grounds of the Presidential Palace in downtown Hanoi. It's a huge park and set within it is the palace which Ho eschewed preferring the more human-sized outbuildings where he lived and worked (his address was House No. 54 if you will). Actually, the accommodation, although Spartan compared with the palace would have been my own choice too. Very well appointed, all polished wood and airy rooms. At every turn, guards in pristine white uniforms, their polished gold belt buckle glistening; all red flashes and holstered pistol, stood at attention daring anyone to smile.

The queue moved more quickly than I'd been told to expect. The mood of those visiting when approaching the sarcophagus was reverential and would, I'm sure, have been enforced had there been any minor act of giddiness (there was none). March in pairs, hands at your side, not in your pockets, no talking. At the ticket office they'd confiscated my rucksack...no cameras... but had instructed me to carry my iPad and iPhone - so I took photographs unhindered except within the sarcophagus itself. The queue walked solemnly round three sides of a glass coffin and the embalmed Uncle Ho looked in remarkable nick, certainly presented better than Lenin was when I'd earlier said hello to him in Moscow. There it was all very dim lighting whereas Ho was lit up like a fairground attraction. It was obvious he's treated as a national hero and his history, while burnished rather, is used to present him as the saviour of the nation.

From there I took a taxi to the Red River having failed to find it during yesterday afternoon's walk...and little wonder. The taxi driver had to cross a busy motorway and proceed down a number of small streets which would have had me lost and confused. It occurred to me that few, if any, taxis would ever visit this poor part of town so I persuaded the driver to wait while I attempted to access the river. Unfortunately, as in Saigon, the riverfront is where the poor build their shantytown and I felt I was prying so took a couple of longer distance shots and retreated to the car. Even there, in perhaps the poorest part of the city, the second language was English. Despite Hanoi being the centre of French colonial power for many decades, the only remnants of their presence seems to be architectural.

Standing in the long queue to board the return plane to Saigon I found myself behind three American men, probably the same age as me. They'd seen service in Vietnam and had returned as part of a tour. Republicans all, they trotted out a litany of conservative bile about President Obama, "Prablam is, Henk, how you gonna put them worms beck in the kenn now he's given po' folks and Latinos health care?" Another…"Ah don't know if ah've a Democrat in ma entire family…'cept a nephew up in Ohio and he teaches class. Sonn'abitch never had to make a pay check in his laaf. Believes in texation!" And a third…"Thing about Danald Trump (The current front runner for the Republican nomination for President) is he don't take no money to run his campaign. He's so rich he just *gives*…the man just *gives*!" After each pronouncement, the other two would harrumph their approval.

I stood behind them hoping they might acknowledge me and allow me access to their world. I wouldn't have denounced them but would have enjoyed a debate, knowing in advance that none of us would have changed the mind of any other.

The queue was delayed rather when a family in front of us apparently attempted to move house via economy class so much baggage was enclosed in boxes and cases.

As the plane took to the sky, it was interesting looking down on the city whose plain was dotted by lush paddy-fields and pock-marked around them like freckles, small similarly sized villages, each of whose population tended the rice fields. It was also nice to see the sun again as we rose above the clouds.

As I over-flew Vietnam going south to Saigon and saw its mighty rivers, impenetrable forests, muscular mountains and began to appreciate just the sheer size and scale of the place, I shook my head at the earlier American notion that it could conquer such a land... and that's not taking account of its major resource; its people!

The taxi from the airport was crazy. The driver spoke not a word of English but presumed I was fluent in Vietnamese. He didn't understand the address I'd shown him but wove through the traffic, his head facing me in the rear in conversation, blethering away all the time. As soon as I saw a landmark I recognised, I asked him to pull over, pretending it was my destination and occasioning a further Vietnamese tirade which I interpreted as, 'They don't make maps the way they used to!'

Waving him off, I found my hotel then took a taxi to the *Cholon Binh Tay* Market in Chinatown. It took me completely by surprise as in any other town I'd been in - even New York and San Francisco where they make great play of the size of their Chinese quarter - it had been but a district of a much bigger city. Here in Saigon the place was huge. It must have been the approximate size of Beijing and took ages to drive through before arriving at the market itself. A cacophony of people shouting, cocks crowing, motorcycles revving, horns beeping and the noise of the sun splitting the trees greeted my exit from the taxi and I wandered around for ages in the sunshine without seeing another westerner; the scent of spices and of street-side cooking filling the air. I didn't know there were so many baseball caps for sale on the planet! I left after a while and went to the *Cua Tay* Market where I bought a selection of Chinese crockery. I was offered my selection of items (I'm determined to master *Pho Bo* when I return to Scotland) at a price of seven hundred and fifty thousand Dong. I then did all the 'too expensive, walking away' routine and in my best actor's voice suggested eventually that very reluctantly, I'd only be prepared to pay 400 thousand Dong (about £12 or $17). She closed the deal at 450 thousand Dong with a speed that suggested that I was still on the wrong end of a bargain.

Lunch at the Rex where I was surprised to be the only person eating in the fresh air until I realised that the sun was so intense it was almost boiling my accompanying Saigon beer. I finished quickly and took refuge in the nearby Intercontinental Hotel where air conditioning and a banana smoothie settled me. As I entered, my three American Republican friends from Hanoi Airport were standing in a huddle debating the big CNN Republican debate that had taken place earlier in the morning local time. Trump still won was the consensus.

One of the regrets I have in leaving Ho Chi Minh City (I'm advised that when referring to the city, you *say* the word Saigon but when writing, you scribe Ho Chi Minh City) is that I hadn't taken the opportunity to drive a car. I'd have been a natural as I drive pretty much the way the locals do here. I'd been put off by stories of police pulling tourists over and asking for bribes - and failure to pay would mean the inconvenience of the slammer for a while just to show who's boss. In the event I hardly saw a cop on the street and still felt that both Saigon and Hanoi were perhaps the two world cities in which I've felt most safe; Tromsø, and Reykjavik being up there as well.

My second reservation now that I'm an expert is that I'd have had no idea how to park a car. There's no space. Motorcycles can easily be hauled to the pavement but a car? If I'd hired a car I'd just have had to keep driving around all day or park in the countryside!

There are two things that Saigon (and Hanoi) people handle with one hundred percent obedience. First, they all wear a crash helmet on their motorcycle (if but a small cap-sized arrangement) and secondly, they all obey the traffic lights. In the urban heart of both cities, important intersections are monitored by police and to assist them, there's a timer attached to every set of lights which counts down from forty to zero. Everyone kind of goes along with it but I noticed that they all start to move off some five seconds before the red light goes to green and stop some five seconds after the light has turned red. They also turn right on red. However, there's a sweet spot between these timings and you're perfectly safe to cross if you presume it's a green light between those points and if you're not knocked down by a motorcyclist travelling against the flow of traffic on the wrong side of the road.

Most of the young women who ride scooters do so wearing a hoodie (pulled up over their head), gloves, a mask covering their mouth and nose, and full length denims. I presumed it was to beat the pollution. "Partly", I was told. "But they're hiding from the sun. They want to be white like Michael Jackson." Influence, even from beyond the grave...

The jockey-styled motorcycle helmets they wear are usually adorned with pretty meaningless slogans in English. *'Pretty Polly; Hello Kitty'*. My favourite...and the one I saw most commonly is, *'Catch Me If You Can.'* To be honest, the traffic crawls so slowly sometimes you'd just require to walk up and tap them on the shoulder!

So farewell, Saigon and Hanoi. Farewell, Vietnam. It's been lovely being in your company. Your citizens have been wonderful except the customs officer who tried to have me bribe him for a visa I didn't need, one nutcase taxi driver who wouldn't stop talking to me in Vietnamese and the taxi driver that tried to cheat me by charging three times the price. With those exceptions, Vietnam has been wonderful.

Don't Mention the War

Salzburg, Braunau am Inn, Berchtesgaden and Munich.

Somehow I'd always managed to avoid travelling through Germany and Austria; something I was keen to put right. I'd earlier been nominated to attend the prestigious Salzburg Seminar, in Austria. Professor Tom Cadbury, doyen of the Labour Party, academic and humourist himself a Salzburg Scholar in the 1960s, had nominated me for the programme which was designed, in rather grandiose fashion and *inter alia*, to school future national leaders. To be accepted for the programme, you had to be nominated by an earlier participant and I had been honoured to be held in sufficient regard by Professor Cadbury.

In essence, the Salzburg Seminar was designed to challenge current and future leaders to develop creative ideas for solving global problems. Legend has it that the Salzburg Seminar was born one winter day on a New York subway. It was there, early in 1947, that Clemens Heller, a graduate student at Harvard University, encountered a Miss Helene Thinig and explained to her that he was organising a summer seminar in Europe that would bring together students from across the distressed continent in an effort to renew intellectual dialogue among individuals whom fate had earlier decreed would be adversaries. In 1947, it seemed an audacious idea given other social and economic priorities.

With the final whistle just blown on the Second World War, many Europeans were still struggling for basic survival. Food and remunerative employment were in desperately short supply. Hundreds of thousands of displaced persons still wandered the streets and country roads of the continent. Germany and Austria lay in ruins.

At the same time, concerns were rising between the former Allies as relations soured between the United States and the Soviet Union. Earlier that year, at a lecture delivered on a trip to Missouri, Winston Churchill had warned that an 'iron curtain' had descended across the continent. The Salzburg Seminar was the result of these geo-political concerns. The Seminar's web site reports that 'In the years immediately following the Second World War, *Schloss Leopoldskron* became the residence of the three young men from Harvard University who set out to create a centre for intellectual exchange in the heart of Europe.

Five decades later, this vision has developed into one of Europe's foremost forums for the discussion of global issues, bringing together future leaders from around the world to meet and work with prominent individuals from virtually every realm of human endeavour: politics, economics, social and environmental concerns, the arts and academia'. "There are hundreds of seminars in the prestige-conscious firmament of *academe*," *Newsweek* magazine has written, "but few can rival the eminence of the Salzburg program."

The Seminar is based in *Leopoldskron* Palace which is situated on a spacious, private estate overlooking the Austrian alps and is located within walking distance of the picturesque city of Salzburg. Dating back to the 18th century, the palace has a colourful history that culminated in 1918 when it was acquired by impresario Max Reinhardt, who restored the palace to its original splendour. Since 1947, *Leopoldskron* Palace has been home to the Salzburg seminar.

My surprise delight upon arrival was to be told that the *Schloss* was the location for the famous Julie Andrews film, 'The Sound of Music'. Certainly there was no getting away from the fact of the absolute opulence of the buildings. The library in particular was a work of just astonishing delicacy and beauty. Whenever I could, I'd take to reading there merely because of the exhilarating beauty of the place. It was gorgeous – as were many others of the rooms.

It was great mixing with people from 57 different countries (typically, only one person from each country would be chosen). That said, there was an additional preponderance of Americans, largely because it was their programme – but they seemed genuinely interested in the work of those attending. However, I felt something of a fraud when I heard some of my new colleagues speak. There was one delegate from Africa who said to us that her ambition was to go home with a lap top computer with telephone internet access – the first in her country as they were so poor. We had a whip round. Another was a young trades-union leader from South America who was living in Amsterdam because if he went home to Peru, he'd be shot. A third was just the brightest person I've ever heard talk, a twenty-something woman from China whose English was superb. It was refreshing, challenging and hugely enjoyable meeting fifty or so charismatic, talkative, focused people from around the world. If and when they move into positions of importance and take up the next generation of leadership, we have nothing to fear. Mind you, as in every group, there were one or two right *eegits* but you have to hope that in later life they only run the civil service or something.

I became a celebrity from the first evening as we all had to stand in a huge circle and, with drink in hand, each offer a toast to our new colleagues in the language of our native land and interpret it if it wasn't in English (the core language of the programme). We had loads of toasts – all pretty anodyne, all wishing the other participants good health or a long life or something until it was my turn. I held my glass aloft and in my best Braveheart, Scottish accent, ventured, *"Poch ma hon"*.

The assembly dutifully repeated the toast and I permitted a beat before interpreting it for them as Gaelic for *"kiss my arse"*. The place erupted and from then on over the duration of the week I couldn't eat my lunch or dinner without some smiling Somalian or Canadian coming up to me and asking. "What was that toast again?"

The city of Salzburg was also a complete delight. It was almost Christmas and the Yuletide village markets they had assembled in the squares in and around the city were quite beautiful.

I'd promised myself I'd return to see more of Salzburg, Germany and Austria so I took the opportunity to hire a small car and travel the fifty miles to visit the building where Adolf Hitler was born in 1889. The apartment building at Salzburger Vorstadt 15, Braunau am Inn, Upper Austria, is a nondescript structure which, at the time of Hitler's birth, was but a modest guest house where his parents rented rooms. His father was a lowly customs officer and the German/Austria border was only yards from their accommodation. Young Adolph moved on aged three when his father was moved to new responsibilities in Passau and just as Adolph had visions of invading the next door playgroup.

I walked around the small, handsome township in a light snowfall and noticed a large stone set in the pavement outside Hitler's house. The stone had been brought from a quarry on the grounds of the former Mauthausen Concentration Camp, near *Linz*, Austria just before the centenary of Hitler's birth and has an inscription in German which reads (translated) *'For Peace, Freedom and Democracy. Never Again Fascism. Millions of Dead Remind Us.'*

I'd no real idea of the controversy surrounding the yellowing apartment or of the stone outside (the only visible indication that the building had any significance) but when I stood in a doorway opposite and began to take some photographs I was accosted by an elderly man who rebuked me in German, unintelligible to my ears. Surprised, I gestured apology for an offence of which I was unaware and put my camera away as he signalled I should do. As we parted company, a traffic warden spoke with me in English (could a Glaswegian traffic warden converse with visitors in German?) and explained that Herr Whateverhisname was a Communist whose parents had suffered during the war and who assumed that everyone who showed interest in the building was a neo-Nazi. I explained that I held views that were far removed from those beliefs and took shelter from the now heavier snowstorm in a nearby café before heading back to Salzburg.

Refreshed, I set off next day to visit the Eagle's Nest, Hitler's mountain retreat high atop the Bavarian Alps. The journey south was only about twenty miles but the snow had fallen heavily overnight and travelling was slow along the two-lane country road. I arrived in the small rural township of Berchtesgaden which is situated in high alpine countryside surrounded by mountains rising to more than 6,000 feet and which consists largely of a ribbon development along the Saalach River. It was very cold and the snow lay deep but the river hadn't iced over, allowing the clear water to run green as it burbled and crashed on to rocks, en route to Salzburg and onwards to the Salzach River.

Adolf Hitler had holidayed in the Berchtesgaden area since the 1920s and had purchased a home in the mountainous Obersalzberg above the town on the flank of the Hoher Göll. He'd begun extensive renovations on his Berghof during his rise in the Nazi Party, inviting senior Nazis such as Hermann Göring, Joseph Goebbels, and Albert Speer for political discussion. As he rose to further power, those around him began to purchase and requisition land in the *Obersalzberg* and in 1937, Martin Bormann acquired the Eagle's Nest as a 50th birthday gift for Hitler. Funded by the Nazi Party, it was completed in just over a year.

The Eagle's Nest or *Kehlsteinhaus* as the Germans would have it, is situated on a ridge atop the Kehlstein, a 6,000 ft. sub-peak of the Hoher Göll rising above Berchtesgaden below. My attempts to reach the peak were frustrated by ever-deepening snow lying on hairpin bends and was abandoned altogether when the authorities closed the road and directed me instead to the nearby *Dokumentation Obersalzberg*, a museum dedicated to the study of National Socialism under Hitler. The original buildings were demolished by the Allies after the war so as not to leave anything that might be used as a location for future neo-Nazi pilgrims. Now a modern building, the centre nevertheless makes use of the honeycomb labyrinth of tunnels which provided fortification for the Nazi high command during the war.

The exhibits were explained only in German which is excusable given the purpose of the centre being to encourage debate among German nationals on the realities of the Nazi regime. However, headphones were available and the commentary was perfectly satisfactory. I tell you this, though; these guys thought big. The tunnels were huge and endless. A nuclear bomb couldn't have penetrated the defences the Nazis built into the side of the mountain.

The German appetite to deal with the consequences and implications of the behaviours of National Socialism before, during and in the immediate aftermath of World War Two is commendable. They appear to have taken the view that their behaviour had to be explicable if unforgivable and that addressing it and challenging it head on so it is not repeated is preferable to having it be the elephant in the room. I was reminded of a trip I'd made as lead officer some years earlier prior to giving evidence on employment in shipbuilding on the Clyde to the House of Commons Scottish Affairs Committee. I'd been sent to East Germany, Hamburg and Berlin at the their behest to assess whether Germany was surreptitiously providing financial support to its shipbuilding industry against European rules as we figured that there was no way they could build and launch ships at the costs they advertised without breaching European missives on subsidy. I was ushered in to the large boardroom of the *Blohm* and *Voss* shipyard in Hamburg. German shipbuilding officials sat opposite with their arms folded denying that any such infraction of the rules had occurred. "But the *Greeks*," they intoned, shaking their heads, suggesting that their high standards of rectitude weren't being matched by their European neighbours in the south.

I was shown round their manufacturing sites and was impressed by their productivity. A single man was responsible for cutting an enormous plate of two inch thick steel the approximate size of a football pitch. As he set it up to be cut using his computer, he pursed his lips, less than satisfied with what he was being told on the screen. Taking a large hammer, he walked out to the edge of this vast platform and hit it hard twice. Content, he returned and pushed a button whereby the lasers went to work and reduced the metal to perfectly sized and proportioned (one would assume) contours.

Following the conclusion of the meeting, I noticed a collection of model ships outside their Boardroom.

"Excellent", I observed.

"Every time ve laanch a zhip zince the yaaad vas fauhmed ve have made a small vezzhion zat ve put on zhow in zees glass cases."

"Excellent", I observed.

Our host then spoke with pride at the total tonnage, the improvements in productivity and the investments in the yards as we walked towards the exit and our car which was waiting to take us to the Aker MTW yards in East Germany.

"Excellent", I observed.

As the party turned left, something drew me to the right hand corridor. I saw that round the corner the show-case continued, but instead of a variety of ships it was an endless encased collection of model submarines – row after row, floor to ceiling - the sum total of the yard's U-boat output during the Second World War.

Our host noticed my discovery.

"Jah... ve alzo uzed to build zubmarines; ze U-boat", he coughed before ushering me out and into the car.

"Excellent", I replied. There was no way they intended airbrushing that important part of their maritime history from the record books. Nor should they.

However, sated by the German museum of their war experience next to the Eagle's nest and slightly worried lest I had to spend the night in the museum, I travelled down the mountain a couple of miles to Koenigsee, a small village on an Alpine lake used for outdoor recreation by Hitler who went boating on the lake. Apparently, Eva Braun liked to sunbathe on its shores. It reminded me of many Highland villages in Scotland with a host of timber-clad shops all trying to sell the same type of duff souvenirs. It was very beautiful though but I didn't want to stay long as I was keen to go down a salt mine back in Berchtesgaden.

I found the complex just outside the town but hadn't been prepared for the concomitant health and safety hassle which ensued immediately I'd bought my ticket. As an inveterate non-joiner, I was disappointed to be issued with a boiler suit and made to join a party of some twenty people who were to be escorted throughout the tour through the salt mine. I understood as soon as we left, mind you as it was quite the most dangerous tour of its kind one could ever imagine...and I could appreciate the earlier focus on health and safety. The group of twenty sat astride a small train akin to a very rich child's toy which proceeded to delve into the bowels of the mountain. It took a while to reach middle earth via a lengthy illuminated tunnel but we arrived at a terminus and everyone disembarked only to find that a second train was necessary but that it could only be reached by sliding down a precipitous wooden chute far beyond anything that has been envisaged by Disney. It was enormous and was contrived of two polished parallel wooden beams that descended forever to hidden depths. No one was particularly keen to be a member of the first foursome to plummet into the gloom but I was selected I suspect on the basis that I didn't appear to have dependents with me and my death could therefore be more easily be covered up.

As with many Disney experiences, an automatic photograph is taken of people just at the most terrifying part of the journey; in our case, to the centre of the earth. While I attempted a relaxed insouciance, my photographed face tells a different story - as did that of each of the other three guinea pigs who accompanied me on the descent to what we clearly assumed was certain death. We sped downwards for perhaps twenty seconds - an eternity when you can't see the terminal point of the drop - before levelling out. I wanted to drop to my knees and kiss the salty earth in grateful thanks for my survival but my motor functions were still scrambled and it was all I could do to remove myself from the chute as the next foursome accelerated towards me.

A long walk through the tunnels, a second train ride and a second chute (not quite as terrifying this time) took the party to a beautifully illuminated underground salt lake which we crossed in a barge. It was sublime. A lengthy train ride saw us back safely to the surface.

I drove back slowly to Schloss Leopoldskron where I'd taken supplementary bed and breakfast in the small monk-like cell which was as basic as it was comfortable.

The following morning I drove north and crossed the border into Germany where I pitched up in Munch prior to flying home. Being something of a football aficionado I wanted to tour the stadium of Bayern Munich which is situated conveniently close to the airport. Having paid my nine Euros fee, I joined a group of five (all males) and was shown round the internal doings. I've visited many stadia and given their architectural requirement to follow the contours of a soccer pitch, they inevitably have long corridors and glazed walls to permit a view of the pitch. Well, Bayern's stadium was no different. What was different was the shell of the 75,000 capacity Allianz stadium which was constructed using ethylene tetrafluoroethylene, fluorine-based plastic sheeting mounded into almost 3,000 interconnected rhomboidal inflated panels incorporating over 300,000 LED lights. Fitted by a team of Austrian mountaineers, the stadium glows in a full colour-changing exterior. It's the biggest membrane shell in the world and looks simply glorious at night. The guide also told me how much it costs to illuminate the stadium for an evening's football. I can't remember how much it was in Euros but in Scotland we'd express it as 'shitepence'!

Also unusual, if perhaps Teutonically so, was the home team's dressing room. Above each changing space were the usual hooks and shelving that permitted tidiness. However, atop all of that was a larger than life framed photograph of the player accompanied by large lettering spelling out his surname. In this fashion, players like Bastian Schweinsteiger, Thomas Müller and Xabi Alonso couldn't fail to find the space in which they were to prepare for the match. Our guide spoke both in German and English. "Of cause, if zay are injured or not in ze skvad zer photograph is removed immediately." He noticed my eyebrows rise and explained. "Iz inzentive to get vell zoon!"

I sat in the departure lounge awaiting my return flight to Heathrow thence to Glasgow. As I sipped at a coffee I was joined by a passenger who arrived somewhat unsteadily on his feet. His shirt tail protruded from the rear of his trousers. He swayed slightly and collapsed rather than sat in the seat opposite. A disinterested observer might have assumed the man was drunk!

Eyes closed, he began a conversation with a fellow passenger and I appreciated instantly by his accent, slurred as it was, that he was a fellow Glaswegian. Unfortunately his victim only spoke German and English and could do little more than smile haplessly.

I intervened and answered his questions about whether he was at the correct stance; was he on time, was the bar open? In short order he seemed satisfied, closed his eyes and after a while, began to sing quietly in a way I've witnessed many times before and since.

Although I couldn't attest that it is a technique completely unique to Glaswegians, it is certainly not uncommon to those who live in that fine city. His song of choice was made popular on this side of the Atlantic by Cilla Black; 'I Can Sing A Rainbow' but on this occasion was accompanied by tightly closed eyes and by small finger gestures clearly designed to conduct the imaginary orchestra that supported his version of the song. Certain of the higher notes weren't even attempted; merely signalled by an open mouth and agonised facial contortions while the note played out inside his head.

He was blessed with a speech characteristic more normally associated with Sean Connery and so his lyric became;

'*Red and yellow, pink and green*
Purple and orange and blue
At this point he departed from the carefully constructed rainbow-praising lyrics of Arthur Hamilton as he approached the hook...
'*I can shing a reindeer, shing a reindeer,*
You can shing one tooooo...'

Well, it *was* almost Christmas. And I was going home.

Our Celtic Cousins

Dublin, Waterford, Arvagh, Wexford and Kilkenny

Christmas having been survived, it was time once again to travel. But first, my penis!

The old penis is a grand thing; handy for picnics. I can't speak for women but for men on those occasions when you have a *just-have-to-go-bladder-busting* situation, it's an easier matter altogether just to walk behind a bush and return minutes later, nonchalantly pulling up a zip, all notions of urgency banished. Well, it transpired that I had to put this handy arrangement into practice once when in Dublin.

My friend John and I were touring Ireland and were over in that fine city visiting friends and taking in a few of Ireland's other wonderful cities and towns in doing so. That evening, as an *aperitif*, we'd had three pints of the best Guinness imaginable in the Palace Bar in Fleet Street; one of my top six bars in the world (the others being Glasgow's Pot Still, McSorley's Old Ale House in New York's East Village, Dublin's O'Donoghue's pub, the Glassford Inn in Glassford of all places and the Rex Hotel Rooftop Bar in Ho Chi Minh City). (If I were ever offered the choice of *seven*, I'd venture the Postgate in Egton Bridge in the Yorkshire Dales on the basis that the warm floral micturition that passes for English beer is avoided). In the afternoon the Palace Bar can be a haven of peace and quiet and of an evening it becomes a more boisterous affair as Dublin comes out to drink. It's a magnificent wonder in polished wood, leather chairs, stained glass and attentive bar-keeping. Anyway, back to my penis.

We'd left Fleet Street and were making our way to O'Donoghue's pub in Merrion Row, to drink further Guinness and listen to the Irish traditional music played there each evening by talented musicians in return, I gathered from some fellow imbibers, for free beer although this was contested by others. Halfway there, we passed along a long row of terraced Victorian properties. My bladder chose *this* moment to tell me that if I didn't attend its needs instantly, I'd need to visit the cobblers the following morning to have them dry out the cheap leather compound from which my shoes were made. Before me stretched unremitting terraced properties. But wait...that shadow, those lights....twenty yards away a lane, a *dark* lane. Could it be? A bistro affair sat incongruously midst the upper-class residential properties whose side lane offered a haven of unilluminated invisibility. Apologising to John, I hurriedly made ground and issued forth; the steam emanating from my ears noticeably diminishing. Halfway through, just as my bladder decided that all was in the process of remedy, a female voice as if from heaven spoke to me through a speaker cunningly affixed to the wall above and to my side.

"Well, you're putin' on quite a show for the six guests we have here lookin' at the images from our security cameras. The three women are definitely not impressed and the three men are laughing at your tiny pisser. Now would you ever put that away and never darken our premises ever again?"

Helplessly I continued, hoping my face would reveal to their camera how hapless I felt. As Magnus Magnusson used to say, "I've started, so I'll finish". I had no way of apologising other than entering the premises, seeking out the young lady (she sounded young...not *that* young)...saying sorry and asking to wash my hands. I rejoined John in the street, who said he now *also* needed to relieve himself. 'Was it okay down there?"

The mischievous part of me wanted to tell him to wire in but I thought of the three unimpressed women and decided against on the basis that he might return telling me that he'd just received a round of applause; apparently from heaven.

We found O'Donoghue's and had a great evening listening to music of the highest standard. The pub...it's a *pub*, not a bar...has spread out over the years and now has a number of different areas where drink can be bought and consumed but there's really only one place to both hear and watch the music and after edging our way forward over a period of about an hour as people left or went to buy another pint, we found ourselves front and centre, drinks in hand, bladders at rest. John and I, amateur musicians both, could appreciate the dexterity with which these boys played. They were gifted in a way that would command big ticket prices in any concert hall but were content to bang away for the price of a pint. Wonderful.

Alcohol has always been associated with Dublin but recently its fame as a drinking town has been compromised rather as hen parties, stag parties and the like turn up, head for the Temple Bar neighbourhood on the River Liffey, throw short drinks down their throat and become uproariously drunk in minutes. Now let me tell you. That's not drinking. Where Dublin excels is in the patient way alcohol gradually infuses the conversation and transmogrifies it into *the craic*; lively and humorous conversational banter. It's almost a metaphor for the way Guinness is poured (the double pour where it's allowed slowly to settle before being topped up to its full measure.)

I love the word *craic*. I even opportunistically added an 'Iain' to my son Conor's full name unknown to my wife, Jean who'd asked that both Robert and Armour be his middle names, he's now Conor, Robert, Armour *Iain*, Culley; *craic*. I've told him that if he ever plays football for Brazil, he can wear his *sobriquet* on his back with pride.

But Dublin more than copes with the younger assault on its drinking culture. Turn a corner anywhere in the city and you'll find another typically Irish pub; some busy, some less so but all devoted to a good pint and decent chat.

John and I had driven down from Belfast where we'd sailed from Cairnryan by ferry. An evening spent in Dublin was, as mentioned, memorable and next morning we ventured up to Glasnevin Cemetery where many of Ireland's poets, authors, politicians and revolutionaries are buried. I'd wanted to find the grave of Brendan Behan; a man of literature as well as a member of the IRA. He took his writing passionately. He took his politics seriously. Did I mention he also took a drink? Well, he did...enthusiastically, and it killed him. Eamon de Valera was another gravestone I sought as I was writing a book ('*The Patriot Game*', available on-line and from all good bookshops) in which he was a central character. Many of the rebels who fought against the forces of the crown in 1916 were buried there and I fancy I bored John somewhat as I'd yelp a name and run off to see the grave of another Irish hero of the Easter Rising much in the way young people today push aside adults to see the inscribed star of Jennifer Aniston on the Hollywood Walk of Fame in Los Angeles.

When first Glasnevin first opened its depths to the deceased of Dublin, the first person to be buried was an eleven year old boy called Michael Carey who had died of an illness, probably tuberculosis, in 1832. Only the family priest and the child's father attended as in those days it was thought too traumatising for mere women to attend. Six years later, the cemetery was standing room only and new land had to be purchased. Today, Glasnevin stretches over two hundred acres and accommodates more dead people than are actually alive in the city of Dublin as a consequence, in some measure of there being cholera pits dotted around the graveyard due to a monstrous outbreak in Dublin in 1849. The pits were created to attempt to contain the disease but underground streams flowed beneath the cemetery and transmitted the disease to a wider population. Beware the law of unintended consequences. Still, it's an impressive and interesting graveyard. I took a photograph of the lift in the visitor centre which showed floors one through four going up but without irony, labels the basement, 'City of the Dead', where I believe resources exist for visitors to learn about the people buried at Glasnevin Cemetery who have had a positive impact on society through politics art, literature, music or engineering.

A statue of Brendan Behan sits on a bench feeding the ducks next to the Royal Canal but, perhaps because of the over-indulgences of the previous evening, we sought it out but gave up when we couldn't find it immediately. Back into Dublin city we met up with our friends Tadhg, Mary and their lovely daughter Anna in a tourist bar on the River Liffey where we'd been promised I'd be able to watch the afternoon's Manchester United match against Liverpool. John and I had had an eloquent sufficiency from the previous evening and were restrained but Tadhg and Mary were throwing it back - Mary matching Tadhg Guinness for Guinness. We caught up on a lot of family and political developments knowing that we'd see them again in a few days down on their farm in Fieries near Killarney. After the match we went on to sink a few further beers in O'Shea's pub on the River Liffey, a pub Tadhg often visits as it's a gathering place for his fellow County Kerry men when they're up in the capital. The live music performed by traditional Irish musicians in O'Shea's was simply magnificent. I avoided all conversation just to listen to them playing jigs and reels. Astonishing musicality.

Wexford was next on our list and the following morning we drove carefully south from Dublin as a ferocious rainstorm drove small bullet holes into the mud at the side of the road so strong was the downpour. As we approached the town of Wexford it was evident as we peered through the windscreen, that traffic was appreciably heavier. The car's wipers were now a blur as they tried to rid the windscreen of rainwater and it was further evident from road signage and the plenitude of fedora hats that a race meet was taking place. Ireland is a great place for the horse racing. Anywhere else the authorities would have abandoned the race meet due to the outrageous weather but they're made of sterner stuff in Ireland. We parked at the side of the road and raced for our lives to the turnstiles which creaked and clanked slowly before permitting us drenched into the course.

As a child I remember James Cagney films where he'd exit an old Auburn 1250 V12 Salon Cabriolet car or some such in the middle of a country road at night in order to shoot some G-men and even to my young eyes, it was clear that the movie-rain that descended on the carnage was so impenetrably-sheeted a deluge that it must be being issued from a fireman's hose off-screen. Well, there were no firemen around but the movie-rain was just as dense in Wexford.

We took urgent refuge in the sole racecourse lounge bar which was stuffed jam-full of people seeking shelter as were we. The course itself was, let's say, *bijou*; tight bends and short straights.

Six bookies had stances outside in the rain and within the bar the Tote was doing great business merely by providing an opportunity for people to bet without having to brave the storm outside. Just as we'd ordered and secured a couple of pints, the electricity failed, plunging the bar into darkness but somehow leaving only the large television screen operational. The bar couldn't open its tills so no more drink was forthcoming and the Tote could no longer take bets. Outside, the electronic screens of the six bookies, still wondrously connected to electricity, continued to show horses and odds to the fury of a table of elderly gentlemen seated near us who insisted that the power had been cut deliberately.

"It was the boys in the ring that done it", shouted the auld guy next to me in frustration, clearly of the view that skulduggery was afoot. "It was the boys in the ring that done it"; the absence of strong drink clearly contributing to his bad temper. Slowly the bar emptied of the more determined gamblers as punters made their way outside through the deluge to the only bookies then able to accept their bets. We stayed.

The inside windows of the lounge bar were so coated in dripping condensation that those closest spent much time clutching the cuff of their sleeved garment and wiping the glass only to see it cloud over within moments thereby providing spectators with only momentary glimpses of the progress of the race. They proved sufficiently clear, however for us to see the two horses we'd backed flounder in mud more reminiscent of the Somme and come in pechin' (auld Scots; 'breathing heavily'), some distance behind the leader. We cut our losses and headed for Ireland's fifth city, the seaport of Waterford.

The sky had somehow managed to darken yet further as we arrived and we took time to wander along the banks of the River Suir close to Waterford Harbour during an interlude in the deluge before a recurrence forced us indoors and into the cavernous House of Waterford Crystal which claims to hold in its vaults, the largest collection of Waterford Crystal in the world; a fact that surprised me not given that we were in Waterford and that they specialised in crystal. That said, the crystal was displayed very well, piercing lighting picking out every glittering edge and cut. Trophies, vases, decanters, even earrings and rings blinded us with their sparkle and spangle.

Previously an important shipbuilding port, Waterford produced an impressive fleet of iron steamships in the middle of the nineteenth century as well as five trans-Atlantic passenger liners. The yards were owned by the Malcomson family which began its climb to commercial success by chartering steamers, later becoming owners themselves. Eventually, over a period of some fifteen years in the 1850s and 60s, they built and operated the largest fleet of iron steamers in the world, including five trans-Atlantic passenger liners. The Harbour has been gentrified some and reminded me slightly of the shipyards of the Clyde which at one time, around 1900, produced a fifth of the world's ships - some 30,000 in all... that's thirty *thousand* ships - employing tens of thousands of workers in the process, not counting those employed in associated industries such as steel manufacturing. I remember in a previous life when I had some small measure of responsibility for the redevelopment of the banks of the River Clyde reflecting that there must have been a point when shipyard workers looked skywards at aeroplanes carrying goods and passengers to points north, south, east and west of the globe, and pondered the future of shipbuilding, their communities and their families. So must it have been in Waterford, if on a smaller scale.

Kilkenny called and at dusk we pulled in to a car park at McDonagh Railway Station across the road from tonight's accommodation; rooms above JR's pub in John Street Upper. JR's looked like a great hostelry but we persuaded ourselves that other establishments might prove more interesting so we stepped out into an unseasonably warm and balmy evening - and found ourselves in a street in which every property seemed to be occupied by a public house...and not just any public house. They each seemed to have character, age and ambiance. We walked the length of John Street - both Upper and Lower, over the River Nore, along High Street and onto Parliament Street before deciding we'd better actually sample a few of Kilkenny's bars and eat something before returning to JR's. We stepped first into Ó Riada's Bar in Parliament Street and found ourselves in the most run-down, tawdry bar, whose shabby and shoogly furnishings were matched by several run-down, tawdry, shabby and shoogly customers. That said, they each had a glass in their hand and were having animated and inclusive conversations about the affairs of the day. There was a lot of smiling and laughing going on and John and I found ourselves welcomed by attentive bar staff and acknowledged by drinkers who all appeared to know one another and spotting two strangers in their pub, toasted us silently; an unspoken invitation to engage with them in conversation should we be pleased so to do.

I remembered being in a pub in Crossmaglen on the border between Northern Ireland and the Republic with our friends Tadhg and his wife Mary some years earlier during what were referred to as 'The Troubles' when that small community was one of the most dangerous places in the Western Hemisphere. Ordering a round of beers occasioned a customer peeling off from another group and standing near us just listening to our conversation before determining to his satisfaction that we could be allowed to finish our beer without intervention. It was a similar atmosphere to the one we experienced in Kilkenny but it was very evident that in Crossmaglen we weren't to be afforded the same friendly welcome; perhaps unsurprisingly given the mistrust and hatred that persisted then. There, we were merely tolerated. However, one *Ó Riada's* beer was sufficient as we wanted to sample a few of the delightful pubs that lined each side of the road. Almost next door to *Ó Riada's* was Cleere's, another ancient establishment within which soft-spoken conversations were taking place and pints of plain were sipped. Very civilised but I was keen to have a look at Kyteler's Inn where alcohol has been served since 1324. They also advertised live music.

We bumped into a large chap who was squeezing past us on the narrow pavement and as we each offered a polite apology, I thought I heard a Glasgow accent.

"You don't sound like a local," I ventured.

"You guys from Glasgow?" he smiled.

"Yeah. Just trying out your pubs for size and looking for some grub."

We shook hands and introduced ourselves to Pat from Govanhill in Glasgow who'd found himself working as a chef in Kilkenny. "Long story," he responded as we quizzed him about how he'd ended up in Kilkenny.

John intervened, seeking guidance. "Paris Texas was recommended."

"Nah. Head chef just left. The new guy is rubbish. He'll poison you! Try Kyteler's."

We chatted further then set off for Kyteler's. Initially impressed, we soon realised that the internal fittings were Irish mock, the music was Irish Rover tourist music and the food was Irish stew basic. We ate and left feeling ever so slightly cheated. They've been serving food and drink for six hundred and ninety-three years and have been reduced to pretty low standard *ersatz* Irish hokum.

Tynan's Bar on the river, however was much more authentic and we joined another crowd of locals who were taking the time to converse over a pint. Now tiring rather, we agreed on one more pub stop where we'd noticed music being advertised along with the promise of a selection of over two hundred Irish whiskeys; The Dylan Whiskey Bar in John Street Lower (so called just because the owner liked Bob Dylan...and whiskey). I'd earlier determined to attempt some Irish whiskey. I'd tried some twenty years earlier and the experience had put me off but decided to get back on the horse. I had a go of Tullamore Dew and Pot Still Irish Whiskey in Dylan's and renewed my vow not to trouble my taste buds for a further twenty years. I'll stick to Speyside malts from now on.

We were instructed in the subtleties of Irish whiskey by an enthusiastic, comely and knowledgeable young lady bartender called Ann who blethered away to us while multi-tasking and serving other customers, cleaning windows and collecting spent glasses. Bar-tending in Ireland appears to be a respected profession. You undertake an apprenticeship before you're let loose on an unsuspecting public. In Scotland I'm more used to students or semi-disinterested staff pulling a pint. Over in Ireland, apprenticeship courses focus upon customer service, cocktails techniques, choosing glassware, draught beer and cellar management, changing kegs, rotating stock and pouring the perfect pint as well as learning the history of every major category of spirits and the methods behind their production. It shows. Everyone who saw to our needs was extremely civil, brisk and efficient.

This being the last leg of our pub-crawl we eased back on the accelerator and sat back to enjoy the advertised band. They took the stage half an hour late muttering to their small audience about a previous engagement over-running although I'd overheard the girl singer, Gill explain to the bar manager that the baby-sitter had been late. There were three of them; a married couple, Phil and Gill Coulter and Evan Grace from the much travelled and successful band *Newfoundland*. Their tardiness annoyed me. They took an eternity to tune up. This further irritated me. They 'one, twoed' into each of the three microphones for ages. This had me narrowing my eyes. Then they started playing (without announcing themselves) and instantly everything was forgiven and forgotten. The quality of the harmonies, the dexterous guitar work, the finger-blurring banjo work on some jigs and reels had both John and I cheering them to the low-slung rafters. Phil's guitar work was sublime. He looked

Scottish, some of his songs were Scottish and his accent suggested Scotland but he had a wide smile which displayed a bright set of white teeth so he was evidently from other parts. Turned out he was from County Antrim in Ireland.

Phil played some standards involving hugely complex guitar riffs by Scottish guitar renegade John Martyn and out-Martyned him. They launched into some jigs and reels more associated with the Chieftains and out-Chieftained them. They were superb and could have held the stage of any concert hall in the world but tonight they were playing for a bar-room of some twenty or so semi-disinterested souls in Kilkenny. We were privileged.

Kilkenny was just a fabulous wee town. Whoever's looking after its commercial interests is doing a grand job. We arrived just as a week-long food festival was ending. The place is famous for its annual comedy festival. But it also hosts the Irish Conker Championships, a European Film Festival, Yulefest, Tradfest, the St. Patrick's Festival, The Smithwick Kilkenny Roots Festival and a Christmas Tree festival. But what took my attention was a large poster advertising 'The World's First Festival of Economics and Comedy!' Economic legends such as Yanis Varoufakis, the Greek economist, academic and politician, who served as the Greek Minister of Finance during his country's spat with the European Union shared a billing with Irish comedian Ardal O'Hanlon. Completely delicious...and they say economics is 'the dismal science!'

Next morning we rose and set off towards Dublin in order to visit Glencullen's famous Johnny Fox's pub.

Situated on top of the Dublin Mountains, Johnnie Fox's is one of Ireland's oldest and most famous traditional Irish pubs, billing itself as the highest pub in the country. I've been there on a number of occasions and found myself lost on each visit, the myriad narrow country lanes defeating me every time.

Sawdust and wood chips on the floor of the pub, antiquated wood panelling, aged artefacts on its walls and photographs depicting famous visitors over the years provided a slightly contrived but not unpleasant character and when coupled with a fine glass of Guinness, provided me with a diverting couple of hours as the rain continued to pour outside. John had drawn the short straw and was driving afterwards, thereby confining his intake to one pint but I was able to enjoy the pub as it was meant to be enjoyed.

We set off north-west to Galway, essentially crossing the length of Ireland from the south east to north-west. En route, I was tempted to make a slight diversion to return to Arvagh in County Cavan where I'd journeyed some years previously.

Aged sixteen, my mother-in-law Anne left the village of Arvagh and went off on her own to find work, telling her father untruthfully that she'd already found employment in Dublin. Now in retirement, Anne had decided to visit her old village almost half a century after she left even though no one she knew lived there anymore. She left as Miss Moran and returned as Mrs Pollock. We had driven from Glasgow and crossed over on the ferry to Larne in Northern Ireland staying overnight in Belfast before travelling down unhurriedly into County Cavan in the Republic the next day.

A bright and sunny day bode well and our entry to Arvagh was complicated only because we couldn't find it on our electronic map and the satellite navigation device wouldn't recognise the place of Anne's birth; so we had to follow the Irish road signs.

Anne steadfastly refused to acknowledge the hinterland as we approached the village; little wonder as the narrow road was heavily tree-lined with great oaks and other evergreens whose spreading branches above enveloped the car, denying any prospect of a view more than a few feet either side. It was as if we were entering the homestead through a leafy tunnel. Forty-five years previously when Anne left, these unkempt monsters would have been but saplings.

We'd journeyed the thirteen kilometres from the county town, Cavan and apart from an occasional farmhouse, had hardly seen signs of human habitation when the trees parted and there to welcome Anne back to her village was a very modern looking Volkswagen garage selling very stylish Volkswagens; not the tractors and trailer parts I'd have expected.

Lying on the borders of Longford and Leitrim, Arvagh is well known as the town where the three provinces of Ulster, Leinster and Connaught meet. It had been a small township; a village, when Anne had left in1955 and so it remained. Perhaps a hundred houses or so, mostly terraced bordered the main street which wandered off into a few short lanes at right angles to the only thoroughfare. Two churches bookended each end of the town and Arvagh National Primary School marked the start of Main Street. *Bijou* it may have been but there was a butcher's, a chemist's, two newsagents', a post office, a fishing shop, a bank, a few shops selling trinkets and knick-knacks and just outside the village, a bakery. Interestingly, above some shops was pronounced, 'Cully's Bakery', 'Cully's Newsagents', Cully's Bakery' and behind the garage, Cully's GAA Football Stadium'. There were also eleven pubs; The Goalpost, Benny's Pub, Hughie's Pub, the Market Bar, Nicholas O'Hara, Thomas Brady, (who interestingly, touted for business both as a publican and a funeral director) JW's Tavern, the Eagle Bar, Paddy's off-licence, Patrick Murtagh's and the Breffni Arms. None admitted their proprietor as Cully.

The terraced houses in Porters Row, which we'd expected to be ruined, had all been modernised; all except number two in which Anne had grown up. Now dilapidated it stood like a gap-toothed smile in the eight-house unpaved street, shored up by scaffolding lest it give way to nature and pulled down the abutting households. Alone it had no roof and had been left to the elements.

I fell to wondering what Arvagh existed to do. I well understand those communities that put down roots to earn a living from the sea or to support a pit. Years ago Arvagh would have housed farm-hands I'd wager, having been settled by Scottish planters in the seventeenth century and the fifty lakes and streams surrounding the village ensures that it remains an important centre in Ireland for game fishing but now I could see no employment in the place other than a few service jobs, a little retail or teaching, Nor was there evidence of a pool of people dependent upon state benefit of one kind or another although I'd suspect that the population was on the elderly side. Arvagh seemed a proud wee township; modest and independent, unspoilt and uncomplicated.

After dinner I walked the main street in the still air, the sweet smell of peat testifying to family fires warming households against the drizzle of fine rain that settled quietly on the village; a *haar* that I'd come to understand back in Scotland would drench the unaware in a moment so fine was the mist.

I noticed a pub set back from the road in Pound Street; Patrick Murtagh's Bar. I went in and joined the two men seated at the bar. Neither spoke. Unusually, (at least in an urban context) there was no music, no television. Just the ticking of a grandfather clock in the corner. After a minute had passed and no barman having appeared, one of the men rose from his bar-stool and asked me my pleasure. He poured me a pint and returned to his seat and his paper while I moved over to a chair beside the warming peat fire to read my book. After some ten minutes of silence, a conversation ensued between the twosome regarding the local football news during which we were joined by a fourth man. It became apparent that the barman was also the owner and his practice was to serve his customers as was required before settling among them to engage as an equal in the *craic*.

Later on he left to attend to something in another room and another man entered, hailing the other two and throwing me a nod in the corner. Laughing with his friends, he walked behind the bar and poured himself a Guinness leaving it standing, one fifth from full until our barman returned and completed the pint some minutes later. There was an informality and sense of friendship that was almost palpable in the bar. Later yet perhaps another half dozen people had joined the company (only one of whom was a woman) and all were welcomed and embraced in the collective conversation.

Too many years as an urbanite had schooled me in a more frenetic, aggressive bar-room culture where everyone has to fight for their space in the chat. The decibel count is higher partly to compete with the football on the television or the Rolling Stones on the jukebox. Jokes and witticisms would spill out and no one was spared a disparaging comment where it was felt it would produce a laugh, no matter how unkind. Here, everyone was listened to and the next contribution derived from the one before. Humour was self-deprecating and the topics were small. The war in Afghanistan, the financial crisis enveloping the world and the prospect of a 'flu pandemic were all ignored. Instead there was a discussion on whether the pitcher of beer at the previous weekend's fair held two or three pints...or two or three litres. Mrs Kelly, it can be revealed, is recovering well from her sprained ankle and the drain at the bottom of the street shows signs of further blockage – which doesn't auger well for the winter rains. The unforced conversation ebbed and flowed easily and silences were allowed to linger while people contemplated their pints and absorbed the import of the previous comment.

Some years ago, a pal, Danny Brennan, found himself a job writing speeches in Brussels for Irish *Teachta Dála*, Pádraig Flynn, a Commissioner in the European Parliament. Danny proclaimed himself to have mastered speech-writing for Flynn as he'd discovered that he would say anything he wrote without change... other than always to score out the word 'people' (which Danny would scatter liberally about the speech) and introduce instead the term, '*ordinary* people'; every time.

It struck me that Patrick Murtagh's bar that night was the meeting place for '*ordinary* people' and that it was me and mine who were the extraordinary – in the sense of the unusual. For all that I couldn't see the purpose of Arvagh initially, it became evident that I'd been in small towns and villages like this many times before in Scotland;

Glencoe, Tomintoul, Auldhouse, Braemar and Haddington to name but a few and had therein experienced the same hospitable, restrained, warm, almost somnolent atmosphere. I'm sure there are villages in Italy, Norway, Morocco, Peru, New Zealand... countries all over the world, that share the same reasons for their existence and the same unhurried civility. And that across the planet there is cause to rejoice in the old Scots' saying, 'We're all Jock Tamson's bairns'. Well, perhaps Jock had rural bairns and urban bairns. In Arvagh, his rural offspring were a credit to him.

Arvagh and its people exhibited all of these characteristics. A lovely wee town but a diversion to relive old memories wasn't in prospect. Galway called.

John and I each wanted to enjoy live Irish music over a few beers but those pubs we visited seemed to have embraced the notion of *ersatz* Irishness in the manner of John Wayne portraying the Quiet Man in John Ford's 1952 movie of that name shot in part in Galway. Old butchers' bicycles hung from walls, *bodhrans* (traditional Irish drums) predominated, Irish road signs offered directions, leprechauns loomed from rafters...it was a false Ireland that might have been overlooked by despondent and celebrating racegoers out on the piss but we wanted something more authentic and traditionally Irish and thought we'd found it when we came upon the Inishmore Bar which promised food, drink and live music starting at 9.00pm, only thirty minutes hence. We settled in.

Two young men took the microphones and started singing the canon of works celebrating Annie and wilderness brought to the world by American minstrel John Denver. We finished our pints and left.

The weather was depressingly windy and wet in Galway, we wanted to move on and did so right after breakfast, to Ennis (Irish, meaning "island") in County Clare on the River Fergus, north of where it enters the Shannon Estuary, some twelve miles from Shannon Airport.

I'd been in Ennis a couple of times before, initially at a time when the town won a *Telecom Erin* Technology award for adoption of new technologies. It was most impressive at that time due to the roll-out of new technologies that now seem commonplace. They'd introduced smart-card technology whereby local townspeople could buy low cost purchases such as a newspaper without cash changing hands and were installing parking meters where a mobile phone was employed to pay the fee. This was back in 1995 when some of these technologies were still considered science fiction.

I was taken to *Scoil Chriost Ri*, a National School for primary age children and was shown a classroom wherein all of the pupils had a computer. This was impressive stuff as most *schools* at that time didn't have even one computer. I spoke to Sister Mary, a nun who taught the class and asked her how she'd managed to combine traditional teaching methods with this raft of new technologies. She was unhesitating in her admiration of her charges. "I'm working as hard as I can just to stay one day ahead of these children. They take to this stuff so naturally. I can see the day when they'll all be using computer technology instead of paper and pencils." How prescient she was!

Ennis on this visit was only a stop over and I decided to go for a haircut while John and I took a break. There were two people in front of me so I figured, ten minutes each, ten for me and I'm back at the car in thirty minutes. I was to be disappointed though as the hairdresser would routinely come round in front of her victim, sit her fat arse on the edge of the washbasin, fold her arms, sip her tea, shake her head empathically at whatever mayhem had befallen her customer before returning her cup to a nearby shelf, cut a few locks and proceed to involve subsequent customers in whatever excitements had just been discussed.

I reflected upon the same unhurried conversation I'd experienced in Arvagh but because I was in a hurry this time, I sat looking at my watch in dismay when I received a text from my beloved wife (a primary schoolteacher) who advised that one of her colleagues had reported during the break that one of her charges had painted a vision of an imagined superhero for an exercise in painting a picture for a calendar. Her text revealed that painting and drawing were strengths of the seven year old boy. However spelling wasn't. The calendar that was now to hang in his parents' kitchen for the ensuing twelve months would show the impressively painted superhero...but the speech bubble that emanated from his mouth said not, "I come in peace" as was intended... but, "I cum in pies". Jean intimated her concern to focus upon spelling next term.

Still, it offered light relief as I waited my turn in the hairdressing chair...where upon selection, I was taciturn to a fault and returned to the street in jig-time. As it should be!

Onwards then, south to Kerry and to meet up again with Tadhg, Mary and their daughter Anna on their farmstead in Fieries but first we stopped off for a glass in the famous Jack Duggan's Bar in Castlemaine. I'd spent my teenage years singing and playing guitar in folk bands and 'The Wild Colonial Boy' made famous by the Clancy Brothers and Tommy Makem was a circuit standard.

'There was a wild colonial boy, Jack Duggan was his name
He was born and raised in Ireland in a place called Castlemaine
He was his father's only son, his mother's pride and joy
And dearly did his parents love the wild colonial boy...'

The pub was empty when we entered so we took our pints of Guinness and sat at a table. Bar staff had adjourned to the cellars so the only noise apart from our conversation was a radio which was clearly of a local nature. It droned on in sonorous tones about the passing of Patrick O'Shea and the sad demise of Mrs Kathleen Brogan, giving details of their funerals and a word of comfort for relatives and friends of the deceased. Further names were mentioned in dispatches until it seemed as if an epidemic had fallen upon the poor souls of the County of Kerry. John and I made inappropriate comments upon how cheery we were being made to feel in the pub but following our subsequent departure, our friend Tadhg explained that in rural Ireland it's a regular and very effective feature of local radio to keep everyone up to date on hatches, matches and dispatches. Indeed, he explained that funerals are taken sufficiently seriously that his brother, a local head teacher and therefore a figure of status in the community, spends a goodly proportion of each of his school weeks attending the interment of relatives of those of his charges.

We travelled the short distance along the road between Farranfore and Castlemaine to the small village of Fieries. It was getting dark as we arrived but although we were rather worn out from our long journey south, Tadhg was anxious to show us the nearby Dingle Peninsula and would hear nothing of our protestations that we might see it in the morning. All five of us were herded into his estate car and having bumped us amusingly along the farm track to the nearest tarmacadamed road surface, took off at enormous speed towards his destination. At first we cooed at the beauty of the landscape but as night fell and in the absence of any street lighting as we passed a scenic viewpoint, Tadhg was reduced to saying, "And over there, if you could see them, are Macgillycuddy's Reeks." Further on he'd point out a site that was used in the 1970 David Lean film, Ryan's Daughter. "But it's a bit dark to see it at the minute". Mount Brandon and Minard Castle would, he assured us, cause us to gasp in appreciation, "But the light's dimming so you can't actually *see* them presently". Presently, we couldn't see the hedgerows at the side of the car, *actually* so he was persuaded after an hour's careering around the highways and byways of Kerry to return to the farm and he did so...without any noticeable reduction in speed or of his commentary regarding the sites of interest we passed..."if only it wasn't pitch black!"

We spent the evening in the kitchen of the farmhouse he'd being improving since relocating his family from Dublin. Tadhg, fiercely intelligent, was also a remarkably accomplished journeyman, able to turn his hand expertly to any of the trades necessary to build, convert, demolish or improve any construction. He'd dealt with all of the rooms of the house beautifully but had yet to make a start on the kitchen and I, for one, was delighted as we sat round the ancient and blackened green cooking range and fed it turf, basking in its warmth as his ancestors had done for the past hundred years and more besides. We talked long into the night aided by an endless supply of refreshments.

The following morning we feasted on a breakfast made by Tadhg which was largely carbon as he ensured that everything in the frying pan was cooked within an inch of its life...just the way I like it but a style of cooking roundly condemned by my wife back home whenever I adopt a similar burnt offerings approach. Bacon, eggs, black pudding, white pudding, sausages, fried tomatoes, soda bread, baked beans and mushrooms fought for space on the plate. I loved every morsel but desisted when I was offered a bowl of porridge. I'd tasted Tadhg's porridge before and suggested instead that he use it to cement the breeze-blocks on the wall he proposed to work on later.

We faced a long drive back to Belfast and home and took our leave secure in the knowledge that we wouldn't have to eat for several days. With an ever-improving weather front, we made the ferry without difficulty and sharing the driving, survived the experience agreeing en route that we'd return again to Ireland as soon as our respective livers permitted.

Closer to Home

Edinburgh, Galashiels, the Outer Hebrides, Lockerbie,
Maybole, Grantown-on-Spey, Dunkeld and Birnam,
Penrith, Carndonagh, Berwick-upon-Tweed, Fenwick,
John o'Groats, Land's End, Kirkintilloch, Balquhidder.

Although my original bucket list included only destinations further afield, I also made a list of places closer to home; some of which were known to me, if incompletely. Some were important to me because of their place in history and others, both unvisited and visited, just hadn't much been written about. Pick up a travel book about Scotland and it'll be full of images and descriptions of Edinburgh, Glencoe, Glasgow or St. Andrews but where might you read of the significance of Fenwick, the train station in Dunkeld or the beauty of Falkland?

Not all of my travels took me to destinations within my native Scotland. I also ventured south into England (if only marginally) and to Carndonagh in Donegal which, for reasons I can't remember, I didn't include in my chapter of other Irish travels.

But to commence my *reportage* of these visits to lesser known quarters, let's start with a place I've just denounced as over-represented in travel books...Edinburgh.

Edinburgh

As a proud Glaswegian, it pains me to say it but Edinburgh is incontestably one of the most beautiful cities in the world; as is Glasgow of course, but Edinburgh really is rather special. When it hosts the annual Edinburgh Festival and Fringe, countless numbers of people crowd its streets trying to avoid the jugglers, mime artists, actors and opera singers each thrusting leaflets which attempt to persuade attendance at their show when all you want to do is meet your pal in the pub.

Its regal, ancient and elegant buildings provide an iconic backdrop which is up there with Sydney Harbour, Paris, Moscow and Rio de Janeiro as being immediately identifiable. It's the place to be at New Year and if we overlook the small matter of it being the AIDS capital of the world for a while due to a worryingly high percentage of its population enjoying a flirtation with heroin, it's a simply wonderful city. In 1983, a sudden outbreak of HIV among intravenous drug users in Edinburgh saw over 60% infected in six months. That makes for a whole lot of human misery but on the bright side, *Trainspotting* was a big hit!

Edinburgh does tourism very well; very well indeed. I'd decided to visit its castle in order to visit the Stone of Destiny. The castle, a rugged fortress perched atop a volcanic plug formed some 350 million years ago in the middle of what is now Edinburgh, hosts the Stone and I was keen to view this historic and controversial piece of sandstone. Since the second century Iron Age there has been human occupation of the rock and it has housed a royal castle since at least the reign of King David 1 of Scotland in the 12th century. Nowadays, the castle is Scotland's most-visited paid tourist attraction with over 1.4 million visitors walking its battlements annually. As the backdrop to the world-wide phenomena that is the Edinburgh Military Tattoo it is Edinburgh's most frequently visited visitor attraction and more than 70% of visitors to Edinburgh pass beneath its portcullis.

I'd visited the castle several times before but hadn't been there for a while. My interest this time had been piqued having read a book about the Stone of Destiny by Ian Hamilton QC; one of Scotland's most celebrated legal minds, a pillar of society, an honest, upright, virtuous, ethical, clean-living and respectable man...that is before he broke into Westminster Abbey on Christmas Eve in 1950 and stole an oblong block of red sandstone that reputedly had been used for centuries to crown the monarchs of Scotland, England and eventually the UK.

Named the Stone of Destiny, Jacob's Pillow or the Coronation Stone dependent upon with whom you spoke, it had huge symbolic appeal in Scotland as it had been used for centuries to crown Scottish kings but, in 1296, it had been taken as spoils of war by Edward 1 of England (not Scotland's favourite monarch) to Westminster Abbey in order to make the point that subsequent coronations in London would bring with them the status of 'Lord Paramount of Scotland', with the right to oversee its royal household and bolstering Edward's claim to the throne of Scotland.

Over the centuries, Scotland and England had pretty consistently been at war. Indeed, Scottish kings had consistently pursued a policy of alliance, *The Auld Alliance,* with France, England's traditional enemy. For perhaps the first time, diplomacy was considered and following overtures from English courtiers, an accession took place whereby James VI, King of Scotland succeeded the thrones of both England and Ireland bringing unification of the three realms under a single monarch on 24 March 1603.

Fast forward to 1706 when two acts of Parliament, the Union with Scotland Act 1706 and the Union with England Act 1707 were passed which put into effect the terms of the Treaty of Union bringing together not only the crowns but also the parliaments of both countries.

Back then, scant regard was had to systems such as the single transferable vote, the mixed member proportional representation, the additional member system or even first past the post. Back then to win a vote in Parliament? Why, you just bribed the nobility.

The proposition before Scotland's establishment was that Scotland could continue with the Scottish legal system, education and church which were important elements in allowing the country to continue to regard itself as a separate entity. However, debates in the Scottish Parliament were heated. Crowds in the streets burned copies of the treaty and threw stones at Parliament's windows. Edinburgh then was said to be in an almost constant state of riot. Its subjects, almost all without a vote, were keen to express their views in the only way they could. A riotous opposition stormed around Glasgow protesting for four weeks but on January 16, 1707, the Treaty of Union was passed by 110 votes to 67.

In 1791, Scotland's national bard, Robert Burns described the sell-out as having been perpetrated by treacherous members of the Scottish Parliament who signed away their nation's independence in his poem, 'Such A Parcel of Rogues In A Nation'.

What force or guile could not subdue,
Thro' many warlike ages,
Is wrought now by a coward few,
For hireling traitor's wages.
The English steel we could disdain,
Secure in valour's station;
But English gold has been our bane -
Such a parcel of rogues in a nation!

Edinburgh historian Michael Fry, author of *The Union: England, Scotland and the Treaty of 1707*, reports, 'You have to admire the English. The bribery was very skilfully done. They succeeded in making a rape look like a respectable marriage.'

Other historians were equally disdainful of circumspection. Many report that the deal was a very poor one for Scotland because Scotland was now required to take on the liability of England's war debts, her customs system and were penalised for exchanging Scots pounds for pounds Sterling. Some made the point that bribes along with more subtle methods of financial inducement such as promises of pensions and important posts were not uninvolved in winning the vote. What is manifestly the case is that the Union of Parliaments wasn't popular in Scotland but the Scots nobility, many of them, prospered substantially.

So Scotland's pretty much always had a complex relationship with its larger neighbour to the south, England. Scratch most Scots and you'll find them experiencing *schadenfreude* when England lose an important football match on penalties and what Scot hasn't found himself saying defensively, 'Some of my best friends...' when accused of being anti-English.

But back to our honest, upright, virtuous, ethical, clean-living and respectable, Ian Hamilton. Back in 1950 he was an idealistic young student studying law at Glasgow University who achieved hero status in his native Scotland when he and three friends staged one of the most audacious robberies imaginable. Aerated about the cause of Scottish Nationalism in the days before it was quite as fashionable as it is today, (although five years earlier in 1945, the very first Scottish Nationalist MP Robert McIntyre had been elected to represent Motherwell) he persuaded his friends that the theft of the Stone of Destiny some six hundred and fifty years earlier was an outrage that demanded remedy.

In both Scotland and England, the stone had mythical properties. According to the Book of Genesis, Jacob was fleeing from his elder twin brother Esau, whom he had deceived. Whilst on the run, Jacob had slept at a city called Luz and had used a stone as a pillow. After waking, Jacob determined that he'd been sleeping in the house of God and that the stone he'd used as a pillow should be consecrated. Subsequent Scottish legend holds that the Stone of Jacob was brought to Ireland by the prophet Jeremiah and subsequently to Scotland where it was used to crown kings, demonstrating their royal lineage to the ancient Israelites. From 1296 until Ian Hamilton set out for London in 1950, it was located in a special throne in Westminster Abbey and used for coronations. For the moment, we'll overlook the minor irritation that geologists have subsequently found the stone to be red sandstone block quarried in the vicinity of Scone in Scotland, and in consequence had neither been transported to Scotland from Ireland, nor indeed from the Holy Land.

Nevertheless, to many Scots it was symbolic and Hamilton had decided it had to be returned to Scotland. In today's culture of high-tech security measures it's almost unbelievable that merely by remaining unseen by a complacent and disinterested abbey night-watchman and by employing a short crowbar to access the Stone and a coat to drag it, Hamilton and his collaborators could remove the stone from beneath the throne and haul it to a waiting car where after some subterfuge it was driven back over the border to Scotland.

The theft made international news and a manhunt to retrieve the stone was quickly put in place - but to no effect. Hamilton was interviewed but evaded arrest. After a period of four months, he decided that sufficient publicity had been drawn to his cause and, draping the stone in the Saltire of Scotland, returned it to the altar at Arbroath Abbey; chosen because of its association with Scotland's Declaration of Independence drafted by Bernard de Linton, Abbot of Arbroath in 1320 which *inter alia* famously declared (in Latin) and is translated thus; *"..For, as long as but a hundred of us remain alive, never will we on any conditions be brought under English rule. It is in truth not for glory, nor riches, nor honours that we are fighting, but for freedom – for that alone, which no honest man gives up but with life itself."* Interestingly, the US Senate Resolution 155 of 10 November 1997 states that, *"The Declaration of Arbroath, the Scottish Declaration of Independence [sic], was signed on April 6, 1320 and the American Declaration of Independence was modelled on that inspirational document."*

Fearing a backlash, the authorities charged no one for the recovery of the Stone of Destiny. Interviewed in his nineties many years after his escapade, Hamilton said, "We drove down the bleak, narrow roads to London to hurt no one; rather to puncture England's pride."

Anyway, the stone was returned just in time as it was used to crown Queen Elizabeth 1st of Scotland, (2nd of England) only three years later.

On St Andrews Day, 30th November 1996, Scottish Tory and Secretary of State for Scotland, Michael Forsyth MP unexpectedly arranged for the stone to be returned to Scotland; to Edinburgh

Castle. "The stone is the property of the Queen and is simply being removed from one part of her kingdom to another," he stated, denying that the then Conservative low polling of 15% in Scotland was pertinent to his decision. "I do not regard this as a political gesture," he lied, bewildered at the very idea.

And so the Stone of Destiny was returned to Scotland amid much ceremony and celebration and placed in Edinburgh Castle alongside the Honours of Scotland. About ten thousand people lined the Royal Mile in Edinburgh to watch a procession of dignitaries and troops escort the stone from the Palace of Holyrood House at the bottom of the mile to the castle at its top.

Well, I wanted to see what all the fuss what about.

Having stepped off the Glasgow train at Haymarket Station, I realised very quickly that it was going to be an unusually hot and sunny day as I strolled along the gradually elevating Morrison Street and along a more testing Johnston Terrace before arriving at the foot of a steep set of stairs leading up to the castle. I could have chosen to walk on and take a more sedate route to the esplanade but figured that if other people could manage the stairs, so too could I.

Jesus, was that a decision I regretted. My thighs were burning as I put one foot in front of the other. My legs shook as I closed on the top of the staircase. Sweat lathered my brow and ran down my backside... (not the same sweat...different sweat...). Old ladies offered me their Zimmer frame and Red Cross ambulance-men rose expectantly from a crouch, nudging each other expectantly as they collected their stretchers, hoping for some first-aid activity to brighten their day. Somehow I reached the castle esplanade, walked its length and wobbled uncertainly through the entrance to a ticket office where a queue like an execution stood in Disney, snake-like fashion pretending to the world that it was short.

A frustrating characteristic of the snake-queue was that every second turn brought me to within touching distance of the bank of ticket-sellers before gradually moving me twenty yards away; returning me and removing me as if a tease. The sales team behind the glass were each bedecked in tartan and spoke in warm Edinburgh tones. As I listened, I noted their very smooth approach whereby almost conversationally they would ask smilingly where the visitor came from, were they here on business, were they staying in Edinburgh and how long were they staying. It was all presented as if a welcoming conversation but was clearly a technique whereby marketing data was being mined. After some thirty minutes I arrived at the front and found myself face-to-face with a young man who was clearly of Cockney origin.

" 'Ello, myte. You wanna tikkit?"

"Yeah."

"Come from rand 'eah?"

"Aye." I wasn't in the mood to be expansive. Hot and bothered, I wished the marketing malarkey over as soon as possible.

"Styin' long ven?"

"Naw."

"Just visitin' then, myte?"

"Aye."

"Bizznizz?"

"Naw." Still drenched in sweat, I wiped a cloth over my face. He smiled in recognition and, perhaps as a consequence of my miserable condition, I thought I sensed a measure of *schadenfreude* as a slow grin spread across his face.

"Cloimb them stezz, then myte?"

"Just gimme my bloody ticket," I nearly growled. Instead, I nodded wordlessly and moved on. He shouted after me.

"Enjoy you visit, myte! 'Ave a goodun!"

An extravagantly uniformed sentry stood at attention nearby, completely stilled. I calculated how easy it might be for me to remove his bayonet, depart sonny-boy from this earth and make it look like an accident.

Immediately I could see why Edinburgh Castle is so popular. It really is a handsome property with simply astonishing views of

Edinburgh and the Firth and was absolutely thronged with people from what appeared to be every corner of the globe. Clicking cameras were noisily ubiquitous as were tour guides with silly unfurled telescopic umbrellas held aloft as a signal to their open-mouthed group of chattering visitors not to stray too far.

Wandering around the oldest part of the castle I took stock of St Margaret's Chapel and was impressed by the Great Hall, the Prison and the Half Moon Battery. I did my share of the tourist stuff as it was in front of me, seemed very well presented, I was interested and the shaded innards of the castle allowed my temperature to drop a degree or two...but my main objective was to see the Stone of Destiny.

Housed along with the Honours of Scotland, it's accessed by means of a nondescript sandstone entrance. I shortly realised I'd been conned into joining another snake-queue which took an eternity to permit me access to the Holy of Holies. Thirty boring minutes were spent queuing slowly in darkened chambers being force-fed animatronics and dioramas of medieval characters milling grain, looking regal or fashioning swords. But, eventually, before me in the dim-lit corridor, people were becoming excited as they closed on the main event.

First up was the Honours of Scotland; a jewel encrusted crown, an elaborate sword and a sceptre. Dating from the fifteenth century, they're the oldest regalia existing in the British Isles.

Frankly impressed by the presentation - and looking to take a photograph having spent the last half-hour in a queue, I was somewhat perturbed as the repetitive growl of a man up ahead gradually entered my consciousness.
"No photographs. No mobile phones."
As I shuffled round the corner I realised that this guy could have been a body-double for Arnold Schwarzenegger had Arnold chosen to have had a somewhat unsightly tattoo inscribed on his muscular right arm acknowledging the affection in which he held

both 'Mum' and 'Hong Kong'. I eyed him up and down, assessing him without him seeing me do so and determined that if push came to shove he could probably dismember me in two seconds flat. But as in comedy, timing is all-important and when he was distracted by a question from an American lady, I took two photographs shown subsequently to be out of focus, squinty and unusable. Still, I'd managed to outwit Arnold so honour was satisfied.

The Stone of Destiny was, frankly, underwhelming. It was what was said on the tin; a large block of sandstone with two metal rings inserted to make for easier carriage. The queue had its own dynamic and no sooner than I made this observation than my back was being pushed forwards by those who hadn't yet realised that they were about to see a large block of sandstone with two metal rings inserted to make for easier carriage. I emerged into the blinding sunlight and immediately looked for somewhere to hide from the heat. Surrounded by historic doorways behind which were myriad tales of adventure and misadventure, I decided that enough was enough and headed off down to Edinburgh's wondrous Grassmarket for a cooling pint and a wee whisky chaser.

The Grassmarket is a venerable part of the city situated in a deep hollow immediately below Edinburgh Castle. Daniel Defoe, he of Robinson Crusoe, the trader, writer, journalist, pamphleteer and English spy, (he was a secret agent working for the crown, reporting on the continuing unpopularity of the then recent political union between England and Scotland) visited the city in the 1724, and wrote that the Grassmarket 'was full of wholesale traders, and those very considerable dealers in iron, pitch, tar, oil, hemp, flax, linseed, painters' colours, dyers, drugs and woods and such like heavy goods and supplies country shopkeepers, as our wholesale dealers in England do'. Nowadays it sells beers, wines and stories in vast quantity to locals and tourists alike. Tourist brochures describe it now as 'lively and vibrant' which is their way of describing a part of Edinburgh in which a greater than usual proportion of those visiting are comprehensively intoxicated.

Surrendering to the relaxed atmosphere of the Black Bull in the Grassmarket and once refreshed, I researched further the Stone of Destiny via electronic means. Given that the Scots had three months to anticipate English King Edward's arrival, there was ample time and not inconsiderable incentive for a switch to be made in order to protect the original relic. Numerous sources suggest that many copies were made and hidden in various sites including Glasgow's Sauchiehall Street and in a location now occupied by Rollo Engineering in Bonnybridge. However, most compelling was a tale of the sad demise aged 99 (in 1999), of a certain Ms. Margaret Pearl Cook, an early founder-member of the Scottish National Party. On her death bed in Wick, Miss Cook reportedly confessed that she'd been involved in matters Destiny and insisted that the stone apparently returned to England in 1950 after the theft, was a fake...and that she knew the location of the real one. As she ebbed, she spoke of a stone, currently under the guardianship of Knights Templar, protected by an iron cage in a church in Dull, Perthshire (pronounced 'Dool' but not unaware of marketing possibilities, the village twinned with 'Boring' in Texas) before going on in ever-weaker breaths to describe a Stone buried in the 13th century on Dunsinane Hill in nearby Scone by monks of that parish. As those around her begged further precise detail she explained in a whisper that these particular monks were more than just men of God, they were *sleekit* men of God and were said to have made a copy of the original stone...just in case!

Just before passing, she raised her head one last time.

"The joke", said Miss Cook, her voice faltering and fading, "is on Edward 1st. The Stone of Destiny never left Scotland in the first place..."

She laid her head on the pillow, crossed the River Styx and joined the choir immortal.

Envisioning a fat fee for a movie script starring Harrison Ford or Tom Hanks (if any acting might be required), I considered buying a bus ticket to Dull. 'Indiana Jones and the Stone of Destiny', anyone? Wee Jimmy Crankie could play Michael Forsyth.

Galashiels

Up with the lark and into the centre of Edinburgh in order to take my seat on a newly refurbished steam train operated by the Scottish Rail Preservation Trust on the equally newly established Waverley Line to Galashiels which was opened by Queen Elizabeth 1st of Scotland and 2nd of England on the day she out-reigned Queen Victoria...a day of *great* celebration in our household I can tell you.

I was early and as I wandered around Waverley Station to pass some time before the train arrived, I was met by a piper playing *"Hector The Hero"*, my favourite pipe tune as, in addition to having a beautifully haunting melody, it always reminds me of my much-missed grandfather, Hector McLeod. Appropriately, *Hector The Hero* is a lament. I took the escalators from the station forecourt and walked past the Scott Monument in Princess Street, the largest monument built to acknowledge a man of literature anywhere in the world. So when you also consider that the birth of Robert Burns on the 25th January is world-wide, the most celebrated birthday of any individual other than the carpenter's son from Galilee, it's fair to say that Scots tend to celebrate the cerebral rather than the warrior... William Wallace and Robert The Bruce excepted.

Back in March1961, at the request of Conservative Transport Minister Ernest Marples, engineer and physicist Richard Beeching took up the appointment as the first chairman of the nationalised British Railways Board with the task of making it more profitable. He set to his task with gusto, producing a report that resulted in the uprooting of 6,000 miles of track (one third of the entire rail network) and the closure of more than 2,000 stations. This boy didn't mess about.

Popular singing duo of the time, Flannigan and Allan sang;

'Oh, Dr Beeching what have you done?
There once were lots of trains to catch, but soon there will be none.'

Not only was the rail network decimated, but it coincided with engineering progress that saw the likes of Mallard, the Royal Scot and Flying Scotsman being replaced by diesel engines; more efficient, more reliable but there was no romance, no steam billowing from their innards, just oil on the track.

And so it was that I walked one of the many platforms of Waverley Station in order to see steam locomotive 60009, The Union of South Africa, which is one of only six remaining of the A4 Class in the world. I boarded a few minutes early and joined a family of five who'd come up by train from Tweedbank in order to catch the steam train *back* to Tweedbank before returning to Edinburgh by steam then catching the regular service back to Tweedbank once more. Immediately upon being seated I found myself offered a glass of Champagne...followed by a quick refill. The train was exactly as I'd imagined; old livery, big comfortable seats, and soot coming in any open window. Marvellous.

My travelling companions were good company and myself and the faither blethered away about the auld days while his two sons enquired of one of the many staff whether there was a wi-fi signal in the 1937-built coach. Used to the smooth acceleration and effortless pace of diesel or electric trains, I'd forgotten the jolt on steam trains when the engine driver disengages the brake; then a slow, very slow, momentum was built before the train reached what seemed its full speed of something around 25mph.

I walked round Galashiels, or Gala as my new pal on the train informed me it was to be called. It didn't take long. It's had its day as a couthy wee town. These days it's pedestrianised, superstores dominate and new housing outnumbers the old. I looked for an old traditional pub but could only see bistros, gastro-pubs and pubs that had been converted into curry-houses. Eventually I found the Auld Mill which had a great wee snug which sheltered me from loud, cursing, raucous and opinionated regulars with whom, when ordering a second pint, I fell into easy conversation about the train and the benefits and disbenefits it'd bring Gala. The conversation took a diversion when one of them noticed my 'Scotland' wristband. I found myself compelled to make the point that the new Borders Rail Link was built and financed entirely by the Scottish Government because support was refused by Westminster 'as the route is not cross-border'. However, Scots taxpayers have financed London's new Jubilee Line and will pay for the high speed London to Leeds line. Better together? In what is traditional Liberal country, they agreed with me to a man.

One of the men, a very short chap who, it transpired, was a street-sweeper having a couple of beers 'for lunch', seemed more the worse for wear but entered the conversation intermittently with some pretty off-the-wall comments - tolerated completely by his fellow topers. He wanted to buy me a pint which I refused because I didn't want to spend much longer in the pub and was keen to see more of the town. I thanked him, politely, finished my beer and left.

As I passed Galashiels Burgh Chambers - a very handsome and quaint building, I gazed upwards and noticed the town's coat of arms which depicts two foxes reaching up to eat plums from a tree. Not perhaps as regal or as distinguished as three leopards leaping or a lion rampant, but nevertheless, I determined to establish its genesis. Again the local library, this one in Gala's Lawyer's Brae, came to my assistance. It would appear that the rustic and peaceful scene of two animals dining on wild fruit has to be explained in a rather more bloodthirsty manner. It seems like it references a skirmish back in the fourteenth century when a raiding party of English soldiers were picking wild, unripened plums close to the town and were caught by a party of Scots who then put them all to the sword. The Burgh's motto is *'soor plooms'*, (sour plums), commemorating, apparently the foolishness of the English soldiers eating plums before they'd ripened. Jesus, back then, you'd think twice before picking the wrong fruit, eh? Mind you, I suppose being a member of a raiding party intent upon doing harm to local people might have weighed equally heavily on the minds of those who found them.

As I walked back towards the railway station, I passed a bin-lorry, whose operatives were busily manoeuvring a large refuse receptacle the size of an Austin Morris towards the business end of the vehicle. Walking towards me to join them was my street-sweeper pal from the pub. For a few moments I enjoyed a rather surreal conversations.

"Oh, hi there, big man. Ye headin' back home?"

"Aye. Need to catch the train."

"See before you do, can I ask you a wee question I wanted to ask in the pub?"

"Sure."

"See if it came right down to it...what would you say your favourite colour was?"

Wary lest he sought the answer, 'plum' so he could skewer me, I answered diffidently.

"Well, it'd depend."

"How's that?"

"Well, I like red because it's the colour of my football team. But I also like blue because it's the colour of Scotland...and I like green because I like green and, I suppose"...I finished lamely... "I also like yellow".

This seemed somehow to satisfy him. He nodded sagely before smiling his understanding as if I'd cleared up a complex problem with which he'd been wrestling.

"Aye...I was just wondering. Ah'm red, tae!"

He wandered off, removing a heavy pair of gloves from his hip pocket whilst leaning slightly to starboard...then port...then... I continued my walk towards the railway station watching his receding form over my shoulder. Distracted, I walked headlong into a bright red, hard-to-ignore pillar-box as if the God of Red was rebuking me for listing other, inferior colours. As my friend the street-sweeper climbed aboard the lorry and joined the driver, I asked myself, *'what if I'd answered, 'brown'?* Perhaps the God of Brown would have had me step in dog *sheuch*? I considered myself fortunate.

The journey back on the steam train was uneventful but equally interesting. Instead of Champagne we were offered a three storey cake-stand high tea which included strawberry tarts, cream cakes and pastries. My favourite cake had an icing covering coloured red, blue, green and yellow.

A doggie bag was offered those who couldn't stay the course.

I managed.

Stornoway: The Western Isles

My son and his family, having moved for purposes of employment to The Isle of Lewis in Scotland's Outer Hebrides, provided sufficient reason for me to travel north to visit with them in their home in Gress, just outside Stornoway. I'd had a few days back in Glasgow to recuperate from my adventures in Galashiels and contemplated my journey north. I could have flown north directly to Stornoway. I could have taken the train as far as Inverness and caught a bus then a ferry. I could have taken the bus all the way from Glasgow to Ullapool but I decided a more interesting approach might be to drive to Oban and catch ferries all the way up the island chain that together comprise the Outer Hebrides, a one hundred and thirty miles arc running from north to south off the north-western coast of Scotland.

Scotland has seven hundred and eighty-seven islands on its coastline, (thereby producing the somewhat surprising answer to the pub quiz question; which has the longer coastline, Scotland or France?) (10,250 miles as opposed to 3,015 miles). I'd be visiting but nine of them, each forming part of that magical concatenation of islands that features so strongly in Scotland's story.

In Scotland, ferries to outlying islands tend to be operated by Caledonian MacBrayne, known to everyone affectionately as 'Calmac'. The company was created in 1851 as a steamship company under the name of David Hutcheson & Co whose main route was from Glasgow through the Crinan Canal to Oban and Fort William and then on through the Caledonian Canal to Inverness.

However, in the late 1870's the Hutcheson brothers retired leaving the business in the hands of David MacBrayne who renamed the firm. MacBrayne grew the shipping company with a mail run to Islay, Harris and North Uist from Skye and a second, from Oban to Barra and South Uist in the Outer Hebrides. However, as new railways began to reach towns on the West Coast - at Fort William, Kyle of Lochalsh and Mallaig - further rescheduling was necessary and at the conclusion of World War One, David MacBrayne found himself operating a much-reduced fleet which eventually resulted in an amalgamation renamed *Caledonian MacBrayne Ltd* – an amalgamation between The Caledonian Steam Packet Company and MacBraynes - whose vessels then carried the red lion rampant contained within a yellow disc in the centre of a red and black funnel recognised instantly from then on by all west coast travellers.

My journey north to beautiful Oban, always one of my favourite harbour towns, was uneventful but upon arrival on the perimeter of its rural conurbation, I found myself stuck in a queue of traffic and was now quite likely to miss my ferry, thereby knocking each of my subsequent bookings out of kilter. I drove at a snail's pace when not entirely stationary, eventually realising that the configuration of a badly designed roundabout as traffic enters Oban was causing the log-jam, rebuking myself for not giving myself enough time and promising to make better provision next trip. All along Oban's George Street, the problems continued, compounded by me as when I reached the turn-off for the ferry at the end of the street, unaccountably I took the wrong turning and found myself back in the congestion. Realising I had perhaps one final chance to make the ferry, I drove carefully but creatively hoping against hope that there would be no enthusiastic police officers on traffic duty that day or, if they were, that they were vulnerable to my effortless charm or disinterested. I saw none and screeched to a halt at the ferry barrier where I was regarded thoughtfully by a hi-viz wearing Calmac employee so small he could have walked under the barrier without stooping. Frowning, he drew to my attention that I was late. The ferry was still in port so I calculated quickly that suggesting he was stating the bleedin' obvious and 'why didn't he just raise the barrier and give me a fighting chance of boarding' might produce poorer results than admitting my delinquency and pleading for mercy, which I did. He shook his head as if to convey, '*I shouldn't be doing this, pal*', consulted his clipboard, sucked on his pencil, pursed his lips in indecision and following reflection which must have lasted thirty seconds, pointed to the vanishing line of cars entering the bowels of the ferry. "Lane ten," he growled uncharitably. I'd made it.

Calmac comes in for criticism from time to time but I find their operation wonderful. Inevitably the seriously wild sea conditions on the West coast of Scotland requires that a ship or two stays in port now and again, causing great inconvenience to islanders but what Calmac does, and does really importantly, is to provide a life-line to the off-shore populations of Scotland.

My ferry, the impressive M.V Isle of Lewis, was heading for the small port of Castlebay, the largest conurbation on the island of Barra. I'd stayed there a year earlier when I'd flown from Glasgow solely because I'd wanted to experience the only scheduled flight in the world which routinely lands on a beach; specifically, the wide shallow bay of *Traigh Mhòr* at the northern tip of the island whose hard-packed, cockle-beach sand allows the De Havilland Twin Otter to deposit and return its passengers six days a week... when the tide's out.

Today however, I arrived by ferry, skimming the handsome thirteen-century Kismul's Castle, protecting Castlebay from its position on an islet just a hundred yards from the harbour in the centre of the bay. It is the home of Clan MacNeil but is currently under a thousand-year lease to Historic Scotland from the MacNeil of Barra. A generous guy, Ian Roderick MacNeil, the current MacNeil Clan Chieftain who made it over for the princely sum of a pound a year and a bottle of whisky! Still, that's a thousand bottles of whisky. Not to be sniffed at.

Because I'd a car this visit, I stayed overnight some two miles outside Castlebay on my route north to the next ferry, in the Isle of Barra Beach Hotel, the most Westerly Hotel in Britain. It was warm and welcoming but the lounge had a piano which guests were encouraged to play. I suspect when the owners came up with this novel idea, they'd ideas of talented amateurs making a decent fist of something from the Great American Songbook or of a visiting troubadour giving it laldy with some Scottish sing-alongs. However, after dinner when all I wanted to do was read and sip at a relaxing (if overpriced) whisky, a young boy aged around seven took to crashing his fists down on the keyboard indulged by his laid-back mother who encouraged his inner creativity by somewhat over-tolerantly telling him quietly if repeatedly to "play properly" while taking no steps to ensure that he did just that. After a few minutes of this musical vandalism, I was in the midst of calculating whether an accurately thrown (empty) whisky glass to the head might (a) knock the wee bastard off his stride and (b) might be contrived to look like a mishap, when a sibling appeared and they both ran off, I presumed to torture and set fire to some protected species outside. Peace reigned until another guest attempted 'Love Me Tender' and I set off to the beach in an attempt to persuade the young pianist to return urgently to his keyboard.

The following morning I left early to catch the first ferry from *Aird Mhor* Ferry Terminal to the nearby island of Eriskay. It was a short hop and in consequence the ferry was rather more basic. However, it made the journey effortlessly and I was soon driving north across the causeway that straddles the Sound of Eriskay and connects it with South Uist where three further causeways brought me to the ferry port in the Island of Berneray. It really is both unsettling and wonderful driving at low level across the sea from one land mass to another. Today I was blessed with a blue sky and a calm sea. Making the same journey at sea level in a Beaufort force-ten gale would defy belief. The onward ferry crossing to Leverburgh was much more thrilling and I stood on deck throughout as the ship navigated several low-lying islands and an assortment of frighteningly large rocks; any one of which if struck, would have seen us plumb the depths.

Now I had finished with ferries and was on the Isles of Harris...
and Lewis. For some reason, the northern part of the island is
called Lewis, the southern is called Harris and both are usually
referred to as if they were separate islands. However, the boundary
between the 'islands' is where the island narrows between
Loch Resort on the west and Loch Seaforth on the east where the
island narrows at Tarbert. Properly, the collective name of the
'Long Island' should be employed but it's a term I've never heard
used; Harris and Lewis it is. It's also a sizeable lump of land being
the third largest island in the British Isles after Great Britain
itself and Ireland. Its east coast is more isolated and has some
of the oldest rocks in the world, being dated at some three
thousand million years old as a result of scouring by the glaciers
in the Ice Ages,

I drove towards Stornoway which is situated towards the northern
tip of Lewis. Initially the landscape was mountainous as around
me, more than thirty peaks soared above 1,000 ft. but as Harris
gave way to Lewis the land flattened, an exception being the
Clisham which reaches 1,874 ft. into the sky making it the highest
peak in the Outer Hebrides.

Thankfully, I was travelling on a Friday as Sundays are a very
special day on Lewis because virtually all commercial activity
ceases and a large proportion of the population attends church.
This makes the character of the islands very different from the
mainland where watching football, going shopping or taking a
trip to the swimming pool is more common. In Stornoway, public
toilets close, the swings in parks are chained so as to deter younger
residents from any activity likely to see them enjoy themselves on
the Sabbath, no one hangs out their washing and petrol is available
from only one supplier; a Norwegian. Recently, Calmac was given
permission both to depart its berth and dock on a Sunday so
perhaps the culture's changing as the tourist pound trumps the
religious beliefs of older residents. As an ocean-going atheist,
I guess I find the Lord's Day Observance culture a frustration as
although I'm a liberal and *tolerant* ocean-going atheist, I tend to

draw the line when someone's beliefs impact on my ability to lead my life as I choose. However, I also understand that people draw comfort and peace from their observance and wouldn't want to hinder their ability so to do. But shutting the pubs on a Sunday when Manchester United are on TV playing in a cup final is rather beyond the pale. Surely pub owners should be allowed to employ part-time pagans like me - non-Sabbatarians, to serve drink and switch on electronic entertainment for those who don't subscribe to the beliefs of the Free Presbyterian Church of Scotland. The church is occasionally referred to as the *Wee Wee Frees* to differentiate it from the Wee Frees, the post-1900 Free Church of Scotland which views itself as being reformed in doctrine, worship and practice and which maintains that all its actions are based on the word of God: the Bible. Each church, however, would deny me my cup final.

Anyway, it was a Friday evening and I had a clear day ahead when I could engage in all sorts of mayhem before someone switched off the lights.

I stayed with my son, Ron, his wife, Lisa and their kids, Arran and Eilidh in their large home in Gress, just outside Stornoway. It was great catching up and on the Saturday, walking the simply astonishing beaches that pepper the shoreline of Lewis. The sand is pure, granular and almost white; the water a luminescent green until it crashes snowy-white onto the beach. Not a single item of jetsam was to be seen. Nor was a single item of flotsam. However, it was as cold as a Tory's heart so after some embracing and windswept walks along the beach, I persuaded Ron to drop me outside one of Stornoway's several pubs.

Stornoway itself is a handsome town of some eight thousand residents. It is home to the islands' council headquarters, the health board and has a particularly sheltered harbour which permits the plying to and fro from the mainland of HMV Seaforth, the lifeline of the island. Shops, pubs, amenities and industrial units support the population.

The Gaelic language is still spoken widely on the island although less so in the town. In Stornoway's library, I found it interesting that up to a third of Scots' Gaelic speakers now reside in urban Glasgow. Perhaps more fascinating, however was the research by Yale University music Professor Willie Ruff that the singing of psalms in Scottish Gaelic by Presbyterians of the Scottish Hebrides; their practice of one person singing a solo before others follow – transmogrified into the call and response of gospel music of the southern United States.

Anyway, the Harbour Bar was jam-packed with young men in their thirties, most of whom were unsteady on their feet as they watched Scotland beat Wales at rugby. I was on a mission to establish which establishment (if any) might show the FA Cup final featuring Manchester United the following day which was the Sabbath. It fitted the bill. Nevertheless I ventured across the road to the Lewis Bar, a somewhat more agricultural affair in which the internal floor of the pub sloped dramatically from one end to the other following the contour of the pavement outside. Certainly wheelchair friendly, the pub at its shallow end offered a bar-top so low it could be sat upon while at the deep end, its sloping floor allowed a bar-top that was chest high. However, it offered a convivial welcome and a coal fire so I sat contentedly sipping at a beer before trying out the County Bar, passing the Criterion Bar on my way there as it seemed possessed of all the relaxing warm ambiance of a white goods shop.

The young barmaid in the County who served me wore an eye-poppingly low-cut top and when I asked in my most charming manner if they might be open to serve strong drink on the Sabbath she tensed and replied, "No! We certainly are not!" Then she spat in my beer.

I made up that last bit about the spitting but couldn't quite reconcile her overtly fruity upper display of flesh Monday through Saturday with her apparent denunciation of someone who sought harmless entertainment on the seventh day.

On the seventh day itself, I walked the family dog, Oscar along a nearby cliff top in mildly benign weather mid-morning. The final leg took me onto the main road and during this twenty minute element, not one single vehicle passed me in either direction. Sabbatarians rule in this part of the islands. Later we went to Ness, at longitude 06 degrees15.71 west and latitude 58 degrees and 30.92 north; the Butt of Lewis and the most north-westerly point of the European Union. We peered timorously over precipitous cliffs to the surf crashing some distance below the lighthouse. In a nearby play-park. Padlocks secured its gate and a notice invited revellers to respect the Sabbath day.

Half-an-hour before kick-off in order to get a good seat, I revisited the Harbour Bar to watch the Cup Final; the same Harbour Bar that had been crammed tight with sports fans the day before...but throughout the duration of the match I was the only person in the place other than a bored barmaid who wanted to tell me how excited she was at having had been appointed postmistress in Stornoway just as striker Zlatan Ibrahimović slotted home a free kick for Manchester United. 1-0. I tried not to appear distracted - but I was. Having said that, I suppose my leap in the air and ear-splitting scream of joy as the net bulged might have been construed by her as my unexpected delight at her new appointment.

Two up, United contrived to see the game levelled at 2-2 and it ebbed and flowed until Zlatan Ibrahimović scored the winner almost at the match end. My frustrations had reached boiling point on numerous occasions throughout the second half and with every red-missed opportunity and defensive blunder, I found myself screeching, "Sweet *Jesus!*" at the TV. The barmaid obviously thought I was a Sabbatarian so passionate were my theological encouragements.

On Monday morning, a slate-grey sky gave way to bright blue as MV (motor vehicle) Seaforth took me back to Ullapool across the Minch. The storm of the previous day had blown through and we sailed on what was almost a flat calm. Upon arrival at Ullapool

I was treated to views of almost transcendental beauty. Snow hung from branches, the sun shone bright in a blue sky. It was freezing but my back was warmed. There was a stillness even as Seaforth docked. Ullapool was dwarfed by sandstone *An Teallach*, a massive mountain that dominates the area and protects a village which although home to only some fifteen hundred people is yet the largest conurbation for many miles around.

Drinking in the scenery, I remembered I was now on the mainland and had a full day's driving ahead of me. Shouldering my rucksack, I headed for my car and home for a brief rest before heading further south, to Lockerbie.

Lockerbie

Exiting the handsome red sandstone railway station at Lockerbie in sunshine, my first sense was of smelling the sweet aroma of a peat fire. Smoke emanating from the Royal Bar, one of two pubs adjacent to the station seemed the likely culprit. Surprised at the presence of peat in the Scottish Borders, my curiosity was assuaged when I noticed a large bag of Galloway Peat for sale outside a convenience store. I hadn't appreciated the existence of peat bogs so far south so already travel had broadened my mind.

I walked only for some ten minutes before standing outside the expensive-looking bungalow at 12 Sherwood Crescent, turning and looking at the green sward of grass opposite where once numbers 13 and 15 had stood. Had I done so just after 07.00pm on the twenty-first day of December 1988, I'd have been crushed to dust and incinerated beneath a section of *Clipper Maid of the Seas* more commonly known by its flight number, Pan Am 103, then *en route* to Detroit, which fell out of the sky as a consequence of a bomb planted in its hold. The explosion tore a hole in the plane's fuselage, sending it into an almost vertical dive. Eight seconds after it exploded, radar showed the debris covering 1.9 nautical miles. As it descended, the fuselage broke up, the mid-section attached to the wings landing first where I stood in Sherwood Crescent. The 200,000 pounds of jet fuel it contained ignited causing a massive explosion and huge damage to surrounding properties. All 243 passengers died along with sixteen crew members and eleven Lockerbie residents. Three years later, following a joint investigation by Strathclyde Police and America's Federal Bureau of Investigation, Libyan intelligence officer Abdelbaset al-Megrahi was jailed for life after being found guilty of 270 counts of murder.

Al-Megrahi always insisted that he had been a patsy; a fall guy. In later years before he was assassinated by the mob, Libyan dictator, Colonel Muammar Gaddafi stated that al-Megrahi, acting alone, had been the guilty man although there remains a substantial body of evidence to suggest that he was innocent (as a by-note, I was much taken by the comment made, I think, by Scottish comedian Frankie Boyle, that Gaddafi couldn't have been much of a dictator if he only made himself a Colonel!)

Pertinent to this presumption of jiggery-pokery is the fact that aboard the doomed plane was a secret, five-man American Defence Intelligence Agency team headed by American Major Charles McKee. A suitcase belonging to McKee was recovered and emptied by the FBI before being returned to the site to be 'found' again. Inside had been a large quantity of heroin, some 'sensitive' documents, plus a large quantity of cash and travellers cheques. These items were removed from official records. It was also alleged that an unidentified body had also been removed from the crash site. No official explanation has been given for these extraordinary examples of evidence tampering although a number of explanations have been offered - all nefarious. Responsibility for the blast was also claimed variously by organisations such as Guardians of the Islamic Revolution, which informed ABC News in New York that the group had planted the bomb to commemorate Christmas. The Ulster Defence League and Mossad, the Israeli intelligence service were also alleged to have claimed involvement.

Further controversy arose when al-Megrahi, having been transferred from Barlinnie Prison in Glasgow to Greenock Prison in 2005, was released on compassionate grounds by the Scottish

Government some four years later when diagnosed with terminal cancer. Following his return to Libya, al-Megrahi found residence in a villa in Tripoli. He survived a further two years and 9 months after his release.

Kenny MacAskill, the Scottish Justice Secretary who released al-Megrahi, wrote a book within which he argued that the UK Government were anxious to veil the circumstances of the bombing, partly to secure £13 billion of oil deals for British firms in Libya. In 2007, Scottish judges announced the completion of a four-year review and decided that al-Megrahi's conviction could have been a miscarriage of justice. Indeed, prominent campaigner Doctor Jim Swire whose daughter was a victim of the bombing was 'entirely satisfied', that al-Megrahi was not to blame for the Lockerbie bombing.

Walking back into the town centre it was as if the place suffered from some kind of tinnitus. There was an ever-present wash of car noise from the M74 motorway and the smaller but equally busy side road that accompanied it. I wondered if locals noticed it or whether it was screened out because of its ubiquity. Lockerbie is a prosperous wee place. Lots of red sandstone villas with high-price cars outside. Its High Street is bestowed with banks, butchers, beauticians and bakers; all the shops needed to tend to everyday needs; I'd include florists, veterinarians, hardware stores and newsagents if only they began with a 'b'. Only two charity shops could I see - and they were both pretty up-market if their window displays were anything to go by. Given that it was once a town whose economy was predicated upon sheep it should have come as no surprise that the main statue in the town centre was a flock of sheep - but it was!

As I was about to leave Scotland in a matter of days to visit Morocco, I thought to exchange an amount of Scottish notes to English ones as Morocco has a closed Dinar currency wouldn't accept Clydesdale banknotes. I passed a bank and wondered if they'd make the exchange. Not only did they do so, it appeared that they traded mainly in English notes and did so enthusiastically. Only twenty-two miles to Carlisle in England. It kind of felt that way.

I was tempted to enjoy a pie and a pint in the Black Bull Inn but the pub with the peat fire opposite, the aged Royal, which still maintained the paint-flaked legend, *'Guinness Is Good For You'* (a completely accurate medical assertion, in my view) won out. A decent enough wee pub, it had a juke box, something I can seldom avoid when I have a glass in my hand. Having glanced through the local rag, the *Annandale Herald* and appreciated that I was now drinking in Scotland's only Conservative-held constituency (out of fifty-nine parliamentary seats, fifty-six of which, as I write, are held by the Scottish National Party) I decided to play some Scottish songs (Runrig playing *Loch Lomond* and the McCalman Folk Trio playing *Melville Castle*). Deciding that it might also be wise to include some English songs given the clientele, I opened a new list featuring English folk singers and found it dominated by Bert Jansch...from Glasgow. Interestingly, as soon as Runrig sang out, two snooker players dropped their cues and ploughed coin into the machine to return the playlist to something more usual to Lockerbie ears. I ordered a small haggis pie (very tasty) while listening and enjoyed the moment as I noticed one or two toes tapping to my choices. I believe I may have struck a blow for freedom.

I returned my gaze to the *Annandale Herald* and continued reading the story of the Lockerbie gunsmith who protested the Scottish Government's requirement that those who own shotguns should hold a licence and be registered with the police. 'It creates a stigma' he fumed. 'Calling a gun a weapon leaves a negative stigma.' He continued, 'A hammer is a tool until you hit someone on the head with it. Then it becomes a weapon. The same applies to a gun!'

Quite!

"Sammy, hand us that shotgun so's ah can put a nail in this fence-post!"

I crossed the narrow station lane to the Bull Inn and found it busy and full of a more elderly clientele, many with zimmers or walking aids. Two baseball-hat wearing guys stood at the bar levering ale into their mouths. Each wore a crew-neck with the motif, *'Britain First'* emblazoned on its chest. Accents all around were of an English hue. Had not the bar-stool coverings been a tartan material I could have been in Weston-Super-Mare. No one played Runrig on the juke box. Queen predominated. *'We Are The Champions'*, sang the pub. The bulky (English) barmaid wore tracksuit and trainers and looked like she'd give Muhammad Ali a run for his money.

I suppose it makes sense that in a unitary democracy comprised of four nations like Britain you'd expect a natural flow of people back and forth across each side of the border but I reminded myself that when I visited Penrith, the Lockerbie equivalent in England, I didn't notice any Scottish accents on the southern side. Very small sample, I'll grant you.

I found Lockerbie a lovely wee town. Comfortable, prosperous, at ease with itself. A typical Conservative town, I'd have said. Having suffered the bombing trauma of 1988 I'd imagine would have had the effect of bringing the town together but it seems to sleep easy these days. I headed back north to Glasgow aware of my intention to engage in another visit to tip my cap at bereavement.

Maybole.

A journey today to salute the memory of my friend, Alan Murray who died too young in his adopted burgh of Maybole where he's buried. The train journey from Glasgow took place under a clear blue sky and a tepid wintry sun which attempted gradually to defrost a Scotland labouring under temperatures of minus five degrees Celsius.

As the train sped past first Royal Troon and then Prestwick Golf Courses, two of the finest links golf courses in the world, I was minded to note the more egalitarian principles of Scotland as opposed to, say, the rest of the world. On each of them could be seen people walking their dog. While I accept that they're not exactly municipal courses, they are still accessible to those who seek to enjoy them without disturbing golfers.

One gently undulating fairway running parallel to the rail track had allowed the sun to warm the green southern flanks of the several parallel hillocks while in the shadow of the northern downslope, a sheet-white frost remained, permitting a scene reminiscent of a large green and white-striped Glasgow Celtic strip. Some of the greens were completely frosted but still, most holes had a foursome lofting balls towards the pin.

Arriving at the railway station above Maybole, the distant Galloway Hills glistened in sunlit snow. As I descended from the station, the place had the feel of a village. My friend Alan Murray had been the local Labour Councillor for many years and had held to left-leaning, conventional, socialist principles throughout. What he'd have made of his party in Westminster these days, abstaining against rather than opposing brutal Conservative cuts in welfare spending is pretty easy to predict - although he was certainly a party loyalist.

For years he lobbied unsuccessfully for a by-pass to ease traffic congestion in his town. Walking along Maybole's High Street, it was easy to understand why as the town happens to sit on the main route north for the gargantuan lorries that exit the Larne, Stranraer/Cairnryan Ferry some few miles away. These monsters are frightening enough when barrelling along a motorway but on a street built in an earlier century to accommodate horse and trap, they're terrifying. And they don't just arrive intermittently. Because they all leave the ferry some miles to the south nose-to-tail, they arrive as if in convoy and then meet their tardy cousins arrowing towards the ferry terminal heading south. It is a physical impossibility for north to pass south at pace and vice-versa. And for pedestrians, my advice would be to crawl along the rooftops. Pavements are perhaps four, sometimes only three feet wide. That there's not carnage is completely down to the good sense and cautious attitudes of local denizens and, to be fair, the lorry drivers.

One observation as I walked towards the cemetery to say, 'Hi' to my friend Alan filled me with hope. On High Street, one terraced red sandstone house, indistinguishable from all others on the thoroughfare bore the brass-plated legend, 'Dr. Rennie'. His doorbells (he had two) were marked 'Day Bell' and 'Night Bell'. How many doctors nowadays are prepared to work from home and be awakened by a needy patient ringing their doorbell at three in the morning?

I was saddened as I paid homage to Alan at his graveside. For the first time, some eighteen months after his too-early demise, I noticed that the grass above his grave now appeared normal, in keeping with all adjacent lairs. Earlier the grave hadn't settled and the turf hadn't knitted giving a makeshift appearance.

I walked back to the town from the cemetery and toasted Alan's memory in his favourite pub, The Maybole Arms (on what is laughingly named Whitehall or the A77 although the thoroughfare would more appropriately be named the Maybole Lane or the Maybole Footpath) and which Alan insisted on calling the Mason's Arms for reasons I can't recall. I sat and listened to the roar of passing lorries outside.

It was my kind of pub; worn upholstery, scabby toilets, disintegrating dart-boards and sticky carpets; the overpowering smell of chlorine in the toilets reminding me immediately of the municipal swimming pools of my youth. The seven unshaven customers (even the *men* were unshaven) that all sat at the bar each continued to wear their anoraks and drank slowly but metronomically, all discussing the small change of their personal lives, all known to one another and all friendly. They discussed their favourite snack. The winner was the barmaid's "Ah like a vanilla cone aff the van an' cheese an' onion crisps thegither!" I was almost sick in my mouth! Later, a question from a woman customer sitting at the bar, "Is France the capital of Germany?" made me worry for the human race.

But this is Burns' country and the Burgh of Maybole is centre stage. When the Reverend James McKnight posted a small notice of marriage banns on his church door in Maybole in 1757, he couldn't have forseen the significance of the announcement. "There is a purpose of marriage between William Burnes, Bachelor, residing at Alloway, in the Parish of Ayr, and Agnes Brown, Spinster, residing in Maybole, in the Parish of Maybole, of which proclamation is made."

Scotland's bard, Robert Burns was subsequently born to the couple in Alloway, only a short distance from the Maybole Arms and many of his poems; 'Sweet Afton', 'Allan Water', 'The Belles of Mauchline', are set in the surrounding countryside. His masterpiece, 'Tam O'Shanter' which draws on the lore of witchcraft, is also set locally. Indeed its hero, 'Souter Johnnie' (whose real name was John Davidson) lived in a thatched cottage (still available to visit) in Kirkoswald, the next village along the road.

Robert Burns is a phenomenon. He was born on 25th January 1759 in Alloway, Ayrshire and this date is celebrated each year by hundreds of thousands of Burns *aficionados* round the world. Indeed, as earlier mentioned, some would have it that his birthday is celebrated more than any other human being other than the carpenter from Nazareth whose celebration takes place eleven months later on 25th December each year. Burns Suppers take place world-wide and Scots and other admirers listen to speakers reciting his poetry. That these events are liberally doused in whisky, haggis and laughter is incidental. What other country celebrates a *poet* as its national hero?

But Burns is real and observably so. His poems written in his own hand are saved for the world and original copies are displayed at his birth-home in Alloway. His likeness is incontrovertibly of him as at least three portraits were painted of him during his lifetime - and they are all recognisably of the same person.

I speak at Burns Suppers most years and now and again enjoy making the point that in comparing Burns with Shakespeare, there is no contest on a number of points. Admittedly, Shakespeare was born in 1564, some one hundred and ninety-five years before Burns; a couple of important centuries. But as a consequence of that, there's much in Shakespeare's history that is at least contestable. We *know* what Burns looked like. But the famous '*Chandos*' painting of Shakespeare, named after Richard Plantagenet Temple Nugent Brydges Chandos Granville, second Duke of Buckingham and Chandos, on a canvas only some twenty-two by eighteen inches, was uncovered at auction in 1856 - some *two hundred and forty years* after Shakespeare's death! People thought it *must* have looked like Shakespeare, but then again, perhaps so too did Nelson Mandela! The image on the Chandos painting had a raffish look about him and wore a gold earring, just as did artists of the time... proof positive, eh? Must be Shakespeare!

Additionally, as Bill Bryson points out in his book, '*Shakespeare*', there are but fourteen words written by Shakespeare's own hand; his name signed by him six times and the words '*by me*' on his will. No one's really sure how he spelled his name. In the signatures that survive, we can attest to Shakesp, Shakespe, Shakspere and Shakspare, the only spelling not available to historians being the one which is now commonly used, Shakespeare.

Finally, in the days that Shakespeare wrote, it was common practice to write as an ensemble, much in the way American comedy is produced these days; as a *team* of writers. And finally, finally; a description of his personality, 'He was a handsome, well-shaped man, very good company and of a ready and pleasant, smooth wit'. Well, this was written more than sixty years after his death by a man who had himself been born ten years *after* that death. So who knows what Shakespeare wrote, what he looked like or whether he preferred Stork to butter.

Burns, however was written about contemporaneously. Sir Walter Scott, who met him when he was aged sixteen said, "He had a poetic eye which literally glowed when he spoke with feeling or interest." By the time he visited Edinburgh on the strength of his book of poems, 'Chiefly in the Scottish Dialect', he was something of a celebrity and in consequence there are scores of testimonies to his personality. One of the number of commentators at the time, a Doctor Walker wrote of 'his innate dignity, his unaffected conduct in company and brilliancy in conversation'.

And he was held in high regard by his contemporaries. In his poem 'At the Grave of Burns', written during his Scottish tour of 1803, William Wordsworth, mused; 'Neighbours we were and loving friends we might have been'. He made no secret of the esteem in which he held Robert Burns;

'Whose light I hailed when first it shone,
And showed my youth
How verse may build a princely throne
On humble truth.'

But it was the man's poetry that set him apart from other mortals. He has been somewhat dismissed by those who prefer the Queen's English because he chose to write in the Scots' tongue, his *lingua franca*. But when he chose to write in the English language, he was in a class of his own. Consider these lines from Tam O'Shanter;

But pleasures are like poppies spread,
You seize the flower; its bloom is shed;
Or like the snow falls in the river,
A moment white, then melts for ever;
Or like the borealis race,
That flit ere you can point their place;
Or like the rainbow's lovely form
Evanishing amid the storm.

His genius can also be found in the simplicity of his language. In his poem, 'A Red Red Rose', a work of some one hundred and fourteen words; five of them, 'newly', 'melody', 'sweetly', 'bonnie' and 'thousand' are of two syllables. The rest are of one single syllable. Genius!

My love is like a red, red rose,
That's newly sprung in June;
My love is like the melody
That's sweetly played in tune.
As fair are thou, my bonnie lass,
So deep in love am I;
And I will love thee still, my dear,
Till a' the seas gang dry.
]Till a' the seas gang dry, my dear,
And the rocks melt wi' the sun:
I will love thee still, my dear,
While the sands o' life shall run.
So fare thee weel, my only love!
And fare thee weel, a while!
And I will come again, my love,
Tho' it were ten thousand mile

Well, Burns strode the streets of Maybole although he didn't have to contend with articulated juggernauts. Had he done so, his poem would have been worth reading.

I left a Maybole whose paved walkways were still crisp in wintry sunshine, my breath visible as I climbed the hill to the train station. My spirits lifted when I noticed the young lady earlier seated in the bar asking confirmation of the capital city of Germany. She collected her young child from the train arriving from Ayr and she was warm, interested, bright and engaged with her offspring. I was reminded that once attending a black-tie dinner in the House of Commons, a very senior business woman leaned over to me and asked if Africa was a country. Maybe it's possible to succeed as a mother or as a business leader while knowing diddly-squat about geography. But if the general population of Maybole are as warm and loving as she whom I scorned as being stupid, it'll be a better environment than, say, Westminster where I have the notion that to a large extent, people are highly intelligent but often bereft of the milk of human kindness.

Madam, I apologise.

Grantown-on Spey

My visit to Grantown-on-Spey in the Scottish Highlands was entirely prompted by nostalgia.

In my early teenage years, my mother each summer took me and my two younger brothers, Alastair and Campbell, to stay in a wee 'but and ben' situated above Bridge of Brown near the main road from Grantown-on-Spey to Tomintoul, the highest village in the Highlands. They were very happy times as we fished in the burn, cooked over an open fire in the small living room, read by oil-lamp and visited all of the towns which cumulatively make up Strathspey, home to over forty distilleries, each producing single malt whisky; in Scots' Gaelic, *"uisge beatha"*, the water of life'.

To we holidaying Culleys, Speyside always started when we reached Dalwhinnie and continued north to encompass Newtonmore, Kingussie, Aviemore and on towards Grantown-on-Spey where other smaller hamlets and villages such as Carr Bridge, Nethy Bridge, Dulnain Bridge and Coylum Bridge (they're big on bridges in that part of Scotland) entranced us. Boat of Garten was always a favourite stop and was possessed of one of the more romantic place-names in Scotland. Right up there with Muir of Ord!

Bridge of Brown was accessed from Grantown-on-Spey by a tightly meandering 'B' road with precipitous drops and an undulating surface. 'Auld Bill' who owned and lived in the croft year round always seemed happy to have us urbanites descend upon him and was full of pithy Scots' aphorisms like ' Never fa' oot wi' yer meat', when someone hadn't cleaned their plate, 'Mony a mickle maks a muckle' when advising on saving money and 'Get up! You're a lang time deid!' whenever someone overslept. I said earlier that his croft was a 'wee but and ben' but I suppose it wasn't. That architectural term refers to an old Scottish cottage where one room is used as an antechamber or kitchen and is the *but*, while an inner room for sleeping, is the *ben*. Auld Bill cooked, lived and slept in a bed recess in one room so making best use of the heating that derived from the small range on the fire. A second room held all of his tools and a third which he'd built using wood from local forests had a few bunk beds which were used to accommodate his guests. The toilet was an outbuilding twenty yards from the croft and there was no running water. It came from the stream nearby when needed. The entire building was infected with dry rot, was damp and was a magnet for the ubiquitous Scottish midge...but we loved it.

However, almost each day we found reason to visit Grantown-on-Spey. If we didn't visit for provisions, we drove there in the evening to sit in a cafe and sip at a soft drink and play the juke-box; Jim Reeves and Wink Martindale being favourites of my mother as I recall. As I walked the town's handsome tree-lined, 'The Square' upon my return I noticed that the cafe was now an Indian Restaurant. Next door, the art-deco Picture House, which we visited each time they changed the movie being shown - no matter its subject matter -, is now host to the British Legion. It seemed somewhat incongruous in this most Scottish of towns to see a large Union Flag flying in the breeze. My curiosity was piqued as in Scotland the charity is known as 'Legion Scotland' although it has the same objective of 'preventing or relieving poverty amongst men or women who have at any time honourably served with any branch of the naval, military and air forces of the Crown'. A glance at their notice-board suggested that it served as much as a social club with darts matches, cake competitions and access to television showing Scottish and English Premiership football matches. Still, it seemed to have replaced the local cinema as a social centre so at least it's not a warehouse or something. I'd imagine, however that it might have a more sizeable workforce than when I attended as a child. Back then, the ticket guy also saw you to your seat via torchlight and sold ice-cream between the 'A' and 'B' movie whilst in-between serving as the projectionist.

I walked round the town, a prosperous burgh, some of whose properties were pretty substantial red-sandstone houses, now converted to hotels. The main street has everything needed for everyday needs. Pubs, cafes, newsagents, hairdressers, mini-markets and estate agents line the thoroughfare and a lonely garage, although well-hidden, serves the automotive requirements of the settlement.

I wandered in to the Claymore Bar for a modest half-pint seeing as I was later to be behind the wheel and sat contentedly reading their notice-board. Perhaps a dozen people sat chatting in groups of two or three. Ceilidhs, pipers for hire, kilt hire and several Scottish Nationalist fliers advertising meetings and marches crowded the cork board. Something wasn't right, though. I couldn't put my finger on it until the barmaid shouted over to a small knot of people drinking near the window. Then it registered...all of the accents - including hers - were English; and Home Counties at that! Perhaps that explained the preference of the Union Flag over the Saltire, I thought. Perhaps not. I was reminded of the argument that in England where there is presently a post-Brexit enthusiasm at the polls for the UKIP party, their objective is to have fewer English people while in Scotland, the SNP seek to achieve a Scotland where there are more Scots - of all backgrounds, creeds and religions, so let's hope that there is an underlying spirit of community in the village. There certainly seemed to be.

The entirety of Strathspey is pine clad. At the side of the roads they stand, pencil-straight like sentries, punctuated every so often by a volley of silver birch. However, I didn't have to walk far out of town before the trees parted slightly and the Cairngorm mountain range came into view. Cairn Gorm itself, Ben Macdui and Cairn Toul are muscled monsters that dominate the range and the valley. In my youth, I'd climbed these and had found myself walking on something that might have resembled the desolation that could have been expected on the moon. Completely barren, hardly any flora and fauna except moss, its rocky, uncultivable surface offers considerable danger for the unaware. It's said that the Cairngorms are the most dangerous mountains in the world because on other ranges; the Himalayas, The Rockies, the Alps, you know in advance what to expect. On the Cairngorm range, however, I've witnessed groups wearing T-shirts having to change into fleeced anoraks and insulating balaclavas following an abrupt change in the weather. From balmy to 'balmy' in minutes! Cairngorm is often used for polar training with snow and ice covering the landscape for much for the year. It is effectively an arctic environment with extreme conditions and rapidly changeable weather. I once skied in a snowstorm where I could only see perhaps six feet in front of me, knowing that cliffs and cornices awaited the slightest incident of disorientation. Not for the faint-hearted or the enthusiastic amateur - which, decidedly I was.

Nowadays, most people ascend Cairngorm by means of a funicular railway which was opened in 2001 and is the highest railway in the United Kingdom. At just over a mile long it ascends the northern slopes of Cairn Gorm, the United Kingdom's sixth-highest mountain and leaves passengers at the Ptarmigan Restaurant, the highest restaurant in the UK. I've dined there. Its food is wholesome but could be procured in any of a thousand restaurants. What the Ptarmigan offers, however, is astonishing panoramic views down to Loch Morlich and across to Ben Nevis. Wisely, those who make their way atop Cairngorm by means of the railway are not permitted to step on to its hallowed and protected surface. A Habitats Directive (hastily drafted by Cairngorm Mountain Ltd. to placate the conservationist lobby in order to speed up the planning process) is designed to restrict access only to serious climbers and scientists in order to protect its biodiversity but frankly, has more likely been designed to protect eegits who figure that because the sun is shining they can wander with impunity on an environment that invites comparison with the surface of the moon.

Beneath this not inconsiderable mountain range, Grantown-on-Spey remains a handsome town and revisiting it brought back many happy memories. I walked back along its High Street and noticed with interest that Mortimer's still remained. This emporium, selling guns, fishing tackle, and country wear seemed to have seen off its sole competition, Ritchies (no apostrophe) and lives on to sell a particular type of Scotland to locals and tourists alike. As a boy brought up in a big city, I used to wander Mortimer's floor open-jawed at the shotguns, knives and rifles that were pinned to its walls. Had I but known, I could probably have visited one of many neighbours in my housing scheme and been shown the same weapons!

Dunkeld and Birnham

When Scotland decides to be beautiful, it pulls out all the stops and can look incredible. I'd planned a visit south to Stranraer but a glance at the morning weather map suggested that I might find kinder weather if I headed north from Glasgow; four below but sunny as opposed to zero degrees and pissing down in southern Stranraer. It was freezing cold, below zero as the sun rose in Glasgow but I headed for the station and caught a train to Dunkeld and Birnam largely on the basis that I'd passed by these towns on many occasions, had stopped off for a coffee but had only briefly walked their streets.

My journey north was rewarded by an azure blue sky, snow-capped peaks and lush green pastures. We passed by Stirling, Bridge of Allan, Dunblane, Gleneagles, Perth - any one of which would have been equally diverting as a destination and all of which looked wonderful, neat and picturesque in the wintry sunshine (I could have spent the day just gawking at Gleneagles Railway Station as it seemed to have been locked in an early twentieth-century time-lock. It was polished, ancient and beautifully maintained; I expected a John Buchan character to step from its ticket-office at any moment. But my goal was Dunkeld and Birnam as I wanted to find out more about a local resident and one of the finest fiddlers who ever bowed strings, Niel Gow.

As the train slowed and approached Dunkeld-Birnam, each town joined at the hip to the other, the train announcer invited caution upon disembarking as 'the platform is slightly lower than usual and the cold weather might make it slippery.' *Slightly lower?* It was, without exaggeration, a full three feet drop and more! An Olympian athlete or a Special Forces free-fall parachutist would have struggled to descend gracefully to the platform. I ventured forth smiling at its ludicrosity, stumbling forward upon hitting solid ground, grateful that the iced platform didn't put me full on my fundament. Three doors along, an old guy, obviously a local used to this lunacy, merely sat on the edge of the train doorway, shuffled forward and dreeped onto the platform. Welcome to Dunkeld-Birnam all you who are aged, disabled, young, blind or drunk! Those who are disabled, young or *blind* drunk may have a particular problem.

I then discovered by means of a helpful sign that Dunkeld lay a mile away from the station, Birnam only a quarter of that distance. However, delighted at my hitherto unknown ability to leap from a train without a parachute or a bungee, I walked into the town in good spirits.

Dunkeld lies on the northern slopes of the River Tay and Little Dunkeld and Birnam lie on its southern flank, nearer the rail-line. Crossing the bridge to Dunkeld provided a lovely view of the town, its buildings completely white other than one householder who'd painted his property in vibrant yellow. I'm betting he's in showbiz!

Dunkeld itself was bathed in sunshine - at least the *tops* of its houses were. A low-lying sun allowed warmth and brightness on certain pavements while crossing the road into the shadows of a frosty gloom saw temperatures plummet by several dark degrees. The town itself suggests prosperity, indeed *comfortable* prosperity in parts. Where houses and buildings have not retained their natural sandstone, they are painted white and where the low sun struck them directly, the glare was ferocious.

For guidance, I sought advice from the Information Bureau in High Street and was delayed beyond the natural length of social interaction as a consequence of the lady behind the counter spilling out all she knew about the 'Wolf of Badenoch' when all I'd asked about was the bust of Niel Gow, accommodated beside Wolf within the cathedral.

"Now, the Wolf of Badenoch was actually the first Earl of Buchan since John Comyn and married the widowed Euphemia, Countess of Ross, but they had no children although he did have a large family by his long-time mistress, *Mairead inghean Eachann,*", she intoned. Before she could get further into her stride, I leapt screaming from a nearby window and walked the short distance to Dunkeld Cathedral (a genuinely lovely place of worship, albeit a smaller version of its kind), in order to see the headstone of Niel Gow which had been taken there by admirers in order to honour him and to preserve his memory. Next to this was the sarcophagus of Alexander Stewart, Earl of Buchan, *Alasdair Mór mac an Rígh,* our friend the Wolf of Badenoch who was the third son of King Robert II of Scotland. He was noted for his cruelty and in one giddy act of abandonment, set Elgin Cathedral ablaze suggesting that forgiveness by the church which now accommodated his remains was a major virtue back in the early fourteen-hundreds.

The cold air drove me into the arms of the *Perth* Arms where a sullen barman asked me 'What d'*you* want?' in the manner of a suspicious landowner finding a trespasser about to fish his river. 'A wee whisky', was the answer. His accomplice, apparently his wife, refused with a heavy humour to give me the password for the establishment's wi-fi, relenting with a silly laugh when she had milked the moment for all of its awkwardness. Still, a blazing fire and the aforementioned wee whisky helped obviate the unwelcoming atmosphere. Unfortunately the noisy, chugging puggy which held centre stage in the bar as a consequence of all of its flashing illuminations, lost the pub points again as I headed for the door and the grave of Niel Gow in Little Dunkeld just on the other side of the River Tay.

The small churchyard in Little Dunkeld accommodates the mortal remains of one of the world's best-ever fiddlers and composers

(Aly Bain claims equal status in my eyes) but as a consequence of the headstone being removed to the cathedral, I found it impossible to determine where he lay in rest. Gravestones dating back into antiquity stood row upon row but the earliest date I could discern was 1805. Otherwise the stones had been wind-blasted into an even surface, obliterating all description of those who lay below. It gave me pause for thought. Unless new sculpting techniques permit a longer-lasting edge to the cuttings or embossments, few of us will be remembered a couple of centuries beyond our demise and given that the world is some 4.543 billion years old, those who seek immortal recognition through the inscription on their gravestone, will likely be forgotten in the virtual blink of an eye. There's every chance that even those such as Donald Trump won't be remembered much beyond a few hundred years once he's largely destroyed the planet.

However, Niel Gow was born in Strathbraan in Perthshire in 1727 before his family moved to nearby Inver when he was but was an infant. His family made use of the Gaelic spelling of Neil which is Niel, often corrected innocently by those unaware of the father's decision. Young Niel started playing the fiddle when very young and at age thirteen had some fiddle lessons from John Cameron, who worked for the Stewarts of Grandtully although beyond that he was essentially self-taught. Despite his being something of a musical prodigy, Gow was trained as a weaver but eventually became a full-time musician when, aged eighteen, he entered a competition that was being judged by John McCraw, a blind Scottish musician, who awarded him the first prize before going on to state that he, "Would ken his bow-hand among a hundred players".

As his popularity grew, his musical abilities were in ever-increasing demand. The Duke of Atholl paid him an annuity of five Scots pounds in return for him performing regularly at Blair Castle, where his portrait by Sir Henry Raeburn is still exhibited in its ballroom.

In 1805, following upon the death of his second wife, Margaret Urquhart he composed one of the most poignant and heart-felt compositions ever; '*Niel Gow's Lament for the Death of his Second Wife*'; one of my personal favourites when played by Scottish fiddle virtuoso, Pete Clark, whose work was introduced to me by my friend and fellow musician, Jim Maxwell.

Although Gow was a very popular musician and travelled widely throughout the highlands playing for the ruling classes (his patrons included the Duke of Atholl and the Duchess of Gordon) he chose to live his entire life in that part of Scotland where he was born. Many of the tunes he composed bear the names of the local rivers, villages and people of his native Perthshire.

Gow himself died on 1st March, 1807, just a couple of weeks before his eightieth birthday. At the time of his death, Thomas Telford's great bridge over the Tay at Dunkeld, the bridge over which I'd just walked, was under construction and the reel, "*Dunkeld Bridge*" was probably his last composition.

I found it interesting that steps had been introduced to the Dunkeld-Birnam south-bound platform to assist travellers descend and that the train south almost stopped in alignment with them. It was standing room only on the train and I had to change at Perth so I disembarked and decided upon a coffee whilst waiting upon the train to Glasgow. I walked past the Station Hotel, the County Hotel, the Queens Hotel (no apostrophe) and the Royal British Hotel before realising that I'd need to walk some distance from the station to find a café that wasn't conjoined with a hotel. The nearby Perth City Social Club was forbidding and seemed a members'-only place so I returned in defeat to the Station Hotel, a very well-appointed establishment, the torrential flush in whose toilets could only be described as astonishing. It was as if the River Tay in spate was descending upon the urinal. Most impressive!

Catching the train south, I couldn't help but notice the modern practice of my fellow passengers who each wore headphones obliterating all external stimuli, I broke with more usual habits, put on my own seldom used earphones and headed south, listening all the way to the melodies, jigs, strathspeys and reels as composed by Niel Gow and played by the estimable Pete Clark.

Just sublime.

Penrith, England

And so, yet further south to Penrith. When I was but a pre-teen child, my grandparents took me several times to the bright lights and entertainment town of Blackpool, Lancashire on the Irish Sea. I always looked forward to the trip immensely not just as a consequence of my anticipation of the destination and its various delights, but because of the overnight bus journey. A journey of any distance was a joy for me but an *overnight* jaunt excited me beyond measure. Invariably I attempted to remain awake and just as invariably I fell asleep in my gran's arms awakening when the bus pulled into Penrith's Market Square in the wee sma' hours for a comfort break. Dopey and confused, I'd head for the pavement along with the adults to stretch my legs as did they. Today I returned to Market Square and it was like meeting an old friend although the George Hotel (in my young day The George and Dragon) is now a shopping mall. Still, the sandstone edifice remains intact sufficient for me to recall stopping there some fifty-odd years ago.

Now, I've passed Penrith many times since but always in a car or on an express train, the town a blur as I whizzed past. Today, I left the train and walked Penrith's byways. It's a handsome town, not particularly photogenic but has a certain charm. I had the sense that it is wealthy enough but also saw deficiencies in the public realm that suggested a local authority not over-endowed with cash, parsimonious or with other priorities. Charity shops dotted the various vennels and tight streets that form the town centre but refreshingly, most pubs and shops seemed to be independent entities and not the more usual conglomerates like McDonalds or KFC although I'm sure they'll be present somewhere in the environs, given that they prosper in more distant outposts such as Outer Mongolia.

One charming feature was the Lonsdale Cinema (formerly the Alhambra) in Middlegate, a cinema with three screens built in 1910 but hosted, for all the world in a building that looks like it should accommodate ye olde public house. Nevertheless, it advertised instead the next Tom Cruise movie as one of its three options. Peppered among shops selling household goods were occasional emporia selling guns, fishing rods, Harris Tweed jackets and sensible shoes; more in tune with the retail outlets I'd expected in this huntin', shootin', fishin' part of the world. Across the road from it was a mini-market whose legend above the door welcomed 'Polish-Latvian-Bulgarian-Romanian' customers. I heard quite a few Slavic/Eastern European accents as I walked the town's thoroughfares so it appears that Penrith is home to quite a few of the immigrants that the current Conservative government want to see returned to their homelands as soon as possible.

I took refuge in the 'Last Orders' pub in Burrowgate (Penrith has a rich collection of 'gates'...Sandgate, Friargate, Middlegate, Castlegate) largely because it advertised free wi-fi, and found myself in a poorly modernised old pub whose clientele seemed to number among those who would welcome repatriation of anyone who wasn't personally acquainted with St. George. Today being the day of the 45th American Presidential election being contested by Donald Trump (he won it the following day) and Hillary Clinton, the conversation was thick with contributions supporting the Republican candidate, mirroring the anger and frustration of the largely white lumpen proletariat of America which just wanted to lash out.

"Ah 'ope he gets in so's ah can get job buildin' that fookin' wall to keep t' Mexicans out!"

"So *what* if 'e starts World War Three? Can't be worse than what we've got at the minute".

"He's backed by the fookin' Ku Klux Klan (he pronounced it *Klu* Klux Klan, in common with half the uneducated world) and by all right thinkin' people in America. Bastid says he wants to drain swamp an' ah thinks he'll shake things oop like they've nevva bin shook up befoh! *Ah* says, mo' powah t'is elbow"

Every second word was 'fookin' and 'bastid' but matters eased when two rucksack wearing young ladies walked in apparently more interested in the toilet facilities than in buying a drink; tourists like me, I sensed.

One toper at the bar reproached the others. "Watch yer fookin' language boys, there's fookin' fanny in now!"

It's nice to know that chivalry is alive and well and living in Penrith.

Temperatures in the minus categories (snow had been forecast) saw me abbreviate my planned walk and take further shelter later on in the Woolpack pub where music by the Police played on a loop almost saw me take to the street before ordering. However, politeness prevailed but as I was looking for a traditional English pub with a low ceiling and wooden beams wherein customers discussed the merits of their Border Collies and drank warm beer, I had one small Glenmorangie and was off again on my perambulations; Sting ushering me from the premises by extolling the virtues of 'Roxanne'.

I passed a prosperous looking Conservative Club, all Union Jacks and blue ribbons and walked uphill to Penrith Castle, now a ruin, which was built at the end of the fourteenth century as a defence against the Scots invaders. Chill temperatures had resulted in a quieter attendance than normal as the park in which the castle is situated was completely empty. It was what might be referred to as a *bijou* castle; not much to look at but I was most impressed by those who built the fourteenth century castle choosing to locate it immediately opposite a main line railway station! What intelligent forethought!

A coffee in the Robin Hood pub en route to the station restored my faith in small scabby pubs that cater to a local population of dart and domino-playing regulars; people who can have a civilised conversation at the bar in the absence of loud music and ubiquitous sports television. The main topic of conversation was the various medicaments each was taking and the variety of deliberate openings that had been made in their persons to permit a surgeon to repair spleens, livers, kidneys and hearts.

"Irritable Bowel syndrome? Ah've 'ad that."

"Chrone's Disease they said it was. Fookin' pain in the arse!"

"I 'ad gout. Too much red meat!" Whereby his fellow drinkers reminded him of his enthusiasm for copious amounts of red wine, brandy, port, dark rum and Guinness. "Yeah, them too," he conceded.

My faith in humanity restored, I headed for the door only to overhear a regular announce to his pals, "That bastid Troomp... Ah fookin' ope 'e *builds* that fookin' wall!"

Chastened, I headed for my train back to Glasgow, clearer, perhaps if not in my understanding of *why* England had recently voted to exit the European Union, at least persuaded of the depth of feeling that had occasioned it.

Carndonagh, Donegal, Ireland

The car-ferry from Scotland's Cairnryan to Northern Ireland's Belfast is a substantial beast; modern and muscular and it whisked me over the *Sheuch* (Scots; ditch) or Straits of Moyle to Belfast in jig time. (When I was a boy my grandfather, Hector used to use the word '*sheuch*' as a polite alternative for 'shite'! 'Ronald, watch you don't step in that dog *sheuch*') Most people assume that they're crossing the Irish Sea from Cairnryan to Belfast but the *Sheuch* connects the Irish Sea in the south, to the seas of the Inner Hebrides of Scotland in the north, so they're crossing the *Sheuch*!

Leaving Derry, I was on the lookout for signs of a border as both north and south had extoled the social, commercial and political virtues of their invisible boundary previously so inked in blood. I saw none.

Driving to my destination of Carndonagh in the county of Donegal in Ireland was rather more complicated than crossing the *Sheuch* however, as motorway gave way to village high street before returning to fast dual carriageway populated by slow-moving tractors whose drivers, I could see from behind that they were grinning from ear to ear in quiet satisfaction at impeding my travelling ambitions; stop/start all the way.

Upon arrival though, Carndonagh revealed itself as a lovely wee township, tidy and bustling. Cars fought for elbow-room in the town square (or triangle, actually); the Diamond, they call it. With a population of only two-and-a-half thousand, it's about as far north as you can go in Ireland, Mallin Head at its tip being just up the road.

Having settled into my accommodation, I drove the short distance to Mallin Head with mounting anticipation as the countryside was both dramatic and gorgeous only to arrive at what should be a celebrated location, the very tip of Ireland to find a magnificently ugly monstrosity built by the British in 1805 as a Napoleonic lookout tower to help defend against a possible French invasion. Now dilapidated, it would benefit from graffiti removal, some paint, some tender loving care and some nitro-glycerine. Given everything that was blown up during the 'Troubles' in the seventies through the nineties, it seems rather delinquent of all concerned not to have reduced this construction to rubble in order to permit the absolute beauty of the place to be appreciated without this carbuncle defacing the view.

Carndonagh has above Donegal average rates of unemployment, partly because of the closure of Kelly's Supermarket which had served the good people of the town for over fifty years and that of the O2 shop which had closed recently.

Robbie Cunningham, manager of Tully's Bar on the Triangle was unequivocal. He finished polishing some whisky glasses and asked me my poison before explaining the change in fortunes of his town.

"The town's quieter. There's no doubt about that. I used to open seven days a week. Eleven in the morning until closing time. Now I open Wednesday through Sunday and I only serve drink from three in the afternoon. No one's drinking like they used to."

At this point I was his only customer and it was three o'clock on a Saturday afternoon.

"Now, I've a small stage back there". He indicated a raised dais in the gloom. "I used to have show-bands from all over play here; groups, maybe seven strong. Expensive, but. Nowadays it's soloists with backing tapes." He pondered my level of interest before satisfying himself that I'd react positively and chanced it.

"I do a bit of the old singing myself."

So saying, he raised his spectacles and affixed them to his forehead, peered at his phone and pressing a few buttons, unleashing a YouTube video of him singing *'Daughter of the Vine'* a country and western melody which was actually very good. He'd a pleasant voice. It was suited to the songs he sang, typical of many Country & Western melodies about blind dogs, divorce, the bottle and/or unfaithfulness.

"I'm actually a drummer! But I gave it up when the show-bands began to decline. People seemed to want to hear me sing so I do a fair bit round about Donegal...I'm up in Aberdeen in a few weeks. Can't remember where. You'll need to come and hear me sing."

Emboldened by the few sips of Guinness I'd consumed I agreed to take a run up to the Granite City with the rider that I didn't intend to wander the streets, my hand cupped behind one ear listening for his dulcet tones. He'd need to let me know where he was playing.

I confess I was impressed by a booking so far from home and even more impressed when he showed me a photograph of his house in Carndonagh, it was a massive pile; probably eight or so bedrooms. Our Robbie must be an exceptional barman, a lucky lottery winner or a popular entertainer. Good luck to him!

I left in order to meet an old friend we'll call Henry for tax reasons, a senior citizen of this parish who'd invited me to a bash he'd organised, "Just to bring the cousins together!"

I puzzled for some time at this excuse for a bash but in the event I understood once the congregation had taken place. In large

Irish families, scattered to the four winds, years can pass before clapping eyes on one or more siblings and their brood and the notion of everyone getting together, flying in from London, Manchester, Glasgow; travelling up even from more distant parts of Ireland just didn't happen - until Henry took the reins.

Simpson's Bar hosted Henry's get-together, a venue reluctantly acknowledged as acceptable by *pubmeister* Robbie Cunningham who agreed that while he would have been delighted to have hosted his friend Henry's event in Tully's Bar - and could have coped with the attendance of sixty, he couldn't have offered the privacy and sole occupancy as could Simpson's - a more modern facility on the edge of town.

Strong drink, dancing (to a solo guitarist playing to a backing tape!) and grub were all subordinated to the *craic* in Simpson's. Genuine affection was evident as yelps, hugs and kisses greeted every curious face that peered round the door, unsure of what to expect of people they'd not seen in some cases, for decades. It was uplifting and life-enhancing seeing how people in concert could generate such a generous and warm-hearted ambience. Interestingly, a recent television appearance I'd made (widely circulated throughout his family by Henry) made me something of a common denominator for those who *partnered* a cousin and who really didn't know anyone other than their squeeze.

"Aren't you that guy..."

I humbly acknowledged my celebrity and allowed them to buy me a drink.

Henry insisted next morning that I visit 'the Hill'. Three miles outside Carndonagh there's a large peat bog run by the council but over which locals claim (or actually *have*) rights. I couldn't say. As a Carndonagh resident, Henry has a site on the bog which he can dig freely and from which he can remove peat.

Approximately seventeen per cent of Ireland is covered in peat bogs. The country has more bog than any other country in Europe other than Finland and with many of Europe's bogs being exhausted, those in Ireland (and Scotland) now have an increased importance among the scientific community, as well as within tourism industry.

Dried out peat sods are referred to as 'turf' and are used as a very efficient fuel. In consequence they have a significant value and are available to any resident (at least in Carndonagh according to Henry) who has 'rights'. A special tool, a peat iron called a *tairsgear* in Scots Gaelic is used which forces the peat to be relieved from the earth in slabs perhaps around a foot in length and a few inches thick. The *tairsgear* has a long wooden handle like a spade but with an angled blade protruding to one side. This permits a slab of peat to be dislodged and with a twist, thrown to one side in order to dry. My friend George Cuthbert – an expert in these matters – insists that the Irish peat iron has its angled blade protruding to the left whereas the Scottish version has it protruding to the right, so giving life to the aphorism that the Irish are all 'left footers'.

Henry explained his introduction to peat-cutting.

"When I was a boy we used to skip school, walk three miles to the bog, spend all day with me da cutting turf and then walk three miles back home where me mum made us spuds for tea. It was back-breakin' work. We'd foot the sod then place five or six sods of turf upright and leaning against each other with the big side up and the wet side out."

"So how do you still manage now that you're getting on in years?"

"Oh, it's all changed now. These days we hire Jack."

"Jack?"

"Aye. He owns a peat-cutter. I phone him up and we agree he'll do an hour cutting and stacking peat with his machine."

"Jack has a machine?"

"It can go anywhere. Through deep mud. Up steep hills. Even through water. His machine...it's a tractor actually...cuts the peat and stacks it for me and I pay him maybe three hundred Euros."

"Jeez, that's a big hourly fee!"

"Maybe. But I can sell that on for maybe a grand!"

"You make a profit of seven hundred Euros by making a phone call?"

"Well there's all of the incidentals."

"And what might they be?"

Henry smiled. "Sure, I'd need to be in when the guy turns up to collect his van-load!"

We continued our conversation and agreed that there was a queer difference between walking six miles and footing turf all day and 'being in' to wait for his cash.

My next door neighbour is Bridie Lynch from Donegal. One mention of this to Henry and a substantial bag of peat was in the rear of my car.

"Tell her it's from her friends in Donegal."

He'd never met her...but he meant it! They are lovely people in Donegal. Just lovely people.

But have not they gone through difficult times? A farewell visit to Robbie Cunningham in Tully's Bar the following day highlighted the change in fortunes for this market town. Still Robbie was cleaning glasses, beer glasses this time, as I walked in. Still I was his only customer. More revelations followed as we settled in to our conversation.

"I was a plasterer to trade, Ron. Worked all over. Me and my three brothers, my brother-in-law and two pals were working on a job in Glengormley, on the outskirts of Belfast. We just couldn't find work here in Carndonagh. So there we were, tired after a hard day's work, driving home. I noticed three guys up ahead on a bridge over the road; the M2, but thought little of it. We were just passing Templepatrick at the time. Heading for home. Out of nowhere the windscreen gets smashed in and these three feckers are firing away at us with a sub-machine gun and two pistols. My young brother's in the front seat and he shouts out, 'I'm hit!' And we drive on, even though they'd burst the tyres."

"It's easy to forget that these things happened. Was your brother all right?"

"Dead as a doornail, Ron. A bullet in the chest. Sixteen years old with his whole life in front of him. May God have mercy on his soul. Fourteen shots fired. This was back in 1973 when the Troubles were at their height and the only reason the British Army could come up with for the attack was that our van was carrying Irish number plates showing it was from Donegal."

"Suspicion would fall on Protestant paramilitaries or the Ulster Defence Regiment, eh?"

"Aye, and the rest." He warmed to his subject. "See, the UDR was an infantry regiment that the Brits organised to defend life and property in Northern Ireland against armed attack or sabotage. At the end of the day they was the largest infantry regiment in the British Army, but they was mostly part-time volunteers and all from the local Protestant community. It was clear that there would be all sorts of cosy relationships between paramilitaries and the British Army but the thing was, only two of us in the van was Catholic. The rest of us was Protestant but religion was nothin' that bothered us. We was all friends and got on great but what they found was that the gun used to shoot poor Henry had been 'stolen' (he mimed the inverted commas with his trigger fingers) from a British Army base in Lurgan the year earlier. The same machine gun was then used to kill two Catholics a year later and although the Royal Ulster Constabulary found the gun, didn't they go and destroy it? They destroyed the evidence!"

"Are you saying there was mischief afoot, Robbie?"

"Feckin' right I am." He raised his spectacles to his forehead again and consulted his tablet-sized phone until he found the article he was looking for and read from the screen. "A report by a Historical Enquiries Team in 2008 said that one of the guns used was stolen from a UDR base. They found evidence of collusion between loyalists and the security forces in the raid on the base and also cited evidence of collusion in the theft of the weapon. An earlier British Army investigation admitted that there was "strong evidence" of collusion between its own Ulster Defence Regiment and loyalist paramilitaries in relation to 'missing' weapons from the UDR barracks." He returned his glasses to the bridge of his nose. "See, back in them days, Ron, the Brits was up to all sorts of funny business. Now we have access to declassified documents that prove that civil servants, government ministers, chief constables and senior army and MI5 officers was all well aware that the UDR was heavily infiltrated by loyalists. They was all aware that weapons was disappearing at an alarming rate and that people was dying as a result." The spectacles were raised again. "Here's one that reads, 'Subversion in the UDR', and"... He read aloud, "it confirms that Whitehall knew that as many as fifteen per cent of the regiment's soldiers were involved in collusion as early as 1973 and suspected that as many as two hundred army rifles and sub machine guns had been passed to loyalist groups."

"Horrible times, Robbie. Is everything settled now?"

"Indeed it is not!" He spoke intemperately. "We're taking legal action against the Ministry of Defence in Britain...and we won't rest until we get some answers. No one's ever been caught, the Brits have kept us in the dark, the government in the south have been as much help as a chocolate fireguard and all the while I've a wee brother dead and buried. The family aren't after money just the truth!"

Now, there was murder and mayhem on both sides. During the seventies through the eighties and into the nineties, I'd sit at home and watch images of the bombings and killings on the evening news shaking my head at man's inhumanity to man, incredulous at the inability of either side to find a political solution and here in front of me, polishing beer glasses, sad and angry, was evidence of what happens when blind hatred trumps political accord and causes actual human victims. More than three and a half thousand people were killed during the troubles of whom fifty-two per cent were civilians, thirty per cent were members of the British security forces, and sixteen percent were members of paramilitary groups. I couldn't help but surmise that at least some of the older, friendly faces whom I'd embraced in drink the night before and others who walked the streets of the town outside the pub would have been involved in some way in the murderous political, ethnic, nationalist and sectarian carnage locals still refer to as 'the Troubles' as if they were years during which there were disputes over bin collections.

Aye, Carndonagh was a lovely wee place - but beneath the surface, many still hurt. Robbie takes refuge in his Country & Western music. Perhaps it's little wonder that he's so popular. When he sings of pain and loss, betrayal and hope, he sings from the heart.

Fenwick

Anyone driving down the M77 from Glasgow to Kilmarnock would pass Fenwick - on the left as the desolate Fenwick Moor eventually gives way to habitation - in a nano-blur. Its small village population of some eight hundred souls live with a constant hum of passing traffic although they have the consolation of mooing cows, baa-ing sheep and tweeting and chirping ornithoids.

Frankly, it offers an ideal village lifestyle for those who'd forego bright lights, traffic lights and supermarkets. Its Main Road consists of an uneven row of well-kept whitewashed terraced cottages, some of which have been discretely converted to surgeries, newsagents or abattoirs, (I made up that bit about the abattoirs). It seems a gentle, well-behaved, kindly community. It also appears wealthy. Once I'd walked away from Main Road the community became instantly more affluent. Large villas predominated albeit with a sprinkling of expensive-looking bungalows boasting large lawns. It doesn't overdo things; a post-office, tobacconist, surgery, tea shop, bowling green and non-fuel garage. Half-a-mile down the hill, a second Fenwick emerges, much like the first but with better street names like Waterslap and Maunsheugh Road.

Fenwick's a peculiar place in that the village is bifurcated with farm fields separating the upper village from the lower. Next to a lower village plaque celebrating the historical significance of the Co-operative movement in Fenwick, a developer is building a series of expensive-looking homes with double garages. They look out of place but in the same cul-de-sac, another carbuncle, the four star Fenwick Hotel seems to cater for those who enjoy their whisky in a square glass...a square glass! Have they no shame? (I infiltrated the premises to check).

However, inside my much preferred hostelry, the wonderfully stone-clad, wood-beamed walls and ceiling of the King's Arms' pub in Main Road in upper-Fenwick, two middle-aged Americans entered the almost empty establishment half way through my first pint asking bus information back to Glasgow - information I knew off by heart. Being American their question had been directed to the entire (half-empty) pub and being Scottish, so was my response.

"Fifteen of, and fifteen after the hour. (I speak fluent American). The bus stop's outside. You'll be back in your hotel in forty minutes."

This was sufficient invitation for them to lift their drinks (still water) and join me.

"You're Scaatish!"

"Well, we're in Scaatland"

"We're from Arizona."

"So was Geronimo!" (I'd been reading about Geronimo).

"Wasn't he a Red Indian?"

"A Native American. And he was in Arizona before you folks." Concerned I may have been a tad cheeky, I thought to reassure them. "But I've been in Phoenix, Flagstaff and"...I had to think, reminding myself by singing the famous Eagles' song to myself..."Winslow."

My visitations excited them and they ignored my mild jibe, consulting a map of the local area, spreading it before me on the table, in the process soaking up some beer spillage that had been annoying me.

"We have relatives who come from Fenwick and we want to know more about the kind of people we come from. One of them was born here but one married someone from Craigie in a church in Stewarton."

"I suppose that makes sense. These places are all nearby."

"Scaatland's so neat. My name's Nancy. This is Eddie." Eddie was a woman.

We shook hands and involved ourselves in a conversation that embraced Donald Trump's Mexican wall (they approved), Scaatish genealogy services in Edinburgh (they approved), Scaattish weather (ambivalent...'Scaatland don't have earthquakes, whirlwinds or dust-storms but she do have rain a 'plenty...although your grass is so *green*!')...and books (they *love* the '*Outlander*' novels of Arizonan author Dianne Gabaldon which features the '45 Scottish Rebellion of Charles Edward Stuart and whose narrative eventually takes the main characters to America as slaves.)

"Thet's pretty much whaa we're here, sah! We just lauuved your Scaattish hero, Jamie in *Outlander*! He inspaad us to craas the paand."

We discussed their current President's economic policy (they approved) and I introduced the political and economic policies that were born here in Fenwick, the Co-operative movement - even if it didn't transfer in its purest form to America.

"You're both basically from Communist stock," I teased.

Americans don't like teasing.

"Don't think so, honey. We'd git shaat back home if we was Caammies!"

I responded in my most pompous manner. "Aye, well the Co-operative movement, once presumed to have its genesis in Rochdale in England, is now unequivocally reckoned to have its beginnings here in Fenwick, only yards from where you sit. Your antecedents would probably have been egalitarians."

They each looked appalled! Equality?

Back in 1761, the year, in case you're wondering, when King George the third of England married Charlotte of Mecklenburg-Strelitz, - yes, *that* year, the Fenwick Weavers' Society was created in Fenwick by local people arranging their matters in such a way as to establish a consumers' co-operative for the benefit of its members. Its original objective was to foster high standards in the weaving craft, but the nascent organisation quickly expanded its range of activities to include the collective purchasing of bulk foodstuffs and books, resulting in the creation of an early library. Now, this was a point in time when, in America, the Pennsylvania Assembly, was reintroducing the scalp bounties, paying $10 for every Native American, male or female killed over the age of ten; eleven years before Scottish inventor, James Watt, created a condenser for steam engines and nine years before Captain Cook sailed to New Zealand (arriving unaware of the presence of French explorer, Jean-François-Marie de Surville, who discovered the place before him - a fact rather overlooked by history!) At that point in time, Fenwick weavers were working on a methodology whereby members could support one another economically. Eat your heart out, Vladimir Ilyich Ulyanov Lenin!

Effectively, the self-employed weavers of Fenwick sought to protect their trade and to help others in troubled times. They organised a community-run school, they made small loans to families in need forming the first credit union, provided loans to permit local people to take advantages of opportunities in the new world and were generally supportive of their neighbours. In effect, they formed the very first recorded consumer co-operative. The movement began in humble fashion when a small group met in secret in the village church to sign a pledge of loyalty to one another and, "to make good & sufficient work and exact neither higher nor lower prices than are accustomed". Revolutionary stuff, as up until that time workers, whether farmers, tradesmen, craftsmen or retailers had been dependant on the patronage of the local landowners and the aristocracy. The notion that the working class could organise itself and cooperate one with another in a way that was fair, mutually beneficial and self-organised was both novel and threatening to the status quo. Meetings continued to be held in secret to avoid any interference by reproachful landowners who tended to the view that workers self-sufficiency was inimical to their own self-interests.

Nancy and Eddie listened silently to me as I allowed them to imagine that their forbearers travelled to America as a consequence of a revolutionary new idea called Co-operatism, an idea based on moral values, commitment, mutuality and the essential dignity of humanity. However, I went on to make the point (not quite as articulately I confess, as I make it here in written form) that far and away the main Scottish contribution to the American economic model was the work of Adam Smith, whose book, 'The Wealth Of Nations' published in 1776 (some fifteen years after the Fenwick Weavers organised themselves) described Capitalism and explained to an innocent world that a nation's wealth is basically the quantity and quality of goods and services that it creates and can sell; effectively its gross national product. However, contrary to the principles of the weavers, he argued that the way to maximise profit and growth was not to restrict the nation's productive capacity by sharing, supporting and assisting but to de-regulate the market and allow the survival of the fittest, most greedy and exploitative.

"Now, thet's more laak it," said Eddie thoughtfully. "Thet's the 'Merican way!"

"I suppose so but when your ancestors left Fenwick, they'd have walked straight into the eight-years'-long American War of Independence which started just as Adam Smith published his seminal writings and would have entered a world where bartering was the main form of exchange. They'd have been much more likely to toast Fenwick than Kirkcaldy where Adam Smith was born."

"Ah guess," said Nancy, worriedly.

They rose to catch their bus. "Food for thought, food for thought...Thank you Raan. Very interesting." which I interpreted as 'we expected to hear dashing tales of ruggedly handsome be-kilted warriors with hair like rock gods, the manners of gentlemen and the soul of barbarians reaching our shores and setting out for Arizona... not this load of bollocks you've dumped on us'.

I wish them well - but would love to be a fly on the wall as they return to their America and its evil triplets of racism, extreme materialism and militarism and explain to their bewildered friends their visit to Fenwick had produced a more complex family tree than the one they'd anticipated.

Falkland, Dunfermline, Culross

It was on impulse.

I'd watched my television screen in wonder as the First Minister of Scotland, Nicola Sturgeon stood before a brilliantly colourful laser and light show that illuminated the pristine

Queensferry Crossing over the Firth of Forth, the longest triple-tower, cable-stayed bridge in the world, and announced it open for business; within budget and ahead of time. On my list of must-visit destinations and one I'd wanted for some time to visit (inspired also by the enthusiasm of Nancy and Eddie for locations shown in 'Outlander') was the village of Falkland in Fife and to get there would have to travel overland via Dundee, cross the River Forth at Kincardine or cross the wider firth using the new South Queensferry Bridge.

A ballot had earlier been offered to those who wished to be the first to cross the bridge as pedestrians because after a two-day hiatus, the bridge would carry vehicles only as they will travel across 'at motorway speeds' and sensibly it was decided not to have people wandering around next to a motorway. 'A once-in-a-lifetime experience' was to be made available before the bridge opened for speedy business. I applied to walk but was to be disappointed. However, the First Minister was heard to announce that the bridge had been completed comfortably within schedule and would be opened to traffic for two days before the pedestrian-only weekend. Today and tomorrow! I was off!

I set off early, confident that I'd be the only person who'd heard the news who would be interested enough to cross the bridge opportunistically. Imagine then my surprise when some two miles out, the easy flow of traffic ran into the sand. Apparently half of Scotland had had the same idea as me and we all crawled slowly towards this new marvel. Having said that, I wasn't in a hurry and an unexpected benefit was to be able to enjoy the structure close up and in detail as leisurely we crossed this wondrous new span.

Upon reaching the far shore in Fife, the sun shone and I drove north passing towns such as Lochgelly wherein was manufactured the barbarous tawse of my schooldays; a thick leather strap which was liberally and forcefully applied to the hands of pupils who'd committed some infraction or other. 'Six of the best' was delivered by teachers and, frankly, was a punishment dismissed with a shrug by parents if not by the pupils themselves. A few years ago my wife and I held a party in a local hostelry and encouraged a 'sixties' theme. Our friend, Rose brought a lot of school memorabilia - including a dreaded leather tawse. The number of normally sensible adults who lined up, gin and tonic in their left hand to be belted on their right by younger members in attendance was remarkable. With a wisdom beyond their years, not one of the teenagers offered their hands to experience the nostalgic searing pain which adults sought - if only once, before turning away with a rueful smile and a slug of their gin; a palliative not available to schoolchildren back in the day, our only remedy then being to lodge the affected hand under the opposite oxter (armpit) as if *that* effected any benefits whatsoever!

Further on, large brown tourist signs pointed the way to 'Scotland's Secret Bunker', an underground Cold War bunker museum one hundred feet underground and the size of two football pitches, housing a BBC studio and switchboard room hidden beneath an innocent Scottish farmhouse. I resisted its appeal and continued on past Glenrothes and the tiny village of Freuchie - best known for having won the village cricket championships at Lord's back in 1985. A Scottish cricket team winning a cricket championship? I remember thinking at the time that it was as likely as a Scottish tennis player ever becoming World Number One!

I'd wanted to visit Falkland ever since as a social worker in my early twenties I had been required to visit a child who had been placed there with a family who wished to adopt her. Then I'd been focussed upon the task at hand in *finding* the place (in days long before satellite navigation) and in returning back timeously (in days long before end-to-end motorways) to Paisley where I worked at the time. Its beauty only registered tangentially and it wasn't until I joined the millions of world viewers who watched '*Outlander*' religiously that I began to appreciate its value.

Set in some measure in Falkland due to its venerable buildings, '*Outlander*' (the Gaelic translation being '*Sassenach*'; someone furth of Scotland, a foreigner) is a televised adaption of a best-selling series of books written by American novelist, Arizonan Professor Diana Gabaldon. It centres on the relationship in 1743, (two years before the 1745 Jacobite Rising in Scotland) between English nurse Claire Randall, the 'Outlander', and her romantic but torrid relationship with Highland warrior Jamie Fraser. Her medical skills earn the respect of her captors but she is nevertheless suspected of being an English spy. I won't go on but essentially the story depicts Scots as bekilted noble warriors, full of humour and possessed of a strong moral code whereas the English Redcoats are ruthless, cruel and perfidious or effete, chinless wonders. Something of a caricature but the series became hugely popular around the world - so popular that then Prime Minister David Cameron successfully lobbied the Sony Corporation, who owned the rights, to delay its showing in Scotland until after the Scottish Referendum on Independence from the rest of the United Kingdom. Had it been shown nation-wide before the plebiscite, it may have aroused such indignation at the way Scots were treated by their English neighbours back in the eighteenth century that Scots men and women would have marched into the voting booths as one and demanded independence.

Falkland is wondrous. A small village of some thousand residents, it was brought into being around 1500 when King James IV commissioned Scotland's best architects and craftsmen to create a 'pleasure palace' for his beloved country pursuits of falconry and hunting. The end result of his vision and efforts was Falkland, certainly one of Scotland's finest Renaissance palaces. The Stuart Kings of Scots were frequent residents and according to legend, Mary, Queen of Scots loved the place as it reminded her of the *chateaux* of the French Royal Court in which she'd grown up. Certainly the palace hasn't lost any of its grandeur and still boasts a Real Tennis Court managed by the Falkland Palace Royal Tennis Club (previously called the Falkland Palace Real Tennis Club). Construction was completed in 1541 and is the oldest tennis court in use today.

However, situated as it is in the middle of the village High Street, the architecture of the palace melds well with the equally astounding design and stonework of the village cottages and gift shops which abound but do not detract from the overall sense of an aged (and monied) settlement.

I delighted in being able to look at a local tearoom and remind myself that that was the location where Claire and Jamie etc etc... or at one of the many households where English Redcoats....

The place is steeped in history both real and more recently conjured by the talents of an American author who has an ear for the Scottish language and an ability to record historical events pretty accurately. Scotland has not been served well over the years as even popular movies such as the cinematically accomplished 'Braveheart' which purported to tell the story of Scottish military hero William Wallace was beset with inaccuracies such as the Scots painting their face with blue woad or one of the movie's centrepiece battles - the Battle of Stirling Bridge - taking place in the absence of a bridge. Robert the Bruce never betrayed William Wallace and our eponymous hero never spoke with a strangulated Australian/American/Scottish accent.

All of that might have been fake - but Falkland is the real deal!

Running parallel to High Street is Black Dykes where a bench at the war memorial is inscribed, 'In recognition of the deep attachment the Cash family in America have for the Howe of Fyfe where the name of Cash originated'. Johnny and Rosanne Cash performed in the village – notably using it to film their US TV Christmas special in 1981 to demonstrate their affection for their ancestral home.

Given my presence in Fife, I decided to move on a few miles to Dunfermline to pay homage at the grave of Robert the Bruce who is interred in Dunfermline Abbey...at least his skeletal remains are; his heart having been buried in Melrose Abbey. Along with the island of Iona, Dunfermline Abbey is the traditional last resting place of most Scottish kings. On his deathbed, Bruce asked

Sir James Douglas to go on a crusade to The Church of the Holy Sepulchre in Jerusalem and take his heart with him. Douglas was killed in battle with the Moors in Spain and Bruce's heart was brought back to Scotland and buried at Melrose - an event recorded in John Barbour's epic 14th-century poem "The Bruce". Lost in the mists of time, a casket containing a mummified heart was unearthed by archaeologists in 1921 before being lost again then rediscovered during an archaeological dig and re-buried at a ceremony at Melrose conducted by the then Scottish Secretary of State, Donald Dewar in 1998.

However, indisputably, the rest of his mortal remains have been secreted beneath the altar in Dunfermline Abbey since 1329. I ventured along the entry-way finding the surrounding graveyard somewhat tousled. Back in 1303, troops of Edward I caused substantial damage to the place following his observation that the Abbey was "not a church, but a den of thieves.....a thorn in the eye of the English throne". Well, they may have spent time and money bringing the old place back to its best but the grassed graveyard was unkempt and apparently uncared for; an empty bottle of fortified wine discarded near the wall suggestive of occupancy, if temporarily, by a den of drunks if not thieves. I followed a clutch of American tourists into the Abbey, each of whom was wearing a backpack laden down with bottled water as if they were intent upon heading off into the Outback to photograph kangaroos rather than make their way from their coach some hundred yards away.

Internally I found the Abbey to be remarkably plain, perhaps in keeping with the Scots' traditional ambivalence about unnecessary embroidery and fuss. A large, coffin-sized ornate brass plate beneath the altar indicates the royal vault within which the warrior king is interred. Brightly polished and well lit, it serves well its purpose.

He was quite a guy, our Robert. For years he attempted to sue for peace with the English King Edward the second. Ignored, he proceeded to capture towns and cities occupied by English troops. For eight years he fought a guerrilla war until in 1314 he met and defeated much superior English forces at Bannockburn. Taking a breath, he invaded Yorkshire and Lancashire before invading Ireland in 1315 at the request of Donal O'Neil, King of Tyrone, purportedly to free the country from English rule and to open a second front in the continuing wars each nation waged with England. Bruce pursued a pan-Gaelic alliance between Scottish/Irish Gaelic populations under his leadership. He wrote to O'Neil calling the Scots and Irish collectively *nostra nacio* ('our nation')...a Celtic precursor to the Sicilians' *'cosa nostra'* (our thing), perhaps?), stressing the common language, customs and heritage of the two peoples. In response, the Irish crowned his brother, Edward Bruce as High King of Ireland in 1316.

That the Bruce died in 1329 is a fact. Whether of tuberculosis, syphilis, cancer, a stroke or an unhealthy diet is less certain. His personal physician, Dr. Maine de Maineri, put it down to Robert's habit of eating eels (although Cockneys I've met argue their benefits.) My own view is that *Signor* Maineri may have had a point!

Dunfermline itself is a handsome town. Lots of old stone buildings, impressive town houses, non-chain shops and estate agents whose windows suggest a brisk trade in bricks and mortar. In its Alhambra Theatre it has retained a gem of a building. Like almost every town in the world these days, its High Street is pedestrianised but due attention has been paid to the public realm and it ends gloriously in a beautifully ornate city chambers and clock tower at its western end where it meets Kirkgate. Interestingly, although the building announces itself as the 'City Chambers', Dunfermline is regarded as a town and is not regarded as having city status. It does fly the Union Flag alongside the Saltire, however, perhaps reflecting the power-sharing political nature of the town's Labour and Nationalist administration.

Onwards then to Culross, a small village on the Firth of Forth where it begins to narrow at the Kincardine Bridge. Home to fewer than four hundred souls, it hosts buildings which the National Trust for Scotland has been preserving and restoring since the early 1900s. Its narrow lanes, cobbled streets and traditionally designed houses have played host to a number of movies and television productions including *Kidnapped*, *The 39 Steps*, *Outlander* and perhaps more curiously, *Captain America* among several others. It really is a beautiful village, steeped in history and very easy on the eye - that is until one turns one's gaze to the view *from* the village. On its western flank, looming skywards is the towering Longannet Power Station, at its peak, the largest coal-fired station in Europe. In 2007, the World Wildlife Foundation named Longannet as the most polluting power station in the UK and, according to a subsequent Greenpeace report, responsible for 4,210 lost 'life years' in 2010.

Across the Forth from the rural loveliness of Culross, spitting flames and spouting black smoke are the multitudinous chimney stacks and vents that so characterise the heavily industrialised port of Grangemouth, a town rivalled only by Middlesbrough for its ugliness, pollution and grime. So...a rose between two thorns; an unrivalled view set beside perspectives of hell, a diamond in the rough. Culross is a genuinely lovely wee township and along with Falkland has accommodated many of the scenes shown in 'Outlander' where it purports to show a Scotland of *circa* 1745 and 1919. In this they each perform magnificently.

Berwick-upon-Tweed, England
To England! Again...

Well, at least, two-and-a-half miles into England! The train from Glasgow to Penzance no less took me comfortably over the border and deposited me in a sunny if breezy Berwick-upon-Tweed to give it its Sunday name. Berwick is the most northerly town in Northumberland and therefore in England. However, as I walked down Marygate past the market selling Scotland football strips, shops advertising Broons Annuals and Scotland fridge magnets, observing buildings on each side of the road unequivocally of

270

Scottish architecture, built of sandstone blocks rather than the small red 'Coronation Street' bricks structurally ubiquitous as the border is crossed on the west coast, I could be forgiven for thinking I was in Scotland.

As I listened to conversations in the Wednesday market and in The Brewers Arms (no apostrophe) it was Scottish accents that predominated. Occasionally I'd discern a Geordie overtone but apart from a Colonel Blimp who conversed in Home Counties bools-in-the-mooth with his (overtly Scottish accented) friend as they exited the large Church of Scotland lunch club on the Parade heading towards the Bank of Scotland on Hide Hill, local people spoke with 'dinnaes', 'haud oans' and 'gauny's'. Even local football team, Berwick Rangers FC play in Scottish League Two, the fourth tier of Scottish football, although their stadium is in Tweedmouth, the adjacent settlement immediately across the river.

Perhaps these Scottish connections are understandable as the town has had a turbulent history having changed hands between Scotland and England no fewer than thirteen times. And with the Scottish Parliament just an hour up the road and the Westminster version some six hours by car, its little wonder that in 2008 when a poll was instituted by ITV to establish local opinion on the matter, the plebiscite determined that 63% of voters were in favour of becoming part of Scotland and but 37% in favour of staying in England. Better financed public services, including free personal health care for the elderly, were cited as the main reasons.

But straight off the bat just let me say that Berwick is just a lovely wee town, really lovely. The railway station, previously the site of Berwick Castle; built in the sixteenth century and demolished in the nineteenth to make way for railway platforms had replaced the fortress, rendered obsolete as a consequence of the construction of lower ramparts around the town. The railway platforms now stand where King Edward took an oath of allegiance from Scottish nobility in 1296, following his ransacking of Berwick. The year before, Scotland had signed the 'Treaty of Paris', initiating the

'Auld Alliance' between them and France, the first mutual defence treaty between any two sovereign nations anywhere in the world. England, not unreasonably took this as an act of war and invaded Berwick where ten thousand of the population; men, women and children were slaughtered to make a wee point. Today some twelve thousand souls safely call Berwick their home following a *'quitclaim'* by Richard 1st in 1187 when he bequeathed Berwick-upon-Tweed to Scotland in perpetuity to help financing his crusading ambitions.

The town itself slopes dramatically from the railway station down to the harbour. The busy Marygate accommodates the usual collection of charity shops, commercial outlets and pubs and is easy on the eye. Half-way down, the muscular Scots Gate (no apostrophe) still stands in order to protect Elizabeth's Protestant England from the Catholic Scots and their allies, the French. Today it marks a boundary between the good pubs; the Brewers Arms, the Free Trade, the King's Arms, from the smelly, plastic, scabby disappointment of The White Horse - although it does serve a decent hot pie; the only foodstuff allowable in pubs seeking my custom. Irritatingly, had I walked a few steps further up the hill, the Castle Bar had sunny windows, no blaring television, no pool table, no slot machines and a decent gantry.

I confess I was almost driven from the Brewers Arms when joined two tables away by possibly one of the most obnoxious creatures it's been my misfortune to encounter in a pub. Four apparent hill-walkers had arrived, removed their small back-packs and leaned their hiking poles against the wall. Two men, two women in their fifties, I'd guess. One of the men, a burly, tattooed, sweaty man presented as a professional Yorkshireman. He'd brook no argument to any of his utterances, told one of the women (presumably his partner...but he was so disrespectful and ill-mannered, it might well have been his pal's wife!) she was stupid, unfit and too fond of the drink...although I grant you that he didn't make all of these assertions in one sentence. That would have been rude.

272

His cadaverous wife ignored his verbal assaults and staring out of the pub window, whistled quietly.

"Whistling women are an abomination unto the Lord. Says so in Bible."

She stopped.

I was mindful of the old aphorism that the Glasgow approach to pub discussion is to master the bare minimum needed to start an argument at the bar and considered offering him honorary citizenship just as he leaned into a monologue about how they were to visit her equally stupid sister and her husband in July.

"T'fat bastid thinks he's done well f'rissel. Stays in big 'ouse. Seen pictures," he said disparagingly, supping his pint. "Lives in New Zealand. S'an island off Canada".

I waited to hear his wife correct him and inform him that her sister stayed in *Newfoundland*. She remained mum but made eye contact with her female friend at the table rebuking him silently; her head shaking ever so slightly in disapprobation as she contemplated her half pint of beer.

Later in the conversation she mentioned that's she'd toothache in one of her rear molars (*All* molars are at the back!). She massaged her jaw tenderly.

Mr Yorkshire was also knowledgeable about dentistry.

" 'Ave it out. You don't need teeth in the back! I don't 'ave none! 'Ave it out!"

I raised my glass to my mouth to drain it before leaving. As I did so, Mr. Yorkshire deposited what appeared to be the contents of a small phial of after-shave on the back of his wrist and applied it to his chin, transforming himself instantly, at least in his eyes I suspect, to a manly scented David Beckham.

Mrs Yorkshire smiled approvingly and directed her comment to her friend. "I love the smell of his colon," she said, emphasising the first syllable.

Now I admit that it's all in the pronunciation; the accent. But my beer threatened evacuation via my nose. Perhaps it was all the shit he'd been talking so I decided that the mispronunciation had been deliberate and that she held no interest in the scent of Cologne!

As I left to go, my back-pack brushed the four hiking poles sending them crashing to the ground. Automatically, I apologised and stooped to collect them.

Mr. Yorkshire couldn't have been more conciliatory. "Not a problem, my friend. Accidents 'appen!"

Perhaps it's just women he abuses.

Berwick very obviously was a strategically important town over the centuries as it guarded the River Tweed right on the border between Scotland and England. Today, its ramparts, the most expensive construction undertaken during the reign of Queen Elizabeth 1 of England, are manicured within an inch of their lives and have pedestrian pathways atop their battlements. Worryingly, there is no protective fencing and only a yard from the tarmacadam the cambered grassed area leads to a sheer drop of some thirty feet and instant death if the slightest delinquent step is taken. A small sign urges caution. I should bloody *think* so! Over the past two decades there have been thirty serious incidents and four fatalities as people have fallen to their death. In response, the local authority have installed glow-in-the-dark studs to advise even the most inebriated that one step to the left might see them meet their maker.

All of the tight lanes leading to the ramparts are gated and each gate invites closure suggesting obsession/compulsion or a healthier regard for safety than perhaps I'd given credit for.

I walked over the utilitarian road bridge crossing the Tweed and photographed both the iconic and beautiful twenty-eight arched Royal Border (rail) Bridge built in 1847 as well as the fifteen-spanned Old Bridge, erected in 1611 some one hundred yards or so downstream. Each of the older bridges was beautiful in construction and looked like they might last for the next thousand years without much effort. The River Tweed shimmered in the sunlight as it headed for the North Sea, the sun warmed my back and the views on all sides were simply magnificent. It was easy to see why the town had changed hands so many times over the centuries. Forget politics and nationalism, these tensions have obviously come about as Scots and English tourists of the past sought to claim this rural jewel as their own.

The long walk back up the hill to the railway station was, frankly effortless. On all sides, picturesque buildings, informative plaques and interesting shops held attention. Even the railway station, upon arrival, was festooned with information about the history of the place.

Berwick-upon-Tweed is a perfect little town - if someone would take a bulldozer to the White Horse Pub, sparing only their pie oven.

John O' Groats – Land's End.

God alone knows how many people have made the journey from John O' Groats to Land's End. Certainly many have made the 874 miles passage by road and countless charities and races have begun and ended at each point on the map. Although I was in peak physical condition and could without breaking sweat have made the road journey hopping on one leg while carrying a bag of coal, I decided that it might be more interesting (and comfortable) to travel between the most northerly and southern points of the UK mostly by rail. As my home city, Glasgow is positioned between both extremities, I decided to travel first north to John o'Groats and then make my way south.

I never fail to be impressed by the beauty of wild Scotland and the journey north to Inverness was characterised by bright sunshine and a blue sky showcasing the natural rugged handsomeness of my country. Arriving at Inverness, another feature materialised for which Scotland is renowned and it absolutely pissed down, materially changing my plan to walk the banks of the River Ness. Instead I elected to seek sanctuary in the Old Market Inn near the railway station. Ordering a beer at the bar, I bumped into two old colleagues who were on a cycling tour of Scotland, one of whom, Jack Law had just completed an album with his band Greenmantle. I promised to buy a copy (and did, later...it was excellent).

The pub was small and is very much a live music bar. On the night I arrived it was populated mostly by heavy, Guinness-drinking, bearded folkies. Jack told me that the place was a favourite drinking place of the popular beat combo, the Proclaimers when north of Leith. We chatted a while before I headed off to get something to eat - in Johnnie Fox's; a major disappointment given the high esteem in which I hold its namesake in the hills above Dublin. When I stepped outside, it was again glorious sunshine. As they say, in Scotland, on any day of the week, if you don't like the weather, just wait a few minutes and your preferred meteorological conditions will soon arrive.

The BBC have taken to using a weather map nightly which purports to show the United Kingdom as if from a satellite positioned above the Bay of Biscay. In consequence, the perspective produced presents the British Isles as if England is very much larger than Scotland. Let me tell you, Scotland's land mass is substantial as I found out the following morning when I caught the train from Inverness (Scotland's northernmost city) to Thurso, the nearest rail station to John o'Groats, some twenty miles further east-north-east. After a hundred and fourteen miles, the train stopped at some twenty-two stations before arriving at my destination. The four hour journey took me from Inverness through Beauly, Muir of Ord, Connon Bridge, Dingwall, Alness, Invergorden, Fearn, Tain, Ardgay, Culrain, Invershin, Laird, Rogart, Golspie, Dunrobin, Brora, Helmsdale, Kildonan, Kinbrace, Forsinard, Altnabrea and Scotscalder before depositing me wearily in Thurso.

I stayed for the night in the Royal Hotel (advertised as charming and quaint, but experienced as tired if functional). Nevertheless, it was well positioned in the centre of Thurso and after walking the town for a couple of hours, showering and changing, I headed off to the nearby seaport of Scrabster and a restaurant recommended me by my pal, Laurie who had dined there quite recently with his wife, Pam and who subsequently claimed it measured up to its reputation as one of the great seafood restaurants in the world. Well, he wasn't wrong!

I entered the smallish Captain's Galley, located right on the fishing port in Scrabster and was welcomed upon entry by owner and chef Jim Cowie who showed me to a comfortable seat, handing me a menu and a laminated copy of a recent award celebrating them as the most sustainable restaurant in Britain because all of the restaurant's seafood is from wild, non-pressured stock species, in season, from local inshore fishermen.

"There's no' many restaurants that can say that their suppliers and their best friends are all the same people," said Jim as he seated me, paraphrasing a quote I saw later repeated in one of their brochures.

Jim and his wife had renovated an old ice-house on the harbour in 2002 and had turned it into a thirty-seat culinary destination for connoisseurs of fine dining and seafood. I enjoyed a superlative meal of sole fillet, chargrilled monkfish and cheese...although on separate plates. A thimbleful of *Sauvignon Blanc* accompanied the spread but it was a quiet night with only one other table occupied. Two thirty-something ladies each with long blonde hair, sat and conversed while *during their entire meal,* flicked and pulled, toyed and swirled, swept and ruffled their hair, all the time agreeing their joint enmity of one of their purported friends. I left seeking a more convivial atmosphere and further thimblefuls.

I found both in spades in the Commercial Bar back in nearby Thurso. I'd asked the taxi driver his recommendation and he'd proffered his suggestion of the "Comm" as it had folk music that evening. As I entered its portals, fiddle and whistles backed by guitars and a *bodhran* frame drum were playing the opening bars of a tune I recognised (having earlier recorded it, playing all of the instruments myself...he said modestly)). It was 'The Cork Hornpipe', a favourite. I ordered a pint and sat enthralled at the musicianship of local imbibers. An elderly man seated with his heavily accessorised wife on bar stools three away from me ended their colloquy as he noticed my enjoyment.

"Good, aren't they?"

I nodded; applying my lips to a glass which I lowered. "I love the *Cork Hornpipe*".

"Aye. Do you know how to tell the difference between a hornpipe, a jig and a reel?"

"By the title of the tune?"

"No, no, no. It's the rhythm of the song. If it's a hornpipe, you should be able to say, 'alligator, alligator' to the rhythm." In my head I began to repeat the words, 'alligator, alligator' as the musicians tore into the hornpipe and to my surprise it worked.

"Now if it's a reel, if you say, 'double decker, double decker' you'll be on the right lines and if it's a jig it's, 'carrots and cabbages' you'd say. That's how you tell."

Throughout the evening I tested his advice against the songs played by the group of amateur musicians and usually found I could ascribe one or other of his prompts to the rhythm. It was great fun. These people performed all evening and were joined from time to time by individuals who entered the pub, removed their jackets, produced their instruments and without seeking permission, sat in and accompanied them. Excellent music and a few drams sent me to bed content.

I'd reserved a rental car from a local garage over the web but when I arrived was informed that it was the owners' car and would I mind not denting it! I promised to do my best and drove the coastal road towards John o'Groats. On the way I drove to the lighthouse at Dunnet Head but recoiled at the fearfully sheer cliff face. I'm not particularly fond of heights and this cliff was terrifyingly perpendicular. I slowly retraced my steps walking backwards from the edge. Safer, now I'd removed myself somewhat from instant death, I took a moment to observe the waters of the Pentland Firth. First of all, I reminded myself, it's not a firth but a strait which separates the north of Scotland from the Orkney Islands and pushes waters from the North Atlantic Ocean to the North Sea (and *vice-versa*) through this tight gap. Its main claim to fame is that exceptionally strong currents of five metres per second make these waters potentially one of the best sites in the world for exploiting tidal power. Indeed, a discarded *Orcadian* newspaper left in the Commercial Bar the previous evening quoted Dr Thomas Adcock of Oxford University who stated that the Firth 'is almost certainly the best site for tidal stream power in the world'. The paper went on to aver that its renewable tidal energy was sufficient to power around half of Scotland.

The most cursory glance at a map of the north of Scotland shows unequivocally that Dunnet Head is clearly and by a considerable distance further north than John o'Groats. But presumably because the Pentland Firth can be accessed at John o'Groats via a harbour and has a more substantial road system it has become fixed as the most northerly point on the mainland. I drove on, stopping briefly outside Castle May, favourite residence of the now demised Queen Mother who'd bought it as a holiday home. Never a big fan of royalty I decided against visiting its interior.

I'd visited John o'Groats a few times before and had left underwhelmed on each occasion. Indeed, in 2010 the place won the 'Carbuncle Award' for being the most dismal place in Scotland, its best feature being reported as its car park. This visit, there was evidence of some pretty decent development with bright new multi-coloured modern buildings tacked on to the revamped old Inn that had stood dilapidated for years. A new modern sculpture, a gift shop and improved car-parking all suggested that the authorities or the tourist board had at last decided to take an interest. The famous signpost had for many years been tended by a photographer who'd take your image after adding to the several directional arrows which were bolted to the pole like porcupine quills, one which pointed towards your home town. However, the man who'd made a living photographing a white pole had left and now a more prosaic signpost, much inferior, points variously towards the North Pole, Orkney, London and Land's End.

Upon visiting previously I'd asked after the background of Mr. Groats presuming him not unreasonably to have been a ferryman named John who'd charged a groat to carry passengers across the firth the six nautical miles to the Orkney Islands. However, the name seems to have been rendered colloquial over the years as it was predicated upon a man called Jan de Groot, a Dutchman, who built a house (whose site is now occupied by the inn) sometime around the turn of the early fifteen-hundreds. He was a ferryman by all accounts but '*groat*' derives from the Dutch for '*large*' so perhaps the Orkneys' ferry fare back in the day was more in keeping with those charged today by the John O'Groats Ferry Company.

Those hardy souls who gather or arrive here having made the journey to or from the most southern part of mainland Britain are to be saluted. I am led to understand that the trek south takes most cyclists ten to fourteen days. I was quite taken to note that while cyclists can cover the distance in ten days, the record for running the route is nine days, two hours, twenty-six minutes by Andrew Rivett who made the run between the fourth to the thirteenth of May in 2002. Impressive! That's around ninety-odd miles a day, every day for nine days. Stunning!

Off-road walkers typically walk about 1,200 miles and take two or three months for the expedition but the most impressive feat was surely accomplished by young Henry Cole who completed the journey from south to north in June 2006, aged four, cycling the route over 31 days. I took an immediate interest in this story as my own four year old grand-daughter was still using training wheels. Did young Henry use training wheels? Well, no. He completed the journey pedalling a trailer cycle attached to the back of his father's bike with his mum following behind in a car. As a proud grandfather I wanted somehow to dismiss the attempt as bogus but at the end of the day a wee four year old boy had made a journey that I couldn't have made - even with training wheels.

But it was time to travel south, following in the footsteps of those mentioned - but by rail. I'm not stupid!

En route, I stopped off in Glasgow to enjoy a beer with friends, Danny, John and Laurie in the city's Pot Still Bar, an older establishment and perhaps the finest whisky emporia in the free world. For once Glasgow basked in glorious day-long sunshine. More used to temperatures in the lower twenties, if not the lower zeroes, I melted noisily convinced of my incipient heatstroke. Eventually the effects of a few 35ml measures (the only sensible quantity of spirit) of Glenfiddich calmed me and as the sun dropped below the tall buildings that bordered Hope Street, I recovered. A good night's sleep and I was up preparing for my twelve-hour rail journey to Penzance, thence to Land's End. I breakfasted early and glanced at the television the better to understand what weather I might expect on my way south. Outside, the sun continued to shine gloriously. A toothy weather presenter gleefully informed a breathless nation that today would be another fine day. He swept his left arm over a map demonstrating the absence of clouds before grimacing.

"Unfortunately, later today, for those in the very south-west, down by Penzance and Land's End, a new weather system is on its way over from France and it looks like they'll experience pretty atrocious weather with severe thunderstorms down there."

Warming to his subject, he nodded at his map as replacing the grey blob depicting rain, was superimposed a violent red and blue representation like a recovering bruise. "Not pleasant," he said. Underscoring his point, jagged digital images depicting forked lightening flashed on and off.

Attempting to offer some salve, he mumbled something about crops benefiting. Like I gave a shit!

Sheesh...Glasgow's too hot and Penzance is to be too wet. The weather gods were not smiling.

Still, Glasgow was bright and sunny as I disembarked my local train in Central Station for my more substantial train south. My heart sank rather as I found my seat and noted that other than me, the carriage had been occupied by a troupe of forty-something, uproarious women off, it transpired later, to York (I'd bet myself it would be Newcastle) who whooped, yelled and sang their way south; and this at 9.00am. Handbags were emptied and bottles of 'commotion lotion', 'wreck-the-hoose-juice', 'Coatbridge table wine' - all Glaswegian references to any alcohol offered in fortified fashion - were handed round. Given that I had just enjoyed an evening much as they were enjoying their morning, my outrage was tempered somewhat but my earphones were called into urgent use.

As we left Glasgow, the Train Manager (there appear to be no Guards anymore) announced the journey.

"This is the nine o'clock train to Penzance calling at Edinburgh Haymarket, Edinburgh Waverley, Berwick-upon-Tweed, Morpeth, Newcastle, Durham, Darlington, York, Leeds, Wakefield, Sheffield, Chesterfield, Derby, Burton-on-Trent, Tamworth, Water Orton, Birmingham New Street, Cheltenham Spa, Bristol Parkway, Bristol Temple Meads, Taunton, Tiverton...and if you haven't lost the will to live (our Train Manager was a bit of a card) ...Exeter, Dawlish, Teignmouth, Newton Abbot, Totnes, Plymouth, Liskeard, Bodmin, Par, St Austell, Truro, Redruth, Camborne, St. Erth and finally..." He was out of breath by now…"Penzance!"

At Newcastle, half of the entire city boarded leaving no seat unsat. The general carriage uproar increased its decibel count markedly. Having reserved a seat upon which to sit, most of them stood in the aisle, chatting.

Around lunchtime, hunger forced me to go looking for comestibles as evidently none was easily to be procured from a trolley. I made my way from my crowded rear carriage all the way to the one before First Class at the furthest end of the train where I found a dolorous, stout uniformed woman pinned against a toilet door. She addressed me as 'Love', confirming my arrival in England. (Had it been Scotland it would have been 'Son' or 'Pal').

"Sorry, Love. This trolley weighs thirteen stone and there's no way I can make it through the crowds on this train. They're cluttering up the aisles."

I reflected that my walk to the front of the train had consisted of me excusing myself repeatedly as the great unwashed sat conversing with their legs splayed across the aisle, they'd placed cases too big for the rack above their head in the aisle, sat their cardboard box full of half-consumed lager next to them in the aisle and stood there conversing with their pals blocking the aisle. Groups of young ladies dressed minimally stood around screeching with laughter around young men who knelt on their seats, holding forth. I understood her point.

I ordered a sandwich and a small bottle of warm white wine. Without waiting for my consent, the stout uniformed lady placed three in my paper bag.

"May as well have three. They're on offer today."

I did a quick calculation. More than half a litre of wine for ten pounds; or one for six.

"That'll do nicely," I heard myself say under my breath lest the woman behind heard of my delinquency and judged me unfairly as I was merely being thrifty.

I asked if the food facility was available all the way to Penzance. She straightened painfully as she struggled with retrieving my choice of sandwich from a lower shelve.

"You going all the way?"

"I am."

She looked at me with mixed concern and puzzlement.

"No one goes all the way."

"Well, I am. This trolley going all the way?"

"Not if it gets quiet, Love." This was a trolley that obviously preferred a lively train.

I 'excused me' all the way back to the rear of the train where I refreshed myself (over a sensible period) with half a litre of warm white wine.

As I enjoyed my *repast*, the Train Manager made an announcement; "Cross Country Trains would like to apologise for the anti-social behaviour of some passengers in coach 'D'. A track-suited girl in a group of Geordie girls a few seats in front of me in coach 'F' immediately scooped up her belongings. "C'mon, yous. This sounds like fun!"

By the time we arrived at Wakefield, a thunderstorm so violent had enveloped the train such that nothing could be seen beyond the tree-lined parameters of the track. I thought immediately of the toothy one's confident sunny weather prediction and consoled myself that he may also have been wide of the mark about the storm that might meet me the morn in Penzance.

I'd earlier been joined at Edinburgh by a quiet young lady, a student who instantly took out a book in German entitled '*Harry Potter und der something or other*,' and armed with a German/English dictionary made her way stoically through the tome, every so often consulting her dictionary and writing the translated word in the margins. She was the perfect travelling companion having regard to the crazies who seemed to occupy all other seats.

To my relief, as the train progressed south it emptied by degrees, noise levels dropped and the scenery became more bucolic. Still, twelve hours seated was pretty gruelling. I checked. Had I been flying, I could have made Seoul or Los Angeles. As the train pulled into Penzance, cars were now using headlights and I stumbled onto the platform mouthing, *Yippee-ki-yi-yay!*

My hotel, the Beachfield was typical of many seaside establishments that would have been thought of as quite the thing back in the day but now it smelled of moth-balls and my first impressions condemned it as tired and rather unloved. However, it had been modernised, was clean, friendly and entirely adequate.

In Penzance, I saw no Union Flags or flags of St. George but there was a preponderance of Cornwall flags, a black rectangle with a white plus sign. It was as if in earlier times local people had decided to mask their piratical nature from the revenue men and had merely replaced the Jolly Roger with a plus sign.

"That'll fool them, Costentyn."

"That it will, Branok. Be a good chap and pass the cider would you?"

I was hungry, having had to make do with only a sandwich all day. The Beachfield restaurant had closed at eight-thirty (it was now nine-fifteen) and so I noticed were all of the several eateries situated on the promenade as I made my way back along to the harbour. I'd earlier noticed a nice looking pub called the Dolphin Tavern which I walked to and found that they still served food. I took a seat and read that the establishment had first opened its doors in 1585 at which time it was used as a recruiting station to persuade Cornishmen to fight the Spanish Armada. The menu's blurb claimed that Sir Walter Raleigh smoked his first puff of tobacco in its bar which was also used as a courthouse presided over by Judge Jeffries, the famous Hanging Judge. This was *my* kind of place...although had I been informed that Christopher Columbus had had his wicked way with Queen Isabella in the back room whilst on his way to discover America, I'd probably have bought that too.

While awaiting my hake dinner I attempted a Cornish lager, *Korev-* a mistake. Its strapline was '*Lager with soul*' but it smelled fishy - more '*Lager with sole.*' Still, I sipped away at it gingerly and read more about Cornwall as I did. I was alarmed to find that at any moment I might find myself subject to '*The Brown Willy Effect*'. I turned the page cautiously wondering whether I should read further within the confines of the nearest bathroom but was relieved to find that it referred to a meteorological phenomenon that sometimes occurs across Cornwall causing torrential rain which then often travels a substantial distance downwind of Brown Willy, the highest point in Cornwall. *Phew*, as they say in the Beano!

I picked up a discarded copy of the *Cornishman* newspaper and read with interest of the activities of the Cornish Nationalist Party, *An Parti Kenethlegek Kerno* which seeks independence from the UK. Given that Scotland presently remains in the grip of this debate I read it with mounting interest. One of their spokesmen argued that Cornwall is a distinct region with a clearly defined economic, administrative and social profile and has a unique identity that reflects its Celtic character, culture and environment. He went on in print to say that his party's philosophy was based on being Cornish, green, left of centre and decentralising.

The article spoke of the problem which has arisen after Cornwall backed Brexit by 56% despite the fact that the area had benefitted substantially from European grant aid. It had been anticipated that between 2014 and 2020, Cornwall would receive over €1,000 per person from the EU Structural and Investment Fund - similar to that received by Romania and Bulgaria. (The Scottish Highlands receives €300 per person). A great deal of trust has been placed in the current Conservative Government that they will replace this money directly and exactly once their departure from Europe has been negotiated. Aye, and pigs might fly!

Still, the Cornwall Independence Party stands for elections and has presently four councillors and around 1.5% of the vote. I'm old enough to remember when the Scottish National Party was similarly subterranean in the polls. I sought further information and discovered that there even exists a paramilitary wing (comprehensively traduced and disowned by the political wing) called the Cornish Republican Army which believes in direct action against the flying of the English flag in Cornwall. Some of their activists have been arrested. Who knew?

I checked both the news and weather before turning in and there again was my toothy weather friend warning of rain of biblical proportions tomorrow.
    "Might be late morning but it's coming!"
    There was a man who loved his job!

After a comfortable night's sleep, I breakfasted and walked back along to the bus station, having been reliably informed that it stood adjacent to the railway station. I searched but there was absolutely no signage and no evidence of a bus stop never mind a collection of them. Two men in yellow hi-viz jackets stood talking, oblivious to my presence.
    I made myself known. "Excuse me. Can you direct me to the bus station?"
    The taller of the two pointed me to a car park across the road. There was absolutely no indication that buses ever entered the space.

"That's it there, mate."

I nodded acceptance of his assertion. "And the next bus to Land's End is at five past ten?"

"No mate, it's nine forty-five."

But your web site says five past ten."

"Yeah. We changed all that."

The bus arrived as they'd predicted - an open-topped tour bus, no less - and my strangled conversations with employees of the Kernow bus company continued unabated.

"A return ticket to Land's End, please."

"That'll be seven forty-five."

I handed him ten pounds.

"Wossiss then? He turned over the note as if I'd just handed him a snottery handkerchief.

I realised I'd given him a Scottish tenner. I explained.

"It's a Scottish note," and then found myself saying the reassuring words uttered by Scotsmen all over England since time immemorial. "It's legal tender. It's subject to the Bank Charter Act of 1844. Currently, three Scottish banks are allowed to print notes."

"Says, 'Clydesdale'." (He pronounced it 'Cloids Doile).

"Yeah. That's one of our banks. They're allowed to print money." I repeated pointing out the word 'Sterling'. He looked me up and down evaluating the evidence before him.

"You certainly *sound* Scottish."

I was about to josh with him and tell him that, yeah, it'd be illegal if anyone born south of Dumfries tried to spend a Scottish note but decided that I was making progress and merely smiled winsomely as he gave me my ticket.

I sat upstairs and took a seat in the open area. It was perfectly pleasant until the bus started moving. Initially I was preoccupied with the exotic plants and trees, thatched rooftops and was counting the skull and crossbones flags draped from people's windows but soon realised that my timbers were shivering and moved to an empty seat which was more protected. I then discovered that the seat was vacant because it was wet! Rather than suffer the indignity of fellow passengers smirking at my discomfort, I pretended that actually one of my seating preferences was sitting in puddles and looked stoically ahead, refusing to move. Inwardly I cursed.

The bus took an hour to travel ten miles largely because of the comically narrow roads. Upon arriving at one of the four million bends in the road, the bus driver had to slow. If a car was approaching in the other direction, a silent negotiation took place to determine who would reverse. However, if a convoy of three or more vehicles came upon the bus and it was a *double* bend, the rear car couldn't appreciate the need to reverse. Quickly, cars would begin to queue behind the bus, creating a logjam. Somehow, through osmosis, resolutions were found and we eventually arrived at Land's End. Nervously, I scanned the sky. Toothy's promised inundation hadn't yet arrived.

For some reason the bus was full of Japanese tourists. This is not a casual ethnic observation but they all looked Asian, some had the red disc of the Japanese national flag stitched to their backpacks and they each seemed acquainted one with another. One lady sat alone and I swear...I *swear* she was the spitting image of Yoko Ono. Even down to the trilby hat. She looked every inch the widow of a dead rock star. So persuaded was I that I almost offered her my hand in friendship, "Hello, Mrs. Ono? I'm Ron!" I decided against it in case she started singing.

The journey south to Land's End passed through some particularly heavily forested areas. These woods were so dense that had the Cornwall Republican Army decided to establish an armed guerrilla war against the flag of St, George, they'd have evaded capture for decades.

Land's End is much more commercialised than John o'Groats probably because it's nearer a larger tourist market in the south of England, Wales and continental Europe. Retail outlets, cafes, museums, visitor attractions, first and last houses, wildlife centres and information centres all squeezed into a sensible built environment which impressed, diminished only by the all-enveloping, thunderous, over-the-top recorded tones of actor Brian Blessed advertising 'Arthur's Quest' in his usual maniacal fashion. I've read about this guy. He's an impressive chap but he doesn't do subtlety!

My backside was still wet so I found a quiet area behind the *'Shaun the Sheep Experience'* and out of view of other tourists, stuck my right hand down the back of my jeans and attempted to squeeze some of the moisture from my nether-garments. As I was thus engaged, and unable to withdraw my arm due to my watch-strap being caught below my belt, a young couple turned the corner. I am famed in all lands west of the Pecos River for my quick thinking and it occurred to me that from their perspective they could only see my left arm and could perhaps be persuaded that I might be a one-armed war veteran of some description rather than a guy with his hand up his arse. I leaned my good arm in their direction, turning slightly as they passed to continue the deception. Initially confident, I was subsequently deflated when I swear the woman caught her partner's eye and gave a look that screamed, 'Darling, I think we've just passed a guy with his hand up his arse'. I made myself scarce and walked on down the footpath to the cliff edge, still damp.

Truth being told, I found Land's End more impressive than John o'Groats. The pathways were well maintained; lots of explanatory notices explained the flora and fauna. A map of the treacherous waters beneath the cliffs showed the frankly astounding number of vessels that had perished on rocks in the English Channel below; rocks passable on a high tide but ready to split open a hull on a low tide. Two rocks in particular, 'Kettle's Bottom' and 'Shark's Fin' had claimed the lives of almost innumerable seamen.

Again I eyed the sky checking on the prediction of Toothy. Grey but no hint of Armageddon as yet. I walked around, taking in the atmosphere of the most westerly point on the British Mainland. After a while and anxious about Toothy's warnings, I headed back to the bus stop and took my seat inside a warmer and drier vehicle. At the first stop, a large woman easily in her seventies, boarded and sat on the front two seats - her girth requiring both. On the journey back to Penzance, she welcomed each and every passenger on to the bus.

"Y'all right, Love?" And, if departing, "Bye, Love."

What I found remarkable was the fact that carrying a walking stick and stooped and elderly as she was, she wore a black hoodie, emblazoned across whose shoulders was the text, '*Black Sabbath*'. On her head sported a baseball cap embellished with the words, '*Iron Maiden*'. I then began to notice that males of this parish tended to baldness coupled with ponytails that emerged from the back of their head; earrings predominated, bandanas were *de rigueur* and beads and necklaces swung from necks. All that was missing were peg-legs...I mean you can take things *too* far! Trust me; the piratical and generally anti-establishment genetics of the local population is secure.

I'd originally intended to walk to nearby Mousehole (pron. *Mowzill*) some three miles to the west of Penzance but my fear of being caught in Toothy's end-of-the-world thunderstorm had me take a bus. Dylan Thomas had pronounced Mousehole as ' the loveliest village in England', and I could see why. (Mind you, his last words before dying were, 'I've had eighteen straight whiskies. I think that's a record.' so what credence can we give his judgement?)

Mousehole lived up to its reputation. It's based around its harbour and its fishing fleet but now tourism predominates. The majority of vessels lying at rest in the harbour these days are pleasure craft. The walking surface of the quay wall is an absolute ankle-breaker and you'd need to be Lance Armstrong when fully topped up with drugs to cope with the precipitous hills that lead from the harbour up to the heights of Mousehole but unquestionably and without demur, it's beautiful.

It's also a pirate's haven. Given its location and its endless coves and inlets, Cornwall was designed to encourage smuggling...and

Mousehole was a major source of irritation to the British Exchequer. Back in 1780, contraband was carried around openly during the day without intervention by forces of the crown. Indeed, when charges were brought against Mousehole officials for accepting bribes and cooperating with smugglers, Richard Pentreath of Mousehole was described by the prosecutor, the Penzance Collector of Customs as '*an honest man in all his dealings...though a notorious smuggler*'; as if to say, 'look he's as guilty as sin - but we're only talking about a bit of smuggling here.'

I'd earlier decided that I was beginning to put on some unwanted timber and had taken the view that for the foreseeable future, I'd eat only salads and drink only water. However, one of my non-negotiable rules is that when travelling I'd eat and drink only local stuff. In consequence, I stepped inside a local café and ordered a Devon Cream Tea (I know I was in Cornwall) and ate the two scones (one jam, one cream) knowing that the fatty contents would go straight to my left ventricle. But it was superb - as is anything with that amount of sugar and fat!

I was served by a local guy...large, twenty stones, earrings, pony-tail, 'Grateful Dead' T-shirt and a hippy demeanour... "'Sup, man?"

I wandered around for a while still eyeing the horizon and decided that Toothy had got it wrong. I took a bus back to Penzance and boarded another to Marazion (pron. Mara*h*zion) as I thought I might yet be able to visit the pretty impressive St Michael's Mount, a small if majestic tidal island in Mount's Bay topped by a castle and chapel, linked to Marazion by a man-made causeway; passable between mid-tide and low water. Again I checked the weather. I began to sense that Toothy may actually be accurate in his prediction as the weather closed in.

Upon arrival at St. Michael's Mount, I examined a board which provided tidal information that permitted access to the isle by means of the causeway. People were still crossing. Large, lumpy droplets began to descend as if to influence my decision. The board suggested that presently if I walked over to the island, I may have to return by means of a boatman in an open ferry whose timetable was not exactly as regular as clockwork. As the rain began to get dumpy, I took the view that it might be wiser to retreat to a pub! I walked up and out of the town, my wife's small brolly protecting my coiffure, in order to find a facility used by locals and in doing so realised how local alcohol entrepreneurs name their pubs here. They merely take the words, 'Inn, Bar, Restaurant, Café, Tavern...even Meadery!' and preface them with the words, 'Pirate, Ship, Smuggler, Captain, Admiral, Cutlass, Brigantine, Brigg, Sloop, Kidd, Blackbeard, Skull and Crossbones, Morgan or Jack' and they have the perfectly named Cornwall establishment.

Toothy's predictions had come to pass and it began to pour down like stair-rods. I took refuge in the King's Arms (which immediately rent asunder my theory about pub-naming) and invited the bartender to recommend a local cider drink. She suggested '*Rattler*'.

"It's six-percent proof," cautioned my effortlessly cheery young lady as she pulled the pint. It's strong stuff!"

I smirked openly at her remark. 'I'm a Glaswegian! Up by, we're used to the drink don't you know!"

After two pints, I sat drooling like an idiot, wiping white foam from the corner of my mouth whilst trying to focus.

"Might you phone me a taxi?" I said enunciating carefully, giving her details.

She made a phone call. "Pint while you wait, sir? They'll be twenty minutes or more."

"Mmmph, mmmphhh."

A further modicum of Rattler Cider passed my lips in the interests of courtesy before a taxi took me back to the Beachfield Hotel where I was welcomed like a long-lost brother.

"Welcome back Mr. Culley. A drink before you go upstairs?"

I looked woozily at their gantry, especially their whisky and noticed that the best they could offer was '*Jacobite Whisky*' and '*House of Campbell Whisky*'; two whiskies never before encountered and in all probability distilled illegally in the hills surrounding Penzance. I demurred but noticed also that they stocked the rather flavoursome 'Rattler Cider' and decided to adopt what I call the Magnus Magnusson approach to alcohol consumption...'I've started so I'll finish!' So, in the quiet and comfortable, bookish, leather-seated lounge of the Beachfield Hotel...in the afternoon...I found myself drinking 'Rattler' and talking to the furniture.

Three hours' sleep afterwards and I felt more able to face the world and set off looking for dinner.

It took some effort but after some trial and error I managed to find the grubbiest restaurant in Penzance; The Luger Inn. I was loath to wander too far from my hotel for grub given the weather and settled for a close-by menu that was immediately withdrawn as I sat and ordered.

"Sorry, sir. Carvery only now!"

My face fell. "And how does that work?"

"Well, I give you a ticket..." A ticket! Jesus! I don't remember much beyond the soggy pastry that accompanied the dried-up beef. I had to pry apart my leathery roast potato. It took strength and patience.

On the bright side, it put my earlier soggy arse into second place in terms of all-time disappointing aspects of visits to Cornwall.

I looked around and saw couples at adjacent tables; the women busily preoccupied with the plate before them; eating mechanically, the men attempting to brush the creases out of their Premiership football shirt. I scanned the menu for *Rattler Cider* to kill the pain. No such sophistication. That said I'd been missing the *Wrigley's* chewing gum I use when driving back in Scotland and so found the roast potatoes both diverting and comforting if less minty.

As I made to leave, an elderly couple consulted the menu outside. I attempted my best semaphore signalling, 'Don't be stupid. Run like fun. Run while you still can. Go...go from here. This place is a dump!' This, I confess, communicated by frowning and waving my right hand from side to side as covertly as possible so as not to incur the wrath of the waiting staff. It seemed to work. They moved on. I paid my bill. My work here was done.

Kirkintilloch

Back in Scotland I decided to visit somewhere closer to home but first, a confession. I lived in Kirkintilloch from age four until aged eight, began my education in Townhead Primary School there and enjoyed my first adventures as a child - worryingly by playing around the gigantic steel wheels of an old (still then operational) steam train shunting up and down at the bottom of the common garden and by making rafts to sail on the slow and murky waters of the adjacent Forth and Clyde Canal. These four years were significant as they were the only years in which I was a member of a traditional family; mother, father and two younger brothers. When we subsequently moved to a Glasgow housing scheme, we lost my father in an accident only months later.

On the other side of the canal of my youth was Peel Park, whose view of the not so distant and majestic Campsie Fells entranced me then, as now. It seemed so high it was almost in the clouds and helped me understand, in later years, how Kirkintilloch was named from the *Gaelic, 'Cair Cheann Tulaich'* meaning 'fort at the top of the hill'.

The township of 'Kirky' as it's known locally was first recorded as a Roman fort during the construction of Antonine's Wall, a turf and stone defensive barrier against the Barbarians of northern Scotland. Named eponymously after the Roman Emperor Titus Fulvus Aelius Hadrianus Antoninus Augustus Pius who lived from AD 86 to 161 and who ruled the empire from AD138 to 161, the wall stretched along the narrowest part of Scotland from Old Kilpatrick on the Firth of Clyde to Bo'ness on the Firth of Forth and took twelve years to complete. Interestingly, although his predecessor Hadrian visited Britain, Antonine never did, preferring to focus upon building temples and theatres, promoting the arts and bestowing honours upon teachers of philosophy. Good for him, I say! One academic, J. J. Wilkes, in his book, *The Journal of*

Roman Studies, states, 'It is almost certain not only that at no time in his life did he ever see, let alone command, a Roman army, but that throughout the twenty-three years of his reign, he never went within five hundred miles of a legion'. Again, good for him, I say. Mind you, he was the adoptive father of Marcus Aurelius; he of *Gladiator* fame, so I'd imagine that sword-play wasn't entirely absent from his family life.

As a child I knew nothing of Kirky's military past nor of its importance due to the convergence of road, rail and canal traffic. I was also unaware of the fact that it was one of only two in-shore boatbuilders in Scotland, Peter McGregor & Sons and J & J Hay, who produced barges and puffers until the yards were demolished in 1954, just as I arrived in town.

I decided to visit to see if my old home town looked the same, if I might recycle the lyrics of mighty Tom Jones.

Well, it didn't.

I was prepared to witness some changes (and frankly to condemn them as outrageous monuments to 'improvements') but a walk along 'Cowgate', the town's Main Street persuaded me otherwise. I've long held the belief that one reasonable way of assessing the impact of a local authority on its citizens is to assess how they deal with their public realm. In many towns I visit, the pavements are cracked, roads pot-holed, paint is flaked and street furniture is rusted. Well, not here in Kirkintilloch. I can't remember the last time I was so impressed with the street-scaping I witnessed in Kirkintilloch. Substantially-sized paving stones were even and secure, the roadway was managed in a way that calmed traffic but avoided the use of speed bumps and colour was used to great effect. It made the town centre look cohesive and, dare I say it, prosperous. Now of those using the pavements, many pushed prams whose wheels weren't true, many a hoodie adorned track-suited young men and women strode along purposefully and walking sticks and Zimmer-frames abounded so I didn't sense that

Kirkintilloch was out of step economically with other towns of its size in Scotland - but it *seemed* so! So all hail the Cowgate Street Design Project dreamed up and implemented by a local partnership of public and private organisations.

I walked down to the Townhead district - or the *Toonheid* part of town where I grew up hoping to see my old primary school. In this I was to be disappointed but I couldn't long hold that attitude as it's been replaced by very impressive apartment blocks. Townhead Primary was typical of schools in my youth; two stories, built of sandstone block surrounded by a playground and contained within a stone and railinged wall. Six long-windows on two walls in each classroom allowed bright and airy teaching space. A later visit to the town's very impressive library allowed me access to old photographs which guided my memory - but it was pretty much as I'd recollected it.

However, one hundred yards further on I came across what I'd presumed from a distance would be a secondary school only to find it was a primary school; Lairdsland Primary school - but how sumptuous! The fenced playground was of artificial grass, surrounded (for traditionalists) by normal grass. Play areas abounded, the school looked modern and bright and was set by the canal where a bustling marina had been formed to accommodate barges and small craft. It looked, frankly, really, really nice. I crossed a 'V'-shaped bridge over the canal and sat on a bench looking at the school as it was now, reflecting upon the improvements in the teaching environment. It just seemed idyllic. The warm sunny day helped this assessment.

I retraced my steps to my old street; Donaldson Street, an earthen and cobbled cul-de-sac where we lived in a two-roomed miner's cottage at number 72. Not only does it not exist anymore but the railway line, the burn that followed its route and the wilderness that lay beyond were all gone. Even the pronounced slope that connected these had been smoothed and levelled. A new business park and a modern-looking police station stood in place of my old abode and were I to guess, I suspect my old home would have been in the car park of the cop shop.

We lived in a two up-two down apartment, two rooms with a communal toilet at the stair-head. Originally built to house the mining community that served the Meiklehill, Solsgirth and Wester Gartshore Collieries just outside Kirkintilloch, the accommodation might best be described as basic. It had a distinctive smell which in later years would cause me to start in recognition whenever it assailed my nostrils. It took me until my twenties to realise that the sweet smell I recalled was dampness. It seems curious now that I remember that smell with some affection.

The miner's cottages whose doorsteps I jumped over when running the short distance to Townhead School had all gone but a decent number of old buildings serving the mines still stood allowing a measure of recognition. The small sweet shop that was such a central part of my young world has now been occupied by a wedding photographer.

My visit to the estimable local library allowed me to investigate further the conditions under which local miners worked. I've seen moving images of miners at work before as have you, but I was genuinely taken aback when I interrogated a document listing the accidents that befell these brave and noble workers. Here's a selection of the descriptions of how they met their demise in local pits;

- *While lying on his side at the coal face using a pick, a fall of coal unexpectedly came away, hit the pick, and drove it into his chest in the neighbourhood of the heart.*
- *He was caught by a wire rope and dragged on to a pulley,*
- *Most regrettably, he drowned in the coal-pit.*
- *He was precipitated from the mouth of the shaft to the bottom, a distance of forty fathoms and killed.*
- *Removing Durie to the surface, his head was observed hanging over the side of the cage and before the engine could*

be stopped his head came in contact with the sneck, whereby his neck was dislocated and death immediately ensued.

- *He was caught between one of the upright beams and a waggon brake, and so severely crushed on the head that he died in a few hours.*
- *A stone fell on his head and killed him.*

And the families of the demised weren't spared either. Having successfully won compensation in court, one miner's family, the Robertsons, suffered a setback when the mine owners, the Woodilee Coal and Coke Company (Ltd.) of next-door Lenzie appealed. The finding was recorded thus;

'The explosion occurred on his striking a match to light his pipe after finishing his piece at the customary knock-off in the middle of the shift. The possession and use of matches in that pit were prohibited by the Coal Mines Act, 1911, and these prohibitions were known to Robertson. Sheriff-Substitute Kippen at Dumbarton found that the explosion was an accident arising out of and in the course of the employment and in law that the appellants were liable to pay £300 of compensation to the widow. The Division reversed that finding, holding that the deceased added a new peril to his employment by striking a match against prohibitions. What he did was for his own purpose, and was innocent enough but did not arise out of his employment.'

And that was that! No matter how unwise to light up a pipe for a smoke during a break, the miner 'woke up deid' and his family faced a life of penury. No safety nets, no welfare schemes, no employment beyond the pits so his kids would have had to follow in his footsteps and face the same dangers as did he at an age when children today are being told they're too young to do a paper round.

I walked the manicured and tarmacadamed tow-path back towards the town centre noting that on the other bank, a series of moorings had been established. A new college campus followed the contour of the canal and on my side sat another brand new school campus, St. Ninian's.

I climbed the steps leading to the Auld Kirk Museum at the end of Cowgate. How pleased I was that I'd made the effort. Whilst small it was stuffed full of information and exhibits, particularly about the period of time when the Romans were the *heid bummers*. They had had to deal with a number of attacks on the forts that punctuated Antonine's Wall and due to a shortage of troops, probably due to re-deployment requirements elsewhere in the Empire, decided enough was enough and left the wall to its fate, abandoning it only eight years after construction. Having made the decision, the departing Romans merely dumped anything they didn't want or couldn't carry down a well. While this seriously pissed off the locals who could no longer access water there, it provided future archaeologists with a treasure-trove of artefacts, many of which were on display; others being available at the much larger and prestigious Hunterian Museum in Glasgow University, Scotland's oldest museum.

It was also Kirkintilloch that was responsible for cocking a snoot at the world domination of the Scotch Whisky industry. As World War One moved inexorably to its conclusion in 1918, one of Kirkintilloch's most regarded general practitioners, Dr. Samuel Cowan, died. He was owed some £514 by those he had treated - a substantial sum at that time. Rather than chase the poor for payment, his widow decided instead that their nine-bedroomed villa could accommodate a lodger and so it was that a Glasgow University chemistry student Taketsuru Masataka from Takehara, Hiroshima in Japan where his family had owned a sake brewery since 1733, took rooms. Two years later he married the departed doctor's daughter, Jessie Roberta 'Rita' Cowan who was then studying medicine at the same seat of learning. Upon graduating in April 1919 Taketsuru took a job with the Longmore Distillery in Strathspey before moving on to James Calder & Co.'s Bo'ness distillery and a final job at Hazelburn distillery in Campbeltown. To cut a long story short, our Taketsuru took his new wife and his new knowledge back to Japan where after more years studying the process of distilling, he started his own distillery producing Nikka Whisky.

The pretty settled world view was that whisky made in the Scottish style, but not produced in Scotland, could never measure up to the standards and tastes of the traditional Scotch whisky distilleries. However, since the turn of the 21st Century, Japanese whiskies have been winning top honours in international competitions. At the 2003 International Spirits Challenge, Suntory Yamazaki won a gold medal, and Japanese whiskies have continued to win gold medals every year since. In Japan, the success of their indigenous product has pleased many – but over there it is consumed often as a long drink with a mixer or with hot water. As any whisky connoisseur will tell you, that's enough to give you the dry boak!

However, 35mls of Scottish malts such as Glenlivet, Glenmoranagie or Glenfiddich with a splash of cold water to reveal the taste – now that's your man!

The citizenry of Kirkintilloch must have the best coiffured hair in Scotland as every second shop in its high street offered the services of a hairdresser; 'the Nut House' being my favourite. Otherwise it was reassuring to see shops selling fish, ironmongery, shoes, holidays, butcher-meat and all other of goods and service necessary in a self-supporting township. Inevitably, charity emporia and low-cost retail outlets found space but I didn't notice too many vacant shops. As Cowgate tailed off into the Townhead area the street-scaping stopped and the quality of the built environment faded. Still, it had been well-maintained and more resembled the Kirkintilloch of my youth.

So the Romans had gone and the miners had gone. So too had my childhood. There are those who claim they are possessed of a memory that permits them to recall in sharp detail their departure from their mother's womb but my memories, supported by old black and white photographs only begin to take shape around eight years old - at which time I left Kirkintilloch for the bright lights and promise of Glasgow. It was lovely returning to visit my old haunts, chastening to update my understanding of the perils faced by the mining community and fascinating coming face to face with the Roman occupation of southern Scotland.

Kirkintilloch has a coat of arms that reflects its Roman heritage and has a motto, *'Ca' canny but ca' awa"* which translated means 'carry on carefully but keep carrying on' or *'Progress With Vigilance'* as was adopted by the local authority in 1975. It seems to me that the town has played its cards well. It's now a modern, prosperous and well serviced township. I wished it continued success as I prepared to head north but discovered that you have to *really* want to visit Balquhidder...at least if you choose to follow the route I decided to take.

Balquhidder

The village stands at the foot of Loch Voil in Stirlingshire and is overlooked by the dramatic pine-clad mountainous heft of the modestly named 'Braes of Balquhidder'. Comfortably a two hour drive from Glasgow, I drove in sunshine and without haste enjoying the simply luscious scenery until I closed on the village. A sign stated without disambiguation that I should take a left turn from the main road and that if I did, I'd arrive in Balquhidder after travelling three miles. Another sign, slightly further ahead, larger and appearing to have been placed there in more recent times, suggested equally that I could journey straight ahead and that if I did so, I'd *also* arrive at my destination having travelled three miles. Given that I'd already gone to all of the considerable trouble of flicking my indicator downwards and in doing so, advising the car behind me that it could expect me to slow and manoeuvre to the left, I decided to maintain my course and turned into a road that rapidly narrowed and tightened until the description 'one-track' might only be presumed accurate if it applied to motorcycles or at a push, an old Austin A40 *circa* 1947. My car, a largish four-wheeled SUV trundled along, its wheels edging the tarmac. Perhaps a further hundred yards along, another sign could be discerned from within the heavily afforested roadside. Helpfully, it repeated the advice that I was but three miles from my destination but added that no passing places would be found whilst making this journey. Reversing the car at that point would have tested the best so I ploughed on noticing as I did so that there were indeed some passing places but that they had been sufficiently overgrown with weeds so that they appeared once again to be part of the countryside that pressed on the road from either side. Headlights full-on I drove cautiously, convinced that a local who knew from experience that no one travelled this road would come barrelling around one of the many tight bends and put an abrupt end to my ambition of visiting the grave of Rob Roy MacGregor, buried in Balquhidder Parish Church grounds since 1734.

Eventually and with nerves shredded, I turned on to an unadopted road whose surface was somewhat pock-marked in that it appeared to have been cratered by protracted aerial bombing. I bumped slowly along seeing evidence of an occasional building through the pines, turning left and right, choosing tracks I figured must lead somewhere but didn't. Every so often I'd see signs suggesting inhabitation only to roll aimlessly onward, completely lost.

A woman wearing a rather sudden yellow jumper walking her dogs appeared from behind a tree so I stopped and opened the car window.

"I'm looking for Balquhidder."

"You've found it. This...," she waved her arm proprietorially... "is Balquhidder."

I looked around and saw only trees.

"I'm actually looking for Rob Roy's grave."

"Ah, yes. That's the church. Take a left along the track, over a hump-back bridge, take a right and you're there. You can't miss it."

I missed it.

Actually, I *passed* it and continued along a metalled road for a distance before turning back and as a consequence of arriving at the village more conventionally, noticed all the signs and arrows that pointed me accurately to the very spot; the very dot on the map. I'd arrived.

I was quite surprised to see so many people visiting the grave. A guy in a kilt with a plummy English accent reminiscent of a cast member of *Downton Abbey* was playing with badged car keys suggestive of ownership of the large Mercedes parked yards away. He was announcing to friends that he was simply *dying* for a G&T. Clusters of Americans talked loudly and took photographs. I wandered round the hinterland of the graveyard until the knots of folk paying their respects to Rob ebbed. Many of the graves were completely abraded or so covered in moss that nothing could be learned of who lay beneath but the stones and those commemorated were clearly of considerable antiquity. Those graves whose wording could be discerned were occupied almost solely by MacGregors, MacLarens or MacLaurins. Earlier research had informed me that the oldest gravestone referred to an Alex Fergusson of Ardandamh who died in 1663 but despite a fairly thorough wander, I could find no evidence of the man. People have worshipped here for millennia and academic research has produced evidence of an 1880bc (that's *BC*, folks) Neolithic temple on nearby Ben Ledi. But I was here to say, 'Hi' to *Raibert Ruadh MacGhriogair,*

'*Ruadh*' is Gaelic for 'red' and relates to the colour of our man's hair, though it was expressed as "Roy" when his name was anglicised from the Gaelic. He was quite a chap, our Roy but was treated poorly by Hollywood as, indeed was that rapscallion, the English Robin Hood who was played variously by Jonas Armstrong (Irish), Sean Connery (Scottish), Kevin Costner (American), Errol Flynn (also American) and Russell Crowe (a Kiwi). Scotsman Rob Roy made the silver screen in the form of Richard Todd (Irish) and Liam Neeson (Ulster). Seems there are problems presenting national heroes using actors who employ the native accent!

But problems emerge when comparing the two. William Wordsworth had a go in a piece of doggerel more reminiscent of William Topaz McGonagall, '*Memorials of a tour of Scotland in 1803.*'

A famous man is Robin Hood,
The English ballad-singer's joy!
And Scotland has a thief as good,
An outlaw of as daring mood;

She has her brave Rob Roy!
Then clear the weeds from off his Grave,
And let us chant a passing stave,
In honour of that Hero brave!

Utter mince!

The thing is, Robin Hood emerges only from folklore...from ballads and stories handed down round the camp fires of the Middle Ages. There exists absolutely no concrete evidence that there existed such a person. Manuscripts in the British Museum purport an account of Robin's life which states that he was born around 1160 in Lockersley in South Yorkshire. Others insist that he was a Wakefield man and was involved with Thomas of Lancaster's rebellion in 1322...I make that nearly two hundred years' difference in the telling.

Nor is there any agreement on his name. An outlaw called Robin Fitzooth is mentioned in dispatches as is Robert Hod, Robyn Hod, Robin Wood, Robin of Loxley and Guy of Gisborne. It has long been suggested that "Robin Hood" was a stock alias used by thieves and indeed that there's significance in the notion that 'Robin' sounds exactly like 'robbin''. In the nineteenth century, the editor and expert on the Middle Ages, Thomas Wright who founded the British Archaeological Society insisted that the character of Robin Hood was mythical and that his name was a corruption of 'Robin of the Wood'. Yet others insisted that he was a wood elf...whatever a wood elf is.

But there can be no question about the existence and legend of Rob Roy MacGregor whose remains lay six feet beneath my feet.

He was born in 1671 son of clan chief Donald Glas MacGregor of Glengyle but took his mother's name, Campbell as the name MacGregor had been proscribed since 1603 in reprisal for some minor delinquency undertaken by the clan. (He presumably achieved some quiet satisfaction by having the final word, causing his gravestone to be etched with the words, *'MacGregor Despite Them!'*)

When aged forty, he borrowed the sum of £1,000 from the Duke of Montrose which he entrusted to his head drover in order to buy cattle. The man carried out his duties meticulously then sold the cattle and headed south with the proceeds never to be seen again despite Rob's best efforts of finding him. Upon returning from his search, he discovered that the Duke of Montrose had bankrupted and outlawed him, seized his lands and evicted his family. Back in the eighteenth century, these boys didn't mess about!

Believing himself to be the victim of circumstance and slightly peeved at the Duke, he embarked upon a sustained campaign of cattle-rustling and general mischief-making highlighted by the kidnapping of the Duke's factor who happened to be carrying £3,000 of the Duke's money at the time. Now this didn't particularly endear MacGregor to the Duke but his knowledge of the Trossachs and the land around Lochs Voil, Lubnaig, Katrine, Lomond, Ard and Venachar allowed him to remain at large. Realising that he appeared to have a particular talent in extortion and intimidation, he began to offer 'protection from cattle-rustlers' to surrounding landowners, in the meantime winning the favour of the influential Duke of Argyll, a long-standing enemy of Montrose. Now with a substantial price on his head for his banditry, he set up home close to the Duke of Argyll's base in Inveraray and went on to play a minor role in the 1719 Jacobite uprising. Captured and escaping more than once, his exploits grew and were exaggerated with the re-telling and in 1723 our friend, the English spy, Daniel Defoe published a book with the snappy title *'Highland Rogue; being a general history of the highlanders wherein is given an account of their country and manner of living, exemplified in the life of Robert MacGregor, commonly called Rob-Roy.'* Quite rolls off the tongue! Probably uniquely at that time, Rob Roy whilst still alive and kicking, was the eponymous hero of a best-selling book whose influence was such that three years later, a Royal Pardon was bestowed upon him allowing him to live out his eight remaining years in peace; a folk-hero and legend in his own lifetime. I gazed down upon the railed slabs that formed his grave lost in my thoughts until I began to appreciate a slight itchiness on the back of my right hand. Narrowing my eyes to focus, I saw an insect, almost too small to be detected. *Shit*, I thought, *it's a midge!* It was around 11.30am (midges are at their peak at dawn and dusk) but it had been raining earlier and there was no wind. Midges can't fly in winds of over seven mph but in cloudy conditions like today biting females (the males die off after mating) are out seeking a blood meal like greyhounds out of a trap. The midge season lasts from early June until September and i began to appreciate that I was standing in the midst of a swarm of midges many of which seemed to be preparing themselves for an attack on my person.

Now, midges exist all over the world but the Highland Midge has the reputation of being the meanest, most persistent, hungriest beast of them all. There are several repellents on the market based upon di-ethyl toluamid, saltidin or dimethyl phthalate. Allegedly, the SAS employ the repellent effects of Avon's *Skin So Soft Body Oil* but I refuse to believe that these tough jungle fighters lie camouflaged in hides whispering to their comrades-in-arms, "Hey, Jimmy. Pass that *Skin So Soft* while I launch this grenade."

Fortunately they have not yet evolved sufficiently to eat their way through glass (although I gather they've a working group looking into this) so I retreated hurriedly to my car and scratched fiercely at the three bites on my right wrist knowing that I'd be dealing with this itch for days to come. Shortly, I also found myself scratching my right ear and neck. Wee bastards!

I'd been looking forward to a coffee in the Old Library Tearoom in Balquhidder but couldn't find it, discovering belatedly that it'd closed. Still, it allowed me reason to journey the fifteen miles to Callander, a small town on the River Teith. It's a popular tourist stop to and from many Highland destinations and it certainly thronged with tourists upon my arrival. I walked the length of its Main Street nosing at shops and enjoying the coffee I'd promised myself before setting off on a journey of reminiscence.

When I was in my early teens, my mother regularly took me and my two younger brothers hostelling under the aegis of the Scottish Youth Hostelling Association. I always found the nomenclature amusing as the hostels were largely patronised by people I considered geriatrics but were probably hill-walkers in their thirties. A popular destination for us was Lendrick Youth Hostel which was to be found some four miles outside Callander near the hamlet of Brig O' Turk on the shores of Loch Achray. It was nearby so I decided to visit.

Normally whatever the weather, my mother would walk us the round trip of eight miles from Lendrick to Callander for a cup of tea and some daily essentials but as I drove the road I had cause to question her parenting skills. The road had some particularly tight bends and although we'd been schooled to walk towards oncoming traffic, we must have faced being batted like flies into the loch had a car turned into a bend as we hugged the same edge of tarmac.

Lendrick Hostel had closed but I discovered that the buildings were now occupied by the Lendrick Lodge Retreat and Spiritual Centre. A leaflet informed me that the lodge rests on ancient Celtic land (Aye, but so does Nitshill) with a magical energy for all to enjoy and offers courses which, while attached to no religion, seek to transform dreams into a beautiful reality. I find that whisky has much the same effect...if in reverse.

I paused at the road-end to Stronachlachar and Loch Katrine which loch supplies much of Glasgow's famous soft water. In doing so I was reminded of a request made of me some several years before when I was invited to contribute to a book that described Scotland's *must visit* destinations. While others wrote of Edinburgh Castle, the Wallace Monument or The Palace of Scone, I wrote of the wonders that comprise the public toilets on the Loch Katrine pier at Stronachlachar. Due to their relative remoteness, they were visited but seldom and were therefore in pretty immaculate and unsullied condition. Dark-stained aged wood complemented copper fittings and elegant porcelain. (Nowadays it's a bistro...a bistro. In the middle of nowhere, celebrated public toilets have been converted to a bistro...Staff told me they'd retained only the wash-hand basins. I almost cried.) I concluded my article with the old joke that walking into the toilets at Stronachlachar was like a taking a deep breath of fresh air. Built to accommodate passengers disgorged from steamship and pleasure cruiser *Sir Walter Scott* which travels the length of the loch, they were a step back in time and all the more wonderful for it. Now they're a bistro! Did I mention that? A *bistro*!

The steamship itself is interesting in that it was built at Dumbarton on the River Clyde as an entire vessel in 1900 then dismantled, its parts numbered before being hauled by horse-drawn cart to Loch Katrine where it was reconstructed and re-launched. When manufactured, it cost £4,269, although a delivery charge of £2,028, almost half its cost again, was charged for transporting it to the loch.

In order to maintain the waters of the loch in pristine condition, the ship was powered by a steam engine fired by solid fuel fed into the firebox by a stoker much in the way a steam-driven railway engine is powered. In 2007, following a refit, the boilers were altered to run on biofuel to maintain the purity of the waters of the loch.

Handsome as the steamship is, it merely provides a platform from which to observe some of the most astonishing scenery on which humankind has lain eye. Driving on over the Duke's Pass, I was now in deepest Trossachs, surely possessed of the most beautiful scenery anywhere in the world. Lochs, heather-clad hills, pine forests and burbling burns all combine to persuade visitors that all must be well with a world where these natural phenomena can combine to form such exquisite loveliness. There are those who'll claim the majesty of the Peak District, the beauty of the Yorkshire Dales, even those who admire the wonder of the Grand Canyon or the Swiss Alps but for me, the heart-stopping, amazing, astonishing and astoundingly dramatic scenery of the Trossachs are unmatched!

This is Rob Roy country. He may have been swindled, rendered homeless, hounded as an outlaw, wounded, imprisoned and eaten alive by midges as he went about his life. But he did so surrounded by scenery which must have compensated handsomely: a legendary man living in a legendary part of the world.

Arabian Nights and African Dawns

Marrakech, Casablanca, Chefchaouen, Tangier,
Nairobi, Mombasa, Zanzibar, Dar es Salaam

My taxi took me from the four-months-old concourse of redeveloped Marrakech Airport straight into a medieval, terracotta-coloured world. Modern roads took me only so far before we pulled up outside the old city wall where every so often a solid black studded metal door suggested occupancy within. Windowless, *Riad Ajebel* permitted entrance where I was greeted by the tall, imposing and distinguished figure of Jean-Paul Courmont, its French owner.

"You must be Ron, from Scotland. You must be tired. Come in. Was your flight okay? Let me take your bag. Would you like a drink?"

And all this while shaking my hand vigorously as if the village water pump.

Classically educated, Jean-Paul was a French national who'd married a Moroccan wife, bairned her, divorced her and settled down in his adopted country, becoming CEO of a large tourist organisation. He was a walking Moroccan encyclopaedia and before showing me to my room, sat with me for an hour in the riad talking through the history of the place, advising against some of my travel plans, "*Trop dangereaux, mon ami*. Some of the valleys of the High Atlas Mountains are verr safe, ozzers less so. I will advice (sic) you."

He was extraordinarily solicitous. "If you are lost in the Medina, just phone me, describe your surroundings and I will fetch you on my motorcycle. Even it is sree o'clock in the morning."

I dismissed his offer immediately because it was way beyond the job description of any hotelier. I suggested that I'd prefer a quiet seat on his roof-terrace where I could write and if he had some wine or beer that would be a bonus. He had both wine and beer.

"But first I will walk with you through the Medina," he declared in a voice that brooked no dissent. Then you dine somewhere I recommend before you return to the roof-terrace. Okay?"

So saying he ushered me out of the rear door directly into the now darkening Medina, through ever-narrower lanes, turning corner after corner. Despite my efforts to recall turning points I was soon hopelessly lost but after an hour of Jean-Paul pointing and describing ancient buildings and mosques, dodging cars and ridiculously speedy motor-scooters, we returned and wearily I staggered into the nearby 'Clock' Café' where I attempted a Lamb *Tagine*. I'd been looking forward to this local delicacy but the lamb was on the bone, didn't seem a particularly good cut, was overly fatty and I didn't really enjoy it. My disappointment was eased somewhat by two musicians; one thumping a booming drum and one playing a stringed instrument that resembled a baseball bat affixed to a hat box. The music was strange to my ears but rhythmic and not at all unenjoyable. I was also distracted by the upstairs waiter who, I swear, when clearing up nearby dropped almost every single dish he lifted from a table. First the knife would slip to the floor from the plate then the rest of the cutlery would fall as he sought to balance things. Soon the plates would slide but he'd catch them just before they slipped from the tray. Shortly he was juggling those contents that remained before settling things down, placing the tray on a vacant table, reorganising his cutlery and crockery and walking carefully downstairs where, after a few seconds, further metallic clattering could be heard. When I finished my meal he approached and collected my *tagine* and accoutrements - and went through the same Buster Keaton routine all over again.

I returned to the *riad* where an ever-concerned Jean-Paul counselled against my idea of a nightcap and some writing on the roof-terrace before bed. "Ees too cold, *mon ami*!"

I assured him that any Scotsman would find the evening temperature in any city contiguous with the Sahara Desert positively balmy and he relented. I spent a peaceful hour there sipping at a brandy and doing some writing. For the first time since my arrival, the air was fresh. Down in the narrow alleyways of Marrakech where pedestrians fought for space with cars and motorcycles, there was an ever-present and overpowering smell of petrol and diesel which watered my eyes and stung my throat. Compounding this was the scent of *Galloises* cigarettes and, occasionally, the smell of raw sewage. It was unpleasant and I was grateful for this respite before bed. Eventually, I bid goodnight to Jean-Paul telling him I was tired - but in truth, I was freezing!

Riad Ajebel is an ancient building boasting a presence of one thousand years, set into the city wall of Marrakech. It is a traditional Moroccan dwelling; a three story building set around an Andalusian-style courtyard within which an enormous palm tree reaches skyward and protrudes from above the terrace. *Riads* are inwardly focussed with an interior garden; the absence of external windows permitting privacy and protection from the weather while a roof-terrace provides for the women who back in the day were not permitted to consort with men outwith their family but could converse at a rooftop level with other women.

My room was centuries old. Windowless, it was quiet; room-phone, television and radio-free but with a comfortable bed, wi-fi and an efficient bathroom. Ceramic tiles and traditional *tadelakt* plasterwork provided a very pleasing effect and I slept soundly.

I awoke to birds chirping in the courtyard trees - and complete blackness! Only once I'd showered, dressed and headed up to the roof-terrace for breakfast was I welcomed by an azure-blue sky and fierce sunshine. Jean-Paul was busily setting out a feast of a creamy yoghurt, various breads, pancakes and crepes accompanied by figs, apricot and honey. A fried egg, some toasted bread and coffee had me pleading surrender. I sat in complete contentment as I enjoyed breakfast whilst my eyes feasted on the snow-capped High Atlas Mountains in the distance.

Once organised, I set off for the more modern district of Marrakech. It stood in complete contrast to the Medina wherein I was resident. Modern hotels shared space with Pierre Balmain and Rolex outlets, and Mercedes and BMWs wrestled each other for parking space. Interestingly, the goodly number of women-only spas each featured blonde, blue-eyed Caucasian models as advertising rather than presenting local maidens as come-hithers.

The main thoroughfare in the city centre is Avenue Mohammed V (the grandfather of the present king) which is lined on either side with leafy orange trees, all of which have had their lower-hanging fruit liberated.

Apparently, the current Moroccan King, Mohammed VI is quite a boy! Having achieved a PhD and being fluent in French, Arabic, Spanish and English, he succeeded his father as king in 1999 and immediately took to television promising an end to poverty and corruption while pledging jobs and improving Morocco's shoogly human rights record. His reforms were opposed by Islamist conservatives and fundamentalists so he simply forbade any discussion of politics in mosques requiring instead that they preach only love and understanding. He then enacted a new family code which granted women more power. Love, understanding and feminism; a veritable hippy, is our Mohammed.

Because of an earlier attempt on the life of Mohammed VI's father by the army (which discovered information pointing to substantial bribes being sought by the king from American inward investors), the present incumbent's palace is now guarded by contingents from the army, navy, air force, the *Sûreté Nationale,* the *Gendarmerie* and his own royal guard. In addition to guarding the royal personage, they are tasked with keeping an eye on each other. Nice move, Mohammed!

That said, the young man is a businessman who would put Donald Trump to shame. Jean-Paul took delight in pointing out the king's various investments and perhaps inevitably, allegations have surfaced suggesting corruption. However, he dodged that particular bullet by decreeing that unlike previous Royals, he would not presume to be sacred or holy but 'the integrity of his person' is 'inviolable'. It's an offence to criticise him. Another nice move, Mohammed!

Wary of Islamic fundamentalism, he banned not the burqa, but the *sale and production* of the burqa, thereby providing for its diminished presence on the streets. Certainly Marrakech has a pretty secular feel to it. It's also alleged that he's heavily backed and supported by the CIA which funded and administers a largely unused airstrip just outside Marrakech which is a fall-back landing place for NASA's space shuttles should it ever be necessary.

I caught a taxi to *Jardin* Majorelle, a twelve-acre botanical garden where Jean-Paul had advised that the ashes of cremated Yves Saint Laurent, the famous French couturier had been scattered in its grounds.

"If you pull a leave from a tree, Ron, you will be in oneness with Yves Saint Laurent."

I couldn't wait. *Haud me back*, I thought. That said, the gardens looked lush and picturesque but they were guarded by a ten foot brick and mud wall atop of which was a further wire barrier. The gate was locked so along with other tourists, I took a photograph through the mesh then caught another taxi - this time to Marrakesh's main railway station. Modern, bright and airy, it sends trains south-west to Agadir, north-west to Casablanca and due-north to Tangier. I'll be catching one in a couple of days.

I decided to visit the famous Marrakech tannery and fortunately took a taxi or I'd never have found the place. Yet again an absolute maze of small alleyways forbid any hope of a return to anywhere I'd want to go under my own steam. The streets thronged with horses and mules dragging carts; the transport of choice in this part of the town. Fortunately the taxi-driver stopped opposite a cave-like doorway which it transpired was the only entrance. I stepped out into the cacophony where I was greeted by a burly doorman who took one look at me and addressed me in English.

Jean-Paul had earlier advised that I'd be asked for cash in return for permission to take photographs and that I should negotiate down. In consequence, I was ready and beat the man down from eighty to forty to twenty Dinar (£1.60). He handed me a bunch of mint herbs which he broke and crushed to accentuate the aroma. "Is verr bad smell in tannery" (It wasn't really).

He explained the various pits. "This one lime and ash. Takes hair off goat. This one pigeon shit. Softens hide. This one for colour."

I took some photographs as he explained that workers from Marrakech waded around in this gunk and gloop seven days a week "But the Berbers, only three days!"

When I asked why, he pointed out that they have to skin their goats way up in the Atlas Mountains and it takes them the balance of the week to prepare themselves for the tannery.

"Is co-operative!"

On the alert for all sorts of scams I paid little heed to anything he told me other than the factual stuff about the preparation of the leather but when he'd shown me round and had taken me into his friend's shop at the exit where a cornucopia of leather goods were on sale, I handed him the twenty Dinars and he promptly handed it to another guy who stood near the entrance. This fellah accepted the note then meticulously entered the sum into a large ledger, timed and dated it.

"Is co-operative," repeated my guide.

Shamefacedly, I headed for the street having denied a really interesting and hard-working social enterprise £3.20.

I wandered along a souk in the searing heat and bought a pair of leather slippers after some protracted negotiation. Gradually the tawdry and untidy alleyway spruced itself up until some of the shops advertised MasterCard and Visa. Turning a corner I found a pretty decent looking hotel which posted a menu that included beers! I entered and ordered a Beer Casablanca which was entirely acceptable. I sat in a shaded area in the bar and watched as a large, fourteen-strong Moroccan family - the women all wearing the all-enveloping black *burqa* - ate a meal while at the adjacent courtyard pool four feet away, two young European couples cavorted, the women each wearing the flimsiest of bikinis. Well-toned bum-cheeks had never seemed so incongruous. And in the interests of disambiguation, I looked at the aforementioned well-toned bum-cheeks only to make and record a sociological and cultural point!

However, perhaps King Mohammed's more secular and tolerant regime is having an effect.

Seeking a European restaurant so I might enjoy a proper drink with my *repas du soir* (my last three meals having been accompanied by water) I returned to the modern and wealthier part of town. Although the avenues were broader and the vehicles more modern, I still suffered the same asphyxiating assault by exhaust fumes. Jean-Paul had earlier made the point that Marrakech was ideal for those suffering from asthma as the air was so dry and there was zero humidity but I fell to wondering what might be the stats for lung cancer when the entire population inhales this toxic mix on a daily basis.

While awaiting my meal I wrote and adhered stamps to old-fashioned scenic cards, sending them immediately so I didn't suffer the ignominy of 'returning home before the postcards' - a jibe often laid at the door of Scottish national football teams which (in my youth) routinely qualified for World Cup and European Champion finals before being turfed out ignominiously at the end of the group stage.

I enjoyed a lovely meal in *Amaia* Restaurant along with a single Beer Casablanca and listened as an American couple next to me conversed and Nat King Cole entertained. The guy spent some time explaining how upon return to the States, he intended going on a road trip with his buddies. His girlfriend (no ring on the fourth finger of her left hand) was reduced to repeating, "*Really* Jaahn?"…"*Seriously, Jaahn?*"…"*Really* Jaahn?" I don't think she was overwhelmingly on-board with the idea.

Before retiring, Jean-Paul spent an hour with me in the *riad's* courtyard talking travel, athletics and politics before pouring over a map to suggest safe and picturesque routes for me tomorrow when I venture into the High Atlas Mountains. His suggestions were excellent but he persisted in attempting to have me cancel the rest of my arranged itinerary and go instead to Fez, "*Mon ami*, it is much more beautiful."

Perhaps so, but my plans have been laid.

Following protracted administrative requirements the following morning, I took temporary ownership of a relatively new Hertz Citroen and drove it timidly from Marrakech Airport. Initially I turned left and found myself deep in a residential area that appeared to mimic the housing schemes I am used to in my native Glasgow other than the fact that the properties were all only two storeys high and the waste ground in front of them had substantial flocks of sheep nibbling at what appeared to be basically rubble. By and large you don't get that in Glasgow.

Some two hours later, an interested observer could not have failed to notice steam being emitted forcibly from each of my ears so frustrated was I at the inability of the road authorities to place signage...any signage that would have allowed me to progress as I intended towards the High Atlas Mountains.

Looking from my roof-terrace on previous days, it had been obvious that reaching my goal would be as complex as hitting a barn door with a banjo. There they stood, majestic, snow-capped and high...very high. They almost *surrounded* Marrakech to the south. They simply couldn't be missed.

However, a heat haze ensured that this morning they couldn't be seen but I was relaxed as I used my native wit to head in the general direction. After some forty minutes driving when the mist hadn't lifted and still no signage appeared to confirm my presumptions, I pulled in at a garage, bought a Diet Coke and asked the smiley guy on the till to confirm my directions, showing him my map. He pulled out a blank sheet of paper and drew directions that had me retrace my steps - right back to the airport. I knew intuitively that his directions were flat wrong but figured I'd better go with local knowledge. Eventually, recognising a road I was on, I returned to my own navigational assumptions and half an hour later I found myself passing smiley's garage again. I thought of popping in to thank him through gritted teeth but decided to press on.

Passing through a green and verdant Tahannaout, the road rose sharply, narrowed and reduced in quality. Traffic lessened and before long I was easing my way round hairpin bends. Every so often a road sign would appear (*now* they appear!) informing me of a bend in the road...just as I'd spent the last half hour taking care not to career over the edge of perhaps a few score of them. Another sign presented an image suggesting I was about to go up a steep hill - this at a point where I'd adopted a driving position broadly similar to that of a Shuttle astronaut on the launch-pad at Cape Canaveral.

I drove on up ever-narrowing roads avoiding donkeys, horses, dogs, cats, camels, cows, sheep, goats, man-eating tigers, (I made that bit up about the man-eating tigers) domestic fowl of all descriptions, smiley kids, wavy kids, cheeky kids, men working at the side of the road, recent land-slips, incipient land-slips, rivulets, dust storms, axel-breaking pot holes...and I loved it.

As the road rose before me, the environment became bleaker but every so often a small Berber village or an isolated and very rudimentary roadside café would appear. The mountainside looked desolate but if I stopped to take a photograph, some kid would appear from behind a bush in the middle of nowhere and try to sell me a purple amethyst crystal. If there were no bushes, an older kid on a motor scooter would glide up and try to sell me a purple amethyst crystal. Instinctively they all hailed me in English. Why don't people presume I'm German or French or Swedish or Icelandic? When I turned corners, elderly men would step out on to the road and signal a direction into their makeshift cafe car park. I refused all blandishments as I'd already identified the dilapidated cafe which I intended to visit on my way back down.

I continued higher, past the snow-line and unexpectedly reached a large grassed plateaux on which some youths were playing on a marked (if sloping) football pitch. Above them on the hillside, a township called Oukaimeden clung to its very existence some nine thousand feet above Marrakech. Just above the village the road petered out at a car park where perhaps a dozen cars had disgorged skiers who swooped and slalomed down a snowy slope serviced by a clunky looking ski-lift. More purple crystals were offered but I desisted, heading back down the way I'd come as my intended stroll in the heights of the High Atlas Mountains hadn't taken cognisance of the fact that while it was thirty-one degrees in Marrakech as I left, it was but a sunny six atop the big hill. Cleverly, I'd worn only a tee-shirt and denims. For the first time I appreciated the benefits of *djellabas*, the traditional, Moroccan long, loose-fitting unisex outer robe with full sleeves. They reminded me rather of the garb usually worn by Friar Tuck in the Robin Hood programmes of my youth. Made of wool, I couldn't figure why people would wear one over their normal clothes in temperatures of thirty plus. Up in the High Atlas, they made perfect sense. Shivering, I drove downwards until I reached my somewhat warmer cafe.

Perched atop a dizzyingly precipitous drop to oblivion, the café centred on an old caravan in which one side seemed to have been peeled away using a can opener. The outdoor dining area beside it afforded magnificent views. Hurriedly an old man (my age) approached and offered me a plastic chair next to his plastic table. I surprised myself by asking for mint tea - something I'd never tried. He urged me to eat something and I agreed his suggestion of chicken.

"*Mais juste un peu, mon ami. Je n'ai pas très faim.*"

He nodded his understanding and I set about taking some photographs of the astonishing views from his makeshift veranda. When he returned he placed a freshly baked loaf of bread before me, straight from an outdoor oven he'd been carefully tending. It looked exactly like an old IRA beret but tasted less woollen...in fact it tasted warm and delicious. Moments later he reappeared with my chicken meal which was smothered in a sauce and vegetables. The meat was a bit tough but the vegetables were tasty. As I peeled away the flesh from the bone, I saw that the bone was six inches long and as thick as my thumb. If it really was a chicken it could have had a walk-on part in *Jurassic Park*. He asked fifty Dinars and I gave him a hundred because I'm the nicest guy I've ever met and because trying to earn a living in these mountains must be near impossible. The mint tea was superb. My new favourite drink.

I saw my first and only dog since arriving in Morocco. It sat contentedly next to a herdsman. I later asked Jean-Paul why there were no dogs. He advised that dogs cost money to feed and people are poor; that people prefer cats as they deal with vermin in doing so, feeding themselves and that the only working dog (and probably the breed I saw) is the *Tichka* or (in Berber) *Aidi*, a breed that has been trained for centuries by shepherds to defend herds and flocks aggressively against intruders and thieves. They are reputedly very protective of their Berber masters.

The Berber are a hardy bunch; an ethnic group indigenous to Morocco and North Africa although there are several tribes with distinctive cultures. Mostly Muslim, they tend towards moderate Sunni and Shi'ah although previously they were Jewish before the creation of Israel. Some seven thousand still practice Judaism in the mountains today. Generally they make a living as tradespeople and farmers. As I descended the High Atlas Mountains, I could have purchased carpets, blankets, pottery, amethyst crystal (although I was warned these would be fake and would have been *dyed* purple), red sandstone slate, glassware, honey, wool, leather and Goodyear Tyres. Cafes abounded. I felt rather abashed at driving past these hard working people in my air-conditioned car. They have a hard life.

I returned my rental car and headed for a glass of *Prosecco* in Marrakech city centre to reflect upon my day. What a pretentious pseud I am! I'd just seen women carrying bundles of washing upon their head that would have ground me into the dust, donkeys carrying wicker baskets loaded with rocks upon whose back the owner then jumped as he bid it up the hill. I saw emaciated horses, *shilpit* sheep, skinny cows, bored camels, harassed horses, uneducated kids and underemployed adults. Everywhere, men, women, kids and beasts of burden walked uphill.

I felt like it was culture-porn...and it was. Sometimes it's easier just going to the beach with other fortunate souls.

But then, as I later sat in my air-conditioned bar, I watched as a waitress, having served me, the only occupant, walk like an automaton around the several tables straightening already straight place-settings. Outside, for the hour that I sipped at my (admittedly two) *Proseccos*, a well-dressed young man, somewhat underemployed as a bouncer, leaned against a lamppost and watched wearily and warily as the world went by. Every so often he'd sip from a tumbler of water he'd hidden in a floral arrangement. Then he'd go back to watching the world go by.

Urban poor, rural poor. But to deal with it, Morocco needs to achieve several things at the same time; decent education, good healthcare, transport and infrastructure - especially for those who live in the mountains, Those are the public investments. But in addition what is needed are market opportunities and employment. That said, Morocco is actually experiencing something of an economic boom having enjoyed a stable economy and continuous growth over the past half-century. Additionally, the IMF notes that its financial sector is sound and resilient to shocks. However, the ace up its sleeve is the fact that controls about three-quarters of the world's remaining good-quality phosphate reserves.

Phosphate, when used as fertilizer, is the irreplaceable chemical driving modern agriculture and its reserves are in decline almost everywhere except Morocco. Most phosphate mines, including those in the U.S., which produces 17% of the global supply, have been in a downward spiral for the last decade whereas Morocco has at least three hundred to four hundred years of rock available; 85% of the world's total.

This single stroke of good fortune could make Morocco a very rich nation in the future and one that would have the rest of the world view it as tomorrow's Saudi Arabia.

Frankly, its only major economic difficulty seems to be unreliable rainfall, a chronic problem that produces drought or sudden floods. Still with its future wealth assured, irrigation becomes an ever-increasing likelihood.

I left the café bar knowing that in doing so, I'd allow my waitress the opportunity to straighten my place-setting and that my young friend outside would watch me leave his world. I'm pretty certain I'd made their day.

As on previous mornings I was awakened by the *muezzin* calling the faithful to prayer from the minaret of a nearby mosque. His invitation sounded somewhat metallic due I suspect, to very loud if inexpensive amplification but it served to rouse me from my bed as I suppose was its purpose.

I had my usual sumptuous if unfussy breakfast on the roof-terrace then took a short walk towards the palace and home again via the souk. Just as I prepared to depart the *riad*, I realised that I'd found my bearings and was step-perfect as I made my way back. I bid a fond farewell to Jean-Paul, jumped in the taxi he'd ordered and alighted at Marrakech Railway Station.

There are two types of taxi in Marrakech; '*petit*' and '*grand*'. The latter is licensed to take travellers to more distant parts but the '*petit*' is tasked with moving people around the city. Jean-Paul had advised assertiveness by encouraging my insistence that the driver makes use of his meter or he predicted I'd be charged a lot more. I did as asked but on many occasions when I'd secured agreement, the driver merely upped his fee by driving me to my destination by a most circuitous route. Where this wasn't sufficiently profitable, it seemed inevitable that they wouldn't have change for any note that I offered. I took to walking around with a pocketful of coins. A further ruse employed was to ensure that once a passenger was ensconced safely in a rear seat, to stop and collect other roadside hailers - sometimes more than one - then take them to their destination. This has the advantage to the driver of maximising his fares but also serves to confuse the original passenger who now has no idea whether any part of his route was subsidised or whether the driver has just been paid twice. Taxi drivers...they rule the world.

I'd earlier reserved a seat to Casablanca; train 608, carriage 1, compartment 4, seat 46. I found it with ease and was first to be seated. From then until the train left one after another, perhaps twenty people argued that their ticket permitted them one of the six seats in the compartment. On each occasion the guard had to officiate and rule on their claim. Several times he consulted my ticket as part of his investigations and on each occasion determined that I was in the correct seat. Confusion had arisen apparently because there were two carriages numbered 1.

The seating was comfortable but slightly cramped as there were more suitcases than there was space above in the storage rack so they sat at our feet on the floor. I slept and read a book about the last song the Beatles worked on as a group ('I want you (She's so heavy)') but found myself engrossed in their rendition of 'I Will' as McCartney actually sang his base notes rather than play them instrumentally. Fascinating and enjoyable in equal measure.

Because ONCF are building a high-speed rail link from north to south on a route which largely follows the contour of the existing line, there were several lengthy stops due to work delays. The new line allows Morocco to join exalted Spanish and French company and whisk passengers to their destinations at speeds of 320 km/hr. The first phase (Casablanca/Tangier) is meant to be opened in 2018. They'd better get a move on. I noticed that few rails had been laid on the extended line although the solum has been formed.

First impressions having walked to the harbour and sauntered round the medina? Casablanca underwhelms! Worse, it sucks! Noisy, crowded and poor, its buildings are tawdry, the built environment and public realm are down-at-heel and surfaces underfoot are frankly dangerous. Stepping on to the road from certain kerbs was akin to leaping from a small dyke. (Scots; Noun. *small wall*) Pavement tiles were missing, footpaths were uneven and litter was strewn everywhere. I looked for a map and eventually found a book store where I purchased one. Tired, I eventually gave up looking for something positive to say and returned to the Atlas Almohades Hotel; decent, clean and well-reviewed. The piano bar looked enticing. I sat in a plush leather seat and wiped my brow. The bartender approached immediately I sat down.

"A Cognac please."

"Eh, sorry, Monsieur. No Cognac." He thought quickly. "We have Campari!"

I returned to the bar menu. "What malt whiskies do you have?"

He looked to the ceiling as if to recall his inventory before shaking his head. "My apologies, Monsieur. We have no whisky." A beat. "Bacardi perhaps?"

I lowered my gaze once more and consulted (the fairly comprehensive) drinks menu. "Perhaps a cocktail?"

A light shone in the bartender's eyes...then dimmed. He pursed his lips. "Once again, Monsieur, I regret..."

"What do you have?"

"Beer...we have beer."

Casablanca beer?"

"Alas, Monsieur...."

I drank a nondescript glass of beer then went to my room and tried to make sense of the television news in French. Apparently the UK is leaving the EEC.

After an hour, I used the Internet to attempt to find a decent restaurant. They seemed thin on the ground in my part of the city and I couldn't be bothered going further afield. I tried to reserve a dinner table at Rick's Café, a relatively new restaurant which attempts to capitalise on the familiarity and affection the world has with the classic Humphrey Bogart and Ingrid Bergman movie, 'Casablanca' (shot almost in its entirety in Hollywood). It was full so I reserved a table for lunch the following day and headed off to an Irish Bar creatively named 'The Irish Bar' a few streets away. Upon entering, first glances reassured me; road signs pointed to Irish towns, fiddles hung on the wall, old-fashioned butchers' bicycles blocked the entrance, framed photographs of Brendan Behan adorned the door to the lavvy...just as one would anticipate. These features describe Irish Bars all over the world.

I approached the bar. "A pint of Guinness, please."

"Alas, Monsieur..."

I eventually was persuaded to drink yet another lager (there was no Casablanca here either) and ordered fish and chips.

It was interesting watching the pub come to life. Young Arab men escorted young Arab women wearing ripped jeans and tight, low-cut, figure-hugging tops (again I only noticed this in order to make a cultural and sociological point), ordered alcohol, chatted and grooved quietly to the musical stylings of Paul Symon. Some of the young women wore revealing attire but also wore the *khimar* headscarf. Casablanca citizens - at least its young people - seem slightly more secular than their elders. The Qur'an (24:31) states that the Prophet (peace be upon him) said;

'And say to the believing women that they cast down their looks and guard their private parts and do not display their ornaments except what appears thereof, and let them wear their khimars over their bosoms and not display their ornaments except to their husbands, their fathers, their husbands' fathers, their sons, their husbands' sons, their brothers or their brothers' sons, or their sisters' sons...or small children who have no sense of the shame of sex.'

There seemed to be a lot of siblings in the pub that night.

As I left I visited the toilet. There were no urinals, just two regular, single lavvies, one for males and one for females. As the male toilet was occupied I popped into the ladies, lifted the lid and noticed a silhouette sign on the door which discouraged young ladies for using said lavvy for purposes of winching young men. Like I said, Casablancan young people seem slightly more secular than their elders.

Upon my return to my hotel, I walked into the (deserted) piano bar again hoping that they might have something close to alcoholic available and noticed that the piano player...he of the piano bar... the guy who gives his name to the entertainment available...the *piano man*...was fast asleep at the keyboard. Unconscious! Brought to urgent wakefulness by the bartender serving me, he launched instantly into a (slightly out-of-tune in the upper reaches) rendition of the 1925 standard, *'Yes sir, that's my baby'* as if it had been an encore asked of him at a Royal Variety Performance; all smiles now.

Being in Casablanca, I was tempted to approach him and venture, "Play it again, Sam," but was aware that this is a universally misquoted reference to Humphrey Bogart's exclamation to Sam (played by Dooley Wilson) in the 1942 film, *Casablanca* where he actually says irritably, "Play it!" I also figured he might have been asked that request before. As I prepared to leave for bed, an American woman approached him and asked the question I'd earlier considered. He drew her a glance and launched into *'Hava Nagila'*. Like I said, I'd bet he'd been asked that request before!

I finished my beer and left, pushing the elevator button for floor seven and behind me I could hear the receding strains of, *'As Time Goes By...'* *"You must remember this...a kiss is not a kiss...a sigh is just a sigh..."* The American's persistence had paid off!

Determined to find positive things to say about Casa (everyone, I'm informed, calls it by its abbreviated name) I rose and dressed taking care to wear a long-sleeved shirt as I thought I might manage a look inside Mosque Hassan II which has a dress code, because lunch was to be at Rick's Café which has a dress code and because my left arm was a blazing red colour as a consequence of driving two days ago with my arm casually leaning out of the window.

I walked from my city-centre hotel down to the mosque and in order to take the perfect photograph which permitted an understanding of its enormity, I walked along a boarded-off seafront following two rod fishermen who climbed a small wall and cut across to the beach. Beach? It was a beach like Largs has a beach! Rocky pools and seaweed strewn pebbles reached out a distance into the breakers of the Atlantic Ocean. Defeated, I walked over to a small pavement café where I ordered a mint tea.

"*Moroccan* Tea!" My waiter corrected me. Poured from height into a shot glass, it was delicious.

The Moroccan people speak French as a second language and many speak a little English. However, on those occasions when I had to converse in the Arab tongue, I confess I was all at sea. It was to my European ears as if my interlocutor was simultaneously having a coughing fit, gargling and clearing his throat. Only my well-honed ability to read people's minds allowed me a modicum of understanding. Much smiling and hand gestures usually saved the day.

I walked along the front towards a prominent lighthouse which was surrounded by a white-walled shantytown. Corrugated tin roofs held in place by large rocks stood in contrast to the many digital television satellite discs also adorning the same rooftops. Accusingly, this small and deprived enclave looked directly across the bay towards the opulence of the Grande Mosque.

I walked further along the Corniche where I was led to believe sandy beaches and frolicking crowds were to be seen. Frankly, it was still pretty scabby and walking along the uneven pathway was fraught with danger. I walked down some crumbling stairs and spent some time on the beach along with perhaps another twenty souls before climbing back up. A petit taxi dropped me at the *Grande Mosque* allowing me thirty minutes to find Rick's Café. I walked past the Moroccan Naval Academy and some extremely expensive looking office blocks, retraced my steps, followed my nose, still quite sure I knew roughly where the café was situated.

But a confidence born of stupidity had seen me leave without actually writing down the address - just the memory of a general location. My 1.00pm reservation came and went as I found myself lost in the city's main Medina. What an eegit!

Tired and sunburned, I found a local restaurant in the Medina; one I suspected did not serve many from beyond the streets surrounding it. I ordered yet more Morocco tea and chose *Poisson Tagine*. When it was delivered and the lid of the glazed earthenware pot was removed, the fiercest fish I'd ever seen stared at me from the plate...that is, it's fist-sized head did, as that was all that was available from this particular fish; a complete fish-head stared at me, unblinking. I poked around looking interested so as not to disappoint the waiter who obviously thought he'd delivered me a real delicacy but all I could think of was that I'd intended being served a chilled cocktail along with my beautifully cooked lunch in Rick's Café but instead was eyeballing an inedible fish dish in the Medina. I ate some of the potatoes, peppers and tomatoes that flavoured the dish before replacing the lid to conceal my lack of appetite, smiling and rubbing my tummy circuitously with the flat of my hand in an attempt to convey to my friend the waiter that I'd enjoyed lunch.

I decided to attempt to buy a charger for my ultra-modern (at the time of writing) Fitbit watch knowing in my heart that this technology wouldn't have reached Casablanca yet. Earlier the hotel receptionist had written an address in Arabic when I explained I wanted to visit a large, modern electronic shop. He knew just the place so I caught a *petit* red rust bucket of a taxi whose driver charged fifty Dirhams to take me to what can only be described as the largest electronic goods market on the planet! Hundreds of small stalls sold every electronic product available to mankind. The sheer tonnage of Apple, Samsung, Microsoft, Nokia, Canon, Sony and Nikon products on sale would have filled the Grand Canyon. I spoke with a few traders about my watch all of whom shook their head until I found one guy who looked optimistic.

"*Ah, oui, mon ami.*"

After a lengthy exchange with his brother, he raced off to find the very man who could sell me a new charger. Ten minutes later he returned and spoke with a new gravitas as if a doctor giving me the news that I wasn't going to make it. He drew his hand across his throat.

"Je suis profondément désolé. C'est carrément impossible."

Nodding, I thanked him and walked round the rest of the market, ever-more impressed by the scale and bustle of the place.

I'd noted that when the taxi driver had dropped me off, it was only a block away from the route of the new tramway system. Seven Dinars (as opposed to fifty) took me back to my hotel comfortably, safely and speedily. An excellent system, it carries over a quarter of a million passengers a day! That said, tram stops have electronic turnstiles. Very sensible, you might think - but they stand at each end of the elongated platform with no other impediments to access. It was like a farmer having a field and a gate but no fence.

After a brief respite I set off again for Rick's Café having organised a 6.30pm reservation. This time I was armed with a map and a compass (I made that bit up about the compass) but the taxi driver couldn't understand my pronunciation of the street-name so I asked him to drop me at the *Grande Mosque* which, according to my map was only yards away. As I emerged I realised I'd put myself in exactly the position I'd been in at lunchtime. I found myself wandering around the same streets no better off than earlier as although I had a map, the street signs were only in Arabic! Eventually, by working out the configuration of streets, I found myself at the point where earlier in the day I'd retraced my steps. Instead of turning around, had I then only taken ten steps more I'd have been at Rick's Café - and my day would have been incontrovertibly the poorer for it!

Let me explain. I arrived at 6.45pm just in time for the doorman to tell me (and the crowd of perhaps another dozen people) that the Café was full up. "You muss get here seex-thirty. Café is verr popular!"

Everyone queueing left but I stayed awaiting an opportunity to take the place of the first person earlier admitted to leave. Half an hour passed and still no one had left. An American arrived, hadn't made a reservation and was refused admission. He got into an argument with the doorman.

"Whaat's your nemm, buster? Ah'm gunna write to your baaas!"

Typical American', I thought. Then another American arrived. He too was told the place was full but like me, he elected to wait and we struck up a conversation. He was self-effacing, intelligent and conversational. As we chatted I realised that when a vacancy occurred it would probably be for two people and suggested that if so, we share the same table or bar stools. Just then an opportunity arose and we were shown in.

What a great restaurant is Rick's Café. It dripped with Moroccan tradition and reeked of Humphrey Bogart. We were shown to the table next to the piano and introduced ourselves.

"I'm Kam," said my new friend. "Short for Kameron. Kam Akhter."

"Jesus...you're almost Scottish. I'm Ron."

"Hi, Raan!"

It transpired that Kam had been travelling the world for five and a half years and had visited every continent except Antarctica. He was on a budget and so asked only for water and a small inexpensive fish dish so I offered to pick up the tab. We conversed until it was time to be thrown out. What an interesting, intelligent and mellow guy!

Initially he was alarmed at my alcohol consumption. "A beer *and* a whisky, Raan?"

But as the evening progressed he found himself amazed at my ability to talk normally after two drinks.

"If I had two drinks, Raan, I'd be under the table!"

"Practice makes perfect, Kam!"

I asked how he managed to finance his adventures.

"When I was younger in Chicago," (he was now in his early thirties, I guessed) "I wrote a book about mind-mapping ('Mind

Mapping. How to improve Memory, Concentration, Organisation and Time Management'...available in all good bookshops) and it took off. Another seven followed. I now get a pretty regular income and it allows me to travel the world...if on a budget!"

We discussed politics, religion, travel, writing, photography, family, food and laughed a lot. He was a really interesting guy. We promised to keep in touch – and did!

At last I had found something positive to say about Casablanca...it does great visitors...and it has the simply majestic Rick's Café!

Travelling north the following morning to Tangier, the day started well. I had an entire six seat compartment to myself and made myself at home. After a while I fell asleep only to be awakened by a kick to the sole of my shoe. I'd slept through the rail stop at Rabat and had been joined by three guys. One of them sat opposite me and passed over a cup of Moroccan tea he'd bought from the trolley. Each of them sipped away at their tea as did I, gesturing my gratitude throughout.

"We from Oman. Where you from?"

"Scotland."

"Is that England?"

"No."

And so we fell into a conversation but as the journey proceeded they became more restive and I took refuge in my ear-plugs when they turned on a mobile phone full blast and began to sing along to Arabian music before starting to pray. I made the mistake of watching an episode of *'Homeland'* on my iPad before the series' theme of Arab terrorists made me uncomfortable. By the time the three guys stepped out to the corridor together I fancied I could hear a ticking sound coming from the single bag they carried between them and had deposited in the rack above me!

A *petit* taxi took me to the very top of Tangier's *Kasbah* and left me there. I'd resigned myself to another bout of aimless wandering when an elderly man (again, my age) took me round a couple of very narrow lanes and pointed me directly at *Kasbah* Rose, a tiny guesthouse at the very pinnacle of the *Kasbah* which itself towers above Tangier. I'd still be looking for it today had he not helped me. In addition, the lanes are very narrow and all involve steps so they don't feature on a map as they are clearly unable to take vehicular traffic.

I unpacked and headed off, stopping to climb atop a cafe with a panoramic view of Tangier. The price was another cup of Moroccan tea and I thought it worth it although the waiter charged me twenty Dinars (£1.50) and upon leaving I noticed that the wall-tariff was five Dinars.

I walked down, down, down to the beach. Tangier old harbour is being redeveloped and a new seafront promenade seems rapidly to be taking shape. A new marina sits empty but once made available I'm sure it'll be oversubscribed. New public space has been created and a system of subterranean retail outlets is well under way beneath a new urban waterfront. The beach was sectioned off for reasons I couldn't discern but it was clean and well used.

I stopped off for a smoothie but instead ordered a citrus drink. Unfortunately the waiter misheard my order and provided me instead with a glass of sulphuric acid. I was afraid my vocal chords might never recover and headed for a famous bar called 'Number One' to treat them with alcohol. Number One Bar is famous as the hostelry in which celebrated novelist of the Beat Generation, William S. Burroughs (battling heroin addiction and where he wrote 'Naked Lunch') and Samuel Becket (in his autumn years) had hung out during the fifties. Yet again I found myself lost as a consequence of a paucity of street signs. I swear to god that when I become King of the World, after I sort out world peace and the cost of printer ink, I'm going to pass a law which requires that every street on the planet has a nameplate attached at each end of the thoroughfare and on both sides of the street - no matter how insignificant the roadway - and in every language. Eventually, at a point where I'd almost lost hope, I stumbled across the bar I sought.

It was a tiny bar but a proper one. The owner, Karim was most solicitous. I was his only customer but he turned off the football on television and played Ella Fitzgerald; American jazz for which the place has become renowned. A brandy took him several seconds and a steady pour to complete; a *stoncker*, as one might say. He began to ply me with *tapas* such that my intention to eat elsewhere was abandoned and I ordered a simple dish of sole. Upon discovering me pounding away on my iPad and discovering that I'd written books, he took a keen interest. "All great writers drink here!"

I thanked him embarrassedly for his remark and handed him a card on which were inscribed each of my eight books to date. Five minutes later he returned insisting that a member of his staff take a photograph of us. Shortly, he showed me with pride a new entry he'd made on his web site incorporating our photograph together and images of my books all set out very professionally along with a testimonial from him. The music had segued into Gary Moore by this time and the minuscule bar had busied up. Very relaxing.

I only had one drink and was about to order a taxi when Karim dismissed the idea.

"*Kasbah* just round corner. You walk. You see Tangier come to life!"

He gave directions which involved me going downhill initially. Given that I'd achieved some height when finding his bar, and was aware that returning to *Kasbah* Rose would involve a daunting climb, I was disinclined but figured if I really *was* so close, taxis wouldn't be keen to pick me up so I walked...and walked...and walked as it became darker and darker. I managed to become hopelessly lost yet again. In the older parts of Moroccan towns, the small lanes are completely labyrinthine, have no street signs - or if they do they're in Arabic and at least in Tangier's *Kasbah*, cover a large, steep area on a hill. Most of the poorly maintained pavements were ankle-snappers in complete contrast to the billiard-table sidewalk investment that's being laid on the shore.

What Karim promised would be a five minute stroll took me two hours of hard and frustrating labour!

I breakfasted late in order to visit the *Kasbah* Museum only steps from my front door but which opened at 10.00am. The owner of the guest house, a Dutch guy called Hans, gave me directions.

"Perhaps fifty metres!"

I got lost again. It really is comical how un-navigable is the Medina. I decided a better course of action was to make sure I knew *exactly* how to get to *Kasbah* Rose from the main *Kasbah* square, photographed turnings for later reference and about ten-thirty, found the Museum. It was closed.

I walked down to the Harbour and bought my ticket for the ferry crossing to Tarifa in Spain in two days' time to avoid any queues and to check out procedures before walking along the corniche beyond the Harbour to photograph the departing 11.00am ferry to Tarifa. When at 11.30am it still hadn't sailed, I returned to the Medina and bought a leather purse, belt and handbag, negotiating half-heartedly and conceding early as these guys scrape a living, the goods seemed to be of decent quality and everything was as cheap as chips. Like Marrakech, this Medina seems replete with artisans rather than retailers as was the case in Casablanca where they specialised in knock-off goods by Ralph Lauren, Nike and the like. Here they were busy cutting, stitching, sewing, planing and weaving the goods they had on display. Ignoring the hand-made products, I bought a fake Nike baseball cap to protect my head from the sun. I negotiated him down from £1.80 to £1.60 and felt horrible doing so.

I travelled out to Hercules Grotto (an underwhelming touristic cave on the coast whereupon waves break). I climbed up to a café atop steep cliffs which were walled off but some twenty-somethings had climbed over the three feet high abutment out on to the rock-face. *Very dangerous,* I thought. I couldn't believe how stupid they were. One slip and they'd fall a hundred feet to the breakers below and would be fish-food. Moments later, the stiff Atlantic breeze whipped my £1.60 baseball cap from my head on to the cliff edge and without thinking, I leapt (get me, *leapt*...clambered) over the retaining wall and negotiated the sheer drop to the ocean to retrieve it. Well, money's money!

Returning to Tangier, I asked the taxi driver to drop me *exactly* where I knew I could find *Kasbah* Rose. Straight down the *souk*, turn right at number 48 and my destination would be directly in front of me. I got lost again and had to pay a boy five Dirhams (shite-pence) to show me to the door. At least it's getting less expensive as I manage to navigate closer each time I get lost.

Up sharp and off to the airport to collect my rental car so as to visit the Berber town of Chefchaouen, a small town in the Rif Mountains some hundred or so miles from Tangier. The *petit* taxis in Morocco in my experience are all different in that in Marrakech they are coloured gold, in Casablanca, red and in Tangier, light blue and green. What they share is that they are all (with very few exceptions) rust-buckets which in the UK wouldn't even be allowed to *test* for an MOT, are driven maniacally and don't have seat belts. The drivers text and phone while driving through crowds of people thronging the street, they talk animatedly over their shoulder attempting conversation while at speed; if animated, it's all spittle and hand gestures, and if unable to pump their horn repeatedly every thirty seconds, they're fined by the authorities (I made that bit up about the fine!)

The car made over to me at the airport was every bit as dilapidated as the taxis I'd become used to but the rental administrator made the effort to walk round the vehicle inspecting every scratch and dent before handing me his findings to sign off - the outline of the car on paper being covered in blue ink dots and scores. It would be difficult for me to scratch the car and invite him to discover it. It would be like a game of 'Where's Wally!' Further complicating my life, he drew my attention to the petrol gauge.

"*Est zéro,*" he smiled happily. "*Pompe à pétrole* round corner." He smiled again. "*C'est très simple. Retourner la voiture à zero.*"

Return the car with an empty tank! I thought it the stupidest idea I'd come across.

I drove to the nearby garage (not *that* nearby) and tried to calculate how much petrol I'd need to get me to Chefchaouen and back via Ceuta, the Spanish enclave opposite Gibraltar. I went with the cash equivalent and put 200 Dinars (£15) in the tank. It almost filled it. Petrol's cheap here.

I was pleased with my journey to Chefchaouen. A toll-road where I made progress soon gave way to a small country road which was in the process of being duelled. In consequence, thunderous lorries carrying spoil trundled along leaving in their wake, queues of frustrated drivers who, once they'd managed to overtake, merely accelerated a hundred yards or so before hauling up behind another behemoth. The route was very pretty however. Mountains loomed and when pine trees and yellow gorse began to make an appearance beside what I fancied were lochs (but were probably reservoirs) I felt I was back in Scotland had it not been for the thirty-eight degree temperature outside.

Chefchaouen is famed for being blue...not depressed...but for having most of its buildings and walls painted the same colour of eggshell blue. A terrific marketing idea which makes the town very picturesque. Delightfully, their *petit* taxis are all painted the same colour of blue. It makes for a particularly fetching prospect. Situated high in the Rif Mountains about a hundred miles from Tangier, it had a bustling air to it. Market-sellers abounded and parking was at a premium. A sandwich lunch took forever to serve for reasons I could not discern but it was a lovely day so I forced myself to overlook the delay and enjoy the laid-back, sunny atmosphere of the place.

It has been suggested that the particular colour of blue used keeps mosquitos away, that Jews introduced the blue when they took refuge from Hitler in the 1930s although I can't for the life of me imagine why, and finally that the elders thought it symbolised heaven and was a reminder to lead a spiritual life. Me? I figure it was a wee marketing guy who sold the town authorities on the idea of colouring the place blue as their Unique Selling Proposition. Whatever... it works well although a lick of egg-shell blue paint here and there might freshen things up a bit.

Chefchaouen is also known quaintly as the main producer of cannabis in Morocco and there are reports that hashish is sold to visitors all over town. I was offered leather handbags and slippers.

Wandering round this lovely town, it's difficult to see it as the centre of a drugs industry. It doesn't have the feel of a Medellin. I saw no pick-up truck carrying men with automatic weapons but the fact is that Morocco is the world's largest exporter of hashish and supplies 70% of the European appetite, with a market value of one and a half billion of your English pounds. European tourism and drug markets expanded simultaneously in the 1960s. Mick Jagger, Keith Richards and the Marrakech Express boys are all owed some thanks by the approximately two hundred hoteliers who now cater to the summer inundation of European tourists seeking chemical relaxation...and I was offered handbags and slippers!

I drove back to Tangier hoping to find out more about Ceuta. Following Brexit, Spain made the repatriation of Gibraltar under their jurisdiction an early condition of the negotiations. The British Prime Minster opposed this, making reference to it being similar to the Falkland Islands over which the UK went to war. Now, I'm hardly an apologist for British imperialism but right across the water from Gibraltar, seventeen miles as the crow flies, the good people of either enclave can watch each other putting out their washing on a clear day. I would never call another nation hypocritical but when Spain recognised the independence of Spanish Morocco in 1956, Ceuta and Melilla remained under Spanish rule. Spain considered them integral parts of the Spanish state despite Morocco's protests. What's good for the goose, eh?

As I drove towards the sunlit peninsula of Ceuta I had presumed that I'd be able to drive across unhindered but I came upon a long queue of cars all being attended to by a host of Moroccans who were offering customs cards and offers of help. I was trapped by a centre barrier prohibiting a U-turn and could see no option other than to go through the entire rigmarole of passport entry and return.

Fortunately I listened to an older Moroccan who merely advised me to undertake a three point turn and drive back to the roundabout some hundred yards behind me, on the *wrong* side of the road and against oncoming traffic.

"Is possible," he pointed out.

I saw the logic of his suggestion and the policeman watching my manoeuvres didn't bat an eyelid! Nor, for that matter, did any of the cars driving towards the customs post. They seemed to take it as quite natural that they'd be headed into an unavoidable collision were one of us not anxious to navigate helpfully and make mutual adjustments to our steering.

Approaching Tangier, the fuel light started flashing causing me to ask myself how much scope a car manufacturer would give someone almost running on fumes. Everything was flashing but I figured that if there was a beeper for not engaging the seatbelt, there must be an audible signal when the tank was down to its last drip of petrol. I was pretty determined to see the vehicle home without putting another red cent of gas into it. I managed it with god alone knows how much fuel in the tank. But that I managed it successfully made me more delighted than words can express.

"*Retourner la voiture à zéro.*"

What a dumb idea!

Afterwards, a couple of beers in Karim's Number One bar relaxed me as did his choice of music. Tonight was country rock. He's quite a character, our Karim. Bringing my Beer Casablanca to my table, he lifted my back-pack from a chair and hung it on a hook he'd screwed on to the side of the table. Quite seriously he told me that people come from all over the world to his bar and take his ideas back home. He had no problem with this, he averred. He just wanted to spread good ideas.

"I invent the idea of hanging things on hook at end of table! Now, *everyone* does this!"

Well, *someone* had to come up with that idea! Certainly he had many photographs on his wall of himself and film stars, most of whom I recognised but could not name. I'd love to visit their homes in Beverly Hills and take a surreptitious look at the ends of their kitchen tables to see if anything dangled.

Next morning I organised myself, bid farewell to Hans and his wife Marit and began to walk circuitously down through the Medina to the ferry terminal to catch the boat that would return me from North Africa to Europe; from Tangier in Morocco to Tarifa in Spain where I intended spending a couple of days in Gibraltar to rest before catching a flight to Nairobi and sub-Saharan Africa. I walked casually down the steep hill from the medina but stepping off a high pavement, found myself pulling up short as a stabbing pain knifed my lower back.

Jeeesus, what was that? I asked myself as I staggered pityingly to a nearby chair in a small cafe, my face contorted as if someone had introduced a red-hot poker to my backside. This attracted the attentions of the owner who arrived hurriedly with a glass of water then retreated to find a cloth as my face was now drenched in sweat. I thanked him for his kindness, ordered a coffee and gathered myself. I'd obviously done myself some kind of pelvic injury. I'd earlier been troubled with back pain stemming from a football injury that saw me hospitalised for a couple of weeks in my youth. It had caused me pain most of my adult life but I'd managed it pretty comfortably. This seemed different.

Given my imminent departure, it seemed that the sensible thing to do was to somehow reach the ferry as planned and travel onwards to continental Europe. Kenya could wait!

I'll say only this. Never again will an ill word about Caledonian MacBraynes cross my lips! The crossing was smooth but the administrative hassles that required to be gone through before actually stepping foot on the boat were immensely frustrating, doubly so because I was now in serious discomfort.

Somehow I made my accommodation in Gibraltar, a berth in a small boat called the *Kasbah Rose* in the harbour. I'd thought it would be a great idea. Inexpensive, different, great location...and it was all of these but it also required me to climb up and on to a shoulder-height bunk. I managed it and hardly left it for a couple of days until I came to my senses, postponed Nairobi and headed painfully home.

My doctor sent me packing to hospital where an MRI scan revealed multi-layered spinal lumbar stenosis. My spine had narrowed at three vertebrae and had pinched my sciatic nerve. It would require surgery. I explained I had an unfinished trip to Africa to complete. The doctor frowned.

"Well, if it remains as a stenosis, it'll just be painful when you walk but this particular condition can become much more serious if it develops into what we call *cauda equina* syndrome."

"Is that bad?"

"Well, let's see. If it progresses to that and you didn't manage to have emergency surgery, you could lose control of your bowels, your bladder, your legs." For unnecessary emphasis, he added, "And your pecker might fall off!"

"But apart from that?"

We both smiled.

"So what do you reckon. Should I travel to Africa? I wouldn't do anything silly like climbing, rafting or hang-gliding."

The doctor pursed his lips in contemplation. "I can't say go to Africa and I can't say *don't* go to Africa. You're a big boy. Presently you have a stenosis...but it might develop. You'd have to have a plan to get back here within forty-eight hours if things deteriorate. The spinal surgeons here at this hospital are the best in the business - so it's your shout! I certainly wouldn't recommend letting some bush doctor have a go at your spine. You could end up in a wheelchair permanently."

Never the brightest chap, I decided to go.

Morocco had been fascinating; from the Medina of Marrakech via the industry of Casablanca to the *Kasbah* of Tangier. The people had been universally kind and helpful. I enjoyed my rail journeys. The quality of life enjoyed by Berber communities in the High Atlas and the Rif mountain ranges allowed me to understand just how difficult it is for them to cling to an existence. But Morocco's a poor country so no easy jibes about its built environment. Let's cut them a bit of slack and remember this. People of Arabian descent, people of Islam have a track record that suggests they might just be capable of huge progress. They invented coffee (and understood its effect on wakefulness). A Muslim mathematician, astronomer and physicist Ibn al-Haitham invented the first pin-hole camera after noticing the way light came through a hole. Indeed, the word 'camera' derives from the Arab word *qamara* foreign meaning 'dark room'. A thousand years before the Wright brothers, generally credited with perfecting the world's first flying machine, a Muslim engineer named Abbas ibn Firnas made several attempts to fly using a machine he'd manufactured comprised of silk and eagles' feathers. He stayed aloft for ten minutes before crashing. Surgical implements such as scalpels, bone saws, forceps, fine scissors for eye surgery and a further couple of hundred medical instruments recognisable to a modern surgeon were invented in the tenth century by a Muslim surgeon called al-Zahrawi. Jabir ibn Hayyan, transformed alchemy into chemistry by inventing many of the basic processes still in use today. As well as discovering sulphuric and nitric acid, old Jabir also invented alcohol and his religious elders promptly decided it was *haram;* forbidden, in Islam. Arabs invented windmills, inoculation and the use of the crank-shaft for irrigation. In the fifteenth century they invented rockets and torpedoes, and finally they invented soap and taught the Crusaders how to use it!

They'll get by just fine...but now I was headed back to Africa, back this time in modest discomfort, to Nairobi.

African Dawns

Nairobi is the capital city of Kenya and I was looking forward to visiting but I also knew I was flying into a potentially dangerous situation following a controversial presidential election. The main opposition leader Raila Odinga had earlier lost to the incumbent president Uhuru Kenyatta who was declared the winner of the contest with 54% of the vote. Odinga then screamed that the ballot had been rigged, the judges agreed and a second national ballot was called for. Odinga then refused to stand citing corruption, and machete-wielding mobs supporting him gathered on street corners in protest. Kenyatta's government then tried to jail the opposition leadership but failed so to do, so had then attempted to seize their passports and remove their bodyguards, jailed a judge who had participated in a mock ceremony offering the presidency to Odinga and then shut down three television stations whose newscasters had carried the story.

Just to calm things down, newspaper reports shouted that water levels were so low that electricity might be compromised and power to Nairobi might have to be cut. Finally, terrorists from *the Al-Shabaab* insurgency, an off-shoot of *Al Q'aeda* whose objectives include 'waging *jihad* against enemies of Islam' were promising action in Kenya having been involved in at least seventeen attacks involving grenades or other explosive devices. Most recently, an attack at Nairobi's Westgate Shopping Mall close to where I was to sleep upon arrival killed 67 people. Today the mall is made secure by Israeli guards under contract as no *modus vivendi* seems in sight.

Al Q'aeda's most devastating bombing had previously been a simultaneous attack on American Embassies in Dar es Salaam and Nairobi which killed 213 people in the Nairobi blast and eleven in Dar es Salaam - all but a dozen Americans, citizens of East Africa. An astonishing 4,000 in Nairobi were wounded, and another eighty-five in Dar es Salaam.

But on the bright side, sometimes I could walk upright without grimacing.

Nairobi was dark when I arrived. I shuffled into my hotel, the 'After 40 Hotel' and readied myself for sleep. I was knackered. Before dozing off, I read the hotel's literature which claimed it was a 'World Class, Four Star Hotel'. It would have struggled to make one star in a developed country but my reaction wasn't one of mocking humour; rather I was touched by their ambition.

The pavement might be crumbling outside, the place might have been drab and tawdry but the reception staff members were outrageously friendly and helpful and believed in their hotel just as much as would have the doorman of the Ritz Carlton. Still, it was indubitably a bit of a dump and had clearly been designed by an architect who'd decided to build an echo chamber and stick some beds in it.

I fell asleep immediately and was awakened by the quotidian, sonorous dirge of the *Muezzin*, the crier who climbs his minaret and calls Muslims to pray five times a day...starting at 5.30 am each morning. I was going to have to get used to this.

First on my agenda was to be a visit to Kibera, the largest slum in Africa, a sprawling mass of tightly packed structures roofed with corrugated tin, accommodating by some estimates, over one million citizens but my guide persuaded me to spend the morning on safari in the nearby Kenya National Park. I'd earlier set my face against the touristy stuff but I was glad I'd listened to David Kabui Kariuki, my *Maasai* guide. (I hadn't realised that a great many Kenyans provide their children with English names whilst keeping their *Swahili* surname. David's two girls are named Fiona and Harriet)

He was what I'd viewed as classical *Maasai* in that he was tall, athletic-looking and slim. He referenced his wife often (and was keen to emphasise any statement he made by saying 'very, very, very' to underscore the importance of what he said. He was also typical of many I spoke with in that his use of English veered towards the dramatic. It was never 'the receptionist has left'...it was always, 'the receptionist has *completely* gone!') Despite telling me his family was everything to him, he explained that in Maasai culture, a woman marries not just her husband but the entire age group. Men are expected to give up their bed to a visiting age-mate guest although he went on to say that these days this practice is practised less. The woman decides strictly on her own if she will join the visiting male. Any child which may result is the husband's child - "But my Alice and me we will not be doing this. Very, very, very not!"

I confess I found the whole safari thing fascinating - not at all the zoo experience I'd anticipated. David drove round the park very slowly pointing out evidence of animal activity. When bouncing slowly round a corner, we saw a lion poised to leap at some gazelles which had wandered down to a waterhole. We waited for a moment and the lion burst forwards all muscle and sinew but the gazelles were too nimble and after glowering at them and promising to catch them next time, the lion retreated to the shade of a bush where he instantly became almost invisible due to his colouring. We waited until he closed his eyes and went to sleep in the simmering heat. Happily I watched lions, water buffaloes, gazelles, giraffes, elephants, eagles, rhinos, monkeys and zebras in their natural habitat. The safari was a happy distraction but I really wanted to visit Kibera.

D'y'know, the British have a lot to answer for! Read any history book and there will be a chapter that begins 'Great Britain took possession of such and such a country', sandpapering the truth by veiling Britain's ruthless colonialism. The British Establishment referred to these previously independent countries as dominions, colonies, mandates, protectorates, territories, overseas possessions, or trading posts but essentially they used the British nation's then land and sea-power to conquer other countries and steal their natural resources. In the late 16th through the early 19th centuries, Britain became, at its zenith, the largest empire in history. But in achieving this ignoble accomplishment, it sowed the seeds of poverty, violence, anger and cynicism in those unfortunate countries it conquered for centuries to come. Nor did we evince any shame about our greedy and exploitative adventures. That roly-poly gangster Winston Churchill boasted in 1920 that Britain was the world's foremost Muslin power in that it controlled the lives of some ninety million Muslims across the globe, roughly the same number which today inhabits Blackburn in Lancashire according to UKIP's Nigel Farage.

There are many uplifting stories about Kibera but in essence it's a triumph of human endeavour over desperate poverty. The shanty-town has grown up since it was founded back in 1899 when the Uganda Railway line was built. The British required a railway headquarters and colonial offices. Migrant workers were brought into Nairobi as indentured labour (slaves essentially as they had no say in their predicament) to work in support of British ambitions, as railway manual labour and to fill lower-level administrative posts in the colonial government.

David introduced me to Richard, a cadaverous fellow *Maasai* guide and one who had lived in Kibera all of his thirty-odd years. Disconcertingly he had a mild ocular condition, strabismus (one eye going to the shops, one coming back with the change) so I was never sure if he was addressing me or David. He explained that even though the shanty-town was comprised of makeshift huts, they had never had running water, sewerage, electricity. Anything they had they had had to establish themselves - but the government still charged them rent; significant amounts of rent that required many families to sub-let to others causing considerable overcrowding, disease and violence. Most people lived on less than one pound sterling a day and could easily go for three or four days without eating.

"Can you wonder people are so angry? The government promise much but do nothing then expect us to vote for them in an election."

I wondered why people then decide to vote for incumbent government politicians given their predicament.

"You can't understand, Mister Ron. (He pronounced it **Meeestaron**) It is about tribalism. There are five tribes that have influenced who is elected owing to their population; the *Kikuyu*, the *Luhya*, the *Kalenjin*, the *Luo* and the *Kamba*."

David interjected, "Our tribe, the *Maasai* are sensible. They don't vote tribally! The *Kikuyu* are most involved. They are stupid!"

Richard nodded as if in agreement and said, "You see, **Meeestaron**, this must be a puzzle to you. You are from the mother of parliaments and vote on a logical basis. You would not vote against your own best interests only because of some tribe you belong to."

I hesitated and decided not to interrupt his flow by directing him to examples of Northern Irish and indeed, Scottish politics where sectarianism still plays its role in political life.

"Here we have a very high incidence of AIDS, rape is common, our young women are not safe. No one has a job - at least not one that pays a decent wage. Education is poor and despite the government saying it is free we still have to pay. There are no books in school." (Again I bit my tongue.) "Most people in Kibera..." He looked round disparagingly and raised his voice indignantly..."In this foul-smelling *slum,* lack access to basic services, including electricity, running water and medical care. Open sewers run through our streets and children play in them then die of cholera, or die of AIDS, or die a violent death or die of malnutrition...but they die. They all die...even if in early old age because of the lifestyle they are forced to endure."

We talked some more and I thanked Richard before David and I left for Nairobi city centre some four miles away. Each of us was helplessly silent in the car, mulling over the words we'd just heard unable to offer any *démarche.*

As we crawled slowly towards the hotel, graffito on a wall amused me. In stark black lettering it announced, 'Chris Died For Your Sins!' I wasn't sure whether it was a simple spelling mistake, the absence of sufficient paint or the anguished declamation of an unsolved murder.

Back in Nairobi I went shopping for razor blades but found none. The 38 degree heat was intense. All around, people (mostly men it must be said) sat slack-jawed on the pavement with their elbows on their knees, their heads drooped or lay on grass borders in a state of utter torpidity. I understood their reaction to the heat and headed slowly back to my small hotel, grateful for somewhere to shelter from the sun.

My evening was quiet and contemplative. I prepared to leave Nairobi and head for Mombasa in the new Madaraka Express managed by Kenyan Rail - Strapline, *Connecting nations. Prospering people.*

I was up before the *Muezzin* woke the neighbourhood and, lathered in sweat even at 5.30 in the morning, made my way down to meet David who drove me to the new Nairobi Railway Station situated miles out of town at Syokimau. We sped along an empty dual carriageway. On the dried rubble-strewn sidewalk many people walked in the dark the long distance into the city and their employment. On the other side, traffic moved achingly slowly towards Nairobi in pursuit of the same end. I arrived comfortably an hour and a half before the stated departure time and found a lengthy and untidy queue stretching before me. My heart sank as standing for any length of time these days remains a matter of some discomfort for me but I soon became absorbed in the particular way Kenya seems to go about its security measures.

Uniforms were everywhere. Police, soldiers, security, railway staff, even a Japanese Admiral (I made that bit up about the Japanese Admiral) swarmed all over the queue, each shouting instructions, the most entertaining of which was when a uniform with a swagger stick instructed that the front of the queue thin out by stepping backwards. Now asking a long queue to move backwards is asking for trouble but asking only the *front* of an unruly queue to move backwards offered sights that couldn't have been bettered by Charlie Chaplin. Those at the rear couldn't hear the instruction and chaos ensued as passengers tripped over luggage and others tripped over them. Then everyone was asked to step away from their cases as dogs sniffed for drugs. Once this was completed, all notions of orderly queuing was abandoned and a rush was made on the security scanning equipment (one for men, one for women, you have to have *some* rules!). When belongings had been collected and a corner turned, another security guy patted travellers down with a wand. A hundred yards ahead, a passport check for foreigners, then a ticket queue formed and once passed yet another luggage scanner had to be endured. Eventually we were invited to step forward and front up at ticket barriers, given an infomercial on how to place our tickets on the scanner, a final passport check and then allowed to board the train and find our seat whereupon a uniformed lady asked again for our tickets and carefully wrote down the name of the person and their seat number in a notebook.

Now this new station (built and operated using Chinese money) is a marvel of marble and glass so it perhaps behoves the authorities to ensure that no one bruises it. I have no business suggesting more efficient ways of managing passengers and am delighted at the number of jobs which must be secured in just getting 1200 passengers on to a train. It must run to sixty or seventy front-of-house security and admin staff - not counting those who service the train once underway.

A second route is planned and has attracted much in the way of local protest as the extension cuts through the Kenyan National Park. Protestors went to court and won but the Government amended the law imposing an automatic halt to a project when a complaint is lodged at an environmental tribunal – burying the change in a completely unrelated Prevention of Torture Act – before the courts yet again ruled against them. The Government then merely ignored the courts and went ahead anyway! I'm impressed... both sleekit *and* disdainful!

I must say that the train journey itself was excellent. We passed a much more managed landscape than I'd imagined. Smallholdings abounded on each side of the line reminding me of crofts in Scotland other than the fact that in serving these small farms, all of the river beds had dried up. This tends not to be the case in Scotland. On a few occasions the train passed through savanna and bush Africa. Giraffes were conspicuous because they towered above the environment but the railway announcer reassured us that many other wild animals were in the bush. My most memorable moment however was surely when visiting the lavatory and photographing the sign which identified the toilet inside it as a *Vacuum Excrement Collector* and sternly instructed users not to put their arm down the lavvy pan to retrieve anything as this could only result in serious injury. 'No shit, Batman!'

The only slightly disconcerting aspect of the journey was the constant patrolling of armed soldiers supported by armed police who wandered up and down the passageway, often thoughtfully lifting their semi-automatic rifles above their head to allow someone to pass.

When we pulled in at each one of several stations, the announcer would say a few words about the town in question and explain that the train would stop for four minutes. And it did. Precisely. As it pulled away, each of the various uniformed people on the platform, soldiers, police, security guards and railway staff all stood rigidly to attention as if participating in a transportational version of the changing of the guard.

Upon arrival at the sparklingly new Mombasa Railway Station at Port Reitz some distance from the city, I began to realise what it must have been like for the Beatles as they left a stage door in the mid-sixties. I must have looked like I had a few bob, or more likely given my unkempt garb, resembled a gullible victim as I was besieged by a horde of taxi drivers each seeking my custom. The most vociferous was Patrick whom I talked down from 3,000 Kenyan Shillings to 1,500. As we left the station, Patrick parted company from other taxis, veered left and squeezed his small taxi between two bollards intended to prohibit entry before taking what he called a short-cut into Mombasa by the simple expedient of driving along a sandy motorway that was only in the early stages of construction. Cheerily he waved good wishes at the drivers of road-rollers, JCBs, diggers and bulldozers, all of which were in the busy midst of creating this new arterial route to the city. He plunged into a freshly established, darkened tunnel only to come face to face with an enormous earth-mover travelling at pace. He threw his vehicle to the right, giggled uproariously at what was almost a fatal collision and ploughed ahead bumping and bouncing his way towards the city. This wasn't doing my poor back any good at all!

Upon reaching metalled surfaces again (replete with huge potholes) he toyed with the ubiquitous *matatus*, (highly decorated mini-buses that serve larger African cities). Very inexpensive, they wander all over the urban environment packed to the gunnels with passengers. They are all highly decorated vehicles, customised with slogans such as, 'One God', 'Blaze of Glory', 'One Big Happy Family' and 'Legend'. I did wonder at the prospect of one *matutu* owner successfully picking up women passengers in his vehicle with 'Crazy Cock' emblazoned on its side.

As we entered the inhabited part of Mombasa, I witnessed the same egregious poverty that beset Nairobi and it just continued all the way into town. Crumbling pavements, torn-up roads, falling down buildings and tawdry shopfronts characterised the route we were following. The city looked like downtown Kabul after the *Mujahidin* had finished with it. I watched mesmerised as the vehicle in front of us drove with an off-side rear wheel that was obviously just about to part company with its axel. I covered my eyes.

It transpires that Mombasan transport authorities are big on sleeping policemen...the speed bump designed to slow traffic that is, not the snoozing, gun-toting rozzers snoring under roadside trees. However, rather than highlight the presence of these devices by painting them or providing them with a smooth trajectory to permit a slow glide across, they merely build something resembling a kerb, a small garden wall if you will. But because Patrick and his fellow driver will have no truck with the authorities, they merely crash into these impediments at speed, spend some time aloft, then crash-land, losing control and sending pieces of their vehicle spinning crazily towards passing pedestrians.

Patrick continued his giggling and dropped me at my hotel, The New Palm Tree in downtown Mombasa. Now, I don't know what the *Old* Palm Tree must have been like but this place was simply the worst hovel I'd ever entered...and I've been in a few hovels, by the way. Paisley comes to mind immediately! The young receptionist looked at my booking slip and asked me if I'd like to look at my room. I demurred. He rephrased his question saying, "I would encourage you to have a look".

I began to get the idea that all might not be well but asked merely if there was a better room available and he nodded conspiratorially, giving me the keys. His card machine wasn't working and I wasn't prepared to pay cash so we agreed I'd pay later and I was shown to my room.

I closed the door behind me and took a deep breath. It was like a junkie's doss-house. Everything was shabbier that the shabbiest shab. The toilet held the remains of the last user's bowel evacuation, a large notice reminded users that drugs misuse and prostitution were not permitted and a smaller notice on the room door explained that in the interests of energy saving, electric power would only be provided between the hours of 7.00am - 9.00 am and 6.00pm and 9.00pm. What tipped the balance was a final notice advising guests to be careful in turning on the shower before turning on the water-heater in order 'to avoid electrocution!' I reflected upon this for all of five seconds before lifting my bag, returning to Reception, explaining my booking was cancelled as it did not reflect the advertised product and caught a passing *tuk-tuk*.

"Take me anywhere...take me to a hotel near the beach," I shouted over the noise of his engine.

He bounced me all over Mombasa until we pulled up at the Nyali Beach Hotel right on the Indian Ocean and parked in the car park. He looked at me for guidance.

Shit, I thought, *this looks too expensive*. But it wasn't. Indeed it was pretty reasonable and I rationalised my decision by figuring that my back would benefit from some R&R.

I spent a quiet evening in my room having taken dinner in the hotel. I'd asked for steak and was delivered of a small piece of meat the approximate size of a pack of cards where that pack had been quartered. I was given of one of the quarters. I ate the potatoes on the basis that the doctor who'd administered the range of inoculations I'd needed prior to my trip had advised that in Kenya and Tanzania, all foodstuffs consumed had to be cooked, peeled or binned.

Another early bed.

I woke early and organised myself before going back to the city centre. Who knew it was hot at the equator? It was only nine o'clock but already I was drenched in sweat. I intended to visit Fort Jesus, a Portuguese fortification at the harbour that goes back millennia but upon approaching the entrance noticed that the Kenyan fetish with security was alive and well. A passport or National Identity Card was required to gain entrance to a museum. I sighed in frustration but rather than admit defeat, brandished my East Renfrewshire bus pass, proclaiming it the Scottish National Identity Card and they let me in without demur. The fort was interesting. Canons protruded from its walls and I was tickled to read a notice saying that the 'Carronade', four large guns pointed out to sea and used to protect the port, were so called because they were made in 1759 in Carron Iron Works near Falkirk just up the road from me. I climbed the uneven steps within the fort before realising that I wasn't the young gazelle I thought I was when attempting to step back down from some of the higher walled gun emplacements.

Early on I began to appreciate the local *patois*. I was constantly hailed by the word, *Jambo*! Now in Scotland this describes a follower of Heart of Midlothian Football Club but over here, it's *Swahili* for 'Hello!' Next favourite was '*Hakuna matatu*', a *Swahili* phrase meaning 'no worries'…'no problem!' I managed '*Jambo*' to enter into the spirit of things but couldn't utter '*Hakuna matatu*' without wanting to break into a song from the *Lion King*!

I wanted to purchase a pair of sandals I'd read were unique to Mombasa in that their soles were made from disused rubber tyres. *Entrepreneurial*, I thought. The first shop I saw was within the fort and was watched over by an ancient white-haired man who looked as if he might deal with perhaps one customer a day. I decided against shopping there as I'd have been tempted to pay double just because I had the means and it would have pleased the old man. I also figured that I'd have problems with the next shop I visited as I anticipated stuffing every Kenyan Shilling in my possession into the hands of the salesman merely to allow me to wipe the sweat from my eyes and rush immediately to somewhere cooler rather than spend time and energy in negotiating in the suffocating heat.

I'd been informed that the production of these sandals was undertaken on an industrial scale in the city and certainly when I entered a somewhat dilapidated shop next to the city market, the overpowering smell of rubber reminded me of visiting a Kwik Fit outlet back in Scotland. I settled on a pair and left to view the attractions of Mombasa market but was constantly assailed by guys who were just trying to make a buck and I can have no quibble about that. One elderly chap figured that I must be in want of spices and followed me around reeling off a list of various herbs and seasonings at his stall that he felt sure I wanted to purchase but when persuaded by a glance I made at a stall selling women's kaftans, started to push them as well. In the time I was in the market I was never allowed a moment to browse. Constant sales pitches accompanied my every step...but as I say, these guys were only trying to make a buck, so *Hakuna matata*.

I walked on and passed by a few mosques within which believers were being assailed by a raised voice. I thought little of it as they were speaking *Swahili* or Arabic or some-such but I also passed one where I distinctly heard the phrase, 'and they take from us what little we have!' They were speaking in English and I was reminded that there was still a great deal of unrest in the country. I must confess, though, I did feel perfectly safe wandering around even though I was the only white face on the streets.

Enervated, I returned to my hotel and made my way to the abutting beach where I tried out my new sandals. What I had assumed would be soft accommodating leather covering my big toe turned out to be somewhat unyielding stiff leather which blistered my feet almost immediately causing me to remove the sandals and walk barefoot. However, the sun was so hot that the ground underfoot was of a temperature normally only found in solar flares and so sent me screaming and hopping to shaded parts, lifting my sandals yelping and hirpling to a nearby table in order to sit, cursing and swearing like a sailor who'd just been kicked in the balls.

The beach was lovely; all white sand, quiet and with a cloudless blue sky and a calm, aquamarine sea; quite perfect. I relaxed and watched a group of young ladies (presumably) each wearing the full-length black burqa sit chatting whilst on the beach before them, another group of young Caucasian ladies, each dressed lubriciously in tiny thonged and strappy arrangements sunbathed. As Jim Reeves used to sing, '*When two worlds collide*', eh?

I'd come to enjoy the local beer, Tusker and sat sipping at a glass while reading the bottle. '*The contents of this bottle will impair your judgement*', it read. I agreed and ordered a second. It's a pleasant lager which nevertheless seems possessed of the unfortunate characteristic of foaming quite explosively when poured requiring a considerable period of time to elapse while it settles down, dissipates and warms up in the heat so somewhat losing its impact as a refreshing drink.

It was that time of day when a man's shadow is twice his height so I decided upon late afternoon tea. The company (everyone else seemed to be a loud Home Counties or loud South African) was entertained by a couple in even louder Hawaiian shirts attempting to sing the entire canon of works of Phil Collins. Whilst keyboards were employed as an adjunct to a prepared backing track, every so often a sudden ukulele would feature. I was reminded that upon taking my seat in the Madaraka Express from Nairobi, I'd slowly begun to appreciate that the music in the cabin was gradually being cranked up - and that it appeared that we were to be entertained by loud reggae music all the way to Mombasa. My earlier assessment of all the uniforms on show had been that the *Capo di tutti capi* seemed to be a Chinese guy so who knew he was also a secret Rastafarian? I'd been looking forward to hearing some genuine African music on my travels; some Afro-rock by Babatunde Olatunji, Miriam Makeba or Hugh Masakela perhaps but apart from that which emanated from a nearby club in Nairobi just as I was attempting to fall asleep on my first night, all I'd heard had been imported. Still, to be fair to the Hawaiian couple, they were pleasant and diverting.

I promised myself that I'd do nothing today as tomorrow would be another day in transit. *I'll sit in the sun and watch the waves break*, I thought. Unfortunately, I don't have the capacity to do that for longer than perhaps four minutes. I'd noticed that the tide hadn't moved in or out since I'd arrived and checking, discovered that 'ocean tides are smaller at the equator because the tidal bulge of the Moon follows along the path on the earth's surface which intersects with the orbital plane of the Moon. This plane is tilted about 23 degrees with respect to the equatorial plane of the earth. The result is that near the equator, the difference between high tide and low tide is actually rather small, compared to other latitudes.' Who knew? I didn't understand a word of that and had always assumed it had something to do with vampires or global warming.

I'll swim, I decided and wandered over to a nearby welcoming pool of cool blue water but noticed that it had no steps to permit a slow entry to its refreshing depths. *No matter, I didn't practice lifting a brick from the bottom of the swimming pool as a schoolboy without learning how to dive*, I told myself. I'd remembered that to complete any manoeuvre, first of all it had to be imagined. Easy! I steadied, tucked my chin, bent at my waist and pushed off with lithe, spring-heeled power into the water like an arrow entering a pond. That is how it was planned. What actually happened was that my bulk semi-collapsed into the pool causing such a *tsunami* that mothers gathered up their children and ran, sunbathers awoke screaming and elderly men called for the pool defibrillator. Later people would point subtly to my reddened chest and belly as I passed and a discussion would commence as to whether it was caused by sunburn or the belly-flop. It was the belly-flop. I don't expose my body to the sun. I expose my body to the interiors of bar-rooms.

That's what I'd do. I gathered up my belongings and apologising to those mothers who still gazed at me open-mouthed, made my way painfully to a chair underneath a straw canopy where I spent half an hour watching my Tusker lager change its appearance from shaving foam to warm micturate.

When in Nairobi I'd noticed that all of the Kenyans who'd self-described as *Maasai* were all tall and slim just like the middle-distance runners I'd seen so often in world Olympics. Now, I'm genuinely not one for loose generalisations or objectifying women but as I sat in Mombasa, I noticed, as I'd noticed since my arrival, that many East African ladies had buttocks that swept out from their body at an angle of up to ninety degrees. Had one stood next to me I could have set my glass of Tusker on her upper backside without spilling a drop. Simple research (I consulted the web, I didn't ask a woman. I'm not crazy!) suggested that this is actually a real physiological phenomenon called *Steatopygia,* a genetic characteristic found in women of sub-Saharan Africa origin, most notably (but not solely) among the *Khoisan* tribe who view this condition as a sign of great beauty. It is diagnosed by modern medical standards as buttocks which are set at an angle of about ninety degrees to the back. Physiologists believe that it is an adaptive physiological feature for female humans living in hot environments as it maximises their bodies' surface-area and retains quantities of fat so that during the dry season, should a food shortage exist in environments like those in the African savanna, *Steatopygians* can live largely off their stored fat. I knew nothing of this. See, new knowledge, just because of a belly-flop! 'Always remain open to learning', as my Grannie never used to say.

The following morning, I thought for a moment about going into the city and watching Bandari FC v Chemelil Sugar but figured I'd be stuck inside a stadium in broiling heat so I hailed a *tuk-tuk* to the nearby village of Mamba where crocodiles were to be found. Inevitably I had to fend off the driver's overtures. "Oh, boss, you don't want to go there. I take you to better place. Not far. You will like." Firm but friendly is the only response or I'd have ended up somewhere miles away with a far heftier taxi fare and a more uncertain destination. As it was, the crocodiles were as soporific as were the staff charged with managing the park. Everyone snoozed. The crocodiles lay motionless in the heat as if constructed of concrete so I took a few desultory photographs and wandered about for a while before returning to the road outside the village. I'd hardly set foot on the dirt track when a motorcycle swept up and braked hard, its rear wheel skidding to a fishtail stop *á la* Steve McQueen in '*The Great Escape*' before he jumps the barbed-wire fence.

"Where you go? I take you."

And so I found myself perched on the back of this motorcycle with nothing with which to steady myself. I felt I was riding bareback as my driver weaved his way in and out of traffic before returning me to the hotel. At least it raised my heartbeat a notch and I didn't suffer the irreversible brain damage I was convinced was to be my fate.

My back, painful earlier in the day, had eased so I walked along the white sand of Nyali Beach. After I'd walked some distance, I noticed that the beach was now much more populous. I realised that the quiet sandy beach I'd been walking and which I'd fondly imagined was a Mombasan secret was actually a private beach. Now, Mombasan couples walked hand-in-hand in the surf, kids played football, youths cycled on a strip of harder-packed sand and people swam. Everyone was black. I felt perfectly safe, everyone shouted '*Jambo!* ' as I walked past and I noticed three things; no one sunbathed (duh!), there was not one single piece of litter and no one made sandcastles. Apparently only imperialist nations teach their kids the need to learn at an early age how to fortify a stronghold using sand in order to maintain and protect that which they have taken by force. I walked until the sun defeated me and sent me scurrying for shade and a refreshment.

Up sharp and off to Zanzibar by air this morning. Upon landing, I smiled my way thorough visa control, visa payment, passport control and customs and walked outside the airport to find my name on a piece of paper signifying that my hired car was waiting. I was delighted at the ease with which I'd negotiated the protocols of entering Tanzania (they pronounce it Tanzania over here) and drove with my hired car guy to Stone Town where I'd be staying. I retrieved my rucksack from the car and opened the rear door to lift my bag. Empty! I realised that while I was congratulating myself on a perfect negotiation of airport bureaucracy, I'd forgotten to collect my large travel bag from the carousel in Baggage Collection. My hired car guy was brilliant, we both jumped back into the car and he drove us back to the airport at breakneck speed.

Upon arrival, I had to make the journey to the carousels in reverse - much to the annoyance of airport staff who shouted that I was going the wrong way. In any European Airport, I wouldn't have got five yards but here in Africa I got all the way through to baggage uplift.

I approached a senior guy, showed him my luggage ticket and said, "I forgot to take my case."

He looked confused. I repeated, "I've lost my case!"

He set his teeth in his lower lip and pondered the situation. "And where did you lose these keys?"

"No...my case!" I mimicked lifting a case.

"So they were *large* keys?"

This went on for a while until the official decided that this was clearly a problem for 'Lost and Found'. Despite horror stories about goods and chattels going missing at Zanzibar Airport, my luminous, light green travel bag sat on the floor of Lost and Found awaiting collection.

Dropping off car hire guy and checking in to the very old-fashioned (in a nice way) Forodhani Hotel in Stone Town near the harbour, I decided to see something of Zanzibar. I decided to familiarise myself with the controls of my hired car. So far, so good, although I tended to turn on the windscreen wipers when indicating left or right but hey, I'll learn. I began to undertake a reverse manoeuvre to start my journey and looking in my rear-view mirror, noticed that at some point the rear window had been broken and had been (I kid you not) replaced with thick glass normally used for a bathroom window! I could see only grey, opaque outlines of anything behind me. *Dangerous*, I figured but then, on the bright side...if I ever needed to pee in the rear seat? The car was very old...some fifteen years, I'd been informed and was typical for car hires in Zanzibar. It didn't have power-steering so wrestling this hulk around Zanzibarian roads was likely to be difficult. I drove a few miles outside town but pulled in and reflected on my next move. Roads were beyond terrible. Axle-deep, cavernous, potholes pock-marked every highway, so yawning that no vehicle ever contemplated driving over them. Instead every driver sought the few remaining square feet of useable highway. The consequence of this was that notions of driving on the left were consistently abandoned and cars and lorries careered over the road missing one another by a hairsbreadth in their attempts to avoid a broken axel. I reflected upon my doctor's advice not to stress my spine and drove back to the hotel, losing my direction several times in the process and parked the car. The wise thing to do would be to leave it parked and write off the cost on the basis that it's just too dangerous. I reflected upon this course of action over a 'Kilimanjaro' beer later on but remembered that one of my ambitions was to visit the famous restaurant called 'The Rock' which is situated on a small rock in the Indian Ocean on the other side of the island. The only way to get there is by car. I picked up my iPad and made an on-line booking. Perhaps if I drive really carefully...

Sleep came more easily than I might have at first anticipated as the authorities had sponsored a concert in the small square outside my bedroom where artist, Zakes Bantwini from South Africa was giving it big licks. At least I was listening to authentic African music but, at 1.00am when he was still giving it laldy, I turned the light out and slept the sleep of the just despite the cacophony.

The following morning I set off in my hired car replete with rear bathroom window. I'd come somewhat to understand the road network immediately surrounding the harbour but had been supplied only with a tourist map which showed that if I simply took the obvious road marked by a big red line to Tunguu, headed for Bungi, took a left to Paje and headed north to Bwejuu, I'd be there in the fifty minutes the web site had predicted. Unfortunately my plans were rent asunder within minutes of leaving Stone Town. There were absolutely no road signs - and a great many roads from which to choose. Occasionally a dirt track would have a yellow sign that pointed out say, 'Darajani Street' - a collection of tin-roofed shacks - but there was no way I could navigate. I drove through a beautiful afforested area before being halted by four armed soldiers who wanted to know why I was driving in a restricted area. By now my frustrations were rising and I wanted to reply, "I'm here on a mission to shoot your commanding officer" but instead said, "I'm trying to get to the internationally regarded Rock Restaurant and appear to be lost." They laughed uproariously at the *mzungu* (a *Swahili* word meaning 'white man') and pointed out that I was travelling in completely the opposite direction. They set me right and I drove on, still mystified about my whereabouts. It was then that I realised a flaw in my plan.

It gradually sank in that all of the petrol stations I was passing had what resembled police incident tape across their entrances indicating the absence of petrol. *Hmmm*, I thought. *I have only a third tank-full* having stuck a derisory amount in at the airport on the advice of the car hire guy. What happens if I get to the other side of the island and have no means of refuelling? I persevered until common sense suggested that my back would applaud a decision to return to base. I couldn't command the availability of fuel needed to complete the journey and the rear-view mirror convinced me that someone behind me was taking a shower. I parked outside my hotel and promised myself that I wouldn't turn the ignition key again. In doing so, a light bulb came on above my head as I remembered the cart-loads of goods that were being hauled around Mombasa market the other day. One of the more popular items was dark blue, plastic jerry-cans. It occurred to me at the time that this was a commodity somewhat aside from the usual haul of materials, sandals and straw baskets that were being wheeled from stall to stall. It shouldn't have taken a genius to work out that petrol scarcity might be a problem on an island in this part of the world. I don't think I'd make a very good spy.

I had two administrative tasks to complete; withdrawing fifty US Dollars and buying my ferry ticket to Dar es Salaam two days hence. Now, honest to God, I really do want to be measured in my assessments of life in sub-Saharan Africa but as I stood in the queue for each purchase I found myself having to force a positive view of the convoluted administrative processes involved in each transaction. Let me start by saying that I am completely enamoured of the get-up-and-go attitude of those who live near the equator. Even the guys who are selling sunglasses, boat hires, taxi journeys, football tops, access to restaurants, earrings, belts...their strike rate must be one in a hundred but still they persevere in heat that melts pavements. "*Jambo*, boss. You want leather belt? Finest quality. I do you good deal. I give discount. Hey, boss, you want?"

Usually a shake of the head and a 'no thank you' suffices but fair play to these guys. They respond by thanking those who have just rejected their ability to earn a few shillings. I'll tell you this, though. If I were tasked with living by my wits in an environment such as I was experiencing, I wouldn't last 'till nightfall!

However, those who manage to secure employment that is not entrepreneurial manage to make bureaucracy into an art form. In the bank I was instructed to convert my debit card into Tanzanian Shillings in the ATM outside and then return. I went to the ATM; broken - as were the next two in a four-unit set up. Pessimistically I moved on to the fourth machine. A woman entered and approached me as I organised myself.

"Parlez-vous français?"

I wanted to show off my schoolboy French but figured that, *"La plume de ma tante"* and *"Ouvrir une fenêtre, s'il vous plaît"* *wouldn't* cut it so instead I admitted, "No. I'm Scottish."

"Ah," she said. "You *looked* French!"

I looked at my image in the reflective panel of the ATM. The sea breeze had tousled my normally coiffured mane which now resembled the wild hair styling of Doc Brown (Christopher Lloyd) in *Back to the Future. This makes me look French?* I thought.

Not for the first time I was embarrassed at the lack of effort I've made over the years in learning to speak another language. Here was a woman (from the Netherlands, it transpired) who was comfortable in French and English as well (presumably) as her native language. Outside, Zanzibarians spoke *Swahili* and English - without much in the way of schooling.

Anyway the lady and her husband were as exasperated as was I at failing to find a working ATM but happily this one spat out Shillings. *Hakuna matata.*

I collected my cash and returned to the innards of the bank, joining a now-longer queue. At the exact moment I got to the front of the queue, the clerk decided to multi-task and deal with a few people at once. Then I was asked to fill out a form in triplicate - the exact same information on each form!!! My forms were stamped and I was guided to another booth where my passport and Tanzanian Shillings were sought and then...and only then, was I given fifty dollars. It took me forty-five minutes.

Later I walked along to the offices of Asam Marine where I'd already booked on-line shipping passage to Dar es Salaam on the African mainland. I just needed to pay for my ticket. At the harbour, I was pointed in several different directions (and I might say, allowed through a number of security barriers without any ID - something being denied locals) before eventually ending up in front of the correct guy. I won't go through the various steps that were taken prior to me being issued with my ticket but this time, four forms were required and I had to fight for space with other local travellers who attempted to distract the clerk's attention while he slowly poked a single finger at his keyboard to complete my application to travel. This simple administrative interaction took, in all, an hour of my time.

A benefit however was that I was sufficiently traumatised by the experience that I had to sit down and have a drink - and realised that I stood outside the restaurant claiming to be the locus of the upbringing of one Farookh Bulsara, or Freddie Mercury as legions of Queen fans would come to know him. Born here in 1946, Freddie apparently played on the beach I presently overlooked before his parents moved to India and then Middlesex.

The bar wasn't going to let a minor early emigration get in the way of profit and so advertised cocktails such as 'Bohemian Rhapsody' (Campari and Rum), 'Fat Bottomed Girls' (a Kahlua base), my favourite, a Monica Lewinski (...find out what a bubbly body can do in a blue dress!) but I chose Freddie's *Baba* (...do you want to find out how to perform in front of 50,000 people? Try this one!) I did, and to my astonishment, as I left and turned the corner, I found myself on an auditorium with 50,000 people asking me to sing *'Bohemian Rhapsody'*. I accepted the microphone...and awoke later in my hotel. That was one strong *Baba*!

The following morning, I looked out of my window at the small off-shore island of 'Prison Island'. Used more in previous years for quarantine purposes against the deadly threat of Yellow Fever, it requires a sea crossing over a busy shipping lane. Today's sea was choppy but manageable and I decided to visit. I awaited the arrival of Hatib, the tour guide with whom I was to negotiate a fare. It was obvious at first glance that this guy was sharp. He was in his twenties, spoke perfect English and seemed genuinely interested in my background. When I told him I was from Scotland, he immediately reeled off information about our political system and engaged me in conversation for quite a while because of his own enthusiasm for Zanzibarian independence.

"You see, Ron (no **Meeestaron** for this guy; he was my equal) Tanzania was formed in 1964 after a revolution overthrew the Arab rulers here in Zanzibar. At that time the politicians decided to merge Tanganyika (the mainland) with my island and we put the two names together; *Tan* from Tanganyika and *Zan* from Zanzibar but it has been bad for us because they are so much bigger than us. All of the money raised from tourists, from the sale of visas all goes to Dar es Salaam. Here people are very poor but we are a small island and although the opposition party on the island wants independence, the government here want to stay attached to the mainland."

He continued his diatribe. "At least in Scotland you have passed the first test and have a government that wants independence. Here, even if we manage that we will still be outvoted by the main Government in Dar!" I refrained from comment.

He went on to recount how at the end of the nineteenth century, the Germans had conquered the on-shore regions and incorporated them into German East Africa. "But after World War One, the Paris Peace Conference awarded all of Germany's empire here to Britain. Can you imagine such a thing, Ron?" One group of countries giving another independent nation to another country? Can you imagine this?

"All too easily," I confessed. "The world is a different place now, Hatib…but in many ways it's still the same. The strong exploit the weak."

He walked me down to his boat (it later transpired he had six of them) and although initially he'd told me I'd have to share the trip with many others, he told me that because of our chat, this boat would be for me only. I was grateful for this if only because the boat (a large covered rowing boat with an outboard motor) was falling to pieces and I counted three flotation devices that would have had otherwise to service perhaps twenty people should anything dramatic have occurred.

The island itself was quite interesting in that it was occupied by huge turtles, some of which were over one hundred and fifty years old. I did my usual 'no need for a guide' routine and headed off alone. I saw everything that others did but at my own pace before wandering into the forest and walking towards the other end of the island.

It was peaceful, quiet and interesting. Some of the trees were ancient. I walked quietly and slowly through the forest when a blood-curdling scream came from behind me. I turned expecting to find a large predator, fangs unveiled, ready to launch itself at me. I'd love to say I dropped into a crouch, lifted a log from the forest floor the better to defend myself before turning to meet my assailant but all I really did was scream like a girl, clutch at my chest and turn to face...a peacock. But in fairness to me, peacocks can do you a bit of damage, by the way. Some of them are ferocious! Not many, but I think this one was one of them. However he turned away and each of us lived to see another day.

On the return leg across the sea, I asked the pilot/driver/guy with his hand on the tiller, to drop me at 'Dreamers' Island' a floating concoction kept above sea water by a double raft of heavy logs supplemented by plastic kegs as buoyancy aids. On board everything was fitted out in 1965 hippy *chic*. Old bits of driftwood and odd bits of jetsam nailed together formed a bar. This thing wouldn't sink in a Level Five typhoon. It was a restaurant/bar but it became obvious that apart from Kilimanjaro Beer, they were out of everything else. (I was offered Robert the Bruce blended whisky but declined as I suspected it had been matured for all of half an hour in a back room nearby). I took a beer and climbed to the upper deck where a cool breeze helped me recover from the peacock attack.

One neat aspect to the raft was a large open hole cut in the middle of HMS Hippydom which permitted viewers to look down into the depths (or indeed swim down into the depths) and witness the truly amazing variety of colourful fish swimming around. With a sandy bottom below and the sun shining above, it was all as clear as day. I was transfixed until the barmaid said what appeared to be, 'That's nothing,' in *Swahili* and threw a few breadcrumbs into the hole. Instantly the entire fish population of the Indian Ocean began thrashing around below seeking sustenance and turning the scene black with small sea creatures.

After a second beer, I asked to be taken to the shore. This was agreed and I was invited to jump into the raft's small boat whose engine, after leaving the relative safety of the floating pub, promptly stopped working and left us adrift on the Indian Ocean. It bobbed *away* from land! I felt pretty safe other than noticing the array of buckets clearly used to bail water from the floor of the boat - already awash with water. After about twenty minutes and a lot of shouting in *Swahili* (from the tiller guy), a passing craft came alongside and took us to shore, me being invited to leap into the rescue boat and catching my thumb between the two vessels as they came together in the process. What a laugh *that* was!

It really is a lovely feeling waking up to a light, blue, sunny sky in the morning and thus far that had been my lot. However, today when I was about to catch a ferry to Dar es Salaam on the mainland, the sky was the colour of charcoal. I dealt with my ablutions, enjoyed yet another perfect scrambled egg made by, I suspect, the world's greatest scrambled egg maker and headed off to the harbour under a threatening sky.

I'd been guided that the experience of getting on the Zanzibar-Dar es Salaam ferry was not for the faint-hearted. All sorts of chaos and confusion had been predicted but having taken the trouble to book in advance and also to complete the appropriate travel documents (even though I was traveling *within* a country, I still had to complete customs and immigration forms to travel from *Zan* to *Tan*), I breezed through in a few minutes. I sat down in my seat awaiting the engines to roar into life when a downpour of cyclonic proportions descended from the heavens and *completely* soaked those who stood behind me in the queue as a consequence of them not having had the foresight to fill in the forms early. I must admit a measure of *schadenfreude* whilst at the same time feeling sorry for those caught in the rain. It was if a huge bucket of water had been poured from the heavens upon the heads of those twenty paces behind me in the queue.

The rain continued as if a tropical typhoon, largely because it *was* a tropical typhoon. For the first half of the two hour journey it continued to pour down in biblical fashion (a journey made at speed by the way; this thing fairly skipped along. I'm an expert on sea speeds and I estimated this at around forty knots!). A mist descended but the driven rain against the window meant that I couldn't even see what I couldn't see. I just trusted that the ship had adequate radar! It was so hot and humid inside the boat that I was probably as drenched as those poor souls who had been caught on the gangplank.

However as we arrived at Dar es Salaam the sun shone once more... and the temperature climbed to the hottest yet! It really was impossibly sultry. I'd done my homework and walked towards Uhuru Street (turn right at the railway station just half a mile from the ferry port) where shopping bargains were to be had. As a large city with Muslim influences, it should have come as no surprise that there wasn't a pub on every corner of every street...and there wasn't! Loads of signs advertised Coca-Cola but nowhere could I see the stuff being sold. I was parched, hot and bothered no match for a determined sales operative in any one of the roadside stalls. I wanted to buy a *Khanga* (a light East African cotton fabric printed with coloured designs, used mainly for women's clothing...I figured my wife might appreciate it one day each year during Scotland's hottest week) in one of the shops that bordered the road. Fortunately I came across Winston who allowed me to purchase several of his wares and by 'bundling' them, gave me a deal that even in retrospect seems reasonable.

Mission having been accomplished, I walked the streets of Dar es Salaam (House of Peace) and found it more developed than either Nairobi or Mombasa. Perhaps the profusion of government buildings added to the appearance of an organised city (despite the city of Dodoma being the formal capital of Tanzania, Dar es Salaam is the *de facto* centre of their universe). Roads were metalled and smooth, street names existed in abundance, road signs made navigation easy, police controlled the traffic and people obeyed their instructions. I could see signs of manufacture suggesting an economy that produced wealth rather than merely distributed it but noticed, however that any vehicle entering a modern hotel had its undercarriage searched by one of those mirrored devices. Perhaps the *Al-Shabaab* threats of terrorism are more concerning than I'd thought.

Almost two thirds of Tanzanians are Christian (while Zanzibar is almost exclusively Muslim) and jointly the two component parts constitute the largest population density in East Africa – partly because the average Tanzanian mother gives birth to a brood which averages 4.77 children. National statistics show that contraception is practiced by only 38% of the population. AIDS and malaria ensure that many fewer children make it to adulthood although these numbers combine overall to create an average Tanzanian citizen age of seventeen years.

After a while, the temperature and the absence of somewhere to sit defeated me and I jumped in a *Tuk-tuk* and went to the Slipway, a more modern part of the city largely on the basis that I figured they might have a hotel there that had air-conditioning. Serious negotiation took place with my driver. I negotiated him down to half the price he'd originally quoted then felt sorry for him and gave him a tip equal to that which he'd sought in the first instance.

The Slipway hotel was admirable. It was situated on Oyster Bay just north of the city but the heat was intense. I'd a new experience when peeing into a lavvy pan. It was so hot, my spectacles slid off my nose and dropped into the pan. My first reaction was that I was fortunate that it wasn't the Vacuum Excrement Collector I'd used in the Madaraka Express, the second, upon retrieving my glasses and washing them was that urine is a very effective lens cleaner.

I stayed out of the sun for the balance of the afternoon but miscalculated my return journey to the ferry on the basis that *leaving* the city in mid-morning isn't as gruelling as returning during rush hour. I tapped my *tuk-tuk* driver on the shoulder, pointed to my watch and told him I'd double his fare (an additional £1.50; there were no limits to my determination to make that ferry back to Zanzibar) if he got to the terminal on time. He agreed but didn't change his behaviour. I tried to help him by encouraging him to mount pavements and negotiate a non-existent lane between two rows of cars. He nodded enthusiastically but continued to invite other drivers to inhabit the space before him. I'd hired the only courteous driver in Dar es Salaam.

With four minutes to spare I jumped from the *tuk-tuk* and handed my passport and ticket to a clerk who was beginning to close his window. I'd made it...just!

While seated on my return journey, the section of the ferry I was in was treated to two (silenced) television broadcasts. The first was an edited account of the Bandari FC v Chemelil Sugar match I'd earlier considered attending. It was fast, interesting, all-action and was played on a pitch that would not have been out of place in Glasgow Green...in the years before they'd improved the surfaces and had then employed a plough to grub up the surface. Poor pitch but an interesting game.

The second offering was Charlie Chaplin in *Modern Times*. The audience laughed throughout, especially at a scene where Charlie's sweetheart (Paulette Goddard) announces she's found the couple a home. The shot cuts to a dilapidated shack which is the very antithesis of a home. It was a dump! The audience shrieked! What I found sad was that the shack was materially an improvement on the properties inhabited by too many Tanzanians.

On my final day in Zanzibar's Stone City, I took to walking its narrow lanes and drinking in its somnolent atmosphere. Apparently it's *de rigueur* to visit the home of Freddy Mercury when visiting Zanzibar but I'd overlooked this until coming across a large group of tourists in Keyatta Street being shouted at by an emaciated (Caucasian) guide who explained helpfully that the apartment block in front of which we stood had been young Freddy's domicile before he was taken off to India. It's part of a hotel block now. I walked on and sat beneath a large, leafy tree and enjoyed a soft drink in the cooling breeze. As I gazed at the sandy beach beneath me I noticed that the small boat whose engine had died when taking me from 'Dreamer's Island' still lay beached on the white sand as an old guy had at its engine with a spanner. *One of the downsides of having a floating bar,* I thought. *No boat? No way to bring customers to your till point!* The bar looked great from the shore but was deserted. No one seemed inclined to swim out.

The breeze freshened and I looked at my reflection in a car's window. Mad Professor Brown from *Back to the Future* had reappeared - my image even scared *me*! I decided upon a haircut and eventually found an out of the way facility that blasted cold air at its customers (me and an American woman who was having her roots treated, it transpired). It was ideal and I took a seat while the hairdresser finished one of the several phases necessary to treat the woman's blonde hair. Whilst a hair styling phase was 'resting', she wittered on, directing her comments to the barber without pause causing me to surmise that she was somehow breathing through her ears. If she started a sentence with the words, *"Back home"* once, she did so a dozen times explaining to the very patient man who was tending to her tresses the various differences she'd found between Zanzibar and Dallas. Grumpily, I almost murmured, 'Aye, for one thing, they don't assassinate Presidents here,' but decided against it on the basis that for all I knew, they'd done exactly that.

I now faced the precarious task of leaving Tanzania by spending exactly the currency I had in hand. The Tanzanian Shilling is worthless outside the country and can't be converted in any *bureau d'exchange*. I'd ordered a taxi from Hatib and he'd costed it at 35,000 Shillings so I enjoyed my first lunch since leaving Scotland in preparation for my tilt at Zanzibar Airport where I was guided not to expect too much in the way of food or drink outlets.

It was impossibly humid when I returned to my hotel room and showered before standing as if awaiting crucifixion in front of the air conditioner in order to cool down. After some time, I felt human again, collected my bag and headed downstairs where my entrepreneurial friend Hatib awaited. We drove to the airport with the windows down but upon arrival I'd hardly stepped from the vehicle when all of my earlier cooling was rendered useless. Instantly I was drenched in sweat and made my way through various unnecessary control points before entering a concrete block with dim strip lighting that had the feel of a 1960's bus station in Vladivostok. It was also a heaving mass of humanity. Every one of the few dozen seats were taken, people lounged on the floor, a long queue awaited purchase of some refreshment, mosquitos dive-bombed as if in Guernica and the noise was simply incredible. They're building a new airport terminal adjacent to the existing one and it won't open a moment too soon.

I managed to find a seat when a flight to Oman was called releasing some and sat reading sweatily until boarding (following an unanticipated further hour's delay) when yet another gargantuan queue formed mostly, I suspect, to get some fresh air at the open door. Although there must have been ten officials standing at the door, each presumably with a task allocated them, only one...that's ONE... managed the ticketing. The other nine looked on or argued with each other. In consequence the queue moved as slowly as liquid pitch.

Kenya International Airport is a modern construct but I was out in a flash by the simple expedient of charming a guy with a badge who, upon seeing a low denomination Kenyan Shilling note in my hand, relieved me of it, pronounced me a Diplomat and ushered me through an empty booth rather than stand at the end of a queue which (I counted) had one million people in it! However, in the best traditions of *karma*, being first out of the traps, I was also guided early to baggage claim carousel A and waited for ages as my bag was delivered to baggage claim carousel C. I left the airport in the wake of the one million passengers who had had to wait in line for passport control.

I stayed overnight in a guest house run by Carolyne and Alfrik. They were a delightful couple and the room was clean, basic and comfortable. They'd promised free wi-fi and air conditioning, neither of which were available but I was so tired I just overlooked this minor delinquency, collapsed on the bed and fell asleep.

I awoke early to the full-throated cry of a rooster and opened my curtains to see that the guest house was located in a secure islet of gated middleclassdom whereas outside, much less salubrious housing was evident. I'd been congratulating myself from having avoided mosquito and snake bites since my arrival in Africa when, upon placing my feet upon the floor, a small lizard ran across my toes and made its escape under the door. Breakfast was my usual scrambled eggs and fruit and my hostess, Carolyne helped me fail to check in to my Emirates flight later in the day. Her cousin, Bassi took me into the city to meet her husband, journalist Alfrik and as we journeyed, we had a long conversation about the trials of attempting to survive and raise a family in today's Kenya.

"If someone breaks their leg?"

"Then they'd better know how to fix it themselves or have a lot of money to pay the doctor."

"Does your daughter go to school?"

"There are government schools where no teaching takes place. We send our daughter to school and it costs $300 every four months."

"Is your main job driving a taxi?"

"There are no jobs so I drive for my cousin, Carolyne. I want to be a rich farmer. My family has sixteen acres near Embu but it has no bore-hole. I need money to dig a bore-hole." He looked at me hopefully.

Traffic congestion was at its peak as we entered the city centre. Smoking booths had been installed as the entire city centre has been declared a non-smoking zone. I thought this a great idea. Very healthy... were it not for the thick fug of petrol and diesel fumes that hung like a throat-clenching cloud over the streets.

We visited the Nairobi Gallery, the National Archives and the Nairobi National Museum. Alfrik was a great admirer of Joseph Murumbi, Kenya's rebellious Vice-President and his fellow politician, journalist and friend who established the Kenya African National Union (KANU), Pio Gama Pinto. He was assassinated in his driveway as he left for the theatre. The suspected assassin, President Jomo Kenyatta, had a watertight alibi that night.

Whilst many of the exhibits in the National Archives were of Kenyan artefacts, weapons and clothing, a decent range was devoted to the evolution of mankind arguing that modern humans evolved from archaic humans primarily in East Africa, exhibiting a 195,000 year old skull as evidence and going into some detail about the Mau-Mau uprising against British rule. Legions of schoolchildren were herded through these exhibitions - particularly the Nairobi National Museum - and I listened in at a respectful distance as kids were told of how in the late nineteenth century, the British first arrived in East Africa as missionaries but when they realised the richness of the soil, the minerals that lay beneath it, the strategic benefits of its ports and the pool of labour that could be exploited, very soon white settlers started arriving and displacing local Kenyans. The East African Protectorate was formed and Britain began introducing draconian laws to protect their investments. African voices were raised against the Hut and Poll Taxes (1901 and 1910 respectively) but it wasn't until 1944 as local soldiers returned from various theatres active in World War Two that a fledgling organisation called the Kenya African Study Union was established. A military wing - the Mau-Mau

- began reprisals against British Colonialism and a brutal campaign was launched, finding its zenith in the mid-fifties.

Now, war crimes have been defined by the Nuremberg Principles as 'violations of the laws or customs of war which includes massacres, bombing of civilian targets, terrorism, mutilation, torture and murder of prisoners of war and detainees'. In addition it cites crimes such as theft, arson and the destruction of property not warranted by military necessity.' After peace had been declared, the British were found to have committed war crimes against Kenyan prisoners such as 'slicing off ears, boring holes in eardrums, flogging until death, pouring paraffin over suspects who were then set alight and burning eardrums with lit cigarettes'. Castration by British troops and denying access to medical aid to the detainees were also widespread and common. One detainee who suffered severe mistreatment was a fifty-something cook named Hussein Onyango Obama, grandfather of a certain Barack Obama, former President of the United States. According to his grandfather's widow, British soldiers forced pins into his fingernails and buttocks and squeezed his testicles between metal rods, all measures considered worthy of repeat application in respect of his grandson by President Obama's successor, Donald Trump.

One photograph, centrally located, intrigued me. It showed the first Independent Republic of Kenyan Government after independence in 1964. Two rows of stern black faces glowered at the camera and in the middle was a magnificent moustache attached to a single white face. Further investigation showed this to be someone called Bruce McKenzie, Kenyatta's Minister for Agriculture. Scarce have I come across a more Scottish name so I delved further. This chap was a prominent Kenyan farmer who, during World War II, had seen action in North Africa, the Mediterranean and European theatres. He seems to have been a bit of a character, our Bruce. In January 1976, McKenzie was involved in the kidnapping of two German and three Arab suspected terrorists wanted by Israel for an attempted missile attack on an El Al airliner taking off from Nairobi. A few months later, in late June 1976, he came to prominence again during Operation Entebbe Some 248 passengers had been hijacked by members of the Popular Front for the Liberation of Palestine who sought to exchange them for comrades held prisoner in Israel and elsewhere. The hi-jacked flight, from Tel Aviv to Paris had been diverted to Entebbe, the main airport of Uganda, one of the countries bordering Kenya. McKenzie persuaded Kenyan President Kenyatta to permit Israel's Mossad to collect intelligence prior to the operation, flying them over the airport in his own private plane to take aerial photographs. Discovering this and in retaliation following the successful release of the hostages, Ugandan President Idi Amin ordered Ugandan agents to assassinate McKenzie. He was killed on 24 May 1978 when a bomb concealed inside a mounted antelope head exploded just prior to his flight. McKenzie had been presented it as a gift from President Idi Amin.

According to the book "Operation Thunderbolt" written by British military historian, Saul David, Kenya's involvement in helping Mossad deal with the Entebbe hijackers had to be kept top secret because had it been made public, it would have badly damaged Kenya's credibility in the eyes of its fellow OAU (Organisation of African Unity) members.'

McKenzie was later revealed as a spy for Israeli's Mossad, M16 and South Africa's Bureau of State.

It had been a long but interesting day as I headed out to the airport to catch my flight back to Glasgow. I said my farewells to Alfrik and Bassi and took a moment before entering the airport to read a security notice outlining prohibited goods in the cabin. These included guns, knives, mace, dynamite...and ten-pin bowling balls. I could only imagine that an earlier attempted hijacking had taken place where an air crew had been bowled over like skittles. I entered and underwent three separate electronic scanned searches before being admitted to the gates. Anticipating Kenya's enthusiasm for yet further security I decided not to replace my belt and just put it in my rucksack. This approach worked well until I was advised that a fourth security check was necessary in order to enter the café!

I mean *really*! I did as requested with as much good grace as I could muster, entered, and asked for a coffee. Swinging my back-pack from my shoulders to pay, my trousers fell down to my knees much to the huge delight of some glum children previously bored of the airport regimen.

At least Kenya's repeated security checks had made *someone's* day!

Hakuna matata.

Homeward bound...

Well, I've visited all of the places I listed back in 2010, some seven years ago. Many of these journeys were undertaken serially, some following some rest and recuperation but all lived up to expectations. Nowhere was I disappointed although Lubbock, Texas came close and Gibraltar was *so* depressing that I couldn't find the wherewithal to write about it lest I might be accused of undeserved vilification... but it was like being in an unkempt English coastal resort.

Almost all of the time I travelled alone but on each of my American trips I was accompanied by two dear friends, John McManus and Laurie Russell and I thank them for their company, their wisdom and wit, if not their driving abilities. Everywhere I found people to be hospitable, welcoming and kind although one or two were out primarily to make a buck. I can't blame them for trying to earn a living and being a bleeding-heart liberal, often colluded with their sales pitch safe in the knowledge that doing so cost me more than might otherwise was necessary. More than once my conscience was pricked and often my hackles rose in response to a world which is quite obviously unequal, unfair, discriminatory and shady. However, it didn't stop me from enjoying cocktails in Ho Chi Minh City or from travelling in air-conditioned splendour by train from broiling Marrakech to searingly hot Casablanca, so I'm as complicit as those I condemn, taking advantage of my socio-economic standing in the world to ease my journey through life.

My travels have seen me visit several bodies of water; the North Atlantic, the *Sheuch*, the Pacific, the Caribbean, the Indian Ocean, the Persian Gulf, the Mediterranean Sea, the East China Sea, the South China Sea, the Gulf of Bothnia, the Bay of Biscay, the North

Sea, the Denmark Strait, the English Chanel, the Gulf of Mexico, the Bosphorus, the Aegean Sea, the Yellow Sea, the Adriatic and the Norwegian Sea. I mention this as many have dived to the sea bed, fished their waters, hunted sharks, swum their shoreline or surfed their waves. I haven't so much as paddled their waters. I'm more of a land-lubber, unpersuaded of the virtues of getting wet unnecessarily.

Although my book is now complete, my travelling certainly isn't. I love planning my adventures and am as happy as it is possible to be when lugging my belongings to the front door of my house before heading to the airport and lands unknown. I now walk with something of a limp as advancing years and a slowly deteriorating frame take their toll but if I am required to use a stick to maintain my balance, then so be it. Travelling is in my blood, although, I'd imagine so is the detrital calcification collected over the decades that will one day slow me down and permit me only memories.

Until then, those memories associated with the destinations described in this book will live with me and permit the occasional wry smile as they are brought to recollection...as will the presently untold stories involving my arguments in the Kremlin, meeting Fidel Castro, climbing aboard an operational space shuttle module in the Johnson Space Centre, illegally entering Palestine and others I mentioned in the introduction to this book.

I am content. Although, as I sit here writing this in blistering heat and intense sunlight in a cafe bar in Nairobi Airport some ninety miles south of the equator, I find myself preparing another bucket list of places I'd like to visit. So far I've listed Churchill in northern Canada, Nuuk, the capital of Greenland and Hammerfest in northern Norway – all townships rather closer to the Arctic Circle and the North Pole than my present location.

It would be nice to cool down for a bit.

I Belong To Glasgow. Ron Culley
Amazon Reviews

This book is a very enjoyable read. There is the nostalgia factor for West of Scotland males of a certain age, however there is much more to this book than a trip down memory lane. The author has done well in his career, but this book is not a padded "list of successes". It is a remarkable story of career progression with stories, many of them humorous, from the author's involvement in the musical scene and his footballing encounters. It illustrates what can be achieved by hard work determination, and the right approach. A real sense of the author's personality shines through due to his honest approach in writing the book. Recommended.

* * *

Like a previous review notes, if you "belong to Glagow" in any way you'll find this book fascinating. It is actually a social history of Glasgow told through the life of the author. So if you now live in Canada, Australia, South Africa or are an ex-pat Glaswegian this is a trip down memory lane. It's funny as well by the way. Oh how I laughed. See me, see mince, ah hate it. See me, see I Belong to Glasgow, ah luv it.

* * *

Now I'm resident in Canada, this book brought back warm memories of a childhood in Glasgow as well as giving an insight into how the author moved from being a working social worker to Chief Executive of a powerful West of Scotland institution. The story is told with humour and no small degree of candour giving a wonderful view into the life of a working class boy, who with ability, drive and willingness to adapt, rose to a position of influence and power in a city & community he clearly loves. It is a great read and will particularly appeal to those who were brought up in Scotland in the fifties and who think fondly of their roots in council schemes and who managed to take advantage of free educational opportunities denied to our children today.

* * *

I got this book as a Christmas gift. I surprised myself by finishing reading it before the year was out. If you "belong to Glasgow" in any way at all, you will find this book a very entertaining and enjoyable read. It was well written, very interesting and very funny. There are not many books that make me laugh out loud.

I loved it!

* * *

This is a fabulous book. A mix of warm, witty and endearing personal commentary coupled with a serious, gritty and revealing insight into a life committed to public service in Glasgow. The book flows effortlessly and provides a social history of a young man growing up in Glasgow, managing to avoid many of the *clichéd* stereotypes, and in a way which begs for more.

The Kaibab Resolution. Ron Culley
Amazon Reviews

This is a tightly written book with a story that hooks you and keeps you reading. It is a pacey thriller. There is intrigue involving Mafia figures. There are elements of American and Irish politics. The characters are well drawn. There is also some romance and some humour, which works very well. All in all a book to enjoy. I'm looking forward to the author's next offering.

**

Cool heroes and beautiful ladies. If you're looking for an action-based thriller that you can skim read, this is for you.

**

I read this book about gun control in America just after the slaying of scores of people in Las Vegas. The book predates the event but captures the lunacy of American weapons policy perfectly. Well written, I enjoyed it thoroughly.

**

The book is billed as being about gun control in America – which it is - but I found the romantic element in the novel completely captivating. I'm a sucker for boy meets girl stories and this one is excellent. I also enjoyed the historical context which places the issue of gun control within the ambit of Mafia (and indeed IRA) involvement. It's also very funny in parts. Recommended.

**

Three cheers for this book. I really enjoyed it. Great escapism.

**

I'd bet that many people don't know about the *Posse Comitatus* that Culley writes about – I certainly didn't. These survivalist groups are located throughout America and are dedicated to resist their own Government by using arms to defend their beliefs. They seem to be scary people and Culley tells the story very well.

Glasgow Belongs To Me. Ron Culley
Amazon Reviews

If you know anything about Glasgow and Glasgow humour, you will love this.

* * *

Very funny, particularly the playground football.

* * *

Glaswegians are hilarious. I laughed long and loud at the jokes in this book. They were all new to me and I thought it was fantastic value. I now expect to re-tell them and claim them as my own when next I'm down the pub.

* * *

I was impressed that none of them really offended good taste but all of the jokes and stories sounded as if they could be actually have been told by Wee Andy, Big Tam and all of the other characters in the book.

* * *

Ron Culley's compendium of Glasgow humour truly hits the mark. Punch lines that actually punch: including possibly the rudest description of Nick Clegg ever published. Just the right balance of in-yer-face hilarity against a background ambience of latent menace. Exceptional and thoroughly recommended.

* * *

I read Culley's thriller and his biography about Glasgow but this is an interesting departure. Very funny indeed. Looking forward to his next offering.

* * *

My favourite joke was the 'cornflakes' joke...but I accept the earlier reviewer's comment about Nick Clegg. Very funny indeed.

* * *

This is a wonderful collection. I have read it through from start to finish but love dipping in at random and I laugh every time. With that marvellous down-to-earth Glaswegian humour shining out of every page, this book will brighten even the darkest days!

* * *

Loved dipping in and out of this book, some real belly laughs too - recommend it to anyone, not just us Weegies. A very funny book and can't wait to read more of Mr Culleys books, well done brings back very good memories.

A Confusion Of Mandarins. Ron Culley
Amazon reviews

This book is well worth a read. Some glorious banter, a gripping storyline with interweaving aspects involving the various characters and a tense climax to the tale. Enough twists and turns to surprise and ensure the unfolding of the drama can't be predicted. Some notable humour too. All in all a very good read.

* * *

A very enjoyable yarn, spun expertly along. The pace never falters from the first chapter to the very satisfying end game. The central characters, the good guys and the villains, are well supported and vibrant The book keeps you guessing and turning as it zips towards its conclusion. A must for anybody who likes their crime well-seasoned, with lively banter and clever nuances. I'll be picking up more of Culley's work.

* * *

A top notch spy thriller with a Glaswegian accent. Brilliant!

* * *

I did not see that ending coming. A very enjoyable holiday weekend spent reading this.
Recommended purchase.

* * *

I enjoyed this very much. The two main characters from Glasgow are both very funny and at the same time quite moving. The story fairly cracks along and I was drawn in to the storyline from the start. To be honest, I suspect that the two SAS soldiers from Glasgow are strong enough characters who could hold a series of books with their presence. Come on Ron, how about a series using these guys?

* * *

The book had me from the early chapter set in Glasgow's Govan. I laughed out loud. It's an unusual spy novel in that from time to time I read it with a great big smile on my face. (I'm from Govan)

Alba; Who Shot Willie McRae? Ron Culley
Amazon Reviews

I always thought there was something a bit fishy about Willie McRae's death, and now I am certain. Great read. Great book & good value.

* * *

Absolutely brilliant read, gripping from start to finish. I would recommend this to anyone who has an interest in Scottish politics, interest in Scotland & an interest in the dark side of Governments. An eye opener!

* * *

This is a story that needed to be told. I read this book cover to cover in three days. It tells the story of how the politicians of the day worked to subvert justice, the rule of law and the democratic values of Scotland. I found it gripping and thought that the characters were exceptionally well presented. Now, no one will ever know what happened to Willie McRae but Culley's assessment at the end of the book said it all for me.

* * *

This book is a must read for all interested in politics, in morality and in Scottish Independence. A real page turner.

* * *

This is a tale of dark doings, laced with political intrigue. The author takes as the starting the factual matrix. This enables him to "fill in the blanks" to provide a full and credible story surrounding the death of Willie McRae. Whether the story as narrated is accurate in its detail may be something upon which different readers have different views. There is, however, no doubt that the book raises important questions which are worthy of consideration. It highlights areas worthy of exploration. With this book the author continues his fine body of work. Recommended.

* * *

A very interesting read. A dramatic story woven around the suspicious, untimely death of Scottish lawyer Willie McCrae. Well researched by the author Ron Culley and I can thoroughly recommend. It won't disappoint.

* * *

A very compelling read, it's a subject that has intrigued and worried me ever since I knew about it. I'm not a conspiracy theorist but I believe Ron Culley has dealt with this very clearly, It's informative and compelling. I thoroughly recommend this book.

Access all of Ron Culley's books via his web site;

ronculley.com

Or via Amazon or Kindle using the book title or author's name.

These books can also be obtained or ordered
through any good book shop.